Elvis Films
FAQ

T0346462

Series Editor: Robert Rodriguez

Elvis Films FAQ

All That's Left to Know About the King of Rock 'n' Roll in Hollywood

Paul Simpson

APPLAUSE
THEATRE & CINEMA BOOKS
An Imprint of Hal Leonard Corporation

Published in 2013 by Applause Theatre and Cinema Books
An Imprint of Hal Leonard Corporation
7777 West Bluemound Road
Milwaukee, WI 53213

Trade Book Division Editorial Offices
33 Plymouth St., Montclair, NJ 07042

The FAQ series was conceived by Robert Rodriguez and developed with Stuart Shea.

Printed in the United States of America

Book design by Snow Creative Services

Library of Congress Cataloging-in-Publication Data

Simpson, Paul, 1961–
    Elvis films FAQ : all that's left to know about the king of rock 'n' roll in Hollywood
/ Paul Simpson.
        pages cm
    Includes bibliographical references and index.
    ISBN 978-1-55783-858-2 (pbk.)
1. Presley, Elvis, 1935–1977—Criticism and interpretation. 2. Musical films—United
States—History and criticism. I. Title.
    ML420.P96S52 2014
    782.42166092—dc23

                                                                    2013038965

www.applausebooks.com

To Mum, Dad, and Tina for introducing me to Elvis;
to Lesley and Jack for keeping the faith;
and, of course, to Elvis

Contents

Acknowledgments

I would like to thank Robert Rodriguez for thinking of me; Marybeth Keating and John Cerullo at Hal Leonard for their forbearance, fortitude, and patience and the company's capable, meticulous editors; Petra Munster for exceptional generosity worthy of the King himself; Bill Bram for showing us all the way with his book *Elvis Frame by Frame*; Mark Ellingham for putting me on the King's trail in the first place; Helen Morgan for her research; Helmut Radermacher for his help with photographs; Todd Slaughter for his permissions; Allan Warren for pictures; and David Troedson for his encouragement over the years.

Introduction

"I Saw the Movie and I Was the Hero of the Movie"

—Elvis Presley, accepting his award as one of the ten outstanding young men in America, 1971

In the last summer of his brief, memorable life, Elvis Presley was haunted by an unfulfilled dream. He told Donna Presley, his cousin, and Larry Geller, his hairdresser and confidant, he wanted to give up touring to make movies. Did he mean it?

Presley was, as Memphis Mafia member Lamar Fike once said, a "true chameleon; they couldn't put up a maze in a castle like what was in his mind," so his real intentions are often hard, if not impossible, to read. Financially, Presley would have been much better off going on the tour his manager Colonel Tom Parker had already scheduled. Yet as Donna Presley recalled: "He still talked about the movies in his final years. He had mastered everything else he set out to do and it rankled with him." In the past three years, Elvis had twice come close to making a movie: nearly co-starring with Barbra Streisand in *A Star Is Born* (1976) and finding the time, will, and resources to start—but, sadly, not complete—the karate documentary *The New Gladiators* (1974). The karate movie was not a vanity project for an out-of-touch, fading star. For Elvis, it was the final manifestation of a dream that wouldn't die. As David Halberstam notes in his book *The Fifties*, "What Elvis Presley really wanted from the start was to be James Dean; it was almost as if the music was incidental. Indeed the star all but said as much, saying, 'All my life I wanted to be an actor.'"

The Revolutionary Significance of Elvis's Movie Dreams

The young Elvis who was inspired by the unmistakable, innovative sound of blues singer Arthur Crudup is the same Elvis who, as a boy, watched and studied films starring silent-movie heartthrob Rudolf Valentino, tough guy Humphrey Bogart, teen idol Tony Curtis, and the pioneers of Method acting, Marlon Brando and James Dean.

When Elvis and his father, Vernon, first went to the movies in Tupelo in the 1930s and 1940s, they did so knowing that, as Vernon put it, "We couldn't tell the church anything about it." The Assembly of God, the church the Presleys belonged

James Dean and Elvis postcard. Presley was merely the most famous of the millions of teenagers Dean inspired.

to, taught that it was a sin to go to the cinema. Despite such guidance, the young Elvis was enthralled by Gene Autry, Fred Astaire and Ginger Rogers musicals, Bing Crosby, and such serials as Flash Gordon, Sunset Carson, and Tarzan.

In 1952, a year before he plucked up the courage to walk into Sun Studios, the seventeen-year-old Elvis was one of many movie fans who turned out in Memphis to see Virginia Mayo and Gene Nelson—who later directed two of the singer's worst movies, *Kissin' Cousins* and *Harum Scarum*—promote their new picture *She's Working Her Way Through College*. A year later, filling in a form at the Tennessee State Employment Security Office, he listed his leisure interests as: "Sings, playing ball, working on car, going to movies."

On the set of *Easy Come Easy Go*, Presley told veteran co-star Elsa Lanchester how much he had enjoyed her performances in Charles Laughton's *The Private Life of Henry VIII* (1933), George Cukor's version of *David Copperfield* (1935), *Come to the Stable* (1949), and *Witness for the Prosecution* (1957). The actress replied: "How sweet of you to say so but I don't believe a word of it—after all, they were mostly made before you were born." To which Elvis replied: "Well ma'am, I used to work as a cinema usher and I caught some of them then. Now I hire the local movie hall and you'd be surprised at the range [of movies] we can get."

He put his moviegoing to good use. He was impressed by the way Tony Curtis styled his hair and used mascara to accentuate his beauty onscreen, the way Valentino projected from his eyes, the way James Dean wore his collar turned up, and the fact that many of the actors he admired—especially Brando and Bogart—didn't smile very much onscreen. He famously watched Dean's *Rebel Without a Cause* more than a dozen times and was, as he proved when he met the film's director Nicholas Ray, word perfect on the script. In an interview in August 1956, for *Teen Parade* magazine, he said: "All my life I wanted to be an actor. And the luckiest thing that ever happened to me is I'm beginning to realize my greatest ambition." It is no overstatement to say that if Elvis hadn't loved the movies—and Brando, Curtis, and Dean hadn't inspired him—he might never have revolutionized popular music.

Presley's passion and purpose were evident in his first screen test for producer Hal Wallis in the summer of 1956. Hal Kanter, who directed Elvis in *Loving You*, saw it and recalled: "I went back to the office and said: 'The man just absolutely jumps off the screen and grabs you by the lapels. You can't ignore him.'" George Cukor, the gifted Oscar-winning director of *My Fair Lady*, spent an entire day enthralled on the set of an Elvis movie in the early 1960s and left convinced that Presley was "potentially one of the most remarkable and extraordinary acting talents I have ever seen." Cukor said: "He'd be a joy to direct. His comedy timing is faultless."

Yet rock writer Nik Cohn captured the orthodox view of Presley's celluloid oeuvre, lambasting the star for "churning out an endless succession of vapid and interchangeable musicals, each one flabbier than the one before. His voice seemed to have lost its edge and his songs were gormless, his scripts formulaic, his films looked as though they'd been put together with two nails and a

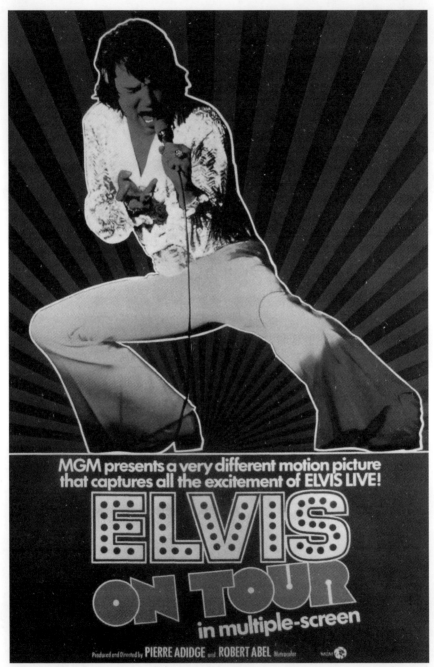

Poster for the *Elvis on Tour* documentary. Elvis's last concert movie was an award-winning farewell to the big screen.

hammer." In his more candid moments, Elvis might not have disagreed too sharply with Cohn, once asking: "Who is that fast-talking hillbilly son of a bitch nobody can understand? They're all the same damn movie with that Southerner singing to someone different."

Reflecting on the biggest professional failure of his life in an interview for *Elvis on Tour*, the singer sounded incredibly magnanimous and genuinely wounded: "I don't think anyone was trying to harm me. It's just Hollywood's image of me was wrong. I knew it and couldn't do anything about it. I had thought they would give me a chance to show my acting ability or do an interesting story, but it never changed. They couldn't have paid me no amount of money to make me feel some sort of self-satisfaction inside. "

The inconsistent quality of Elvis's movies should not blind us to their significance for him. He had set out for Hollywood in the summer of 1956, intending to be the next James Dean. In one interview he said, "People ask me if I'm going to sing in the movies, and I'm not." He soon learned otherwise. Four songs were shoehorned into his debut movie, which was renamed *Love Me Tender*. That hasty change of priorities set a precedent for Hollywood's view of Elvis. He was not a talent to be developed—like Brando or Dean—but a commodity to be exploited, like Rin Tin Tin, Tarzan, and Dean Martin and Jerry Lewis.

Presley told Wallis: "My ambition is to be a motion-picture actor—a good one, sir." The producer of nine Presley pictures initially said: "When I ran the test I felt the same thrill I experienced when I first saw Errol Flynn on screen.

Love Me Tender EP cover. Presley's anachronistic hip-swiveling helped sell his film debut.

The camera caressed him." He also found Elvis "a natural in the way that Sinatra was." This may have just been the kind of stuff producers say to ingratiate themselves with new actors. Wallis later said of Elvis that there was "absolutely no point in pushing him." This was certainly how he briefed Allan Weiss, who wrote six Presley pictures for the producer. The writer said: "In viewing the test one thing was clear: it would be a mistake to try to force this strong personality into a preconceived role. His parts must be tailored for him, designed to exploit the thing he did best—sing." Joe Pasternak, who made *Spinout*, agreed with Wallis's unflattering verdict, once telling Elvis's manager, "He doesn't have it. He really can't act."

Yet Michael Curtiz and Don Siegel proved otherwise when they directed Presley in *King Creole* and *Flaming Star*, respectively. Walter Matthau, Elvis's co-star in *King Creole*, called him a "very elegant, sedate, refined and sophisticated actor, who was intelligent enough to understand what a character was and how to play the character simply by being himself through the means of the story." In his memoirs, Siegel sounded haunted by Elvis: "Elvis could have been a singing and an acting star; also, he would have been much happier. You could see that he had a lot of layers, a lot going on. God that boy had potential." Yet with dismay, the director noted that the interchangeable musical comedies turned Presley into a "joke as an actor in Hollywood."

To watch the best Elvis movies—such as *Flaming Star, Follow That Dream, Jailhouse Rock, Loving You, King Creole, Viva Las Vegas*, and *Wild in the Country*—is to see that Quentin Tarantino wasn't exaggerating when he said: "He's the biggest tragedy of all rock stars. He could have been a truly terrific actor if he had worked with a lot of other real actors. If I ever see *Orpheus Descending*, I think Elvis would have been the best person to play that part." Sidney Lumet, who directed *The Fugitive Kind*, the movie of *Orpheus Descending*, admitted later that he wished he'd cast Presley, not Brando, as Tennessee Williams's antihero. And yet, as the director confided to Elvis's biographer Elaine Dundy, "As I look back on it now, it would have been death to have cast Presley. There's snobbism in America that gets doubly vicious about its own."

Lumet hit upon the central tragedy of Elvis's fourteen years in Hollywood. As a singer, he had changed the world. As an actor, he couldn't change Hollywood's view of him.

Squandering the King's Promise

Before Elvis served in the U.S. Army, he looked poised to emerge as a screen actor with the ease and magnetism of Frank Sinatra. Debra Paget, his love interest in *Love Me Tender*, recalled: "Had anyone told me he'd never had a dramatic lesson, never stood in front of a movie camera, I wouldn't have believed it. His acting was convincing, he always knew his lines, picked up like a trouper the purely technical aspects, like moving in and out of camera range, and the many other tricks of the trade that usually take months and years of experience to learn."

And he kept learning. He built on the success of *Love Me Tender* and *Loving You* with the noir-ish musical melodramas *Jailhouse Rock* and *King Creole*. As Dolores Hart, his love interest in two of those films, put it, "Elvis had a charisma that fed off other people. When he was with excellent actors, he became excellent himself." For an actor with just four movies to his name, this was a promising body of work. Elkan Allan, the respected British film critic, said of *King Creole*: "His best film. If he had taken this as the starting point for a serious career, he might really achieved something."

His first post-army movie, the musical comedy *G.I. Blues*, was well-crafted family fare. Two last stabs for artistic credibility—*Flaming Star* and *Wild in the Country*—presented Elvis with a dramatic challenge but were commercial disappointments when compared to the triumphant escapism of *Blue Hawaii*. This entertaining, formula-defining musical comedy was the eleventh-highest grosser in the United States in 1961—and the fourteenth in 1962—and produced a soundtrack that topped the Billboard charts for twenty weeks. Probably the

Blue Hawaii was so successful—on celluloid and record—it changed the direction of Presley's movies for good.

most-watched Elvis movie ever, *Blue Hawaii* was—alongside *Viva Las Vegas*—the best of what the star later referred to as "the Presley travelogues." For Parker, these movies, usually packed with sun, sea, and song, were a manageable substitute for the world tour that he—as an illegal immigrant without a valid American passport—might have found hard to organize and control.

The formula reigned supreme—with such notable exceptions as *Follow That Dream* and *Kid Galahad*—until 1968. In the hands of an experienced director like George Sidney, and blessed with a sexy, charismatic co-star such as Ann-Margret, the machine could produce a musical comedy travelogue as classy and entertaining as *Viva Las Vegas*. At its worst, with competent second-unit director Michael Moore promoted to the director's chair, you get the tired, repetitious *Paradise, Hawaiian Style*, a musical comedy that its star, judging by his expression of incredulous amusement, found funnier than most cinemagoers. Most of the other formulaic musical comedies fall between these two extremes with *Fun in Acapulco, Girl Happy, It Happened at the World's Fair, Roustabout* (in which he seems roused by the challenge of playing off Barbara Stanwyck), *Speedway*, and the breezy *Tickle Me* probably the best of the rest.

A brief flirtation with producer Sam "King of the Quickies" Katzman produced *Kissin' Cousins* and *Harum Scarum*, low-budget exercises mainly notable for all the wrong seasons. Of the latter, *New York Times* reviewer Vincent Canby said the star acted with all "the animation of a man under heavy sedation but then he had read the script."

Presley was not stupid or unrealistic about his acting ambitions. As a boy, he had enjoyed Crosby's musical comedies—even paying tribute to his boyhood idol with his version of *Blue Hawaii*, a song written for Bing's 1937 musical *Waikiki Wedding*—and he wasn't averse to making them. But he wanted them to be of a certain quality, and he didn't, as his friend Jerry Schilling put it, "want to make ten musical comedies one after the other."

Elvis's escapist musical comedies found their most loyal audience in the Deep South and outside America. In Thailand, moviegoers were enthralled by what one fan called the "beautiful things and beautiful sounds" on offer in Elvis's movies. In 1965, *Tickle Me* enjoyed an eight-week sold-out run at the 2,500-seater State Theater in Sydney. Because Elvis wasn't on TV, and didn't perform live between 1961 and 1968, each movie—no matter how dire—was the fans' only chance to see him. Their patience was sometimes rewarded by a song that showcased the real Elvis. Think of the sweet beauty of "Can't Help Falling in Love," the finger-snapping charm of "Return To Sender," the stomping, sassy "Bossa Nova Baby," and the soulful sophistication of "I Need Somebody To Lean On."

By 1966, the Elvis formula had begun to eat itself. *Blue Hawaii, G.I. Blues*, and *Viva Las Vegas* had made so many millions that Presley was sent back to the fiftieth state for the third time in *Paradise, Hawaiian Style*, played a racing driver in *Spinout* and *Speedway* (and a speedboat racer in *Clambake*) and was back in a uniform in *Paradise, Hawaiian Style* and *Easy Come Easy Go*.

Double Trouble in Hollywood

In Hollywood terms, Elvis had become a double anachronism. He was locked into a multipicture contract—with no approval of songs, scripts, or co-stars—at a point in movie history when many actors were becoming free agents who selected their own roles. To make things worse, Elvis was floundering in a sinking genre, his celluloid destiny shaped by the film musical, which misplaced its mojo in the late 1950s.

The geniuses who had had made Hollywood musicals so great—like Busby Berkeley, Mitchell Leisen, and Gene Kelly—had become marginal figures by the 1960s. Even George Sidney would make only one more musical after *Viva Las Vegas: Half a Sixpence* (1968) with Tommy Steele (the first "British Elvis" before Cliff Richard inherited that mantle). Most of the artistically and commercially successful American musicals of the 1960s—*West Side Story*, *My Fair Lady*, and *The Sound of Music*—were adapted Broadway hits. Many high-profile musicals—from *Camelot* to *Hello Dolly!* and *Dr. Dolittle*—flopped spectacularly. Some musicals that did succeed—*A Hard Day's Night* and *West Side Story*—were distinguished by a kind of social realism that seldom characterized Presley musical comedies. Critic Roger Ebert made this point in his review of "pleasant, polite, sweet, kind and noble" *Speedway*, concluding: "If the late show viewers of 1988 will not discover from it what American society was like in the summer of 1968, at least they will discover what it was not like."

The actors who had inspired him—Brando and Dean—helped wreck the old Hollywood studio system. Presley was a victim of Hollywood's painful rebirth. Persuaded by Parker—and driven by his urgent desire to emulate his idols—he unwittingly placed his celluloid destiny in the hands of those who had built Hollywood's glorious, but stifling, past rather than whose who were shaping its dangerous, exciting future. While the Beatles worked twice with gifted young director Richard Lester, nine Presley pictures were directed by the dutiful Norman Taurog, a filmmaker renowned for his technical competence, and rapport with child actors, who had won a Best Director Oscar in 1931 for the kids' movie *Skippy*.

Many suspected that Elvis was too dumb, jaded, or apathetic to realize what was happening. The record doesn't support that view. Though he may have had reservations about meeting the Beatles, he didn't hide from the threat they posed on celluloid. When Ray Connolly met the singer in Vegas in 1969, they began discussing Mal Evans, one of the Beatles' assistants, who was a big Elvis fan. Presley recalled: "Yeah, he's the guy in *Help!* that kept swimming." Not only had the singer watched the Fab Four's second movie, he had remembered it in detail.

The certainties that shaped the worldview of a movie executive like Paul Nathan (associate producer on all nine of Wallis's Elvis films, who had cut his teeth on the Martin and Lewis quickies in the early 1950s) would quickly become irrelevant as Hollywood sought, desperately, to create a new working model. It wasn't just the Elvis formula that broke down in the 1960s as the studio system decayed: the beach-party movie, the Doris Day movie (like the sex comedy from which it sprang), and the Jerry Lewis comedy had all run aground by around 1966.

You would never guess from the less distinctive Elvis movies of the 1960s that the Beatles, Bob Dylan, and the Rolling Stones had revolutionized popular culture again. The disconnect astounded W. A. Harbinson, author of *Elvis: An Illustrated Biography*, who lamented: "So the new music follows Dylan, and the Beatles and the Stones, while their hero, Elvis Presley, now well-fed and slick, makes strange movies with such titles as *Girl Happy*, *Tickle Me*, *Harum Scarum*, and *Paradise, Hawaiian Style*. It's not real. It's a weird scene, man."

As a singer Elvis helped invent the generation gap. As an actor, he was plagued by it. His wholesome 1960s movies appealed especially to young girls—younger, or more innocent, than those screaming at the Fab Four—so producers labored to make him up-to-date by importing or inventing dance crazes like the Twist and the Clam, creating stereotypical contemporary milieus (like the clichéd hippies in *Easy Come Easy Go*), and drafting in such innocent ingenues as Anne Helm (*Follow That Dream*), Laurel Goodwin (*Girls! Girls! Girls!*), and Annette Day (*Double Trouble*) as romantic leads. The idea, presumably, was to encourage girls to believe they could kiss Elvis too—a point made oddly explicit in *Double Trouble* when Day is shown in a school uniform. (Worry not—her character is just four days shy of her eighteenth birthday.) Such casting forced the King to maintain a certain decorum in his romancing. Until *Live a Little, Love a Little*, when his character goes to bed with Michelle Carey, the motto seemed to be: no sex please, this is Elvis.

The best way to respond to the Beatles' threat was to make better music and sharper movies. Instead, the people who sold Elvis to the masses tinkered. They pointlessly lied about his age in *Clambake*: his character's driver's license says he's twenty-seven, when he was thirty-two. With upbeat numbers dominating the charts, RCA sped up the title song "Girl Happy" in the mistaken belief that this would make it sound more contemporary. They cast him as the lead singer in a foursome in *Girl Happy*, *Spinout*, and *Double Trouble*. The latter's European setting—though Elvis never left Hollywood during shooting—was an oblique, half-hearted attempt to take on the Beatles and the Stones on their own turf and marked the final bow for the Elvis movie as surrogate world tour.

In 1967, *Easy Come, Easy Go*, Elvis's twenty-third movie (and his last with Wallis) was probably his first not to cover its costs on initial release. Arnold Laven, co-producer of *Clambake*, said that United Artists made that film only because under the deal the studio had struck with Parker "it was 'pay or play': if they didn't make the movie, they would simply give Elvis Presley $750,000 and have nothing to show for it." So UA effectively outsourced the film to Laven, Jules Levy, and Arthur Gardner, believing they would cut their losses if the movie could be made for $1.5 million.

With Wallis, Paramount, and United Artists all losing interest in 1967, only MGM and a few minor studios were willing to work with Presley. Even the studio with more stars than in heaven was sticking with Elvis partly out of contractual obligation. *Double Trouble* was produced by Irwin Winkler, then a thirty-five-year-old novice on the MGM lot, who later won a Best Picture Oscar for *Rocky*. Elvis had almost given up by then too, telling Marlyn Mason, his spirited co-star in *The Trouble with Girls* (1969), "I'd like to make one good film before I leave. I know this whole town's laughing at me."

His last movies were, at least, less predictable. The willingness to experiment didn't always pay off. The spaghetti western *Charro!* (1969) stumbled, despite an intriguing buildup. *Live a Little, Love a Little* (1968) was a screwball comedy that very nearly worked. Despite the obvious relish with which Elvis played Native American rogue Joe Lightcloud in *Stay Away, Joe* (1968), this odd comedy western didn't really gel. A plot might have helped. Yet *The Trouble with Girls* (1969) was almost Altmanesque in its swirl—good enough for the normally stern *New York Times* to call it a "charming comedy." Elvis was sympathetic, if idealized, as a groovy doctor in a New York ghetto in the half-decent *Change of Habit* (1969), looking cooler in a football shirt and jeans than he had in many of the more elaborate outfits he had donned in his travelogues.

Sadly, this change of strategy didn't prevent *Change of Habit*, his last feature, from becoming the first American movie to have its British premiere on television. For a man who had declared that becoming an actor was his greatest ambition, it was an ignominious end to a movie career.

Technical Advice from the Colonel

William A. Graham, who directed *Change of Habit*, has recalled one conversation with Parker (credited as technical advisor on twenty-four Elvis films) that helps explain why the star's dreams were so cruelly dashed: "Parker said: 'I hear you've been going up to Elvis, sonny.' And I said, 'Yeah, that's right, we've been working on the acting and he's coming along very well.'" To which Parker replied: "Let me tell you something, we make these movies for a certain price and they make a certain amount of money, no less and no more. Don't you get goin' for no Oscar sonny, because we ain't got no tuxedos." Graham understood the warning but ignored it.

This philosophy meant that, unlike other actor-singers such as Crosby, Sinatra, and Dean Martin, Elvis would ultimately make movies designed only to appeal to his own fans, and, as budgets were trimmed, the decent ensemble casts that distinguished the likes of *King Creole* and *Flaming Star* became the exception, not the rule. Elvis's global fanbase was massive, even unprecedented, but this proved a myopic, self-defeating strategy. Only two of his movies—*Blue Hawaii* and *Viva Las Vegas*—made more than $5 million at the U.S. box office on their initial release. As a point of comparison, *Von Ryan's Express*, Sinatra's highest-grossing film of the 1960s, raked in $17.1 million in the United States. By shining

George C. Scott as General Patton. *Patton* was Presley's favorite film: he often cited the line, "All glory is fleeting."

in ensemble casts in movies such as *From Here to Eternity* and *Rio Bravo*, Sinatra and Martin reached out to cinemagoers who never bought their music.

Between 1960 and 1967, most of Elvis's films—and roles—were driven by the need to sell soundtrack albums. The movies sold the music, and the music sold the movies. Commercially, the logic was flawless. The soundtrack to *Girls! Girls! Girls!* sold 600,000 copies, 100,000 more than his most creatively satisfying studio album, *From Elvis in Memphis*. Yet the sheer volume of soundtracks—and the goofiness of such numbers as "A Dog's Life" and "Petunia the Gardener's

Daughter!"—began to reduce demand. By 1968, when the *Speedway* soundtrack peaked at number 82 on the Billboard charts, an all-time low for a Presley album, even Parker realized the game was up.

This modus operandi probably explained why Elvis wasn't given an acting coach. The official explanation was that tuition would stifle his natural talent, a rationale Elvis publicly went along with. Yet in March 1956, asked if he would like to "study acting at some place like the school that Brando went to," he was quick to say, "I'd like to, I sure would like to do." And then he added—and this is where he seems partially culpable for his disappointing movie career—"I'm busy right now, but if it came to the point where the people wanted me to, I would."

"The people"—certainly Wallis and Parker—didn't want him to. Parker was pretty explicit about it, telling the press: "Elvis movies will never win any Academy Awards, all they're good for is to make money." If you make movies as fluffy as *Clambake*, the last thing you want on set is a disciple of The Actors Studio boss Lee Strasberg trying to identify the motivation of Elvis's singing, millionaire raceboat driver. Sensing Elvis's frustration during *Girl Happy* (1965), director Boris Sagal advised him to cut back his movie schedule and study acting in New York. With commerce, not art, directing Elvis's movie career, it was not advice the star could easily heed. Yet Strasberg might have welcomed him. After watching *Wild in the Country*, the man who had taught Brando and Dean told friends that Elvis was a great acting talent going to waste.

Elvis the Movie Buff

One of the most humiliating aspects of Presley's failure was that he knew a good movie when he saw one. He watched *Dr. Strangelove* sixteen times. The list of other movies he truly loved is notable for its eclectic discernment: *Across 110th Street* (which made such an impression he memorized—and once recited—the entire script), *Bullitt, The Godfather, It's a Wonderful Life, Miracle on 34th Street, Monty Python and the Holy Grail, Dirty Harry, Mr. Skeffington, On the Waterfront, Patton, Rebel Without a Cause, The Man with the Golden Arm, The Pink Panther, Executive Action* (a conspiracy thriller about the JFK assassination, a subject that deeply intrigued Presley), *The Wild Bunch, Wuthering Heights*, and *To Kill a Mockingbird*. He particularly loved *Patton*, often quoting the line "All glory is fleeting." Two outliers in his list of personal favorites are Max Ophüls's artsy sentimental masterpiece *Letter from an Unknown Woman* (1948) and Victor Fleming's drama *The Way of All Flesh* (1927), for which Emil Jannings won the Best Actor Oscar as the bank clerk who goes tragically astray.

As Schilling recalled: "Sometimes, I would wonder—why are we looking at this three times? Elvis would pick up something, not from the major star necessarily, and use that. He would pick up little things you never knew about."

His curiosity about movies was almost boundless: in September 1963, in nightly sessions at the Memphian cinema house, he watched the Roger Corman horror *The Terror*; a worthy documentary about native culture in New Guinea called *The Sky Above, the Mud Below*; the musical *Hootenanny Hoot*; and *All the Way Home*, a film of James Agee's autobiographical novel about his Tennessee childhood and his father's death. Even in the 1970s, as depression took hold, Elvis found solace at the movies, dropping into the Memphian night after night when he was home.

As he knew so much about movies, reading some of the scripts he was given sometimes left Elvis nauseous. Yet he never entirely lost his curiosity about movie making. John Rich, who directed him twice, once recalled how interested Presley was in the process. "One day he walked by my cutting room and he said 'Can I watch?' The editing process fascinated him. But about five minutes later, the guys came by and said, 'C'mon Elvis that's boring.' I always regretted that because he had a real interest in what I was doing."

The on-set presence of the Memphis Mafia—the retinue of friends he paid to keep him company, serve him, and protect him from the outside world—put a barrier between the star and his writers and directors, but their presence—like the star's country-boy politeness on set—probably reflected his own deep insecurity. Certainly their pranks became more pronounced as the movies became interchangeable. In between scenes, Elvis often released his frustration with karate sessions behind his trailer.

Though he was usually polite, even gracious, he seemed increasingly to insulate himself against Hollywood, a community that he felt thoroughly misunderstood him. In a way, he was doing his manager's bidding. As David Hajdu noted in *The New York Review of Books*: "Parker effectively kept Elvis out of the film world: they [his movies] have always existed in a self-contained, unchanging sphere all their own, unrelated to developments in film during the same years."

The star's reticence frustrated some directors such as Rich and Sidney who recalled, after *Viva Las Vegas* was shot: "What you knew about Elvis 15 minutes after meeting him was about all you'd ever know. He was like a piece of glass. At the end of a long day shooting with Frank Sinatra, Dean Martin, Clark Gable, you'd sit around and have a lot of laughs. Not with Elvis. He had his troupe and you couldn't get close to him."

Put the Blame on Who?

Once, Schilling recalls, Elvis was angered enough to confront producer Hal Wallis. Interviewed on the set of *Becket* (adapted for the screen by Edward Anhalt, co-writer of *Girls! Girls! Girls!*), Wallis had said it was necessary to make the "commercially successful Presley pictures" to do "artistic pictures." Schilling says that Elvis was so angry he went up to Wallis and said, "Mr. Wallis, when I do get to do my *Becket*?"

Such defiance hardly sounds like the "yes, sir, no ma'am" Elvis of popular legend, but Wallis's remark clearly stung: Peter Guralnick and Ernst Jorgensen note in their chronology *Elvis Day by Day* that he complained about Wallis's remark in that interview often in his last years.

Blaming Wallis was easy but not entirely fair. The producer became, like Fike, a surrogate for Parker, the misdirected focus of Elvis's rage at his manager. Even Wallis dreamed of doing something different with Presley—pairing him, for example, with John Wayne in the classic western *True Grit*. He may have despaired of breaking the manager's hold over his star and challenging the soundtrack-selling status quo.

Elvis could have, as Priscilla Presley remarked later, demanded better scripts. Then again, the King had, as his first mentor Sun Studios founder Sam Phillips observed, "the biggest inferiority complex of anyone I ever knew." For all his disgust and discontent, he avoided the confrontation that could have redefined his movie career, and publicly, as he did an interview with *Parade* magazine in 1962, he defended the status quo, saying: "You can't go beyond your limitations." Yet by the mid-1960s, even Weiss began to lose faith in the formula, complaining that Wallis wanted everything "kept pretty shallow" and noting that the depressed star was "walking through the movies. All that natural gift, the extraordinary ability he had, squandered."

Elvis never did *Becket*. And many of his movies have long been regarded—even by their disgusted star—as a kind of freak show. In the worst of them, it's hard to believe he is the same star whose pelvis almost gave Ed Sullivan an aneurysm. As the critic David Thomson put it: "Is there a greater contrast between energy and routine than that between Elvis Presley the phenomenon live and on record and Elvis the automaton on film?"

This paradox makes Elvis such a perplexing yet charismatic figure. He is simultaneously the most famous person in the world and, as the Albert Goldmans of this world would have it, a puppet. In his second film, director and screenwriter Kanter had tried to warn Elvis of the pitfalls ahead, having his star—as vulnerable young singing sensation Deke Rivers—ask his agent: "That's how you're selling me, isn't it? Like a monkey in a zoo."

In Presley's best films you can see, as Kanter said, "Here's a good actor, who given time and better scripts and less reliance on lyrics and money and singing could have been a superb actor." Though Elvis never disappeared into a role in the manner of Robert de Niro, his work did suggest that his instantly recognizable persona had many facets and complexities. Unfortunately, as an actor, he was a victim of his own genius. As a singer, he had been dubbed "Brando with a guitar." Yet as an actor, without a guitar, he was no Brando. The alchemy Presley achieved in a record studio on such songs as "Mystery Train," "It Hurts Me," "Long Black Limousine," and "Heartbreak Hotel" was never quite matched by anything he did onscreen.

Sometimes, when you watch the better movies, there are moments when it is hard not to be moved by Presley's predicament. Acting was his boyhood dream. When he came to Hollywood, that dream, like Jay Gatsby's, must have seemed so close he could barely fail to grasp it. But fail he did. Although he had enough talent to suggest he could have flourished as an actor, by the time he left Hollywood in 1970, he was glad to go, to leave the scene of (as he saw it) the greatest failure of his career. As he told Lanchester when they were discussing her movies in 1967, "You see, ma'am, I had an ambition to be a proper actor myself once."

The King's Most Surprising Comeback

Although Pauline Kael once said: "Elvis starred in 31 movies which ranged from mediocre to putrid, and just about in that order," critics are gradually reevaluating Elvis on celluloid. Andy Warhol adored the "vacant, vacuous Hollywood style" of Elvis's musical comedies, arguing, "They don't really have much to say, that's why they're so good." Some Presley movies have been reappraised as effectively extended music videos, precursors of a genre that became industrialized with the birth of MTV in 1981. The verdict on others has changed, as such writers as Danny Peary have challenged the critical orthodoxy. Peary's book *Cult Movies* (1981) was a landmark in the reappraisal of films. If a movie like Jerry Lewis's *The Nutty Professor* (1963) could be hailed as a cult classic, couldn't the same be said of many Presley pictures?

Peary was particularly impressed by *King Creole* for "mixing genres, going into a serious dramatic musical, already an odd form, into pure 1940s drive-by-night film noir" and for giving Presley the chance to play a "full-fledged, contradictory human being." While eulogizing that film, he recalled discussing *Viva Las Vegas* with Slobodan Šijan, the director of the great Yugoslav comedy *Who's Singing Over There?* (1981). Šijan had gone to see the Presley musical with a friend and came out of the cinema feeling he'd wasted his afternoon. His friend challenged him: "You like musicals, don't you?" Šijan admitted he did. Under further questioning, he also agreed that he liked Ann-Margret, Las Vegas, and Elvis. At this point, Šijan had, Peary wrote, "an epiphany: he'd become an insufferable elitist, the worst kind of prude. He'd been lying to himself: actually, he'd enjoyed *Viva Las Vegas*." (He's in good company: Steven Spielberg once told the actress and dancer Teri Garr it was his favorite movie—not his favorite Elvis movie, but his favorite movie, period.)

The elitism Šijan repudiated still leaves many critics to underestimate even Presley's better movies. A handful—most obviously *Roustabout*, which inspired Peter Ormrod's whimsical homage *Eat the Peach* (1986) and *Speedway*, one of the stepping stones for *Pulp Fiction*—are genuine cult classics. Others—notably *Harum Scarum*, in which he plays a singing assassin—are odd enough to intrigue, baffle, and alarm. Some of his later efforts—notably *Change of Habit* and *The Trouble with Girls*—are significantly better than they are given credit for. And there is plenty of unpretentious fun to be had at times in *Blue Hawaii*, *Fun in Acapulco*, *Frankie and Johnny*, *G.I. Blues*, *Girl Happy*, *It Happened at the World's Fair*, *Kid Galahad*, *Speedway*, *Spinout*, and *Tickle Me*.

The movies also inspired a lot of Elvis's most iconic music. If Presley had never worked in Hollywood, we might never have enjoyed such classics as "Love Me Tender," "Teddy Bear," "Jailhouse Rock," "Young and Beautiful," "King

Creole," "Trouble," "Hard Headed Woman," "Wild in the Country" (a lovely, seriously underrated ballad), "Can't Help Falling in Love," "Return to Sender," "Bossa Nova Baby," and "Viva Las Vegas." Or such minor gems as "Almost," "Clean Up Your Own Backyard," "In My Way," "Let Yourself Go," "A Little Less Conversation," "Party," "Suppose," and "Treat Me Nice."

Leonard Bernstein said once: "Elvis Presley is the greatest cultural figure of the 20th century. He changed everything—music, language, clothes—and a whole revolution—the sixties—sprang from it." You can't understand that without watching the movies even if you will occasionally wonder how Bernstein's great innovator, applauded by Gene Kelly as he shimmied his way through *Jailhouse Rock*, ended up singing a ditty like "Queenie Wahine's Papaya."

And with each successive Elvisless year, the movies are, at their best, the most powerful visual reminder of his indispensable genius. Because with Elvis, it was never just about the music, it was about the look too: the flashy outfits, the curling lip (about which he quipped: "I got news for you, baby, I did 29 pictures like that"), and the rare, almost Byronic, physical beauty. The vocal pyrotechnics that make "Trouble" such a classic are even more striking when you see Elvis, at his most electrifying, performing the song in *King Creole*.

The Only Elvis Autobiography We Have

There are also, as Elaine Dundy explored in her book *Elvis and Gladys*, powerful autobiographical undercurrents to many Elvis movies—even the most disposable ones—which suggests there is more going on than first meets the eye.

The best-known aspects of his life—his intense bond with his mother, his stillborn twin, his Svengali manager, his southern character, his military service, and his womanizing ways—are reflected and distorted in many of his movies. These resonances were so noticeable that when George Kirgo was hired to write the screenplay for *Spinout*, the first thing he and co-writer Theodore J. Flicker did was try to "imagine what Elvis's life was like." Their first script was returned with Parker's verdict: "When I do Elvis Presley's life story, I'll get a hell of a lot more than a million dollars for it."

As fiercely as debate over every aspect of Elvis Presley's life, times, and career has raged, one central mystery remains: what kind of man was Elvis? Many fans—especially those too young, too poor, or to distant to see him live—feel the best hope of answering that question lies in footage of the man himself.

Sometimes the clues may be small: an expression, a reaction, or a song. Often the most revealing moments are relatively innocuous: the way he walks down a street in *Change of Habit*, erupts into laughter during *The Trouble with Girls* and sneaks away from a party with a friend's girl in *Stay Away, Joe*. Very occasion-ally—especially in his recollections of his dead mother with psychologist Hope Lange in *Wild in the Country*, his anger at his mother's funeral in *Flaming Star*, and the exchanges with his ineffectual father Dean Jagger in *King Creole*—we are given a telling glimpse of the man behind the myth. Or, as Lamar Fike might say, the chameleon behind the myth.

Did Hollywood Save the King?

The ultimate irony about the movies, one that even loyal Elvis fans are reluctant to acknowledge, is that they may have saved his career. Michael Streissguth, the associate professor of English at Le Moyne University in Syracuse, New York, wrote that "by dumb luck, the movie years had the effect of preserving Elvis economically while the wild music environment passed over. Elvis was not spent from years of musical rejection, so when the time was right and people were ready to see him in concert, he was fresh and ready to pounce on the opportunity. Inadvertently, Parker's decisions in the early and mid-1960s gave us the great Elvis music of the very late 1960s and early 1970s."

There was nothing intrinsically stupid about taking Elvis to Hollywood. The same strategy had prolonged the careers of Crosby and Frank Sinatra. Presley's initial success had persuaded Beatles manager Brian Epstein that this approach would work for his group, but acting didn't excite the Fab Four as it did their idol. The execution of the Hollywood strategy began to go awry for Elvis when three movies a year—almost all musical comedies, became the norm. "They don't need titles, you could just number them" said one MGM executive. This was the treadmill Presley was referring to when he said, onstage in one of his first Vegas concerts, that his career had got "stuck in that big rut by Hollywood boulevard."

Yet if he had stuck to making records in the face of the British Beat invasion in the mid-1960s, how would he have fared? Very few artists had remained at the top for as long as Elvis—between 1956 and 1963, when "One Broken Heart for Sale" stalled at number 11, every regular single made the top ten in the Billboard Hot 100. Even if he had been cutting better songs, the Beatles and their successors—notably Herman's Hermits and the Monkees—would probably have brought that run to an end.

The movies gave Elvis one competitive advantage: they provided good promotional vehicles for singles like "Bossa Nova Baby" and "Viva Las Vegas." Only between 1965 and 1967 did Presley really struggle on the charts, as the films attracted smaller audiences and the songs churned out by Hill and Range's music factory deteriorated in quality. Even Parker knew better than to try to pick a single from the *Paradise, Hawaiian Style* soundtrack. Yet this strange retreat, a move some have portrayed as the King's abdication, helped maintain his stardom at a time when his kind of music was no longer fashionable.

Though many fans gave up on him altogether, others—even those who felt the movies had become, as one writer put it in *Elvis Monthly*, "animated puppet shows for not over-bright children"—just stopped watching them and waited for the real Elvis to return. Which he did in 1968. The tragic irony is that the TV special—and the Vegas shows that swiftly followed—extended his career and probably shortened his life. Many of the problems that marred his later years—of which depression, drug abuse, ill health, and insomnia were merely the most visible—became apparent while he was working in Hollywood, but the punitive live schedule (he played over 1,100 concerts between 1969 and 1977) exacerbated them and isolated the star from those who might have helped him.

The Final Word

The aim of this book is to tell you things about Elvis's movies you don't already know and, where appropriate, to persuade you to reconsider some things you think you already know. In exploring some of the controversies—over scripts, co-stars, even hairstyles—that have made Presley's film career so thoroughly misunderstood, this book aims, above all, to send you back to the movies to watch them afresh.

In a perceptive appreciation of Presley's film career in the *Los Angeles Times*, Mark Olsen pointed out: "Even all these years later, having made 33 theatrically released films, he is still somehow at once completely familiar and utterly unknowable. His film career leaves us with fixed images—Andy Warhol's iconic gunslinger Elvis comes from *Flaming Star*—but also with open ideas and possibilities." Even the most indifferent of his movies really do, as Olsen suggests, "add to the dynamic of his mystery and the enduring vitality of his talents."

Loving Who?

Love Me Tender to King Creole

In early 1956, Warner Bros lawyer Joseph H. Hazen received a phone call that would change Elvis's life. His sister-in-law Harriet Ames, a member of the wealthy Annenberg clan, rang to tell him, "Look at that fellow on the television, Elvis Presley. He's a terrific dancer. He's quite a character." Intrigued, Hazen turned over to catch Presley on the Dorsey Brothers' *Stage Show*. One glimpse was enough to convince him to call movie producer Hal Wallis and urge him, "Turn on the TV, the kid is terrific."

Hazen, fifty-seven, and Wallis, fifty-five, were partners in a venture that produced movies for Paramount to distribute. Hazen managed the finances, while Wallis made the movies. The producer was just as smitten by Presley: "There was something about his eyes, a solemn look . . . an expressive face, a new personality that I knew was definitely star material for the screen."

Though Wallis didn't know it, becoming such a star was the dream that had inspired this singing sensation since he had first sneaked into the cinema to watch Gene Autry, Rogers and Astaire, and a cowboy serial starring a now forgotten character called Sunset Carson. Elvis's movie tastes had broadened since then. His favorite actors included Humphrey Bogart, Marlon Brando, Tony Curtis, James Dean, Kim Novak, and Richard Widmark, and the films he cherished varied from *Rebel Without a Cause* to *The Student Prince*, the Mario Lanza musical in which the tenor sang but couldn't appear because he was too portly.

Elvis may have been desperate to go to Hollywood, but his manager wasn't about to let his guard down. Wallis and Hazen bombarded him with calls, but Parker, cannily, ignored them until both partners had learned the crucial lesson he was not to be rushed. Eventually, he stopped playing it cool. Presley flew out to Hollywood, landing with a camera around his neck, as if he was tourist in town to take pictures rather than a star who wanted to make them. On March 26, 1956, at Paramount Studios, Presley played two dramatic scenes from the Burt Lancaster–Katharine Hepburn drama *The Rainmaker* and mimed "Blue Suede Shoes."

In the light of what happened in the sixteen years and thirty-three movies to come, it is worth reexamining the reactions to that initial test. Allan Weiss, who wrote six Presley movies for Wallis, later recalled that the star acted "with amateurish conviction like the lead in a high school play" but was "absolute dynamite when he stepped up and started lip-synching the words to his familiar hit." This was the verdict he used later to justify some of his screenplays, insisting, "It would be a mistake to try to force this strong personality into a preconceived role: parts must be tailored for him, designed to exploit the thing he did best—sing, he was much more successful in lighter pictures that cast him as a singing personality." That might explain why Weiss didn't write any of the three movies that are generally regarded as Presley's best: *Jailhouse Rock*, *King Creole*, and *Flaming Star*.

In other interviews, Weiss has sounded more impressed with Presley as a young thespian, saying once: "No one had any expectations; he was such a strange, quiet fellow—so completely foreign—but he sang, read a scene from *The Rainmaker* and answered questions asked from off-screen—and it was phenomenal. It was one of those life-changing experiences."

In Wallis's memoirs, he said he was impressed by Presley's "originality" and the way the camera caressed him. The eloquent advocacy of Abe Lastfogel at the William Morris Agency (which represented Elvis in Hollywood) convinced him that he could use Elvis to tap into a youth market still mourning its dead idol James Dean. Yet the shrewd producer was also impressed by the singer's record sales, and music seemed to offer the surest commercial reward for him, Paramount, Elvis, Parker, and RCA.

"The idea of tailoring Elvis for dramatic roles is something we never attempted," Wallis declared years later. "We didn't sign Elvis as a second Jimmy Dean. We signed him as a number-one Elvis Presley." Wallis's ringing defense of his management of his star is slightly undermined by the sense that, for the producer, "number-one Elvis Presley" was in movie terms roughly on a par with a number-one circus attraction.

Wallis's verdict suited Parker (who privately doubted whether "his boy" had the ability to become the new Dean or Brando), but it wasn't the universal view. Hal Kanter, who directed the first Presley/Wallis picture, *Loving You*, had initially been skeptical yet, after watching the screen test, found Elvis "charming, witty and completely unafraid of the camera." William Morris did not back Lastfogel's faith by playing hardball in talks with Wallis. Young agent Lenny Hirshan was instructed to get Presley as much work as he could before the singer's star waned. So the agency advised the Colonel to accept Wallis's offer of a deal for one picture, with options for six more. The sums sounded impressive—with a $150,000 fee for Presley's first film—but when production of *Loving You* started, Parker was furious to discover that Lizabeth Scott and Wendell Corey were being paid more than his star. He never trusted William Morris's advice on movie contracts again.

As he would for much of his movie career, Presley remained oblivious to such machinations. He was simply glad to be in Hollywood, mingling with actors like Natalie Wood, Dennis Hopper, and Nick Adams, who had co-starred with Dean, whom he believed had been "a genius in acting." He also met—and fascinated— Nicholas Ray, who directed *Rebel Without a Cause* and was desperate to cast Elvis in his western *The True Story of Jesse James*. Inevitably, the idea came to nothing, and Ray made do with Robert Wagner while Presley made his screen debit in the B western *Love Me Tender*, originally titled *The Reno Brothers*, which had been revamped to give him a significant supporting role in which he could sing four songs.

The cast and crew on his first movie weren't sure what to make of him. His love interest Debra Paget summed up Hollywood's preconceptions when she said later: "Before I met him, I figured he must be some sort of moron." On

Elvis and Debra Paget in *Love Me Tender* (1956). Paget got on well with Presley considering she feared he was a moron.   *20th Century Fox/Photofest*

set, his humility, charm, and industry overcame such skepticism, but it could do nothing to shield him from the critical abuse that greeted the movie's release on November 21, 1956. The *Hollywood Reporter* dismissed Presley as "an obscene child" but did note that the new hero possessed "mannerisms by Brando out of the Actors Studio" and concluded: "The new hero is an adolescent. Whether he is twenty or thirty or forty, he is fifteen and excessively sorry for himself. He is essentially a lone wolf who wants to belong." That last line pretty much sums up Elvis's status in the movie industry as his film career progressed and, you could argue, the tragedy of his life and death.

Yet in the winter of 1956, Presley was just glad to be acting. Reassured to see *Love Me Tender* grossing $540,000 in its first week—second only to *Giant*, the epic Dean/Liz Taylor/Rock Hudson western—Wallis rushed ahead with *Loving You*, a heavily sentimentalized, lightly fictionalized account of Presley's rise to fame that celebrates and satirizes the tricks showbiz uses to sell its stars. By January 1957, when *Loving You* started shooting, Kanter had to close the set to keep secretaries, executives' wives, and the heirs of Hollywood's moguls at bay. America's curiosity about Presley was almost as intense, and *Loving You* peaked at number 7 on *Variety*'s box-office survey. He was the fourth-biggest box-office star in America in 1957. That was some achievement, but Presley would have noted that the third-biggest attraction was his friend and rival Pat Boone.

Although *Loving You* focused on the generation gap and cast Presley as a very vulnerable, misunderstood young hero, the movie was infused with the kind of can-do optimism that reflected the traditional values of such showbiz biopics. In the Kanter/Wallis version of America, no differences were so profound that they could not be overcome by a rousing rendition of "Got a Lot of Loving You to Do." The presence of Elvis's mother, Gladys, clapping her son on in the finale, obliquely emphasized that the generation gap could be closed.

Though all is well at the end of Presley's next two movies—*Jailhouse Rock* and *King Creole*—they are not infused with the same kind of sunny spirit as *Loving You*. These films were darker, complex, more challenging for Elvis's fans and for himself as an actor. The obligatory happy ending cannot quite erase the issues and injustices they spotlight.

His performance in *Jailhouse Rock* is eloquently captured by Clarence Worley, the protagonist Christian Slater plays in Tarantino's script for the movie *True Romance*: "In *Jailhouse Rock*, he is rockabilly: mean, surly, nasty, rude. He couldn't give a fuck about nothin' 'cept rockin' and rollin', livin' fast, dying young, and leaving a good-looking corpse."

Jailhouse Rock was received so enthusiastically by its target audience that it grossed $4 million on its initial release and sparked a mini-riot in Oakland, California, when some male cinemagoers took Presley's dialogue ("That ain't tactics, honey, it's just the beast in me") too literally and grabbed several girls as they walked up the aisle. In *King Creole*, a kind of *Rebel Without a Cause* with rock and roll, he is so convincing as rebel with a cause Danny Fisher that Howard Thompson declared in the *New York Times*, "Cut my legs off and call me Shorty,

Elvis Presley can act." Friends say the *Times* review made him happier than they had ever seen him.

Though Wallis had declared there was no point in trying to build a dramatic picture around Elvis, he came very close to that with *King Creole*. Hiring Michael Curtiz to direct hinted at greater artistic ambition. So did the cast: Dean Jagger, Carolyn Jones, Walter Matthau, and Vic Morrow were merely the standout performers in a strong ensemble. And the care that Curtiz, Wallis, and Hazen put into the story—they even likened the central clash between father and son to the dysfunctional relationship between Brick and Big Daddy in Tennessee Williams's *Cat on a Hot Tin Roof*—suggested that all concerned had loftier ambitions than showcasing a dozen new songs.

They may have been inspired by the thought that they had competition for Elvis's services: Robert Mitchum had been desperately keen to use the King in his cult moonshine movie *Thunder Road* (1958). It was hardly the kind of film Parker would have wanted Elvis to make, but the star was intrigued and flattered by the offer and impressed by Mitchum. The offer does suggest that Elvis's growing confidence on the screen could have opened up all kinds of roles if Parker had handled his client differently. The same thought had occurred to Hazen, who suggested that if Elvis had had a lawyer, Parker could never have run his client in the way he did.

At the end of shooting for *King Creole*, Presley walked over to Curtiz and said, "Thank you very much Mr. Curtiz. Now I know what a director is." Commercially, the story of Danny Fisher was less successful than its predecessor—though it peaked at number 5 on *Variety*'s box-office survey—but here was proof that he could look like Brando without a guitar. His cousin Billy Smith said, "That was his best film—if he'd been able to do more dramatic pictures like that the whole story might have been different."

It's a showbiz cliché that professional triumph must be accompanied by personal tragedy, and, only six weeks after *King Creole*'s release, Presley's mother, Gladys, died on August 14, 1958. Although Elvis had bought her the antebellum mansion Graceland in 1957, her spirits had sunk as fame separated her from her son. She turned to alcohol for consolation and to diet pills in an attempt to look good for Elvis in public. The news that he had been drafted—remember the Korean War had ended only in 1953—made her anxious and exacerbated her depression, and she died, at the age of forty-six, after problems with her liver. Elvis was distraught. He was already the most famous man in the world and, at twenty-three, looked destined to achieve his greatest ambition, to be a "good actor." Yet suddenly, it all counted for nothing.

Love Me Tender, Twentieth Century Fox, 1956

Director, Robert D. Webb; Screenplay, Robert Buckner (based on a story by Maurice Geraghty); Music, Lionel Newman with suggestions by Ken Darby; Producer, David Weisbart; Running time, 89 minutes

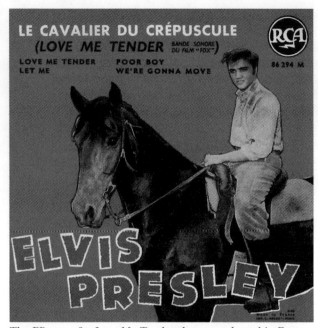

The EP cover for Love Me Tender that was released in France.
RCA ensured *Love Me Tender*'s music crossed the world.

Cast: Elvis (Clint Reno), Richard Egan (Vance Reno), Debra Paget (Cathy Reno), Robert Middleton (Mr. Siringo), Mildred Dunnock (Martha Reno)

Clint (Elvis), the youngest of four Reno brothers, stays behind to run the family farm while his elder siblings go off to fight for the Confederacy in the Civil War. News spreads that Vance (Richard Egan), the eldest of the four, has been killed in battle. Yet reports of Vance's death prove to have been greatly exaggerated, and he is shocked to discover on his return that his old sweetheart Cathy (Debra Paget) has married Clint. Life isn't made any easier by the fact that Cathy clearly still loves Vance.

The romantic tensions are exacerbated by the complicated repercussions of a robbery the three eldest Reno brothers staged on a federal payroll without realizing that the Civil War was over. A posse turns up on the farm to arrest the three, but Clint, convinced they are innocent, stages a rescue and can't understand why Vance is insistent the loot should be handed over to the authorities. After various misunderstandings, Clint comes to believe that Vance and Cathy have double-crossed him and, having lost the plot even more conclusively than the scriptwriters, shoots Vance and is fatally shot in return. Sibling rivalries are ultimately set aside as Clint lies dying in Cathy's arms. In the final shot, Twentieth Century Fox made a half-hearted attempt to placate fans who had been outraged by the leaked news that their idol died in the film by having a ghostly close-up of Elvis crooning "Love Me Tender" as the family leave his grave.

Essentially a B-movie period western, initially called *The Reno Brothers*, this was a very odd star vehicle for Presley, who has a secondary role in a part for which many other young actors—including Robert Wagner—had been considered. Even the decision to rename it *Love Me Tender* and insert four songs (so much for Presley's initial contention that he wasn't going to sing in his movies) couldn't obscure the fact that Egan and Paget are central to the movie, while Elvis is essentially a guest star. He doesn't even appear until the twentieth minute, and even then he is behind a plow. This low-key introduction does at least reduce the pressure on him to act. Apart from the title song, the other numbers—"We're Gonna Move," "Let Me," and "Poor Boy"—seem either slightly or hilariously anachronistic, especially when Elvis starts shaking his hips while performing "We're Gonna Move" on the front porch.

Wallis had loaned out Presley to Twentieth Century Fox, letting the studio test the market for his new protégé. Though *Love Me Tender* recouped its costs in three days, the film's hasty, incomplete makeover may explain why one fan reviewer complained about his "totally unsuitable role and the almost childish persistence of the other stars in trying to 'better' Elvis's lines." Wallis was almost as unimpressed. His associate producer Paul Nathan told Parker "very confidentially and as man to man" that the film was "crap."

Presley got kinder notices from his fellow actors than from Wallis or the critics. Egan mused: "They seemed to put him in front of a backdrop and have him sing a song. He could do that easily but he had much more depth. He showed extraordinary ability to catch on." Paget was impressed by how quickly he understood the technical aspects of the trade that many actors took years to master. The young singer was encouraged by the thoughtful tuition of director Robert D. Webb, who would take him aside before scenes and help him visualize them.

Infuriated by the hype surrounding the film—and by the threat to society its star seemed to personify—many critics were simply vicious. *Time* magazine famously inquired: "Is it a sausage? It is certainly smooth and damp looking . . . Or is it a Walt Disney goldfish? It has the same sort of big, soft beautiful eyes and long, curly lashes . . . Is it a corpse? The face just hangs there limp and white with its little drop-seat mouth, rather like Lord Byron in the wax museum."

In the *New York Times*, Bosley Crowther was only a shade nicer, calling the picture a "slight case of a horse opera with the heaves" before adding, "Mr. Presley's dramatic contribution is not a great deal more impressive than that of one of the slavering nags." Crowther did pay Presley the compliment of saying that "he goes at it as though it were *Gone with the Wind*," while damning Egan for lethargy and Paget for her melancholia. The only actor Crowther actually liked was Mildred Dunnock as Ma Reno, although he added, "She loses the viewer completely when she shows enthusiasm for Mr. Presley's songs." Gossip queen Hedda Hopper didn't even need to see the film to know she wouldn't like it, complaining that the fans "screaming and yelling left me cold."

For someone who wanted to be an actor, this should have been hard to take, but Presley was enough of a realist to admit, "If you play yourself, you're much better off. Like Jimmy Dean, Marlon Brando. With *Love Me Tender*, I couldn't play myself because this character I was portraying was so far from me, it wasn't even funny."

Presley was being too hard on himself. There are times when his acting is wildly off-key, or you can see him getting his breath before a key moment, but he is appropriately sincere and sweet as the younger brother who idolizes his elder sibling. He is much less assured when his character goes bad, though, to be fair, the screenplay doesn't make the transformation especially plausible.

Ultimately, the reservations of Crowther, Presley, Wallis, and *Time* magazine didn't matter. In today's money, *Love Me Tender* took $36 million at the box office. Although the movie was famously given its premiere at the Paramount Theater in Times Square, with a giant Elvis poster titillating the girls who had waited outside since 10:00 a.m., business in the Big Apple wasn't as sensational as elsewhere in America. Within twelve days of release, business in the city's cinemas was merely "uppish and downish." Such relative indifference would be taken into account. His movies would in future premiere in other cities and, even in the late 1960s, remain stubbornly popular in the South and West.

Still, who cared about the critics or New York? *Love Me Tender* had made a colossal profit. That was the only verdict that mattered to Parker.

Loving You, Paramount, 1957

Director, Hal Kanter; Screenplay, Herbert Baker/Hal Kanter (based on a story by Mary Agnes Thompson); Music, Walter Scharf; Producer, Hal B. Wallis; Running time, 101 minutes

Cast: Elvis (Deke Rivers), Lizabeth Scott (Glenda Markle), Wendell Corey (Tex Warner), Dolores Hart (Susan Jessup), James Gleason (Carl Meade), Ralph Dumke (Jim Tallman)

Cunningly crafted to sell Elvis to mainstream America without alienating his millions of teenage fans, *Loving You* is the archetypal Hollywood rags-to-riches success story distinguished by some decent rock music, Hal Kanter's cynical yet sweet script, and some compelling performances, not least from Presley, who at times shows the kind of stillness that characterized such screen greats as Spencer Tracy.

This was Wallis's first Presley movie, and he took some care to make sure the investment paid off, casting two capable actors he had on long-term contract—Scott and Corey—to support his inexperienced star. Wallis had a script that, he said, needed something. When Kanter asked what it needed, he was told: "A complete rewrite."

At Wallis's urging, the director created an entertaining story that seemed specifically designed to counter a recent suggestion by New York congressman Emmanuel Celler, who was investigating the record industry, that Presley's "animal gyrations are violative of all that I know to be in good taste." Looking back, the director realized how fortunate he was to work with Elvis at such an early stage in the singer's movie career: "There was no formula at the time. It hadn't been established yet. I was lucky and naive. I was marching to my own drummer."

Deke Rivers (Elvis) is a young truck driver whose talent for belting out a song catches the eye of scheming press agent Glenda Markle (Scott), who sees him as the "gimmick" that can help her ex-husband Tex Warner (Corey) turn around his career as the leader of fading country band the Rough Ridin' Ramblers.

Deke is mesmerized by and half in love with husky, worldly "Miss Glenda"—the way the character addresses her reflects the rather formal manner in which Presley instinctively addressed older or more experienced co-stars—but also attracted to demure young singer Susan Jessup (Dolores Hart, who is so wholesome it's as if she has already decided that one day she'll give all this up to enter a convent).

Elvis and Dolores Hart in *Loving You* (1957). Innocents abroad: As Deke and Nellie, Presley and Hart learned showbiz's cynical ways.   *Paramount Pictures/Photofest*

It's obvious that Deke has the talent to make it to the top, but just to help him on his way Glenda manufactures a riot, creates a fictional benefactor, and parlays a ban on one of the kid's concerts into a live nationwide telecast that will surely be his ticket to the big time.

Unfortunately, the young singer doesn't like the rap he's getting. When he complains that "they make it sound like they ought to be ashamed just to hear me sing," Kanter is feeding Presley the lines with which to disarm his critics. By the end of the movie, after Deke has driven off into the night, spilled all his secrets with a dreamy vulnerability that had girls swooning, and been reconciled to his newfound fame, even flint-hearted moviegoers are forced to conclude that here is, as Ed Sullivan had famously put it, a "decent fine boy" who was "thoroughly all right."

It's all cleverly done. Scott's agent (Kanter's amusing take on Parker, whom he described as a "King Con") is Machiavelli Lite, redeemed by her love for the endearing if ineffectual Corey. Watching this movie, you get at least a glimpse of the impact the real Presley had on America and the impact fame would have on its star. The lack of privacy—Deke can't even go out for a meal without being asked to sing, and his cars are covered in lipstick love letters—would define Elvis's life in ways he could barely have imagined at this point in his career. The use of shadows to highlight the hero's mythic qualities also points to the godlike aura that would come to surround the singer.

Kanter had watched Presley on tour, and this is the performer's story, albeit as observed by a sympathetic yet cynical outsider. Raw, naive, yet immensely gifted and blessed with enough intuitive intelligence to discern that he is being sold like a monkey in a zoo, Rivers is an appealing hero, made all the more convincing because Kanter has so craftily blurred the distinction between character and actor, a sleight of hand that works spectacularly well during the presentation of such rock-and-roll classics as "Got a Lot of Livin' to Do" (during the reprise of which you can see Gladys, in the audience, applauding her son's performance), "Party," and "Mean Woman Blues," which are such sublime representations of his 1950s stage act these scenes are now almost of historic value. At the same time, with such ballads as the title song and the soft, self-parodying rock pop of "Teddy Bear," the movie reached out to millions who might not have thrilled to "Hound Dog."

Presley's growing self-confidence onscreen is reflected in the way he has made over his image. The blue eyes are even more striking when contrasted with the inky jet-black hair he had styled after his idol Tony Curtis. His new look completes what is, for all the sentimentality, a near definitive introduction to its celluloid star. When "Miss Glenda" defends rock and roll as protected by the American constitution, the movie has rammed the point home. As presented in *Loving You*, the Presley story, as author Susan Doll has noted, is really just a more up-to-date version of the Al Jolson story. And if Jolson wasn't a threat to society, then neither, surely, is Elvis.

The movie's presentation of a gyrating Elvis that the world outside North America had never seen had some unexpected consequences. In 1961, a fifteen-year-old French boy named Hervé Fornieri took the name Deke Rivers and, as the lead singer of Les Chats Sauvages, decided it was his mission to bring rock and roll to France.

Jailhouse Rock, MGM, 1957

Director, Richard Thorpe; Screenplay, Guy Trosper (based on a story by Ned Young); Music, Jeff Alexander; Producer, Pandro S. Berman; Running time, 96 minutes

Cast: Elvis (Vince Everett), Judy Tyler (Peggy Van Alden), Mickey Shaughnessy (Hunk Houghton), Vaughn Taylor (Mr. Shores), Jennifer Holden (Sherry Wilson), Dean Jones (Teddy Talbot), Anne Neyland (Laury Jackson)

If *Loving You* was a film rose, Elvis's third movie was a hard-bitten film noir that largely portrayed the music business as a racket run by sharks that exploited the young and credulous. At one point, the industry's ethical standards are unfavorably likened to those among convicts, when Presley's defiant hero points out that in prison they might steal from you but they'd be too honest to claim what they'd stolen was theirs.

In *Jailhouse Rock*, Elvis is a sneering, embittered antihero who stops being a heel only in the final reel when, after a career-threatening punch in the throat, he bursts into a verse of the achingly beautiful ballad "Young and Beautiful." The unpleasantness was all too much for America's Parent–Teacher Association, who dismissed the movie as a "hackneyed, blown up tale with cheap human values." Posterity has been rather kinder, with some critics—notably Leonard Maltin—suggesting this is Presley's best film.

Singer Vince Everett (Elvis) is sentenced to prison after defending a lady's honor by accidentally killing a man in a barroom brawl. The injustice—and the tuition of his experienced cellmate, a fading country star called Hunk Houghton (Mickey Shaughnessy)—teaches Everett to "do unto others as you would have them do to you—only do it to them first." The point is reinforced when Elvis is ruthlessly and, for many teenage girls watching, thrillingly—whipped after a minor role in a prison riot. The young star later takes Hunk's advice far too literally, smashing his guitar on a heckler's table and storming out of a party given by the parents of pretty Peggy van Alden (Judy Tyler) because they are misguided enough to ask his opinion about dissonance and modern jazz.

In jail, Vince discovers he has musical talent and, mentored by Houghton, steals the limelight at a concert broadcast from the penitentiary, with a heartfelt performance of "I Want to Be Free." From this point, when Hunk looks at his young cellmate he sees only dollar signs. He persuades Vince to sign away 50 percent of his future earnings in return for unspecified management services.

Only on Vince's last day in jail does he realize he has been conned: Hunk had persuaded the prison staff to hide all the fan mail he received after the telecast.

On release, Vince's guitar-swinging ways intrigue petite record-plugger Peggy. His version of "Don't Leave Me Now" is ripped off by a big label called Geneva Records (prompting the remark about ethics in jail and in showbiz) and given to a big star called Mickey Alba. Enraged but determined, Vince and Peggy set up their company, Laurel Records. He owns 51 percent, she owns 40 percent, and their ruthless lawyer Mr. Shores (Vaughn Taylor) has 9 percent. After Peggy sweet-talks DJ Teddy Talbot (Dean Jones, years before he made his name alongside Herbie, the VW Beetle with a mind of its own) into promoting their new record, they have a hit on their hands. The title of Vince's hit, "Treat Me Nice," must surely be ironic, as he doesn't treat anyone nice. When Peggy reprimands his "cheap tactics" after he grabs her, Vince sneers, "That ain't tactics, honey, that's just the beast in me."

When Hunk comes out of jail, even he is taken aback to realize how well his protégé has learned that lesson about doing unto others first. He is kept as a hanger-on—for 10 percent of Vince's earnings—and looks on with disapproval as his boy goes to Hollywood, dates actress Sherry Wilson (Jennifer Holden) despite her daffy costumes, sings "Baby I Don't Care" at a Hollywood swimming-pool party, rocks through "Jailhouse Rock," and finally sells his 51 percent of the company to Geneva, the very label that had ripped him and Peggy off. Seeing the tears in Peggy's eyes, Hunk decides it's time to give Vince what's coming. The beating stops when Vince is caught in the throat and can't breathe (a story that eerily parallels a real-life emergency in which Elvis had to have an operation to remove a tooth cap that had gotten stuck in his throat).

Ultimately, the sound of Vince's voice bursting into life resolves everything. Peggy forgives him so completely—and Hunk looks so convincingly penitent—we don't even think to ask how all the loose ends have been tied up. After all, Peggy has still lost the company that was her life. Presumably, the fact that she is united with this new, ethically improved Vince is sufficient compensation. As for the antihero himself, he has mysteriously contrived to regain his soul without having to give the rest of the world back.

Jailhouse Rock takes risks. As written by Guy Trosper and directed by the prolific Richard Thorpe, Presley is presented as a brooding antihero in the Dean/Brando vein. Yet the backstory doesn't really explain Everett's grudge against the world, and the *Los Angeles Times* reviewer, offended by the "crime, greed, profanity, vulgarity and brutality" in the film, pointed out: "The kids flock to see and hear Presley sing. Yet in this picture, the leading character plays a vicious, rude and unpleasant individual." It is a tribute to Elvis's magnetism that we continue to care about such an arrogant jerk.

The central implausibility of the movie—that an ex-con with a habit of slapping record executives and smashing guitars could rise to the top of the entertainment industry and even advertise his crimes with a song like "Jailhouse Rock"—may, as Elaine Dundy has suggested, mirror the Presley's tragic family secret about Vernon's incarceration in Parchman Prison in the 1930s. It also mirrors the plot of Elia Kazan's "A Face in the Crowd," a jaundiced meditation on celebrity and the power of TV, in which the guitar-playing hero Lonesome Rhodes goes from inmate to idol.

There are echoes of Parker's own past in *Jailhouse Rock* too. On the cell of Hunk's wall is a picture of Hank Snow, the Canadian country singer with whom the Colonel had briefly managed Presley. Nobody quite knows how Parker ended up as Elvis's sole manager, but the most likely explanation is that Parker, sensing the youngster's potential, asked Snow to invest more money in their client and when the Canadian demurred, cut him out of the deal. Snow's picture could be coincidence, but Houghton also mentions he had once toured with Eddy Arnold, Parker's biggest client before Presley.

You don't have to see *Jailhouse Rock* as a full-blown conspiracy to expose Presley's secrets, as Dundy does, to detect something odd about this film. Parker seemed unusually interested, advising producer Pandro Berman that they call the film *Don't Push Me Too Far* or *Trouble Is My Name*. In a visit guaranteed to unsettle his client, he brought the impresario Jim Denny, who had rejected the singer for the *Grand Ole Opry*, onto the set. When Denny assured Elvis he had always had faith in him, the singer said, "Thank you, Mr. Denny," and then turned to the Jordanaires and whispered, "That bastard thinks I've forgotten how he broke my heart." This was also the film where Presley walked out of the studio after MGM ordered his backing singers not to join in a gospel singalong.

The unflattering light the movie sheds on the record industry is intriguing given that *payola*—the practice of bribing DJs to play records on air—was a household word in the 1950s. In 1959, the scandal led WABC Radio to fire Alan Freed, the pioneering DJ who claimed to have coined the term *rock and roll*. Yet the indictment in *Jailhouse Rock* isn't as harsh as it initially seems. As John Mundy writes in *Popular Music on Screen: From Hollywood Musical to Music Video*, the movie implicitly acknowledges the need to move away from Mickey Alba's sentimental balladeering and Hunk Houghton's hillbilly gospel to the more authentic, youthful style showcased by Elvis in such confident rockers as "Treat Me Nice," "Baby I Don't Care," and the triumphant "Jailhouse Rock." As a girl tells Vince after "Baby I Don't Care": "When you sing, it's really Gonesville." The respect with which these numbers are presented implies that show business is ready, willing, and able to embrace rock and roll.

That embrace is at its most glorious when Elvis performs "Jailhouse Rock." Choreographer Alex Romero started out with a different routine that Elvis, though he tried to learn the steps, never felt at home with. Eventually, he fessed up and told Romero he didn't think he could do the dance. The shrewd choreographer asked Presley to perform "Hound Dog" and "Don't Be Cruel" for him and said: "I'm going to go home tonight, and I'm going to take what you do for a routine, and it's going to be you, what you normally feel comfortable doing onstage, but I'm going to choreograph it." He was as good as his word. The next day he laid out the new steps and, Romero recalled, "Elvis whipped through it." The result was a glorious fusion of Presley's own moves and the stylized choreography that had distinguished MGM's greatest musicals.

Presley's attitude toward the film changed when his co-star Tyler and her young husband were killed in a car crash just days after shooting had ended. Stunned at her death, he said he would never watch it again. A pity, because he more than holds his own in a thoroughly watchable movie that benefits from Thorpe's brisk direction.

Widely condemned on release—even Donald Zec in the British newspaper *Daily Mirror* declared it was guaranteed "to turn even the best-insulated stomachs"—*Jailhouse Rock* was a smash, generating $32 million in box-office revenue in today's money. Today the film is prized as surviving evidence of Elvis as the rebellious icon who upset parents, moral guardians, and politicians across America. When Elvis's character says, "I come have a little beer and first thing you know some old broad's pushing me in the corner about some stupid question . . . Shove their conversation! I'm not even sure they were talkin' English," teenagers in cinemas around the world felt like cheering.

The movie has had a significant influence on rock music. Was this, one reviewer wondered, where the Who's Pete Townsend got the idea of smashing his guitar? And is Presley's leering glare one of the inspirations for Bob Dylan's disdain in "Don't Look Back"? And then of course there's the title track itself, which enthralled the young David Coverdale, the lead singer of Whitesnake, and has recently inspired a video homage by the ubiquitous One Direction. As performed by Elvis, this unforgettable blend of MGM and Memphis anticipates the birth of the music video. The great Gene Kelly watched one of the run-throughs and burst into applause when Presley and his crew were done.

King Creole, Paramount, 1958

Director, Michael Curtiz; Writer, Herbert Baker and Michael Vincente Gazzo from Harold Robbins's *A Stone for Danny Fisher*; Music, Walter Scharf; Producer, Hal B. Wallis; Running time, 116 minutes

Cast: Elvis (Danny Fisher), Carolyn Jones (Ronnie), Walter Matthau (Maxie Fields), Dolores Hart (Nellie), Dean Jagger (Mr. Fisher), Liliane Montevecchi ("Forty" Nina), Jan Shepard (Mimi Fisher), Paul Stewart (Charlie LeGrand), Vic Morrow (Shark)

When Elvis performed "Trouble" on the *King Creole* set, actor Tony Russo (who played Chico, the bartender) was mesmerized. As he told Bill Bram, author of *Elvis Frame by Frame*: "I knew I was witnessing something terrific. I ran home that evening and said to my wife, 'My God, I just witnessed one of the greatest performances I've ever seen!' He had such magnetism, vitality and energy."

King Creole remains the Elvis movie where that magnetism, vitality, and energy is displayed most triumphantly. In the context of the King's film career, Curtiz's

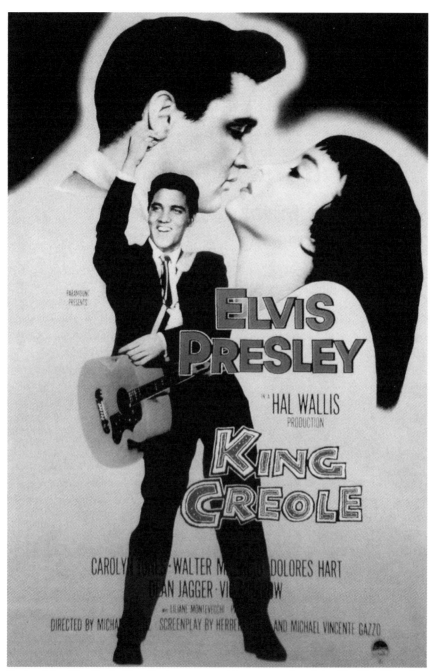

Postcard for *King Creole*. *King Creole* was so good it even convinced the *New York Times* that Elvis could act.

movie seems almost miraculous. It is as if all concerned—even the hard-nosed Wallis—got carried away and decided, first and foremost, that this was going to be a good movie and that taking care of the usual business—providing a hit single and a chart-topping soundtrack album to placate Parker and RCA—could come later. Wallis's inspired decision to ask Curtiz to direct may have changed the mindset. An industry veteran who had made all kinds of movies, from *Charge of the Light Brigade* to *Casablanca* (for which he won the Best Director Oscar), Curtiz was no mere hack, and, although he could be tyrannical and unpredictable on set, he quickly made this movie his own and won his star's respect. When the director told him to change his hairstyle and lose fifteen pounds, Elvis duly obliged. As Jan Shepard (who played Danny's sister Mimi) recalled later: "No matter what Curtiz would ask of Elvis, he would say 'Okay you're the boss.' Curtiz said he thought Elvis was going to be a conceited boy but when he started working with him, he said: 'No, this is a lovely boy, and he's going to be a wonderful actor.'"

As the following, rather breathless, synopsis of the story makes clear, *King Creole* is not one of those Elvis movies that skimps on plot—if anything, there's almost too much of it. A movie that used the Harold Robbins novel *A Stone for Danny Fisher* as the springboard for a melodramatic tale of adolescent angst with a noir-ish ambience that found time to weave in eleven Elvis songs could have, in the hands of a lesser craftsman, degenerated into a shambling mess. Curtiz pulled it off, an against-the-odds triumph that was probably his last truly satisfying movie.

Feeling his troubled life is "fixed—like a crooked fight," Danny Fisher (Elvis) blames his ineffectual, unemployed father (Dean Jagger) for the family's poverty and sweeps up at a nightclub to earn extra money. The job introduces him to some shady characters, including Ronnie (Carolyn Jones), a moll who is virtually owned lock, stock, and barrel by gangster Maxie Fields (Walter Matthau).

After being expelled from school—for poking a kid who taunts him about Ronnie—Danny has to save the moll from further agony at Maxie's brutish hands by singing the song "Trouble" at the nightclub. His magnificent rendition dispels Maxie's suspicions and prompts Charlie LeGrand (Paul Stewart), owner of the King Creole club, to offer him a job. Torn between his love of virginal Nellie (Dolores Hart) and bad girl Ronnie, and desperate to avenge the humiliation of his father by an arrogant boss, Danny gets embroiled with a street gang run by Shark (Vic Morrow). After Danny is set up, by being implicated in the gang's attack on his father, he has no choice but to sign on with Maxie. Seeking retribution against Shark, Danny suffers a serious knife wound. Ronnie whisks him away and nurses him back to health. Yet their hideaway is discovered by Maxie, who kills his moll—and is killed by a dumb gang member Danny had been kind to.

Almost all is forgiven: Danny returns to the King Creole and is reconciled with his father. In time, we are led to believe he may be reconciled with Nellie too, although in the final scene, he is crooning a song Ronnie loved called "As Long as I Have You."

King Creole is so chock full of plot that, especially in the second half, the film almost becomes a rapid-fire sequence of melodramatic events. Yet it remains compelling throughout. Some of the musical sequences—the opening duet with Kitty White on "Crawfish," the glorious abandon of "Trouble," the plaintive "As Long as I Have You," and the stuttering "New Orleans"—are sublime. Even the lesser songs have great lines: in "Dixieland Rock," a green-eyed darling on the loose at the Golden Goose gets the drummer so nervous he loses his sticks.

For once, Elvis is as compelling when he's acting as when he's singing. Advised by a great director, he was also surrounded by some of the finest actors he would ever work with. Hart later said of her famous co-star, "When he was with excellent actors, he became excellent himself." That is precisely what happens in *King Creole*, especially in the scenes with Matthau and Jones. When flirting with Jones's temptress, he makes the most of such lines as "That's a pretty piece of material—you ought to have a dress made out of it someday." He interacts well with Matthau, whose expertise as a character actor later turned him into a star. As Matthau recalled later: "Curtiz would call him Elvy and me Valty. He'd say, 'Elvy and Valty, come here: now, Valty, this is not Academy Award scene, don't act so much. You are high-price actor. Make believe you are low-price actor. Let Elvy act.'"

Presley's scenes with Hart are worth close study. At first glance, Hart's Nellie seems too saccharine to be true, yet she actually gives a superb, nuanced, portrayal of a girl next door compelled by the irresistible force of her attraction to Danny to take risks she would never have contemplated before. Her love isn't blind. After watching him distract customers with his singing while the store she works in is robbed, she says: "You were in on it, weren't you?" Yet when he invites her to follow him into a hotel room, almost as if she were a prostitute, she is so entranced by Danny she doesn't instantly turn away, as a good girl should do. Hurt and confused, she asks: "I don't know, I've never been to a place like this before, but I want to see you again. Is this the way?" That final question is heartbreaking and resonant.

That is just one instance where Wallis, for once, doesn't seek to soften the edges. His associate producer Paul Nathan sent him a memo saying, "The business of Danny using two broken bottles as weapons in one scene is unacceptable." For once, Wallis ignored him. This unusually uncompromising approach dismayed Britain's *Monthly Film Bulletin*, which lamented the film's "calculated violence and viciousness." Most reviewers were—and have since been—much kinder.

In a thoughtful appreciation, film writer Danny Peary (author of *Cult Movies*) praised the film—and Curtiz for its complex mix of genres and for a noir-ish fatalism that recalled the work of the great Fritz Lang. As Peary points out, when Ronnie and Danny are on the run from the mob, the low-key lighting and ambience in one scene—in which the troubled Danny is asleep in the car while the anxious, exhausted Ronnie frets at the car wheel—pays homage to Sylvia Sidney and Henry Fonda "bouncing along the dark highway in Lang's *You Only Live Twice* (1937)."

Acting on a film that felt designed to make the most of his talents, rather than exploit them, Elvy blossomed. Curtiz had noticed the anger that lurked beneath Presley's polite exterior and encouraged him to express it even if he wasn't sure where this resentment came from.

This may have been Presley's happiest time on a movie set. The fact that he bumped into—and shook hands with—Brando in the studio commissary must have seemed wondrous and serendipitous to the young star. The collective memories of cast and crew, as reflected in Bram's book and in many subsequent interviews, convey how much affection and pride they had for this film. That pride may have been swelled by the retrospective realization that they had helped create a movie that won unusually fulsome praise from the critics and has been judged by many as the best Elvis ever made.

The second-worst review the film got—after the *Monthly Film Bulletin*—was from Robbins, whose novel *A Stone for Danny Fisher* was the bastardized source for the story. His intensely personal novel about a boxer in New York had been turned into a musical melodrama about a New Orleans singer. Though he never publicly complained, his verdict on the film was just four words long: "I got the check."

2

Where Do I Go from Here?

G.I. Blues to Kid Galahad

When Presley returned to Hollywood in April 1960, he was haunted by his mother's death, unsure of his appeal to his fans, and even slightly ill at ease in his traditional realm, the studio. Fearing that rock and roll, as much as he loved it, might be a fad, and surprisingly lacking in confidence in his ability as a ballad singer, Elvis saw the movies as his best hope of prolonging his career.

Although so much had changed—even his idol Brando was not enjoying the same kind of critical and commercial success as in the 1950s—Presley was probably reasonably optimistic about building on what he had achieved in *King Creole*. Yet he wasn't enthused by the script for his first post-army movie, *G.I. Blues*, and, when he saw the songs, he told Parker half of them ought to be cut. The absence of any Leiber and Stoller numbers—for what the Colonel euphemistically described as "business reasons"—symbolized a new direction for Presley.

The rebel was to be tamed, turned into a bland all-round family entertainer, whose musical comedies would promote smooth, best-selling soundtrack albums. The makeover was officially recognized in 1962 when *Parade* magazine declared Elvis was "a paragon of virtue." To be fair to Presley, Wallis, and the Colonel, they were, in part, adjusting to changes in popular culture that had left most of the singer's old rivals—Chuck Berry, Fats Domino, Jerry Lee Lewis, and Little Richard—marginalized. Rock's popularity had abated, and even a star as big as Presley had to take note. A recent resurgence in old-style Hollywood musicals—with the success of *Gigi*, *South Pacific*, *Porgy and Bess*, and *Can-Can*—seemed to suggest an obvious career path for Presley as a film star.

Managed properly, the change in emphasis in his movie roles could have reflected the increasing diversity of his music and his softer, more romantic ballads, like "It's Now or Never," that would sell millions. Yet Wallis, who would produce seven more Presley pictures, was never as creatively energized by his star as he had been on *King Creole*. The shift in priorities was indicated by Wallis's choice of director: instead of the marvelous but unpredictable Curtiz, *G.I. Blues*—like eight other Presley pictures in the 1960s—would be directed by the obedient, diligent, technically competent industry veteran Norman Taurog.

Presley's mood on the *G.I. Blues* set wasn't improved by the ribbing he was getting from his buddies (who were being dubbed "El's Angels" prior to their emergence as the Memphis Mafia) at some of the scenes he had to play. It must have been a jolt for Elvis to suspect, as he was directed to make ineffectual efforts to calm a screaming baby, that he was no longer cool.

Presley's friend Alan Fortas says the star made his reservations known to the Colonel, who hit back: "You can do the greatest movie in the world, and the greatest acting job, maybe even win a hundred Oscars, but if the movie doesn't make any money, you're a flop." Elvis could see the brutal logic and, as Don Siegel would later observe on the set of *Flaming Star*, was probably too insecure to press the point, but he still yearned to build on *King Creole*. Initially, he may have acquiesced to *G.I. Blues* as a way of reestablishing his power at the box office. The musical comedy did that job brilliantly, raking in $33.5 million in today's money, becoming the fourteenth-highest-grossing movie of 1960 and, by the end of the decade, making back more than twice its cost in box-office revenues.

The soundtrack strayed on the Billboard chart for 111 weeks and, unlike the King's vastly superior studio album *Elvis Is Back*, was rewarded with a Grammy nomination. He must have been alarmed to note that many outsiders—his manager, critics, and even millions of his fans—were more interested in the synthetic Elvis than the real thing.

G.I. Blues invented the formula that the star came to refer to as "the Presley travelogue," in which our beautiful hero wooed beautiful women in beautiful locations while singing enough songs to sell an album. This "singing personality" genre, as the screenwriter Weiss dubbed these movies, would find lucrative expression in *Blue Hawaii.*

After underlining his enduring popularity in *G.I. Blues*, Presley tried to branch out with the bleak, violent western *Flaming Star* and the small-town melodrama *Wild in the Country*. Neither was a great commercial success—Siegel's western spent just one week on *Variety*'s box-office survey, at number 12—though the record doesn't suggest that, as Presley came to believe, they lost money. Wallis was irritated that *Flaming Star* had been released so soon, only a month after *G.I. Blues*, but the proximity probably did more damage to the western's takings.

The pity is that *Flaming Star* rivals *King Creole* as the King's best film. The British film director Bryan Forbes later called it a "superior Elvis Presley film which demonstrates he had more acting talent than many critics gave him credit for. Elvis spawned many imitations, but he was possessed of extraordinary charisma, projecting a sullen, brooding talent that, like James Dean, captured the imagination of a generation. He had a unique talent, both as a singer and a screen personality."

Yet by the time *Wild in the Country* was being shot in December 1960, Parker was finagling with producer Jerry Wald to see if they could insert some more songs, much to the chagrin of director Philip Dunne and Elvis. Twentieth Century Fox's marketing department made no great effort to convince a wider audience of moviegoers that either film was a different kind of role for Elvis. Nor did they forewarn Presley loyalists that their idol would not be belting out his usual quota of tunes. The poster for *Flaming Star* explicitly says: "Hear Elvis sing" and then lists four songs, including two—"Summer Kisses, Winter Tears" and "Britches"—that had been cut from the film. Siegel later said: "The studio made a mistake. They should have put a campaign saying that Elvis emerged as an actor in the film. If they weren't going to sell it properly they shouldn't have released it."

Parker felt his point about Oscars and flops—which he had made public in an interview with the Hearst media empire in June 1960—had been underlined. So it was back to Wallis, musical comedies, and eye-pleasing scenery with *Blue Hawaii*. Intriguingly, Parker had suggested this locale in a letter to the producer in December 1958, while Elvis was serving in Germany, noting the popularity of Hawaiian music and Elvis's "good voice for that type of singing."

This entertaining romp was monstrously successful, Elvis's second-highest-grossing movie after *Viva Las Vegas*. It was also the first Wallis/Presley movie where the producer worried about his star's appearance, urging the Colonel to get Elvis to lose weight and tone up. With an eye for detail that was intermittently applied to Presley's scripts, Wallis even recommended the actor buy a Hanovia ultraviolet tanning lamp. Such precise advice was probably useful, as *Blue Hawaii* paved the way for the popularity of the Frankie Avalon–Annette Funicello beach party movies.

The fanaticism that greeted Elvis's arrival in Honolulu meant he had to hide behind round-the-clock security and spend most of the time in his hotel suite. When the shooting moved to Kauai, and he was less likely to be mobbed, he relaxed in the hotel bar singing duets with Patti Page, his mother's favorite singer, who was married to the movie's choreographer, Charlie O'Curran. Page recalled, "Elvis would come in and bring his guitar and we would sing. We did a lot of gospel songs, a lot of the old hymns we grew up with. That was a fun time."

Such fun times became increasingly rare, although the practical jokes Elvis presided over on many films can be seen as an attempt to lighten the mood. Suspecting he was being treated as a commodity rather than a personality, the star increasingly withdrew, using his entourage as a protective screen. Though he often took it upon himself to play the genial host on his movie sets, his remoteness frustrated such directors as Siegel and George Sidney (*Viva Las Vegas*) and saddened Boris Sagal (*Girl Happy*).

Blue Hawaii was the second-highest-grossing movie in America when it was released on Thanksgiving weekend in 1961. The soundtrack album was just as lucrative, quickly selling five times as many copies as *Elvis Is Back*. The only person who wasn't giving thanks for this success was probably Presley himself, who was, by this point, shrewd and cynical enough to read the runes with depressing accuracy. You could argue that *Blue Hawaii* is the most important film he ever made, such a smash that the singer would be doomed to make what *Variety* called "romantic non-cerebral musicals" for years to come.

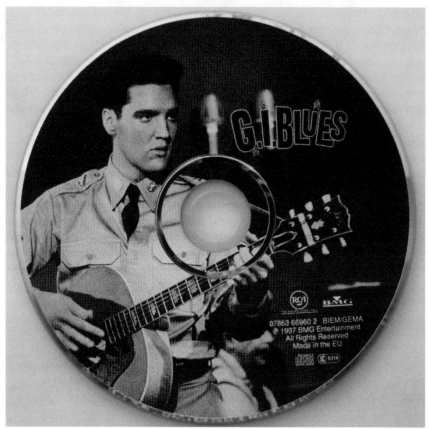

An all-round family entertainment, *G. I. Blues* proved Presley's popularity hadn't waned.

Before the final triumph of the Presley travelogue, Elvis made two modest movies with United Artists: *Follow That Dream* and *Kid Galahad*. The former, an amiable comedy directed by the experienced Gordon Douglas and scripted by the gifted cynic Charles Lederer, was a minor classic, even if the hilarity didn't quite live up to its British poster billing as "His funniest, happiest, wildest, motion picture!" Yet there were only a handful of songs, and the backdrop (a small beach off a highway in Florida) was hardly spectacular, so *Follow That Dream*, after reaching number 5 on *Variety*'s box-office survey, disappeared from the listing after just two weeks.

Kid Galahad was an intriguing failure. The blend of comedy, music, action, and fight-game corruption didn't quite gel in the hands of director Phil Karlson. The movie was a remake of Curtiz's 1937 classic melodrama of the same name and might have been more coherent if, as Presley had hoped, the inspirational genius behind *King Creole* had returned to direct. Once again, there was no obvious hit single, and, though most Elvis fans now regard the movie fondly, it grossed even less than *Flaming Star* on release.

On the set of *Kid Galahad*, actor and stuntman Nick Dimitri had asked Elvis, "Do you really want to be an actor?" He replied, "Yes, I want to be like Marlon Brando." Yet even before these United Artists features were released, this Brando wannabe was ordered back to Hawaii, to sing about shrimps and dainty little moonbeams in the next Wallis/Taurog opus, *Girls! Girls! Girls!*

When he was interviewed at the start of shooting of *It Happened at the World's Fair* by *Parade* magazine's Lloyd Shearer, Presley felt obliged to justify his film career: "I've had intellectuals telling me that I've got to progress as an actor, explore new horizons, take on new challenges, all that routine. I'd like to progress but I'm smart enough to know you can't go beyond your limitations. They want me to try artistic pictures. That's fine. Maybe I can pull it off someday. But not now. I've done eleven pictures and they've all made money."

The most depressing aspect of such observations is that Elvis sounds like the ventriloquist for his master's voice. The Colonel himself couldn't have put it better.

For much of the 1960s, Elvis's comedy musicals would serve as surrogates for the world tour he was destined never to make. Tom Diskin, Parker's aide, said: "The Colonel always said Elvis's films could reach fans in the remotest corners of the world—something it would take the best part of a lifetime to do in concert appearances."

G.I. Blues, Paramount, 1960

Director, Norman Taurog; Writers, Edmund Beloin, Henry Carson; Music, Joseph J. Lilley; Producer, Hal B. Wallis; Running time, 104 minutes

Cast: Elvis (Tulsa McLean), Juliet Prowse (Lili), Robert Ivers (Cookie), Letícia Roman (Tina), James Douglas (Rick), Sigrid Maier (Marla), Arch Johnson (Sergeant McGraw)

"Why did Presley allow this?" That was the blunt question posed by Jack Good, the famous British TV producer of the pop music series *Shindig.* "Are his fans morons? The apparently infallible Colonel Parker seems to have made a mistake."

Parker would have been baffled by talk of a mistake. His boy had come home from the U.S. Army and starred in a well-made, if exploitative, musical comedy loosely inspired by his experiences—the key word there is *loosely*—that generated $33.4 million in today's money.

The rebranding of Elvis as a clean-cut all-American boy—with, as *New York Times* reviewer Bosley Crowther put it "honey in his veins instead of blood"—was deemed an unqualified success by Parker and Wallis. They never paid too much heed to critics anyway, so what did it matter if even the august *Variety* complained of the songs: "Presley sings them all as a slightly subdued pelvis."

For Jack Good and his ilk, it was as if their idol had been shorn of his power. As G.I. Tulsa Maclean, Elvis sings to puppets (a prospect that apparently freaked him out at first), to babies, and, in one of the weirdest scenes in the entire Presley movie canon, in a bar where one bored soldier turns on the jukebox, insisting he wanted to hear "the original," and selects a song called *Blue Suede Shoes* by an artist called Elvis Presley.

At best, this scene is a very clever in-joke—the real original was by Carl Perkins, who wrote *Blue Suede Shoes*, and the jukebox doesn't play Elvis's original version either but a softer cut, recently rerecorded in what RCA satirically described as "Living Stereo." At worst, it's an early example of what Dundy has interpreted as a series of jokes—against Elvis, his background, and his sex appeal—that punctuate his movies.

Wallis had been dreaming of making this musical comedy since the summer of 1959, starting filming while Elvis was still in Germany. At one point, the movie was to be called *Café Europa* (after the nightclub at the center of the plot). Such a cool title might have signified a very different kind of movie, and in September 1959, Wallis settled on the much more blatant *G.I. Blues*.

The producer and his writers took a few known facts about Elvis—he was in a tank unit in Germany, he has Native American blood, he sings (in a trio, only this band are the Three Blazes, not the Blue Moon Boys like Elvis, Scotty, and Bill)—and used those to deck out an age-old plot borrowed from *The Fleet's In* (1942), in which sailor William Holden's buddies bet that he will be able to defrost an icy nightclub singer known as the Countess (Dorothy Lamour). *The Fleet's In* had been produced by Paul Jones, who worked with Wallis and *G.I. Blues* director Norman Taurog on the Dean Martin/Jerry Lewis comedies. This time around, the exotic ice queen is Lili (Juliet Prowse), a cabaret dancer who, as W. A. Harbinson puts it in his *Elvis: An Illustrated Biography*, "walks away with the movie with an erotically charged routine that makes Elvis look tame." Tulsa's rationale is that if he wins the bet, he'll have enough money to open his own club back in Oklahoma.

While Tulsa is trying to win—or at one point call off—the bet, Taurog keeps us busy with plenty of songs; romantic subplots in which Elvis's buddies, Cookie (Robert Ivers) and Rick (James Douglas), woo Letícia Roman (Tina) and Marla (Sigrid Maier); and a running gag about how dumb, credulous Sergeant McGraw (Arch Johnson) can be conned into supporting the Three Blazes. Although Tulsa says he has a Cherokee grandmother, nothing is really made of that revelation other than a quip about his uncle Leaping Bear being a swinging clarinet player and therefore, presumably, much cooler than the finger-snapping, hip-swaying, hand-clapping soldiers who try to convey their enthusiasm for the light, comic wail with which he hurries through the song "Frankfort Special."

Peter Nazareth, author of the intriguing essay "Elvis as Anthology," has suggested that the chorus of the title song "Occupation G.I. Blues" is a subtle swipe at U.S. imperialism or occupation overseas and even the historical colonization of indigenous lands. The track was written by the Brill Building's most industrious twosome, Sid Tepper and Roy Bennett. Anyone searching for subversive subtexts in the duo's other Elvis soundtrack numbers—which notoriously include

"Song of the Shrimp" and "Petunia the Gardener's Daughter"—would be forced to conclude that they felt messages were best left to Western Union (which happened, coincidentally, to be the title of a "Return to Sender" clone they wrote, which was released as a "bonus" on the soundtrack album for *Speedway*).

The songs Leiber and Stoller presented—"Dog Face" and "Tulsa's Blues"— sound more challenging than anything Elvis sang but didn't make the cut, presumably because Parker had decided they were a threat, stirring up his boy with funny ideas. The best number, Pomus and Shuman's subtle ballad "Doin' the Best I Can," is interrupted by "Blue Suede Shoes" and the ensuing, inevitable brawl. The children's songs "Wooden Heart" and "Big Boots" are beautifully sung but not as effective as two numbers that trace the progress of the Prowse/ Presley romance: the smooth rocker "Tonight Is So Right for Love," sung over a restaurant table to show what he means when he says music has to "ooze," and the pretty "Pocketful of Rainbows," which Elvis sings to Prowse in a cable car, underlining the spell their characters are casting on each other. "Didja Ever" makes entertaining use of Elvis's drawl and is rousing onscreen, if not on record. The other songs—"Shoppin' Around," "Frankfort Special," and "What's She Really Like"—are decent, if not earth-shattering, and significantly better than the title track, which is, as Harbinson said: "the first really bad song to come off the conveyor belt."

Yet when you're watching *G.I. Blues*, it is easy to forget such variations in quality. The King is so glad to be back in America, making movies and recording songs, that he handles many of these numbers as if they were gems. Though he doesn't swivel his pelvis, he moves his body in performance with a freedom, panache, and confidence that he wouldn't display later in, for example, *Paradise, Hawaiian Style* or *Double Trouble*.

Elvis's morale, commitment, and performance were often influenced by the quality of his co-stars. In *G.I. Blues*, he was surrounded by a strong, experienced cast and given Prowse as a leading lady. The affection between them (they had a fling on set even though Prowse was engaged to Frank Sinatra) is obvious, and with her unconventional charisma she grounds the movie. *Time* magazine panned the film and Elvis, and added that Prowse was "absolutely out of place in this picture. She looks human."

Wallis's production makes a difference. There are some slip-ups—in one shot you can clearly see that the couple entering a building are doubles for Prowse and Presley—but *G.I. Blues* has a wonderful glow about it, a patina that reeks of Hollywood's heyday and owes a lot to the accomplished cinematography of Loyal Griggs.

The ultimate failure of *G.I. Blues*, as Elvis's best biographer, Peter Guralnick, has pointed out, is that the new Elvis it presented "did not even begin to suggest either the complexity of the real Elvis or the real world that Elvis had begun to know." Then again, as the star himself joked: "It's not about my real experiences in the Army. They couldn't film that." One of Presley's experiences in Germany that couldn't be filmed was meeting a fourteen-year-old schoolgirl called Priscilla

Beaulieu. At this point in his life, she was still in Germany, listening to his complaints about the script and the songs over the phone.

The caustic reservations expressed by Good and Guralnick are understandable: their hero is no longer taking on the establishment—in this musical comedy, he is joining it. Yet *G.I. Blues* is relatively easy to watch if you can suspend disbelief for the duration, enjoy Elvis's obvious relish, and resolutely ignore the issue of the kind of films he could have been making instead of this one. And Presley transcends his material. Watching him perform "Frankfort Special," with his smiles and in-jokes—there's a lovely moment when he looks down at his jiggling leg, as if acknowledging his former image—is much more fun than it has any right to be.

Flaming Star, Twentieth Century Fox, 1960

Director, Don Siegel; Writers, Clair Huffaker and Nunnally Johnson (from Huffaker's story "The Broken Lance"); Music, Cyril J. Mockridge; Producer, David Weisbart; Running time, 101 minutes

Cast: Elvis (Pacer Burton), Barbara Eden (Roslyn Pierce), Steve Forrest (Clint Burton), Dolores Del Rio (Neddy Burton), John McIntire (Sam Burton)

"Certainly he's no Brando. On the other hand, Brando's no Presley." With those eleven words, Weisbart broke the news to Don Siegel that *Flaming Star* would star Elvis, not the mumbling king of Method acting, as its tragic half-breed hero.

The switch meant there was, as Siegel tactfully put it, "a need to refocus on the script," which Nunnally Johnson had written from Clair Huffaker's novel *The Brothers of Broken Lance*. When Johnson huffily refused to change a word, Huffaker volunteered to help. They set out to create a script in which Elvis sang just once—a period number at a party in the opening minutes.

While Huffaker was rewriting, Siegel urged Weisbart to convince the front office that Presley couldn't sing ten rock-and-roll numbers if he was to convincingly convey the anguish of a man torn between two worlds in a violent corner of the American West in 1878. The director won that battle but lost another—over the casting of tall, British brunette Barbara Steele as the leading lady. Luckily, the rushes—especially her strange faux Wild West accent—won that argument for him. Steele was relieved when Siegel broke the "bad" news and Barbara Eden was cast, performing capably even if her hair was a tad too coiffed and her clothes too smartly tailored to look authentic in the small western town where the story is set.

The son of a white father and a Kiowa mother, Pacer Burton (Elvis) lives a peaceful existence with his family on their ranch in Texas until a new chief, Buffalo Horn (Rudolph Acosta), stirs up the Kiowas to massacre the Burtons' neighbors. The Kiowas want Pacer to join them, but he keeps them waiting until he and his mother, Neddy (Dolores Del Rio), can talk to her family. On the way back from the Kiowas, a deranged survivor of the first massacre attacks them and Neddy is fatally wounded. With his half-brother Clint (Steve Forrest), Pacer tries to get help, but they have to effectively kidnap Doc Phillips (Ford Rainey), and by the time they have returned—with Clint's girlfriend Robyn (Eden)—it is too late.

Enraged and in grief, Pacer tries to kill Doc, professes his secret love for Robyn and, after saying farewell to his father (John McIntire), rides off to join the Kiowas. Yet he soon realizes he is not at home with them either, especially after they kill his father and seriously wound his brother. Knowing his actions will effectively sign his death warrant, Pacer helps Clint escape to safety and turns to face his pursuers. The next morning, badly wounded, he returns to tell his half-brother that he has seen the flaming star of death and—with Clint chasing him in similar manner to Brandon de Wilde running after his departing hero at the end of *Shane*—rides off into the mountains to die.

The pessimistic mood of this bleak, violent, liberal western is succinctly captured by Clint's observation, as the frontier war rages, "It's just pure hate now with everybody ready to kill anyone who's not like them." This reflection has greater resonance because, although he's no villain, Clint is infected by the same racist attitudes as the other white settlers. The point is made explicit when he upbraids his brother: "Good God, Pacer, you're a civilized human being." To which Pacer—this exchange takes place after the struggle to treat their dying mother—replies: "No, the people at the crossing are civilized, not me." Even Robyn, who loves the Burton family, is stained by the same prejudice, unable to see that Pacer is in love with her because he is part Kiowa.

The movie does occasionally telegraph its messages—such as when the dying Pacer tells Clint: "Maybe someday . . . somewhere people will understand . . . folks like us"—yet for the most part Siegel and Huffaker offer no easy answers or comforting clichés.

Although the Kiowas, as the *New York Times* reviewer A. H. Weiler put it, "are not simply presented as 'heavies' but as beleaguered men being ruthlessly deprived, in their view, of their lands," they are not idealized as they are in such liberal westerns as *Broken Arrow*. Their retribution is brutal. Neddy's own sister rejects her for marrying a white man. Racism is so culturally entrenched that Pacer is forced to recognize he has no people. As the movie closes, with Clint limping and shouting after his dying half-brother, the camera pans out to echo the scene where Neddy had crawled to her death on the range.

The movie ends in such convincing despair, it's tempting to wonder if Siegel is trying to draw parallels between America in the 1870s and the 1960s, possibly even highlighting the complications that could ensue as the civil-rights struggle progressed. The film even raises the issue of miscegenation, at a time when racial segregation was becoming a cause célèbre for the right and extreme right across America, especially in the Deep South. This theme was enough for the newly apartheid South Africa to ban the film and led some critics to call it a "civil rights Western."

Flaming Star isn't perfect. There are too many day-for-night shots, Cyril J. Mockridge's score can be intrusive and melodramatic, the final twenty-five minutes feel a bit rushed, and some of the dialogue, especially when the Kiowa chief is speaking, sounds self-consciously poetic. Yet these are minor flaws in a thoughtful, dramatic western that refuses to offer the comforting certainties of a traditional John Wayne horse opera and is too dispassionate in its analysis to rouse liberal indignation like a Stanley Kramer movie. In an America intoxicated by its own audacity in electing John F. Kennedy as president, *Flaming Star*'s despair was ahead of its time. By the end of the 1960s, after assassinations, a traumatic struggle for civil rights, and war in Vietnam, Siegel's pessimism would be reflected in the violent, revisionist westerns popularized by Sergio Leone and Sam Peckinpah.

Siegel highlights the isolation of the Burton family with some stark, beautiful compositions. When the mother is buried, he shows us the five mourners standing around the grave at different levels, with each turning toward the house in ascending order of their closeness to the dead woman. The scene ends with McIntire, standing alone, as the others fade into the distance. The landscape overwhelms him—and them—underlining just how vulnerable they are in the face of history and prejudice.

The role of Pacer terrified, tested, and ultimately inspired Presley. Although Guralnick found his performance insipid, most critics were impressed, with Britain's *Monthly Film Bulletin* saying that "it gives Presley a good role and he makes the most of it." His performance isn't showy, but he draws off his talented co-stars (especially Forrest, McIntire, and Del Rio) to subtly convey the anguish of a man who discovers he has no place in this world. As his friend Fortas said: "He knew something about being an outcast even if he wasn't a Kiowa."

Although Elvis struggles with some of the Kiowa dialogue, he shows just what he could have been capable of in the moving scene after Neddy's funeral. In rapid succession, he attacks Doc, wrestles with Clint—before pulling a gun on him—and reveals his love for Robyn. His interaction with the other actors is so credible you almost feel you are in the cabin with them as their lives spin out of control. He shines in many less obvious moments too, giving a sublime emotional resonance to the scene where he smilingly embraces his mother after beating off the trappers who had tried to molest her.

After his shock at that initial casting switch, Siegel was certainly satisfied, saying later: "I found Elvis sensitive and very good—with the exception that he was very unsure of himself. They tried to get him to sing throughout the picture. They didn't want him to get off a winning horse. But when I was able to calm him down, I thought he gave a beautiful performance."

That beautiful performance wasn't watched by that many cinemagoers. Twentieth Century Fox and Parker had ignored Siegel's semi-serious suggestion that the posters should proclaim "Elvis acts!" in the same vein as the "Garbo laughs!" slogan used to promote *Ninotchka*. The inevitable result was that *Flaming Star* peaked at number 12, on the *Variety* Box Office Survey.

Although Siegel had a high regard for his star, he decided he didn't want to work with him again. Even by Hollywood standards, the behind-the-scenes machinations were a headache, and Presley frustrated him: "I had always had problems getting through to him, when I wasn't alone with him. Those were rare precious moments, since he avoided being alone with anyone. I wasn't very interested in working with him after this because he was, well, so distanced."

Wild in the Country, Twentieth Century Fox, 1961

Director, Philip Dunne; Writer, Clifford Odets, based on the novel *The Lost Country* by J. R. Salamanca; Music, Kenyon Hopkins; Producer, Jerry Wald; Running time, 114 minutes

Cast: Elvis (Glenn Tyler), Hope Lange (Irene Sperry), Tuesday Weld (Noreen), Millie Perkins (Betty Lee Parsons), William Mims (Uncle Rolfe), John Ireland (Phil Macy), Gary Lockwood (Cliff Macy), Rafer Johnson (Davis),

"It's like I'm always walking around with a cupful of anger, trying not to spill it." That line, uttered by Elvis as troubled Glenn Tyler in his seventh movie, reflected his real personality much more accurately than most fans would have suspected at the time.

Presley epitomized smiling, obedient professionalism in many of his musical comedies. He was an essentially gentle man but could be as short-tempered as his antihero in *Jailhouse Rock*. By 1960, when he shot this movie, his boyhood dream had come true, though not at all in the manner he had envisaged. His grief at the loss of his mother two years earlier must have been stirred by his father's marriage, four months before shooting for this melodrama started, to Dee Dee Stanley. The swirling emotions infuse his performance in *Wild in the Country*, and when he discusses his late mother with psychiatrist Hope Lange in this movie, it is almost as if Elvis himself is having therapy for his bereavement.

There must also have been anger about the way his movie career was progressing. *Flaming Star* had not rocked the box office, so five songs were hurriedly inserted into *Wild in the Country*. Presley must have sensed that his dream of becoming a good actor was already in danger of extinction. He didn't spill his anger about this often. Maybe he would have been better off if he had.

Yet he clearly identified with Tyler, a character that playwright Clifford Odets had loosely modeled on Thomas Wolfe, whose most famous novel is *Look Homeward Angel*, and gives an intensely personal performance in a decent, if flawed, movie that has enough confidence in its own appeal not to yield to convention until the finale (and even then, the happy ending comes with caveats).

Many critics have agreed with biographer Guralnick that Presley was out of his depth in this melodrama: "He simply seems lost in the role, alternating between bouts of sullenness that start and end with bombastic declamation and equally silly posturings of trembling sensitivity." Guralnick even blamed

Presley's rapid-fire delivery of some dialogue on the star's amphetamine use. Elvis's performance has its uneven moments, yet it is much more rewarding to watch him wrestle with Odets's slightly overheated script—at times it sounds as if the writer is trying to channel *Peyton Place* and Tennessee Williams—than to see him smirk through *Paradise, Hawaiian Style*.

The role of small-town outsider suits him far better than singing beach boy. And two scenes—when he is lamenting the death of his mother and kissing Lange in a motel room—are as good as anything he ever did onscreen. One of the incidental delights is a scene where, to show his intrinsic goodness, he is asked to quote and translate Jesus's cry from the cross. The quiet reverence with which he says "Eli, Eli, lama sabachthani?" and explains where it can be found in the Bible is touching.

Tyler is a troubled young man who escapes detention only because his uncle Rolfe (William Mims) takes him into custody and he agrees to see psychiatrist Irene Sperry (Lange) once a week. The usual romantic triangle is replaced with a romantic rhomboid as Glenn is torn between wild child Noreen (Tuesday Weld), childhood sweetheart Betty Lee (Millie Perkins), and Irene, who encourages him to fulfill his literary ambitions. The budding romance between psychiatrist and patient causes a scandal that she seeks to resolve by agreeing to marry suitor Phil Macy (John Ireland). Macy's son Phil (Gary Lockwood) starts spreading rumors about Glenn's motel tryst with Irene. Furious, young Tyler punches Phil and inadvertently—because the Macy boy has a weak heart—kills him, in a twist that recalls the opening of *Jailhouse Rock*. As the town's mood turns ugly at a coroner's inquest, Irene tries to kill herself but is rescued by Glenn, who, as the film closes, is heading off to college to see if he can become a writer.

That breathless summary omits some events—such as Rolfe's attempts to charm, cajole, and force Glenn into marrying his niece Noreen, who has an illegitimate baby, or Betty Lee's father threatening Glenn with a rifle—but captures part of the problem with the movie. There is too much going on, and the script spends too much time telling you what's going on. It might have been easier if the hero's romantic dilemma had been simplified. The contrast between Weld's sensual Noreen and Lange's sensible psychiatrist is so effective that Betty Lee seems underwritten and underdeveloped or, as Glenn says at one point: "flat and dried out."

By the time shooting started, Odets had been fired, leaving a script that was twice the required length—and still had some key scenes missing—so Philip Dunne, while directing his first movie, had to cut and rewrite during production. Though he did a reasonable job, the script has its pretentious moments and occasionally sounds downright florid. The role of the older woman Elvis falls for had been written for Simone Signoret (who had tempted Laurence Harvey in *Room at the Top*), but she was too expensive. (She was an odd choice to play a therapist in small-town America anyway.) Luckily, Lange stepped in and is one of the best things in the movie.

Presley and Lange intrigued each other, and the movie is at its most compelling when they share the screen and are given the right lines. In one marvelous exchange, Elvis protests: "I'm an ignorant country boy, ma'am," only for Lange to berate him: "Oh, stop boasting." Their hesitant embrace in a motel room is touching and thoroughly believable in its stop–start awkwardness. Where they do falter, the fault is often with the dialogue. When Elvis describes the reaction to his character's literary ambitions by saying, "You'd think I'd set a blowtorch to the American flag," it seems so out of proportion as to be almost ludicrous.

Presley is just as effective when sparring with Weld, a sexy, almost feral, presence as the small-town slut who "never stood a chance in life." It's devastatingly clear why the brooding hero finds her so hard to resist, but she also represents a tempting opportunity for him to live down to the community's expectations of him. The glee with which Weld, challenging Lange's attempt to inspire her protégé, laughs and says, "She means like Jesus, Glen," is all the more effective because it seems visceral, instinctive.

The movie would be better if it were shorter, more focused, tauter, and more ambitious. The screenplay doesn't go as far as either Williams or Odets in his prime might have, and the conflicts don't quite have the requisite dramatic clout. At times, this is more like "Mild in the Country." The uneven tone is partly explained by Parker's insistence on inserting songs. Dunne does his best to integrate them into the film—"In My Way" accentuates the downbeat mood beautifully—but the nadir is when Presley is forced to sing "I Slipped, I Stumbled, I Fell" to Perkins in the car. The scene belongs to an entirely different movie, and Elvis knew it. Perkins remembered him complaining to her: "God, this is so embarrassing. Nobody would ever do this in real life."

Such compromises—on top of all the other difficulties—doomed Presley's last, best shot at a career as a serious actor. The critics sneered. In the *New York Times*, Bosley Crowther was unequivocal: "Nonsense, that's all it is—sheer nonsense." And, more crucially, it was marketed as if it were another musical comedy (the poster bore the slogan: "Elvis sings of love to Hope Lange, Tuesday Weld, Millie Perkins") and became only a modest commercial success. The movie's reputation has risen considerably since. It remains indispensable viewing for any Presley fan, and at least Elvis liked it, which is more than can be said of many of the movies to come.

Blue Hawaii, Paramount, 1961

Director, Norman Taurog; Writers, Allan Weiss, Hal Kanter; Music, Joseph J. Lilley; Producer, Hal B. Wallis; Running time, 101 minutes

Cast: Elvis (Chad Gates), Joan Blackman (Maile Duval), Angela Lansbury (Sarah Lee Gates), Nancy Walters (Abigail Prentice), Roland Winters (Fred Gates), Howard McNear (Mr. Chapman)

Blue Hawaii is the definitive Presley travelogue, the ultimate expression of the musical comedies Weiss dubbed the "singing personality" movies, and gave the star one of the defining songs of his career, "Can't Help Falling in Love," which he used to close his concerts.

As Chad Gates, Elvis is the heir to the Great Southern Hawaiian Fruit Company and, returning from his military service, decides to shun the pineapple business to get a job with the tourist agency where his sweetheart Maile (Joan Blackman) works. This declaration of independence infuriates his mother, Sarah Lee (Angela Lansbury, who was only ten years older than Elvis when the film was made), and perplexes his father (Roland Winters). Life gets even more complicated when Chad is asked to help guide teacher Abigail Prentice (Nancy Walters) and her students around the island. Oversexed and underaged Ellie (Jenny Maxwell) is so troubled by her crush on Chad he has to spank her to make her behave, and Maile mistakenly assumes that her beau is having a fling with the teacher. Luckily, all is resolved, after Chad and the boys have spent a night in jail, his mother has fainted, and Prentice has fallen for pineapple tycoon Jack (John Archer). Sarah Lee is reconciled to Maile when she realizes her future daughter-in-law is Hawaiian royalty, and Chad, discovering a hitherto unsuspected flair for diplomatic compromise, finds a way of doing his own thing and helping the family business: by launching his own tourist agency, which will arrange tours as incentives for the plantation's sales force.

The bare synopsis doesn't convey the charm of this entertaining, if innocuous, movie. Blackman said afterward: "There was something magical about *Blue Hawaii*. The other beach movies tried too hard. There was something very sweet about the film. Elvis had a lot to do with it, but there was chemistry between us that added flavor." Some might balk at the idea the movie was "magical," but there is something in Blackman's theory that the movie is mysteriously greater than the sum of its parts.

The scenery is spectacular, especially during the Hawaiian wedding ceremony that gives the finale a rare romantic grandeur. The songs are better than usual: "Can't Help Falling in Love" is perfect, while "Blue Hawaii," "Hawaiian Wedding Song," "No More," and "Rock a Hula Baby" are all good and, apart from the novelty number "Ito Eats," even the lesser numbers like "Beach Boy Blues," "Island of Love," and "Moonlight Swim" are pretty and catchy. Presley had trouble not laughing as he sang "Beach Boy Blues," especially the line "I'm a kissin' cousin to a ripe pineapple and I'm in the can."

For films that were designed as musical comedies, Presley movies could be surprisingly light on laughs, but this time the intentional humor is supplied by parents Lansbury and Winters and by Howard McNear (best known as Floyd the barber in *The Andy Griffith Show*) as the implausibly vague tourist-agency boss.

Lansbury's southern belle is a delight. Confident that her son has got all his foolishness out of his system after the war, she is reminded by her patient husband: "Sarah Lee, how many times do I have to tell you he was not in a war?" To which Lansbury replies, with just the right amount of dolefulness: "I know you're right, Daddy, but if I don't tell myself there was a war, I have a most depressive feeling Chadwick's just wasted two years." Later, she greets her son's return from his night in the slammer with the cry "My baby's home from the big house!" One of the recurring pleasures is seeing how long Lansbury can stretch her errant son's name: "Chaad-wick!!!"

Blackman and Presley do have chemistry, although Goldman, for once, is right when he says they relate more like brother and sister in this film. (Their romance is much more convincing in *Kid Galahad*.) You can't help but wonder whether the love story would have had more heart if Juliet Prowse had played the role, as originally intended. Her demands—to use her own hairdresser and have a secretary on the shoot (essentially for someone to talk to)—infuriated Wallis, who dropped her. Still, it's hard to imagine her as a French-Hawaiian beauty, and her particular charisma might not have suited the story and setting.

Yet in one way, the South African actress would have felt utterly appropriate. At times, *Blue Hawaii* does seem like an informal sequel to *G.I. Blues*, in which she played Presley's love interest. The two films were even re-released together in 1974. Maybe her presence would have made the movie's Tulsa-goes-to-Polynesia shtick a tad too obvious.

The biggest disappointment is Elvis's character. There are strong, well-defined characters around him, but Chad, as written by Weiss and rewritten by Kanter, doesn't give Presley much to work with. Weiss had originally described his hero in these terms: "Essentially a loner who appreciated women—preferably in quantity—but whose underlying attitude was audacious and arrogant, even a little contemptuous. Presley fitted this characterization pretty well." That description hinted at subtexts the movie was never going to explore, so Chad becomes a handsome, personable, free-spirited kind of guy who wants to make his own way in the world and, though he is obviously attracted by—and attractive to—women, is almost always true to Maile. There is a hint of Weiss's darker characterization when Maile rebukes Chad that he can't spend the rest of his life on a surfboard and he replies: "Sure I can. The G.I. Bill of Rights says I get my old job back. This is my old job."

Elvis carries this off pretty well for the most part; having so many scenes with Lansbury and Winters seems to have inspired him. He even manages to sound reasonably convincing when he is obliged to spank Ellie or, as he calls her, "Miss No-Breeches Bardot." The spanking—to show her that someone cares for her enough to smack some sense into her—is forceful enough for the teenager to show the seat of her discomfort at breakfast the next morning. Maxwell later confided that it was almost as painful in real life. In a rare quest for realism, Taurog had Elvis redo the take several times and, as Maxwell recalled: "He had to spank me hard to make it look good. But my skimpy costume was wet and there wasn't much between Elvis and what he was spanking." Such scenes were a staple of the western genre—John Wayne was still doling out such punishment in *McLintock* (1964)—but it seems out of place in such a musical comedy.

Presley had loved Bing Crosby's movies as a boy, and *Blue Hawaii* is, in effect, a Crosby musical with Elvis in the starring role. The title song came from the 1937 musical *Waikiki Wedding*, in which Crosby, a smooth-talking PR man, is hired by a pineapple company president to escort Shirley Ross, a Miss Pineapple Queen contest winner, around the islands. The Crosby film features "Sweet Leilani," a pretty Hawaiian-tinged ballad Elvis liked to sing at home. The similarities are striking. One of the principal differences is that Crosby's PR man is, even within the confines of musical comedy, a significantly more rounded character than Chadwick Gates.

Variety paid the movie a backhanded compliment, saying this "slim but convenient" fare was sure to succeed at the box office. By 1969, *Blue Hawaii*'s box-office rentals in the United States had risen to $4.7 million, roughly on a par with the star-packed spectacular *Gunfight at the OK Corral*. Presley tried to be pragmatic about the change in his movie persona, telling gossip columnist Louella Parsons: "My fans are growing older. The old wiggle is on the way out." Yet his real feelings were reflected in the high jinks, practical jokes, and karate sessions that would increasingly accompany the making of his movies. If he couldn't take pride in them, his attitude seemed to be, he could at least enjoy making them.

Follow That Dream, United Artists, 1962

Director, Gordon Douglas; Writer, Charles Lederer (from Dick Powell's novel *Pioneer, Go Home!*); Music, Hans J. Salter; Producer, David Weisbart; Running time, 110 minutes

Cast: Elvis (Toby Kwimper), Arthur O'Connell (Pop Kwimper), Anne Helm (Holly Kwimper), Joanna Moore (Alicia Claypoole), Jack Kruschen (Carmine), Simon Oakland (Nick)

When *Follow That Dream* was released in May 1962, it was dismissed by America's most influential movie critic, the *New York Times*'s Bosley Crowther, as "laboriously homespun and simple-minded . . . cornmeal mush." Yet when Hal Erickson came to review it for the paper's website years later, he characterized it as a "leisurely musical comedy with a homely appeal that will delight even non-Presley fans." That critical shift is probably the most significant reevaluation of any Elvis film and is, frankly, no more than *Follow That Dream* deserves.

This tale of innocents abroad was sympathetically adapted from Richard Powell's funny novel *Pioneer, Go Home!* by Charles Lederer, who had written or co-authored such gems as *His Girl Friday*, *I Was a Male War Bride*, and *Gentlemen Prefer Blondes*. Powell was not over-enamored of the idea of Presley playing in the film. He told producer Weisbart and veteran director Gordon Douglas: "My only real fear was that Presley would say to himself that this was a funny story and so he would have to act funny. The humor in the book was character humor which had to be played straight to bring it out . . . They assured me that he would play the role straight, which he did, and he did a very good job."

Elvis stars as Toby, the naive but responsible member of the itinerant Kwimper clan, which also includes Pop (Arthur O'Connell), their attractive former babysitter Holly (Anne Helm), adopted twins, and a young orphan

French poster art for *Follow That Dream* (1962). *Follow That Dream* was a vastly underrated comedy, with Presley underplaying the doofus.

United Artists/Photofest

girl, Ariadne. When they get stranded on a strip of unclaimed Florida beach and decide to become homesteaders, pompous official H. Arthur King (Alan Hewitt), sex-crazed child welfare boss Alicia Claypoole (Joanna Moore), and two gangsters—Carmine (Jack Kruschen) and Nick (Simon Oakland)—do their utmost to displace them. Yet, largely through the sheer force of Toby's innocent goodness, the Kwimpers prevail over all their enemies.

Officially, the division of responsibility within the family is defined by Pop when he tells Toby and Holly: "I'll take care of the brain work and you take care of the work work." Yet Pop's ignorance of the real world is even greater than Toby's or Holly's. When the Kwimpers start up a fishing business, Holly thinks they need a bank loan to expand and has to explain to Pop that banks charge interest on the money they lend. At this point, O'Connell's patriarch leans forward as if the scales have fallen from his eyes and says, in exactly the right astounded tone: "Oh, so that's how they do it!" The comic moment that best sums up Pop isn't the running gag about the pressure in their makeshift toilet, it's the quiet pride with which he comes back from town and announces he has bought some "luxury items," which turn out to be the "john" and the wood to house it in.

The bank scene, in which Toby inadvertently contrives to give the impression that he is trying to rob the bank, flows amusingly. The mystification of bank vice president George (Howard McNear, Blackman's befuddled boss in *Blue Hawaii*) when Toby offers the Kwimpers' toilet as security for their $2,000 loan, is amusing too. Bank president Mr. Endicott (Herbert Rudley) recommends that the bank give a character loan on the grounds that "Honesty might be the only real security there is."

When Claypoole, who is supposed to be judging the family's moral fitness, tries to make out with Toby, he goes as far as to kiss her but uses his education—his habit of counting the multiplication tables—to keep his cool. Before her attempted seduction, she gives Toby a word-association test, which provides some of the biggest laughs in the movie. When Claypoole says, "Help!," Toby says, "Help!" back. Admonished for repeating the word, our baffled hero explains: "Nobody just shouts help! They shout 'Help! Help!' so I was waiting for you to say "Help! again and when you didn't say it, I said it for you."

Holly is so outraged by this flirting, she pushes Claypoole into the river, ensuring that the welfare department's vengeance will be terrible and swift. (The onscreen romantic triangle is even more piquant because it mirrored what was happening on set, with Helm replacing Moore in Presley's affections.) The twins and Ariadne are taken into the department's care, and the Kwimpers are invited to a court hearing to determine their fitness as guardians.

While all this has been unfolding, the Kwimpers have been coexisting none too peacefully with the gangster crowd who have taken advantage of the beach's uncertain legal status to run a mobile casino there in the belief that this strip could become an eastern Las Vegas. They are initially baffled by Toby, but then, when he is appointed sheriff and tries to impose an 11:00 p.m. curfew, they decide to be rid of the Kwimpers. Their own goons, hired hit men, and a bomb all prove equally ineffective. Finding that one of the heavies has left a jar under their makeshift house, Holly returns it—and the nitroglycerine it contains—to the gangsters' trailer with predictably devastating results. As the indestructible Toby, Presley plays it beautifully deadpan as Nick and Carmine count down to the explosion: "Well, I'll be doggone. Your place done blown up, Nick." The court scene rounds off the comedy nicely, with dyspeptic but decent Judge Warman (Roland Winters, Elvis's dad in *Blue Hawaii*), perplexed, outraged, and finally grudgingly impressed by Toby's homespun advocacy.

Follow That Dream is not a cool Elvis movie—as say *Jailhouse Rock* and *King Creole* are—so the quality of Presley's acting has often been overlooked, but his speech defending the Kwimpers is one of his finest moments on celluloid. This is the point at which the movie could have gone awry but Elvis's shy, sincere eloquence is just perfect. He wins the day, and after Pa has confused the judge even further by promising to make up with the government and start taking relief again, the scene is set for the expected romantic climax between Holly and Toby, with the alluring ballad "Angel" setting the mood. Even here, the romance is lightened by humor. When Holly tries to stroke Toby's forehead, like Claypoole did, to persuade him to kiss her, she asks, "Like this?" Toby replies, "Not so much like she was ironing a shirt."

There is a certain irony in the fact that Elvis gives one of his best performances as a character who is, as biographer Goldman would later portray him, dumb white trash. His brown hair and bulk suit the role, making him look young enough to still hang on Pop's every order (or pretend he does). In a talented supporting cast, O'Connell stands out as ornery Pop, a role he reprised in *Kissin' Cousins*. Though his moral authority is qualified by his habitual reliance on government handouts, O'Connell's indictment of the city official ("You do nothing for a single solitary soul because you're pretending to do something for the public") seems more resonant than ever. Lederer didn't tinker too much with Powell's novel—his biggest change was deleting a hurricane scene—and versatile veteran director Douglas is largely content to draw out the story and the cast.

Follow That Dream has flaws. Looked at today, the romantic denouement seems a tad dubious. True, Holly is nineteen, but she was the family's babysitter and has lived with them for six years. The comedy would have been odder if wild child Weld had gotten the role. If either her or Connie Stevens—who were both in the running—had been cast as Holly, it would have unbalanced the movie.

Sometimes—for example, when Toby lifts a car over a log with superheroic ease—the movie tries to force the comedy, and there are some strange touches; we never understand why such a large crowd has come out to watch the Kwimpers' custody case. And the songs, the best of which are "Follow That Dream" and "I'm Not the Marrying Kind," are subordinate to the story, so they aren't always staged that innovatively or—in the case of "Sound Advice" —that well. They did, though, change the movie title. The usual tunesmiths couldn't find a rhyme for "pioneer" for the title song, so the movie couldn't be called *Pioneer, Go Home!* Eventually Sid Wayne and Jay Livingston wrote "What a Wonderful Life" (which is played over the credits), but the working titles *Here Come the Kwimpers* and *It's a Beautiful Life* never really worked, so the film came to be called *Follow That Dream*.

If, as Tony Pellum suggests on the website Flickdom Dictum, you take the film on its own terms—as a slightly daffy, optimistically patriotic, Capraesque fantasy—*Follow That Dream* stands out as arguably one of the best Presley comedies. In Britain, *Monthly Film Bulletin* praised the film's "charm, humor and liveliness."

For a modest musical comedy that did reasonable but not spectacular business, Elvis's ninth movie casts a long shadow. During shooting, he was introduced to a young Tom Petty (whose uncle worked on the film), who was so blown away ("He stepped out radiant as an angel," the founder of the Heartbreakers recalled later) he brought every Presley record he could and started dreaming of being a rock star. In 1978, Springsteen completed one of his greatest songs, "The Promise," in which the narrator says he followed that dream just like those guys do way up on the screen." The allusion became more overt in the 1980s when Springsteen started performing his own radically reworked version of the song "Follow That Dream."

Kid Galahad, Mirisch / United Artists, 1962

Director, Phil Karlson; Writer, William Fay (based on the novel by Francis Wallace); Music, Jeff Alexander; Producer, David Weisbart; Running time, 92 minutes

Cast: Elvis (Walter Gulick), Joan Blackman (Rose Grogan), Gig Young (Willy Grogan), Lola Albright (Dolly Fletcher), Charles Bronson (Lew Nyack), David Lewis (Otto Danzig)

"For a film about a singing prize-fighter (which is silly enough) it will do." The *New York Times*' Bosley Crowther's verdict sums up *Kid Galahad* pretty well—which is a pity because, after this, it would be travelogues all the way (some of them decent) until *Stay Away, Joe* in 1968.

Curtiz's original *Kid Galahad* was a classic, noir-ish fight picture in which Wayne Morris's rise as a tyro boxer leads to tragedy as his manager Edward G. Robinson is shot by gangster Humphrey Bogart for failing to fix the boxer's big fight. This plot, taken from the eponymous novel by Francis Wallace, was recycled as *The Wagons Roll at Night* (1941), with the action transposed to a circus and Bogart again starring. It seemed an odd story to tailor to suit Presley. Some elements harked back to the film that *King Creole* could have been if it had been closer to *A Stone for Danny Fisher*, and at least it was no travelogue. Wallace's novel had originally been sold with the cover slogan "Gamblers, girls and a soft-hearted kid with a killer instinct," and that still applied in this third screen adaptation.

The King swings into action in the musical comedy fight movie *Kid Galahad.*

The central flaw in the movie—which, as Crowther grudgingly admitted, makes for "moderately genial entertainment"—is that it can't really decide what it wants to be. The songs are hardly likely to appeal to fans of boxing pictures; the boxing scenes (despite the coaching of legendary trainer Mushy Callaghan) are too implausible to convince the sport's aficionados and too long to thrill Presley's usual fans. With no credible suggestion that events might turn out tragically, the drama loses much of its, well, punch. This must have been depressingly obvious to Presley, who apparently watched the Curtiz original forty times before shooting started.

Some of that confusion is evident in the presentation of Elvis's hero Walter Gulick, aka Kid Galahad, a young man who has just come out of the U.S. Army and wants nothing more than to run his own garage and settle down in Cream Valley. A "hero with a halo," Walter chivalrously knocks out a goon who tries it on with delightful Dolly Fletcher (Lola Albright), who is hopelessly in love with Willy Grogan (Gig Young), a small-time boxing promoter with gambling debts. Willy decides the surest way to settle them is to exploit this unusually docile young man's knockout punch. To keep his meal ticket alive a bit longer, Willy persuades trainer Lew Nyack (Charles Bronson) to give Galahad a few tips. This arrangement is convenient for everyone until Rose (Joan Blackman), Willy's gorgeous sister, turns up and falls for Galahad and gangster Otto Danzig (David Lewis) orders Willy—and Galahad—to throw a fight.

Good's triumph over evil is rapid and—if you ignore the blows to Galahad's head and Nyack's hands (broken by Danzig's henchmen)—pretty painless. The amusingly cynical Willy comes good, agreeing to marry Dolly (after the two briefly break up) and telling a young district attorney (Ed Asner, in one of his first movie roles) he'll testify against Nyack's assailants. He doesn't even object when his sister and Galahad are left alone in the changing room for a celebratory embrace after Elvis has won the big fight.

In Curtiz's original, Robinson's doomed promoter is the central figure. Writer William Fay has tried to shift the focus to Elvis. This works occasionally, especially when he's singing and, in one compelling scene, where he warns Willy: "I'm a grease monkey that won't slide so easily." Yet for the most part Elvis's singing boxer is a one-note character, so straight—he even proposes to Rose very soon after their first embrace because it's the "safest" thing to do—that he seems almost remote. In the 1937 movie, Bette Davis—in Albright's role—also falls for the kid, and it's a shame this doesn't happen in the remake, as the early scenes between Albright and Elvis, highlighting the contrast between her hard-won cynicism and his naive innocence, provide some of the best moments.

So Elvis almost becomes a supporting actor in his movie as Young's amoral fixer dominates the story. The actors didn't gel offscreen. Young was semipermanently intoxicated and, in Elvis's eyes, treated his wife Elizabeth Montgomery (the star of *Bewitched*) abominably. You wouldn't guess as much from their scenes in the movie, and Young certainly makes the most of his one-liners, such as his gleeful assessment of his protégé's potential: "He's got an ax in his right hand, and a bowling ball for a head."

Elvis had issues with Bronson too. Young liked to amuse himself by putting down Bronson, who, in turn, took a swipe at boxing trainer Mushy Callahan and refused to be impressed by the King's on-set karate demonstrations (especially after he tried to emulate Presley but failed to break a board). Stung by his co-star's surly indifference, Presley uncharacteristically told his buddies Bronson was a "musclebound ape." Once again, the animosity doesn't affect their rapport onscreen. Bronson would later claim to be ashamed of this movie—although others might regard *Death Wish 4: The Crackdown* as a bigger blot on his copybook—but his performance as the trainer is natural, proportionate, and convincing.

Presley made the most of the rare opportunity to act like a tough guy by sparring with three professional boxers and developing a special rapport with Callahan, the former light welterweight champion who supervised the fight scenes. Jack Driscoll, one of the boxers, told Bill Bram: "Elvis had extraordinary physical ability: his coordination was outstanding. It didn't take him too long to catch on to the hand movements, but he couldn't do the footwork the way he wanted it: he was too heavy [he weighed about 178 pounds] and I remember reading reviews that said 'blubbery Elvis.'"

As Graeme Clark noted in his review for *The Spinning Image*: "Parker is credited as a technical adviser and with that in mind, it's surprising that the film should feature its hero being ruthlessly taken advantage of an unscrupulous promoter for most of the running time." On set, Parker did his best to live up to the Svengali image, hypnotizing Elvis's bodyguard Sonny West to berate director Karlson so vehemently that the director had him thrown off the set until the joke was explained.

A musical comedy-drama about a singing prize fighter poses certain problems for Karlson. For once, the songs are subjugated to the story, but only the soulful "Home Is Where the Heart Is" and the swaying "I Got Lucky" really stand out. Sadly, the numbers are staged about as unimaginatively as the boxing scenes, in which Presley shows as much paunch as muscle. It's possible that in the hands of a more seasoned director, the movie's unorthodox mix might have come off. Karlson does his best, but he might have relished his task more if the story had struck to its tough, noir-ish roots.

Kid Galahad is still one of the King's more watchable movies, and it insults the intelligence less often than many of those that follow. Fay's script has its moments, especially when the cook comments on his boss's sudden doting on Dolly: "For a bum like Willie, it's beautiful." One of the best lines in the movie—when Elvis leans over and asks the trainer of the boxer he's knocked out whether he will still get his five dollars—was ad-libbed by Elvis. The film's comparative commercial failure—the initial gross was around $1.75 million in the United States—legitimized the return to the formula with *Girls! Girls! Girls!* For Elvis, the next six years in Hollywood would be a kind of artistic slavery.

3

Please Don't Stop Loving Me

Girls! Girls! Girls! to Roustabout

In 1961, Presley had been the tenth biggest box-office draw in America. In 1962, with *Blue Hawaii*, *Follow That Dream*, *Kid Galahad*, and *Girls! Girls! Girls!* all on the circuit, he was the fifth-biggest draw in the United States and second in the UK. Commercially, he remained a potent attraction in 1963 (7th in the U.S.) and 1964 (6th in the U.S.) but, by the end of 1964, his reign over America's popular culture was unceremoniously ended by four of his most ardent fans, the Beatles.

When *Girls! Girls! Girls!*, the third Taurog/Wallis musical comedy in three years, was released in November 1962, it shot to number 6 on *Variety*'s box-office survey. Yet the initial gross—$2.6 million—wasn't as impressive as it looked. By 1964, the movie had made only $30,000 in profit. As Presley and Parker took the lion's share of that money, that performance must have been of some concern to the Colonel and was probably one of the reasons he started looking for a different kind of business model.

That quest would lead him to Sam Katzman, a producer known as the King of the Quickies, who prided himself on frugality. Their common philosophy meant, inevitably, that Presley made two pictures for Katzman: *Kissin' Cousins* (which may have been one of the most profitable of the star's career) and *Harum Scarum* (which signaled the beginning of the end of Presley's film career). *Kissin' Cousins* marked a defining moment in Elvis's movie career—and not because Presley played two roles in the same film. He would make good movies after that, but once Katzman had proved you could make an Elvis film for $800,000 that generated $2.8 million in North America, budgets shrank, schedules shortened, and the quality of the co-stars diminished. The fact that the Gene Nelson–Gerald Drayson Adams script for this faux hillbilly romp was nominated for a Writers Guild of America award for Best-Written Musical Screenplay can only be regarded as a devastating indictment of the guild's artistic standards.

Yet before that desperate detour into exploitationsville, Presley made some decent, if formulaic, musical comedies. *Girls! Girls! Girls!*, *Fun in Acapulco*, and *It Happened at the World's Fair* all had a certain Hollywood gloss. The star looked as handsome as ever. Some of the songs—notably "Return to Sender," "Bossa Nova Baby," and "They Remind Me Too Much of You"—were memorable. Yet even in

1963, the box-office take showed signs that the travelogues were losing their appeal, even for Elvis fans. Official confirmation of the King's declining influence came when "One Broken Heart for Sale," the most commercial song on the scandalously brief soundtrack to *World's Fair*, didn't even make the top ten on Billboard's Hot 100.

A special Elvis edition of *Films Fortnightly*. Though some British fans hated his films, many stuck with the King's movies through thin and thinner.

The problem wasn't just the quality of the material. Elvis had signed up to the old Hollywood star system at the very point it was rotting away. By the mid-1960s, the system's fragility was blatantly obvious. As Frank Rose put it in *The Agency*, his insightful portrait of William Morris: "The glamor days were over for all of them. Wallis, Lastfogel, the Colonel—they were fighting a losing battle. Show business as they knew it was dying and Elvis, who helped kill it, was trapped in the carcass." Even such durable box-office attractions as Cary Grant, Elizabeth Taylor, and Doris Day were finding audiences harder to come by. Only John Wayne and, bizarrely, Jack Lemmon seemed commercially immune to the sudden, surprising, and mysterious shift in popular culture that was given the reductive label "the Swinging Sixties."

The way Elvis's movies were being handled left producers, studios, Parker, or Presley little room for maneuver. Thanks to his star's pulling power, Parker had negotiated some impressively lucrative contracts for his boy—$600,000 plus half the profits for *Follow That Dream*, an offer even Wallis felt he couldn't match—but this meant that the star accounted for 70 to 80 percent of the film's cost. That left little to spend on co-stars, script, or, as the films progressed, the songs. Even Joe Pasternak, who produced *Girl Happy* and *Spinout*, warned Parker he couldn't make movies that way. But Elvis's manager was resolute. As Pasternak recalled: "He said 'I'm sending you Elvis Presley.' He didn't want to boost the price up, but he wouldn't budge on Elvis, and he'd want to save on everything else."

This wasn't actually what the star wanted. As Schilling said, "He knew they were spending all the money on him and none on anything else, especially the co-stars. He couldn't have cared less about the money, he just wanted to be in a good film." The tight budget for co-stars posed a particular challenge because as early as 1964, appearing in an Elvis movie had for many actors, as Sue Anne Langdon (*Roustabout* and *Frankie and Johnny*) put it, "become a take-the-money-and-run kind of thing."

Elvis had attempted to save face on the set of *Kissin' Cousins*, telling leading lady Yvonne Craig that the Colonel would know when it was right for him to return to dramatic roles. Yet by the time *Roustabout* was being shot, in the spring of 1964, Presley's faith in Parker—and Wallis—was evaporating. On the last day of shooting, the *Las Vegas Desert News and Telegram* ran a story that pointed out that Presley's commercial success was financing such critically acclaimed productions as *Becket*. The piece quoted Wallis as saying: "In order to do the artistic pictures, it is necessary to make the commercially successful Presley pictures." Perhaps sensing the trap he had fallen into, Wallis added, "But that doesn't mean a Presley picture can't have quality too." The story so rankled with Presley that, Schilling recalls, he actually went up to the producer and asked, "Mr. Wallis, when do I get to do my *Becket*?" The answer, of course, was never.

Neither *Roustabout* nor *Viva Las Vegas* were as acclaimed as *Becket*, but they did suggest that, with challenging directors like John Rich and George Sidney, gifted co-stars (Barbara Stanwyck, Ann-Margret), and some decent songs, Presley could still make decent movies that didn't embarrass him, his co-stars, or his fans and could, all being well, increase his audience. Yet that wasn't the direction Parker was interested in. More impressed by Katzman's frugality, he had a completely different agenda for his client.

In September 1964, at the Memphian Cinema, Elvis got to watch *Becket* and had *Dr. Strangelove* screened three times, explaining to Larry Geller that Peter Sellers was so subtle an actor "you don't always get him the first time, or even the second or third." Even at this stage, he was trying to learn his craft through observation. Three months later, the Colonel signed a new deal with MGM that finally guaranteed his star $1 million a picture. As good as that contract may have looked in the short term, it came close to rendering Elvis culturally irrelevant.

The point was made explicit by the *New York Times* when it greeted the British Beat invasion in 1964: "Multiply Elvis Presley by four, subtract six years from his age, add British accents and a sharp sense of humor. The answer: it's the Beatles (yeah, yeah, yeah)."

Girls! Girls! Girls!, Paramount, 1962

Director, Norman Taurog; Screenplay, Edward Anhalt, Anthony Weiss; Music, Joseph J. Lilley; Producer, Hal B. Wallis; Running time, 106 minutes

Cast: Elvis (Ross Carpenter), Laurel Goodwin (Laurel Dodge), Stella Stevens (Robin Gantner), Jeremy Slate (Wesley Johnson), Benson Fong (Kin Yung)

Dreck. That was Stella Stevens's emphatic, succinct verdict on the script for *Girls! Girls! Girls!* The actress felt so strongly about it that she refused to play her part until she was threatened with suspension and promised a role opposite Montgomery Clift that never materialized. Ironically, this script was, in part, the fruit of Oscar-winning scriptwriter Edward Anhalt's labors. Like Stevens, he was helping out against his better judgment. The man who had written such intelligent screenplays as *Panic in the Streets* and *The Young Lions* (with a breakthrough role for Presley's idol Dean Martin) had agreed to polish Anthony Weiss's script only on the understanding that he was given first crack at *Becket* (1964), a Wallis production that earned Anhalt his second Oscar. As for the star, he wasn't too keen either. His co-star Laurel Goodwin told Tom Lisanti, author of *Drive-In Dream Girls*, "Elvis didn't like *Girls! Girls! Girls!* Didn't like it at all."

The final script certainly doesn't contain any Oscar-worthy flourishes. If anything, the screenplay stands out for a variety of sexual innuendoes, often at Elvis's expense, and a meanness of spirit that gives what was intended to be a heartwarming musical comedy an odd flavor. When the heroine rings her father to ask for $2,000, does the script really need to blatantly advertise the fact that Daddy thinks she has to pay for an abortion?

The plot is even thinner than usual: as nautically minded free spirit Ross Carpenter, Elvis wants to buy his late father's boat *Westwind* and falls for pretty young Laurel Dodge (Laurel Goodwin), who, a bit like Elvis's character in

Laurel Goodwin and Elvis in *Girls! Girls! Girls!* (1962). In *Girls! Girls! Girls!* all the romance seemed to over-excite Elvis on screen.   *Paramount Pictures/Photofest*

Clambake, is trying to keep her fortune secret to find out if people like her or her money.

Despite the double entendres—the Chinese proverb that "man remember small things very big" being merely one of many—for a self-proclaimed "red-blooded boy who can't stop thinking about girls, girls, girls" Elvis seems more interested in the boat than either Lauren or Robyn (Stevens), the sultry nightclub singer who is passionately in love with him. Still, as the reviewer on Brilliant Observations On 2120 Films points out, "They probably didn't see much promotional value in a movie entitled *Boat! Boat! Boat!*" To mask the insubstantial plot, Elvis is given two sets of surrogate parents: the Stavroses, a Greek couple who sell *Westwind* to unscrupulous businessman Wesley Johnson (Jeremy Slate) and the Yungs, a Chinese family in Paradise Cove whose cute, slightly twee young daughters provide an excuse for such songs as "Earth Boy."

Goodwin is a spirited leading lady who, given the choice of marrying Elvis or living in sin, daringly asks for a bit of both. They spar well, especially during the number "The Walls Have Ears," which is ridiculous but fun. This scene is most famous because Presley, at this point in his life, often didn't wear underwear, and at one point "little Elvis," as he called his penis, is clearly visible. ("Look at that," he complained to Goodwin. "It's sticking out like a thumb. Sort of like a thumb." Taurog never even noticed.) This may or may not be why Cameron Crowe chose this as one of his thirty-six coolest musical moments on film for *Empire* magazine.

At this point in proceedings, Stevens is an increasingly marginal figure, though she does get to perform "The Nearness of You" (although her vocals were dubbed by Marni Nixon), the second-best number in the movie. Yet despite our hero's mysterious decision to relinquish his dream of owning the *Westwind* so he can settle down with Goodwin, she is virtually a spectator as the movie ends, for no apparent reason, with Elvis and a multinational cast of girls! girls! girls! performing *Girls! Girls! Girls!* in Paradise Cove. Quite how—or why—these girls happened to turn up on such an inaccessible, if beautiful, spot is a mystery neither Anhalt nor Weiss care to shed any light on.

While romancing Goodwin and scheming to buy his boat back from Johnson (who seems to pour himself a drink in almost every scene but never gets drunk), Elvis has to burst into song at regular intervals. The haunting ballad "I Don't Want To" was cut, and Leiber and Stoller's title track, despite a storming sax solo from Boots Randolph, really ought to have been. Instead the song is reprised for the finale, so lucky Elvis gets to sing "Crunchety crunchety crunchety crunch" twice in the same film.

The highlight of the soundtrack is undoubtedly "Return to Sender," performed in the Pirate's Den nightclub, so Elvis can give a proper performance. He uses the scene to pay tribute to one of his favorite singers, Jackie Wilson. As Guralnick wrote in his sleevenotes to *Elvis: The Great Performances, Volume 2: The Man and His Music*: "Elvis gives back a witty, almost flawless interpretation of Wilson's act with this rich R&B-flavored Otis Blackwell song. The hand gestures, the boxer's shuffle that stands in for the Twist, the self-amused little shoulder shrugs, even the facial expressions, all suggest Wilson." The homage was prompted by Elvis's long-standing admiration of the singer.

Even for an Elvis movie, "Song of the Shrimp" is an odd number, a pretty little calypso about a tragically naive crustacean sung with delicacy and astonishing sincerity by a star who, Nazareth suggests, is acknowledging the influence of the calypso king Harry Belafonte. Nathan wanted to cut this number too, saying after a preview: "I know we all like the shrimp song, but honest to God, it got nothing last night."

This was the second time in four movies the Elvis travelogue had been set in Hawaii (although, bizarrely, the location is never mentioned in the movie). The choice smacked either of ruthless commercial calculation or lack of imagination. The same mindset influenced the choice of director—Taurog returning for the third time—and casting. Hart would almost certainly have starred in her third

Elvis movie if she hadn't become a nun. Slate had already appeared fleetingly in *G.I. Blues*. Ken Becker, a drunk in the Pirate's Den, had already popped up briefly in *Loving You* and *G.I. Blues* (and would make his fourth and final appearance in an Elvis movie in *Roustabout*).

Stevens had never appeared in an Elvis movie and, as effectively as she plays off her leading man onscreen, she hated it—and the star, whom she later accused of being drunk when he performed "Return to Sender." (Her suggestion that he always had a large glass of rum in hand sounds questionable. Even Goldman never accused him of being a lush.) Stevens later said she asked him why he didn't demand a better script or director, only to be told: "Why mess with success?" Privately, Presley shared her reservations—the fact that he broke forty karate boards in his hotel room some nights until Wallis ordered him to stop probably indicates the depth of his frustration—but may have felt obliged to save face with an actress who, Goodwin says, put on so many airs on set that the crew dubbed her "Queen Stella."

Stevens's fears must have been realized when, on release, *Variety*'s reviewer complained she "was wasted in a standard role as a sultry torch singer who has given up ever really nailing the guy." Goodwin attracted better notices, with the reviewer saying she had the "cute, homespun potential of a Doris Day." Presley was praised for breezily playing himself. That certainly did the trick as far as Parker and Wallis were concerned. The movie grossed around $2.7 million, significantly more than Presley's last two, more artistically ambitious vehicles *Follow That Dream* and *Kid Galahad*.

Girls! Girls! Girls! has not exactly been reevaluated in the decades since its release, but the current critical consensus is probably best summed up by *Time Out* magazine, which calls it "one of Presley's better lightweight vehicles." It certainly isn't as painful as some of the travelogues to come. The central quartet—Presley, Stevens, Goodwin, and Slate—do enough to make us care about the outcome. And though the soundtrack is varied, "Return to Sender" is one of a handful of truly great songs to illuminate one of Elvis's post-army movies.

It Happened at the World's Fair, MGM, 1963

Director, Norman Taurog; Screenplay, Si Rose and Seaman Jacobs; Music, Leith Stevens; Producer, Ted Richmond; Running time, 105 minutes

Cast: Elvis (Mike Edwards), Joan O'Brien (Diane Warren), Gary Lockwood (Danny Burke), Vicky Tiu (Sue-Lin), H. M. Wynant (Vince Bradley), Guy Raymond (Barney Thatcher), Kam Tong (Uncle Walter)

As Mike Edwards, a pilot who spends all his money on clothes and women, Elvis turns out to be a sheep in a wolf's clothing. As the story starts, he has an address book that contains so many women's names he can't even remember what the first woman he tries to seduce is called—she is Dorothy Thompson (Yvonne

Craig). Inevitably, coitus interruptus intervenes in the form of an incandescent, trigger-happy father. It will take more than stray bullets to persuade Mike to change his ways. And by more we mean true love.

Even though our hero is preoccupied by the need to raise $1,200 so he and errant buddy Danny (Gary Lockwood) can get their plane back, he agrees to take a seven-year-old Chinese girl, Sue-Lin (Vicky Tiu), he has met around Seattle's World's Fair after spotting a vivacious blonde in the crowd.

Even for an Elvis movie, the King's initial pursuit of the opposite sex seems a tad obsessive but the movie effectively steals his wolf whistle, as Danny might put it. Mike's character is sweetened by his sudden, initially unrequited passion for nurse Diane Warren (Joan O'Brien), a development that sparks the best song in the film, the haunting "They Remind Me Too Much of You." He is so besotted he fakes an eye problem and, when rebuffed, pays a fresh young kid (Kurt Russell, who would play Elvis in the John Carpenter biopic) to kick him in the shins. This works well initially—the two smooch as Mike croons "I'm Falling in Love Tonight" in the restaurant at the top of the Space Needle—but when that pesky meddling kid turns up and asks our hero if he wants to be kicked again, Warren splits, fearing she has been deceived by a pathological liar. Despondent, Mike returns to the trailer he shares with Danny (paid for, presumably, with the winnings from his buddy's gambling school) and sings "One Broken Heart for Sale." This strikes such a chord that neighbors and random strangers leave their trailers to sing along with surprising proficiency.

The smoking gun that proves Mike's innate decency is the way he accepts responsibility for Sue-Lin when her uncle goes missing. Many of the children in Presley's movies turn out to be more cloying than cute, but Vicky Tiu is genuinely adorable, and her rapport with Elvis gives the movie more heart than most of his musical comedies. This relationship never quite unbalances the film, but it does mean that Elvis sings as many songs to the child as he does to his leading lady. In 1978, RCA released a compilation called *Elvis Sings and for Grown Ups Too*—featuring "Cotton Candy Land" and "How Would You Like to Be?" from this movie—and that album title effectively sums up the modus operandi here. The confusion is most apparent when he sings "A World of Our Own" to the woman he loves, but the tone, tempo, and feel are almost indistinguishable from Sue-Lin's lullaby "Cotton Candy Land."

Inevitably, Sue-Lin masterminds a reconciliation between the star-crossed lovers, faking a temperature so Warren comes over to the trailer where Mike is looking after her. This unexpected revelation of Mike's compassion moves Warren and they kiss again before drunken Danny, fresh from another night's gambling, spoils the mood. As the nurse drives off, Mike's buddy whistles: "You didn't tell me she was put together like that." Mike's reply, "Can't you tell a nice girl when you meet one?" tells us—and him—that he is irrevocably in love.

Desperate to get Sue-Lin out of the trailer so he can host gambling nights there—and keen for his buddy to resort to his old roving ways—Danny persuades an old flame to pretend to be Warren and report the girl to Child Welfare. With

Sue-Lin out of the way, all seems set for the buddies to fly a mission for crime boss Vince Bradley (H. M. Wynant). But the little girl disappears, Mike sets off to find her, and Vince gets impatient and urges Danny to fly solo. The movie changes key in the penultimate scene as Vince pulls a gun and tries to hold

Some critics weren't sure what the 'it' was that happened at the World's Fair.

Sue-Lin and Warren hostage to force Mike and Danny to smuggle furs across the border. In the ensuing fight, good prevails. All ends well when Sue-Lin's uncle is found and Mike and Diane stroll off into a happier future, singing "Happy Ending." It isn't such a happy ending for Danny, who has lost a buddy and co-pilot but, just possibly, may find an unlikely May–September romance with child welfare officer Miss Ettinger (Dorothy Green).

The question that has intrigued many critics about *It Happened at the World's Fair* is exactly what "it" is. Strip away the missing uncles, conniving gangsters, and poker games and all you really have is the age-old tale of a woman coming between two buddies. This isn't necessarily a criticism—almost every Hollywood musical comedy starts with the premise that a happy couple will embrace in the final scene. The art lies in making that destination as enjoyable as possible.

Looking back on the movie, O'Brien told Lisanti: "The premise of Elvis caring for a little girl was unique and different. It showed a side of him that was the real thing—a very sweet gentleman. A child-like attitude even emerged from him which I enjoyed watching. I also liked the fact the film was relatively uncluttered. It didn't have all these women falling out of the sky and dancing to bongo drums. From that standpoint, *It Happened at the World's Fair* was a better-than-average Elvis film."

The repartee between the buddies gets the movie off to a decent start—it is oddly pleasing to see Lockwood and Elvis doing something as mundane as trying to hitch a lift—and then the Chinese family and the romance take over. Taurog sets the action against the backdrop of the World's Fair and, drawing on the craft of cinematographer Joseph Ruttenberg, shoots as much footage as possible on location so that, although there is some back projection, the end product feels more colorful, optimistic, and authentic than *Fun in Acapulco*. The fight scenes—with poker players and Bradley—are quicker and slicker than usual too.

For once, the romance is nicely judged. O'Brien's nurse is initially resistant, yet intrigued, and handles the inevitable separations and reconciliations adroitly. It also makes a change to see Presley falling in love with an intelligent, beautiful woman who seems to be about his own age. *Variety*'s reviewer found he "effortlessly executes his customary character—red-blooded wolf on the crust, clean-cut nice guy at the core," but there's a hint of maturity too, clad in Sy Devore's sharp suits, Elvis looks sensational (even if sometimes he's wearing a little too much makeup) and seems almost to be grooming himself for a career as a Cary Grant–style leading man. For an Elvis hero, his desire to work at NASA is so constructive it's almost radical.

What slows the movie down are the ten songs. None of them are as great as "Return to Sender" or "Can't Help Falling in Love," none really rock, many are fluffy (though pleasant onscreen), and collectively they put the brakes on the story. *Variety*'s reviewer felt the movie would have been better paced if three had been cut. Yet Taurog knew that the movie had to produce a soundtrack album, and even with all ten songs on the record, the LP only lasted just over twenty minutes.

Although *It Happened at the World's Fair* is of no great historic significance as a movie, it works well on its own terms and as a snapshot of a more innocent, optimistic America, a country whose faith in the infinite technological possibilities of the future is symbolized by our snappily dressed hero's application to fly for NASA. He celebrates this initiative—and his romance—by singing "Happy Ending" in a scene that seems to belong to *The Music Man*. Even though this is performed in front of a marching band that seems to have strolled in from some Ruritanian romance, there's a sense in which the happy ending isn't just for Elvis, O'Brien and Tsiu but for America, and millions of fans watching in cinemas around the world.

There was a happy ending at the box office: earning $2.25 million at cinemas in the United States. The critics were generally unimpressed. Though the *New York Herald Tribune* called it "inoffensive, escapist fluff," British critic Elkan Allan was vitriolic: "If it didn't have Elvis Presley, this could be dismissed as a lousy film that desperately uses the World's Fairground in an effort to inject some novelty. With Elvis, it's a lousy film with ten musical numbers that desperately uses the World's Fairground."

Fun in Acapulco, Paramount, 1963

Director, Richard Thorpe; Screenplay, Allan Weiss; Music, Joseph L. Lilley; Producer, Hal. B. Wallis; Running time, 93 minutes

Cast: Elvis (Mike Windgren), Ursula Andress (Marguerita Dauphin), Elsa Cárdenas (Dolores Gomez), Alejandro Rey (Moreno), Larry Domasin (Raoul Almeido), Paul Lukas (Maximilian Dauphin)

Fun in Acapulco's got mariachis, muchachas, amigos, and an inordinate number of scenes where Elvis is superimposed on whatever footage the production crew could glean from a quick whizz around Acapulco. There are almost as many rumored reasons why Elvis wasn't allowed to go down Mexico way as there are songs in the movie. The most favored explanations are, in no particular order: rumors that the star had made derogatory remarks about the country or its women, worries about the expense of the security required if El went south of the border, or Parker's paranoia about his client leaving the United States to work in a country where his movies were banned (after *G.I. Blues* triggered a riot in Mexico City). So Elvis, who had been so keen to go on location he bought a matador's cape, stayed in Hollywood, masking his disappointment by taking lessons to improve his Spanish pronunciation.

Like every other Wallis/Presley movie of this era, *Fun in Acapulco* would not deviate from the musical-comedy travelogue formula. Yet Elvis might still have been enthused by the musical challenge. In the early 1960s, his music had acquired a Latin flavor, an influence that even Ernst Jorgensen, the greatest living authority on the King's recording career, admits he cannot explain.

Femme fatale Elsa Cárdenas tries to tempt Elvis in *Fun in Acapulco*.

Some of the tracks on his 1962 album *Pot Luck*—notably the lovely "Fountain of Love"—had Latin rhythms and moods, and he had just revamped Cole Porter's "Begin the Beguine" into the yearning "You'll Be Gone."

In *Fun in Acapulco*, only "Bossa Nova Baby" is on a par with Porter's classic, but Elvis gives his utmost, even on such nonsense as "There's No Room to Rhumba in a Sportscar," simmers beautifully through the finger-snapping "Margarita" and the suave "You Can't Say No in Acapulco," brings an insane conviction to "El Toro" (a song about a morose matador), and soars to meet the considerable technical and linguistic challenge posed by Pepe Guizar's "Guadalajara."

O'Curran's staging of "Bossa Nova Baby" is one of the musical highlights of Elvis's movie career, almost up there with some of the numbers in *King Creole* as a musical spectacle. The song, the suit, the beat, the urgent vocal are so effective you don't even mind the fact that the instrumental break sounds like Saturday night in a Mexican brothel.

Even the hard-to-please Roy Carr and Mick Farren say in *The Illustrated Record*: "The movie soundtracks were now coming thick and fast and, by the standards of the average Elvis film, this was one of the better examples. At least part of its success was due to stickling closely to the Mexican theme, rather than trying to shoehorn a bunch of unrelated songs into a minimal plot."

The plot in *Fun in Acapulco* was still minimal. Elvis is Mike Windgren, a trapeze artist haunted by guilt after dropping—and killing—his brother, who has come to Acapulco to find himself. Funnily enough, the rest of the Windgren family seem—a telegram suggests—to live in Tampa, Florida, Colonel Parker's hometown.

After getting sacked from his job on a boat (after spurning the advances of his boss's Lolita-esque daughter), he gets a job as a part-time lifeguard (cue for a few too many scenes of Elvis climbing onto the diving board and looking angst-ridden) and, through the offices of a precocious, loquacious, engaging boyish Svengali called Raoul (Larry Domasin), moonlights as a singer at Acapulco's biggest nightspots and hotels. He catches the eye of Dolores Gomez (Elsa Cárdenas), a highly sexed lady bullfighter, and the beautiful Marguerita Dauphin (Ursula Andress), director of entertainments at the hotel where he is working. Marguerita already has a boyfriend—champion diver Moreno (Alejandro Rey)—and her father (Paul Lukas) is a famous chef desperate to work north of the border. The predictable complications ensue, with Raoul doing his best to muddy the waters ("Girls are trouble, Mike, and if I'm your partner, half the trouble is mine"), before Mike conquers his fear of heights and assuages his guilt by making a 136-foot dive off La Perla cliff. This feat helps resolve the romantic quadrangle, as he is reconciled with Andress, and Rey makes do with Cárdenas. All that remains is for Mike to celebrate with a rendition of "Guadalajara" that is so rousing it sounds as if every man, woman, child, and stray dog in the neighborhood has been pressed into service.

The denouement is obvious from the very moment we see the first dive off La Perla, but director Thorpe does his best to make reaching that destination as fast and painless as possible. Cinematographer Daniel L. Fapp (who won an Oscar for his work on *West Side Story*) brings the tale to life, basking many scenes in vibrant colors, but is let down by the slapdash way Elvis is superimposed onto so many backdrops of Acapulco. This is the first time this kind of expediency has had such a visible onscreen impact on a Wallis/Presley picture. Sadly, the same techniques would later mar *Paradise, Hawaiian Style* and *Speedway*.

Though Elvis's backstory is reasonable enough, the revelation that he accidentally killed his brother comes so early in Weiss's screenplay, it dissipates the tension rather than building it. This construction of the romance between Presley and Andress is similarly flawed, with little opportunity for them to show genuine passion. As clinches go, none are as steamy as the brief moments of contact to come in *Roustabout* between Elvis and older woman Sue Anne Langdon.

Inevitably, though Andress and Elvis have reasonable empathy onscreen, their romance never catches fire. (The same happened on set, possibly because her jealous husband John Derek kept finding excuses to drop in.) The actress looked far more convincing making her iconic entrance onto the beach in *Dr. No* than she does in any scene in *Fun in Acapulco*, where the producers dictated her costumes to make sure they're not too sexy. Her loss is the movie's loss. At times, especially when she's walking away from the camera, her hideous costumes make this beautiful actress look almost malformed.

The same Puritan morality decrees that when Elvis dates Cárdenas, whose character is, by the standards of Elvis's family films, virtually a nymphomaniac, they are frustrated by steering wheels, brakes, and other impediments that a generation of American teenagers had mysteriously managed to circumvent on their drive-in dates.

By marginalizing the romance, the producers ensure that the warmest relationship in the movie is between Elvis and Domasin, easily the most endearing of the many Parker-style managers that recur in Presley's pictures. The boy-agent's antics—whether managing his client's social life or negotiating an increase in fees—have an amusing charm. That wouldn't always be the case with the allegedly adorable moppets Elvis would be obliged to interact with in forthcoming movies.

The critical response varied. Howard Thompson in the *New York Times* said, "Mr. Presley has never seemed so relaxed and personable." *Variety* predicted, "Presley fans won't be disappointed," but went on to add: "Presley has come a long way and is deserving of better material than is provided in this Allan Weiss screenplay." Another critic vehemently agreed, lamenting: "Elvis might have had some fun counting the money . . . from the rotten movie, but it doesn't extend to us."

Elvis's thirteenth movie, *Fun in Acapulco*, proved the stereotypical Wallis musical comedy travelogue could still generate decent returns. It was number 5 on *Variety*'s box-office charts for a week and generated over $3 million in rentals in North American cinemas, making it the highest-grossing movie musical of 1963. The single "Bossa Nova Baby" made number 8 on the U.S. charts. One Elvis fan who bought the 45 was John Lennon. In 1971, when he was trying to select a playlist for an Elvis-only jukebox, this Leiber/Stoller number was one of the singles he owned that didn't make the cut.

On their fall 1964 U.S. tour, the Beatles made a point of catching the movie at a Miami drive-in. If Lennon didn't like "Bossa Nova Baby," he must have loathed "There's No Room to Rhumba in a Sports Car." *Fun in Acapulco* finds Elvis the movie star at a crossroads. What he's doing is still commercially successful enough not to require imminent change, but all the old assumptions that underpinned his movie career would be challenged. The Fab Four arrived in America in February 1964, greeted by thousands of screaming teenagers at New York's JFK Airport. A month later, the singer who had inspired them most would release the low-budget quickie *Kissin' Cousins*.

Kissin' Cousins, MGM, 1964

Director, Gene Nelson; Screenplay, Gerald Drayson Adams, Gene Nelson; Music, Fred Karger; Producer, Sam Katzman; Running time, 96 minutes

Cast: Elvis (Josh Morgan, Jodie Tatum), Arthur O'Connell (Pappy Tatum), Glenda Farrell (Ma Tatum), Yvonne Craig (Azalea Tatum), Pamela Austin (Selena Tatum), Cynthia Pepper (Midge), Jack Albertson (Captain Robert Salbo)

Something unprecedented happened during the making of *Kissin' Cousins*. One day Elvis did not turn up for shooting. As Donald Woods (who played General Alvin Donford) told Eric Braun in *The Elvis Film Encyclopedia*: "Elvis wouldn't leave his dressing room because he had not come to terms with the blond wig he hated wearing as his hillbilly cousin." It took a few minutes for director Gene Nelson to coax him onto the set. After that, Woods recalled, "he was, as always, totally co-operative and offered to stay on after his 6:00 p.m. deadline to make up for the delay." Indeed, actress Cynthia Pepper recalled: "Usually on a set, the main star's demeanor sets the tone for the working environment. With Elvis it was always fun."

Yvonne Craig wondered if the issue was that he dyed his hair. It's possible. He might also have been disturbed by the movie's blatant allusion to his childhood and his stillborn twin, Jesse Garon. A proud southerner, he might also have been appalled by the movie's patronizing, stereotypical presentation of its hillbilly cast as Internal Revenue–fearing, moonshining, inbred white trash. Then again, he might have read the script, counted how many times Craig had to curse "them dang kittyhawks!" and wondered how he had sunk this low.

Lance LeGault, the actor who was Elvis's stunt double in many films and rehearsed with him, told Presley biographer Jerry Hopkins: "We shot *Kissin' Cousins* in 17 days and that was the turning point in Presley films as far as shooting. Up until that time, certain standards had been maintained. But it seems to me from *Kissin' Cousins* on we were always on short schedule. Once they realized they could take this guy and do a film that quickly, we were on quick pictures."

The strain on Elvis—who was playing two lead roles and had eight songs, which he rehearsed after hours or during lunch breaks—must have been immense. As dark-haired Josh Morgan, the air force officer who has to persuade his cousins, the Tatums, to sell some of their land on Smokey Mountain for the government to use as a missile site, Elvis does his best but at times can barely disguise his irritation with the material. As blond Jodie Tatum, an inarticulate, Kittyhawk-chasing yokel who challenges every stranger on the mountain to a wrestling match, Presley is surprisingly oafish, almost as if he's decided to make this dim-witted hillbilly alter ego as ludicrous as possible. His character—and this isn't Elvis's fault—is so one-dimensional, his only redeeming quality is his singing voice, especially when he opens his heart to croon "Tender Feeling." Credibility is always a relative concept in Elvis films, but it's hard to fathom why feisty, curvaceous typist Midge Riley (Pepper) succumbs to his charms.

The only consolation for Elvis is that some fine character actors are sinking with him. Arthur O'Connell does his darnedest as ornery patriarch Pa Tatum (a role *Variety* described as a "mountainous waste of talent"), and Glenda Farrell is an astonishingly plausible Ma Tatum. As Elvis's boss Captain Salbo, Jack

Albertson generates most of the few laughs in the movie and seems to lift Elvis's spirits and performance in their scenes.

When he first arrives on Smokey Mountain, Elvis is attracted to both Tatum girls: Azalea (Craig) and Selena (Pamela Austin). His dilemma inspires one of the film's best songs, "One Boy, Two Little Girls," which Elvis sings with such refinement and reverence that it stands out from the rest of the film. "There's Gold in the Mountains," another number on the same theme, is so well crafted that, as trite as it is, it's plenty listenable and hard to forget. Yet Austin's character almost disappears about halfway through, as if her scenes had been left on the cutting-room floor. In consequence, Craig has to shoulder most of the responsibility for cursing the Kittyhawks, a group of desperate, man-hungry women, led by Ronald Reagan's daughter Maureen, who live in a valley where no men have been born for twenty years—a phenomenon that would have intrigued Charles Darwin.

Eventually Josh wins obdurate Pa Tatum over, by saving his life and making the military agree that no Revenuers can trespass on the family's land. The deal is settled at a real—i.e., utterly fake—hillbilly hoedown where the Elvis twins sing "Barefoot Ballad," the spritely "Once Is Enough," and the rocking "Kissin' Cousins." The lyrics of the closing number ("I got a gal and she wants a lot of love") have the directness of some of Elvis's great hits of the 1950s, but the song lacks the same sparkle. The soundtrack is significantly better than the film, though if Elvis was really expecting to encounter grizzly bears (as he sings in "Smokey Mountain Boy") in Tennessee he must have been bitterly disappointed.

Some of the muddled thinking and cost cutting are clearly visible onscreen. Albert's air force captain is wearing an army uniform—as are all the enlisted men. In one number, a dancer clearly falls over—presumably Nelson and Katzman decided it was too expensive to reshoot. The cutting from Josh to Jodie as they jointly sing "Kissin' Cousins" at the finale is amateurish. In some scenes, you can see the shadows of the camera equipment. Occasionally the editing is so shoddy you realize one of the Elvises isn't the King at all.

Though some fans liked the dual role—and still love the film—for the critics it marked a new low. In the *New York Times*, Thompson dismissed it as a "broad, meandering rehash of Li'l Abner," referring to the famous hillbilly comic strip. *Variety* went further, spelling out some of the "little things" Katzman had forgotten: "a well-developed storyline and characterizations that are at least remotely related to life." *Time Out* magazine's reviewer was more succinct: "So thin it barely exists." The final scene, in which O'Connell and Albertson hold up a paddle to spell out "The End" looks like a belated, unsuccessful bid to convince us of ironical intent.

While some of Elvis's star vehicles—notably *Harum Scarum*—are so bad they're good, this should be filed under so bad it's dull. The scariest aspect of the movie—apart from the script—is the fact that, in today's money, it took around $21 million at the box office. Katzman had set a dismal precedent, although even Parker realized this was pushing things. Tensions on the set, largely created by the punitive shooting schedule, occasionally got so high he dropped in to perform a few morale-boosting stunts. This was probably the first movie Presley had made that he felt completely embarrassed by.

Viva Las Vegas, MGM, 1964

Director, George Sidney; Screenplay, Sally Benson; Music, George Stoll; Producers, Jack Cummings, George Sidney; Running time, 85 minutes

Cast: Elvis (Lucky Jackson), Ann-Margret (Rusty Martin), Cesare Danova (Count Elmo Mancini), William Demarest (Mr. Martin), Nicky Blair (Shorty Farnsworth)

At the very point when almost everyone—especially Elvis and his fans—began to fear the worst for his movie career, along came this thoroughly entertaining musical comedy, probably his best in the genre.

The movie was blessed with gifted director George Sidney (whose most notable previous works include *Anchors Aweigh, Pal Joey,* and *Kiss Me Kate*) and charismatic co-star Ann-Margret, who had been hailed, with Hollywood's yen for stereotyping, as "the female Elvis Presley." Sidney had worked with the actress on *Bye Bye Birdie* (1963), an Oscar-nominated musical comedy inspired by the brouhaha that surrounded Presley's induction into the U.S. Army, and would shoot her again in *The Swinger* (1966), a lurid comedy in which her body is photographed in such detail and from so many angles, the movie occasionally feels voyeuristic, virtually a public acknowledgment that the man Ann-Margret always referred to as "Mr. Sidney" was obsessed with her.

Sidney wasn't the only crew member who was smitten. According to Alan Fortas, one assistant director, who had dated the actress, was still in thrall to her beauty and ordered a cameraman to focus on her. Certainly when Elvis starts singing "C'mon Everybody," it is hard not to be distracted by the camera's invasive focus on Ann-Margret's gyrating bottom. (Was this the scene that so outraged Catholic priests on the Maltese island of Gozo that they persuaded the authorities to ban the movie?)

As the filming progressed—and the camera angles kept favoring Elvis's co-star, who was also given two songs to sing—Parker's rage mounted. The situation became even more complicated—for the Colonel—when his client fell deeply, passionately in love with the actress. The manager's standard tactics weren't as effective as usual—the film was being produced by George Cummings, who as the son of MGM's old boss Louis B. Mayer had more clout than many producers on other Presley films. Even so, Parker managed to kill one of the duets (the saucy "You're the Boss"), have one song reassigned to Elvis, and ultimately put a cap on the budget overrun. This was especially crucial, because it affected how much he and his client would make from the film. Parker's lobbying may explain why at the finale it takes less than a minute for the hero and heroine to wed, head off on their honeymoon, and halfheartedly reprise the title song.

The Colonel was, as he saw it, doing his utmost to protect his client's interests, yet in the long run this philosophy would prove counterproductive, even when you saw it purely in the terms Parker understood best: cold, hard cash. *Viva Las Vegas* was Elvis's most commercially successful movie, generating around $39 million in revenue in today's money. One reason for that commercial success was that, because of the chemistry between the stars and the quality of most of the songs, it was so entertaining to watch.

Elvis and Ann-Margret in Viva Las Vegas (1964). Elvis's chemistry with Ann-Margret thrilled cinemagoers—and terrified his manager.

Lucky Jackson (Elvis) is a racing driver who has to work as a hotel waiter to raise the money to buy the engine for the car he hopes to win the Las Vegas Grand Prix in. Yet his focus on this goal is hardly absolute, as he is, unsurprisingly, distracted by the considerable charms of Rusty (Ann-Margret). His rival for the race and the girl is Italian count Elmo Mancini (Cesare Danova). The denouement is inevitable from the outset, even though Rusty can't understand why Lucky won't give up racing for love. In this respect, the plot mirrors the tensions that killed the stars' romance. Although Elvis was so overwhelmed by his feelings for the actress he asked Parker to manage her, her unwillingness to give up her career to become his wife was one of the factors that ultimately ended their affair.

Viva Las Vegas has such momentum that the plot is even more incidental than usual. There are some half-decent lines, courtesy of Sally Benson, whose biggest hit was "Meet Me in St. Louis." When Ann-Margret drives into the garage and complains that her engine whistles, Elvis responds: "I don't blame it."

Sidney had studied Presley's previous movies and thought the camerawork was all wrong: "He had all the close-ups. It was boy, boy, boy, when it needed to be boy–girl." He proved his point. One of the qualities that makes *Viva Las Vegas* so easy to like is the way the romance between its principals is given time to blossom even if, on their day out, we learn a few too many statistics about the Hoover Dam.

The songs are significantly above average too. "Viva Las Vegas" is easily Presley's best title song since "King Creole." Though not stupendous on record, "C'mon Everybody" is compelling onscreen—and not solely because of the focus on the actress's derrière. "What'd I Say" (mysteriously added at the last minute, to Parker's irritation), "If You Think I Don't Need You," and "Today, Tomorrow, and Forever" all have their appeal. Ann-Margret's numbers—"My Rival" and "Appreciation," which allows her to channel Marilyn Monroe—are better than many that Presley sang in his later movies. The romantic duet between the stars on "The Lady Loves Me" is, despite the occasionally unsubtle lyrics, comically effective.

Yet the standout song—and scene—is the moody, reflective "I Need Somebody to Lean On," in which Elvis ponders his failed relationship. This sequence could have suited one of the great Gene Kelly MGM musicals, and, as Guralnick says, "You can sense the quiet satisfaction Elvis must have felt as words, music and image come together for once." This affecting scene, hinting at an emotional depth you don't find anywhere else in the movie, is in a class of its own.

That leads, indirectly, to the question of whether Ann-Margret steals the film from Elvis. The critical consensus is she does—and there are scenes where Presley almost becomes her straight man. Yet there also moments when it is hard not to be irritated by what the *New York Times* reviewer Howard Thompson dubbed her "cutey pie grimacing." When they are dancing together in "C'mon Everybody," it is almost as if she is thinking that if she yelps at a certain point or touches her hair in a certain way, she will look even sexier. Presley's performance, though more low-key, stands up pretty well. The competition might have done him some good—during "C'mon Everybody" he moves his body with a freedom not seen since *King Creole*.

Viva Las Vegas is worth watching for all kinds of reasons: its appealing portrait of Vegas in the 1960s, the chemistry between the central duo, and because, when all is said and done, it is one of the most entertaining musical comedies of the 1960s—and one of Steven Spielberg's favorite films. As Thompson noted in the *Times*, "Whatever it isn't, *Viva Las Vegas* remains friendly, wholesome and as pretty as all get out." The fans agreed. The movie was the eleventh-highest grosser of 1964 and has probably generated more revenue—$39 million in today's money—than any other Presley film and broke box-office records in Manila and Tokyo.

Sadly, MGM, perhaps spurred on by the cost-conscious Colonel, drew all the wrong lessons from such a smash. Elvis would be stuck in races in *Spinout*, *Clambake*, and *Speedway*—as if *Viva Las Vegas* owed its popularity to the grand prix scenes. The more obvious lesson—that the audience for an Elvis film could be expanded significantly with the right co-star and the right music—was completely ignored.

Roustabout, Paramount, 1964

Director, John Rich; Writers, Anthony Lawrence, Allan Weiss; Music, Joseph J. Lilley; Producer, Hal B. Wallis; Running time, 96 minutes

Cast: Elvis (Charlie Rogers), Barbara Stanwyck (Maggie Morgan), Joan Freeman (Cathy Lean), Leif Eriksen (Joe Lean), Sue Anne Langdon (Madame Mijanou), Pat Buttram (Harry Carver), Joan Staley (Marge)

The sneer, the leather jacket, and the rebellious attitude made a welcome return to the Elvis canon in *Roustabout*, in which he plays antihero Charlie Rogers, a nomadic, singing tough guy who ends up falling in love with his very own carnival queen, Cathy Lean (Joan Freeman).

Weiss's original script heretically had Rogers being drummed out of the army after deserting under fire. This detail was soon cut—"Wallis wanted everything kept pretty shallow," the writer said later—as the veteran producer decided this was the wrong kind of G.I. blues for Elvis. Shorn of that motivation, Rogers's deep resentment of the world seems to be inspired solely by the fact that he is an orphan who hails from a "swamp outside Shreveport, Louisiana."

Having tinkered with the script, Wallis indulged in his favorite pastime, writing to Parker and ordering him to get his star into shape. As a "lean, hard-hitting tough guy," the producer warned, Elvis could not be "pudgy looking . . . he must train down to get the look or his character will not be believable." In the same letter, he took a pop at another favorite target, Elvis's hairstyle, saying he wanted all the "dye and the goo" taken out. Though Elvis looks reasonably trim in the picture, he wasn't going to change his hairstyle for Wallis—especially with his pride still stung by the producer's remark to *Variety* that he used the money from Presley pictures to finance artistically significant movies like *Becket*.

Despite Wallis's fudging, the plot was stronger than usual. Elvis's singing louse loses his nightclub gig after provoking a few rowdy college boys into a fight, an incident that leads to the obligatory scene of Presley in a cell. Spurning the waitress Marge (Joan Staley), who paid his bail, Charlie rides off into the distance on his Honda motorcycle. A few miles—and one song—later, he is run off the road by cranky carnival manager Joe Lean (Leif Eriksen) after flirting with his daughter Cathy. Carnival owner Maggie Morgan (Barbara Stanwyck) offers to pay for a new guitar and to fix his broken Honda motorcycle. With Japanese motorcycle parts in short supply in this part of America, Charlie has to spend a few days at the carnival and agrees to become a roustabout, partly to prove to the owner he's no softy, and partly so he can pursue Cathy.

For once, the storyline is substantial enough to have a backstory. We realize that Joe's unlikable ways stem from his guilt at drunkenly fixing a ride that killed a customer. To pay off the victim's family, the carnival had to turn the bank, but—and here the story does descend into cliché—with revenues falling, the carnival is struggling to repay the loan. Remorseful and resentful, he suspects that the "bum" Rogers is being hired as his possible successor and does his best to get the youngster thrown off the lot. That isn't going to happen, because his singing soon proves to be the carnival's best hope of paying off the bank. Tensions come to a head when Joe is accused of stealing the wallet of an obnoxious customer (Steve Brodie, whose irritating antics sparked the brawl in *Blue Hawaii*, returning here for some more pointless pugilism). While Joe is hauled off to jail, Charlie returns to the scene, finds the wallet, teases the fortune-telling femme fatale Madame Mijanou (Sue Anne Langdon), and, after a coffee and a kiss with Cathy, decides he'll let her father stew in jail.

The next morning, in a scene that inspired the Irish comedy *Eat the Peach* (1986), our hero is goaded into trying to ride a motorbike around the Wall of Death. When he falls—and the vital wallet falls out of his pocket—he is deemed to have broken the carny code of honor. Stung by the disgrace—and Cathy's rejection—he quits, riding off to work for Harry Carver (Jesse Buttram), a ruthless carnival mogul known as the Undertaker because he only buys rivals that have gone bust. This being an Elvis film, the heel turns into a hero after a touching appeal by Cathy, and his return is enough to placate the bank and prompt an instant, implausible change of heart from Joe.

Although *Roustabout* was not as critically or commercially successful as its predecessor *Viva Las Vegas*, it is in some ways a more significant movie. For once, Parker earned his keep as a technical adviser. The carnival background, which he knew so well and spent a weekend discussing with Weiss, is convincingly drawn, right down to the jargon. Maybe Weiss got more out of this weekend than Elvis's manager realized, because Carver (drolly played by Buttram) seems a sympathetic parody of Parker. When the owner of Carver's Combined Shows tells his new singing sensation, "Around here there's just one reason the show must go on: the gross," it's as if the Colonel himself is speaking.

Instinctively more comfortable as a misunderstood bad guy who turns good, Elvis gives one of his best post-army performances. He idolized—and was initially terrified by—Stanwyck, a true Hollywood great. There are differing accounts over their relationship—Langdon said she was too strong a character for Elvis and broadcast her displeasure at having to appear in an Elvis film—but Elvis's bodyguard Lamar Fike said Presley enjoyed the picture and that "she helped him as an actor." She later described him as "a fine young gentleman with impeccable manners." Mae West had originally been offered the part but turned it down after Wallis refused to rewrite the film so she had the starring role and Elvis had a small part opposite her.

Stanwyck looks stunning in the tightest blue jeans that legendary costumier Edith Head could design. The sparks certainly fly when she and Presley argue onscreen. At one point, Stanwyck tells him he needs to start living "from the waist up," an intriguing allusion to Elvis's appearance, shot from the waist up, on *The Ed Sullivan Show* in 1956. In their scenes, Presley interprets his character shrewdly. He is just bad enough; any darker and he would unbalance this musical-comedy/drama.

Presley's rapport with Stanwyck is matched by his interplay with Langdon's fortune teller. After she shows off her legs, Elvis tells her, "Marlene Dietrich did it better," only for Langdon to hit back, "But she's not here." Unfortunately, the King doesn't have the same kind of chemistry with Freeman. It's not entirely her fault. Her character is required to flounce off in a huff a few times too often. It doesn't help that apart from a ride on the Ferris wheel while Elvis sings "It's a Wonderful World," the soundtrack doesn't contain any numbers to bond the lovers. In the best ballad, "Big Love Big Heartache," Elvis is pining for his girl.

In a sympathetic essay on Presley's movies in *Elvis* (Phoebus, 1977), Jeremy Pascall says that, compared to the Beatles movies, the star looks out of touch in films like *Roustabout*. That's not quite true.

Roustabout is almost two movies in one. The opening scenes at Mother's Tea House are much sharper and cynical than what follows. The astringent tone is set when the owner Lou (Jack Albertson) teasingly introduces Rogers as an artist who would undoubtedly be playing in San Francisco "if the authorities didn't misunderstand him." In her movie debut, Raquel Welch plays a young customer who asks the waitress, "How come they call this place a teahouse?" Marge replies: "It was something that was in and now is almost out so we'll rename it either something further in or further out," which must be one of the smartest putdowns in an Elvis movie. After Presley sings "Poison Ivy League" (which pokes fun at the sons of the rich who give him an itch), an enraged college boy complains, "I've seen more action in a zoo." To which Elvis, his sneer gloriously back in place, replies, "From which side of the cage?"

When Elvis rides away from lovestruck Marge, he rides into a more conventional movie. There are enough clichés to understand why *Variety* dismissed the movie as "nonsense," but the film has plenty of spirit and enough emotional depth to keep you watching, and it is mostly well played and gorgeously shot by Loyal Griggs. What does let the movie down—especially if you compare it to *A Hard Day's Night*, which was released four months earlier in the United States—are the songs. The classic "Little Egypt" stands out, and "Hard Knocks" and "One Track Heart" have plenty of energy, but many of the songs are just too carny-tastic for the movie's good.

On release, one reviewer described *Roustabout* as "slightly improved jollity," and this is one of Elvis's best post-army movies, successful enough artistically and commercially to suggest that the old rebel image, even in this slightly synthetic form, had resonance. Elvis's performance also suggested that, with the right cast, he could still give his all. He even did his own stunts—cutting an eye in the karate fight outside Mother's Tea House, an accident that director John Rich covered up by making the star wear a Band-Aid in some scenes.

The soundtrack topped the U.S. album charts, and the movie grossed $3 million in the United States, the twenty-eighth-highest grosser of 1964. *Roustabout* also featured probably the most entertaining argument between Elvis and one of his directors. Years later, Rich said he set out to tease a better performance out of Elvis. Egged by on the Memphis Mafia, and insecure at sharing the screen with Stanwyck, Elvis seems to have been uncomfortable with this approach at times—even though the results onscreen suggest Rich knew what he was doing.

At one point the star insisted he wanted backing singers on a number he was singing on the road. Rich demurred, on the grounds of realism, asking Elvis where they would put these backing singers. His star replied, "Same damn place you put the band." Touché.

Watching the film later, Presley must have sensed that Rich's approach had worked. As Nathan noted in a memo in March 1964, after the film had enjoyed a good preview: "Elvis saw picture recently and told me it is the best picture he's ever made . . . He is not given to praise and his comment, if ever, is 'it's pretty good' or 'it's ok..'"

4

A World of Our Own

From *Girl Happy* to *Clambake*

In 1967, Presley dropped out of the top-ten box-office acts. In Quigley's list of box-office champions, he had slipped from tenth in 1966 to sixteenth. Though Elvis didn't stop making feature films until 1970, he would never return to the top ten. His last major box-office success was *Girl Happy* (1965), which made about $23 million in today's money. The wonder, given some of the fare he was starring in and the competition he now faced, was that it took him so long to fall out of favor.

Few other stars could have survived such misfires as the Rudolph Valentino homage/parody *Harum Scarum* or the repetitive brain injury of his third Polynesian sojourn in five years, *Paradise, Hawaiian Style*. It is roughly at this point in Elvis's movie career that even the critics gave up making wisecracks or honing insults. The star himself told Pierre Adidge and Robert Abel in a candid interview that never made it into *Elvis on Tour*: "The pictures got very similar. If something was successful, they'd try to recreate it the next time around. So I'd read the first four or five pages, and I knew that it was just a different name with twelve new songs—and the songs were mediocre in most cases. That's what might have made it seem like indifference. But I was never indifferent. I was so concerned that's all I talked about. It worried me sick."

The movies Presley was starring in between 1965 and 1967 seemed to exist, as the writer Howard Hampton put it, in a "self-referential nirvana." Even Parker was shaken by some of them. His advice on the strategy to sell *Harum Scarum* was at least honest: "Book it fast, get the money and then try again." The movie is worth watching as a curio because, as the author Joe Queenan wrote: "When you see a film like *Harum Scarum*, where Elvis sets out to the Middle East on a State Department goodwill tour, crosses the Mountains of the Moon, is then abducted by bandits, gets gussied up in lime green pants and a golden cummerbund, dons a turban, and leads a peasant's revolution against the wicked oppressors, you can only shake your head in disbelief."

Although a few of his musical comedies in this era—notably *Tickle Me* and *Spinout*—were distinguished by occasional satirical intent, they came out so often that they really could, as one MGM executive had said, have been numbered. Unfortunately, while Parker was bedeviling Hazen and Wallis to sign a new contract, the canny ex-carny had failed to notice how much buzz—and business—the Beatles' movies were generating.

A Hard Day's Night had been hailed as the *"King Kong* of jukebox movies" by *Village Voice* magazine, while *Help!*, less satisfying for audiences, critics, and the Fab Four, was still easier on the eye and ear than *Harum Scarum*. Parker was arguing over contracts when, even if he had just followed the money, he should have sensed that fundamental changes in the system were required.

The only major change he initiated was to agree to save Allied Artists' money by not having Elvis record a single new song for *Tickle Me*. He could just use some of the numbers from his extensive back catalog. Presley's terse telegram accepting the deal—"Arrangements with records okay"—hinted at his disgust or despair. That deal was symptomatic of a more worrying trend: the inability of the Hill and Range music factory to provide his client with any big hit songs.

At least Wallis could sense that things had changed. He didn't know what the answers were, but as early as November 1964, days after *Roustabout*'s release, he announced he wanted Elvis's next film to feature the star as a character who had a chip on his shoulder but did something about it. Presumably he gave up that idea, or, by the time Anthony Lawrence and Weiss had written it up, it mutated into *Paradise, Hawaiian Style*, in which Elvis plays a helicopter pilot whose main grievance is that the world assumes—correctly—that he's an irresponsible womanizer.

For their star, the studios, and some of the writers, Elvis's movies had become a treadmill. The one exception to the prevailing ennui was Taurog, who kept working hard, trying to make the most of what he was handed and encouraging his star to do the same. Yet he didn't have the clout to make the necessary changes. And after the making of *Double Trouble*, he complained: "The women still think he is a kid . . . they want him to remain an adolescent. Because his fans are so close to him, we have to be very careful about the way we cast him. We can never make him smart alecky or leering with sexuality. He can never lose a fight, and we can never dress him like a slob. His pictures have to be upbeat, as if the character he plays is living out the dream life of his audience."

For *Loving You*, writer/director Kanter had been able to meet and observe his star before shooting began. By 1966, when MGM was wrapping up *Spinout*, writer George Kirgo was allowed to meet Presley only on the last day of filming, for five minutes, to be presented with what the scribe later described as "one of the most hideous, most horrible oil paintings of himself," which the star duly signed. With such a modus operandi, any creative engagement between star and scriptwriter was all but impossible.

The sheer remorselessness of Presley's movie schedule in this period now looks like an act of desperation, a determination to extract the last dollar and fulfill contractual obligations. In 1967, three movies—*Easy Come, Easy Go; Double Trouble;* and *Clambake*—were released within six months. The only good thing about this strategy—as far as Elvis was concerned—was that it wore out the formula more quickly.

In 1966, after the release of the period musical comedy *Frankie and Johnny*, Charles Boasberg, head of Paramount's distribution, warned Wallis the film was "dying all over the country, and this is his second poor picture in a row." By 1967, Paramount was of two minds about whether it was worth releasing *Easy Come, Easy Go*. Wallis had seen enough by then: that was his last Presley picture. Much to Parker's chagrin, the producer had refused to spend money on more—or better—songs for this film, a decision director Rich later dismissed as lunacy: "By this point, the songs were the only things that were selling." To be fair to Wallis, the system had failed him. As he wrote to Parker's aide Tom Diskin, "We have now had from the music company fifty-five demo records and in our opinion . . . forty-three are just no good at all."

Although he could be hard-nosed, Wallis was pained by the way Presley's movie career had played out and by the star's obvious increasing disenchantment. He may also have felt that the rewards were no longer enough to justify the hassle of handling Parker. In a memo in March 1967, Nathan reported to Wallis on *Easy Come, Easy Go*'s performance: "The five days in 30 theatres in here took in $64,000, and they estimate it will take in $84,000 for the Easter week. This compares to *Paradise* which took in $93,258 in 29 theatres for the first week in June . . . obviously the star is not as big an attraction as he was."

Paradise, Hawaiian Style had been the last film to be included in Wallis's contract with the Colonel, and talks over a new deal took seven months, with Elvis's manager arguing over almost every clause. Ultimately, this rather unproductive negotiating stance led to a deal for one new movie (*Easy Come, Easy Go*), and, after Parker complained he had spent too much of his own money promoting that film, Wallis sent him a check for $3,500 and never worked with Presley or his manager again.

United Artists only made *Clambake* because the bosses decided they would lose less money than if they paid the financial penalty for not exercising its option—and they subcontracted the film out to producers Arthur Gardner, Arnold Laven, and Jules V. Levy, telling them not to spend more than $1.5 million (roughly half what had been spent on a typical Elvis movie before Katzman's frugality had taken its toll).

Even Elvis's loyal fans were fretting. One wrote to Wallis: "I realize that there is not much you can do if Elvis doesn't care and sometimes I doubt that he does." Some exhibitors felt that Elvis's appearance suggested there must be something "radically wrong" with him.

For the most part, Presley took his decline with good grace, trying his best to rally morale on the set. He managed to distract himself from the indignity of *Harum Scarum* by beginning an unending quest to discover some meaning in life—both life in general and in his life in particular. His verdict on this film is contained in the inscription on the autographed photo he gave to director Gene Nelson: "Someday we'll get it right." Pills and practical jokes helped too. He could rely on his bodyguards to do his bidding along with, as the movies came and went at ever shorter intervals, a corps of trusted dancers and extras (many of them women).

Many stars had what they call a "request list," and Presley was no exception. As Michelle Breeze, who had a bit part in *Double Trouble*, told Bill Bram: "Elvis had a group of us girls and he wouldn't do a movie unless we were there for him, especially when he did his musical numbers. It gave him comfort to know he was singing to people he was familiar with." People who wouldn't, presumably, titter when he sang about Old MacDonald's farm or Queenie Wahine's papaya.

During the shooting of *Paradise, Hawaiian Style*, he was, at times, listless, detached, even slightly cruel when Herman's Hermits singer Peter Noone came to interview him—although it is clear, from his sardonic aside to DJ Tom Moffatt ("Tom, this is probably the best interview you've ever had"), that his anger is directed as much at himself as at his visitor. Shepard, who worked with him on *King Creole* and *Paradise, Hawaiian Style*, was shaken by the change in his personality between 1958 and 1965, saying, "It was as if he'd aged 30 years emotionally."

His equanimity usually returned, even though before each movie he had to make an increasing effort to slim down. His crash diet before *Clambake* was so drastic, on top of some of the other pills he was taking, that he fell over, knocking himself out. Alarmed by his star's torpor, fearing that success was slipping away, Parker stepped in, banishing Presley's recently acquired spiritual guru Larry Geller and playing a pivotal role in the star's marriage to Priscilla Beaulieu on May 1, 1967. Two months before the wedding, the Colonel had written to MGM urging them to do away with the scenarios focusing on girls in bikinis and nightclub scenes "which have been in the last 15 pictures . . . I sincerely hope that you are looking in some crystal ball and coming up with some good strong, rugged stories."

Girl Happy, MGM, 1965

Director, Boris Sagal; Screenplay, Harvey Bullock, R. S. Allen; Music, George Stoll; Producer, Boris Pasternak; Running time, 96 minutes

Cast: Elvis (Rusty Wells), Shelley Fabares (Valerie Frank), Harold J. Stone (Mr. Frank), Gary Crosby (Andy), Joby Baker (Wilbur), Jimmy Hawkins (Doc), Nita Talbot (Sunny Daze), Mary Ann Mobley (Deena Shepherd), Fabrizio Mioni (Romano), Jackie Coogan (Sergeant Benson)

The awkward tagline "Elvis jumps with the campus crowd to make the beach 'ball' bounce!"—complete with those thoughtfully applied quotation marks around ball—accurately captures this musical comedy's genre-straddling ambition to fuse the college-vacation frolics of producer Joe Pasternak's hit *Where the Boys Are* with the beach-party vibe of *Blue Hawaii*. The surprise here is that, despite such limited ambitions, a below-par soundtrack that prompted its star to walk out of the studio in disgust, and some ill-conceived attempts to help Elvis compete with Beatlemania, *Girl Happy* is one of the King's more entertaining musical comedies.

For once, Elvis isn't chasing girls. His mission as bandleader Rusty Wells is to stop boys chasing one particular girl: Valerie Frank (Shelley Fabares), daughter of gangster-cum-nightclub-owner Mr. Stone (Harold J. Stone). The task isn't made any easier by the fact that Valerie is heading to Fort Lauderdale, the most famous beach resort in Florida, for a spring vacation with her friends and, as Rusty warns her father, "Thirty thousand sex maniacs." Mr. Frank is all for canceling his daughter's trip until Rusty suggests that he and his buddies in the band are willing to head down to Florida to act as secret chaperones.

Mary Ann Mobley was the unhappy girl in *Girl Happy*.   *Metro-Goldwyn-Mayer/Photofest*

He just about succeeds in his mission, despite being distracted by sultry beauty Deena Shepherd (Mary Ann Mobley) and the fact that cosmopolitan playboy Romano (Fabrizio Mioni) has the worst of intentions regarding young Valerie. Romance between watcher and watched blossoms until Mr. Frank clumsily reveals the truth, prompting the hitherto innocent heroine to stage an impromptu striptease at the Kit Kat Club. Disaster is averted only when Elvis starts a chaotic fight. When his love is arrested, he breaks into jail just as she is leaving on bail and has to escape in drag, the only cross-dressing scene in his thirty-one feature films. Luckily, the complications are ironed out, giving Jackie Coogan the opportunity to amuse as a cop who doesn't like jailing students. After a final performance by his combo during which Elvis wryly observes, "It has been sociable," Mr. Frank mysteriously gives the romance his blessing and the King and his queen are reunited.

There's nothing new about any of this—you can almost see *Girl Happy* as a complement to Pasternak's 1960 hit *Where the Boys Are*, which sees the Fort Lauderdale spring break from the female point of view—but it works, partly because Sagal never lets the pace slacken. The young director bonded with his star (even advising him to take a break and learn his craft at the Actors Studio, a proposal that would have given the Colonel an aneurysm) and draws out one of the King's better performances. *Variety* hailed his "growing naturalness" while British pop star Mike Sarne, reviewing the film for *Films and Filming Magazine*, suggested Presley had become a "first class comedy actor."

One minor mystery is why, given that this is partially a beach party movie, Elvis never bares his chest, even wearing a jacket while water-skiing. That apart, he looks in his prime. Lean, tall, with his trademark immaculate blue-black hair, he is sexy without looking sleazy. As a reviewer on website The Sheila Variations has pointed out, there is, for example, none of the crude ogling that marks the allegedly sophisticated sex comedy *The Seven Year Itch*.

It helped that the star quickly developed a good rapport with both his love interests: Fabares, in the first of three films in which she would be his leading lady, and Mobley, a former Miss America who was from Presley's home state, Mississippi. Onscreen he has real chemistry with both, even if he is destined to end up with the good girl rather than the vamp. Fabares is especially adroit, giving the right emotional weight to some scenes, notably her tearful phone call when her father tells her he's paying Elvis to watch over her. Her strip show is probably the most erotically charged nightclub scene in a Presley musical comedy since Juliet Prowse strutted her stuff in *G.I. Blues*.

Writers R. S. Allen and Harvey Bullock had learned their craft on the 1960s sitcom *The Andy Griffith Show* and make sure the movie is never too far away from a gag or a song, creating one comic setpiece in which Latin lothario Mioni is unceremoniously dumped—with his yacht—in the swimming pool at the Seadrift Motel. They drew inspiration from Pasternak's *Where the Boys Are, Some Like It Hot* (Elvis's drag scene), and, inevitably, *A Hard Day's Night*. To appeal to a newer generation of teenyboppers, the King was cast in a fake Fab Four—with Bing

Crosby's son Gary, Joby Baker (who had met his wife Joan Blackman on the set of an Elvis film), and Jimmy Hawkins as his indistinguishable bandmates—and forced to enter a shaving-cream fight to emulate George Harrison's shaving scene in Richard Lester's classic rock musical.

The repercussions of Beatlemania didn't end there. The fluorescent opening-credits sequence is obviously designed to be seriously groovy in a way that Austin Powers might have appreciated, and director of photography Philip Lathrop has given the film an interesting Day-Glo, Pop Art color scheme. The soundtrack was slightly more rocking than for *It Happened at the World's Fair* and *Girls! Girls! Girls!* but not significantly more interesting or contemporary. Nothing in *Girl Happy* was as classy as "Return to Sender."

The falling-in-love ballad "Puppet on a String" reached number 14 on the U.S. charts, but the other distinctive numbers didn't always stand out for the right reasons. "Fort Lauderdale Chamber of Commerce" has one of the Tepper/Bennett partnership's cleverest hooks and works well in the movie as Elvis tries to distract Fabares. The title track, a collaboration between Doc Pomus and Norman Meade (who wrote the Erma Franklin classic "Piece of My Heart"), might have worked if the master hadn't been speeded up so much that Presley began to sound like Mickey Mouse. Thanks to Sagal's nifty direction, "Do the Clam" isn't too painful onscreen, but on record it is easily the worst in the microgenre of dance-craze numbers that started with "Dixieland Rock," gave us "Rock-a-hula Baby," and peaked with "Bossa Nova Baby."

The most seductive number—literally and musically—is "Do Not Disturb." Yet strangely, after thirty-six attempts to record this sly little song, Elvis stormed out of the studio. He was clearly dissatisfied with his material, and some of the rather strained rock numbers he was cutting for this film—which included "The Meanest Girl in Town," a reworking of the Bill Haley number "Yeah! She's Evil" —must have rankled, especially with the Beatles surpassing him as the music industry's best-selling act. He had inspired them, and now he was being ordered to imitate them. He would not record again for eight months.

The soundtrack may explain why, despite relatively kind reviews, *Girl Happy* never became a firm fan favorite, but it has proved one of Elvis's more durable musical comedies. As with many musical comedies from this era—not just Elvis's—there are moments when the singing is out of sync, electric guitars let rip even though they're not plugged in, and the comedy turns chauvinistic (as when Elvis says tells his cronies he'd love Deena even if she wouldn't make out with him: "I'd miss her, but I'd still love her"). Yet for all of that, this is very watchable. For once, Elvis is simply a singer and there is no car or speedboat to be fixed against the clock. The dialogue is snappier than in many Elvis movies, and the cast give it their all, delivering a slick, quick sex comedy in which nobody has sex.

Although Presley wanted to be a serious dramatic actor, he shows in *Girl Happy* that he had a natural flair for musical comedy. Reviewing Elvis's movie career for the *Los Angeles Times*, Mark Olsen said: "The film shows that Presley at half-speed still exudes more talent, charm and charisma than most performers." This view has been echoed by critic Stuart Griffith, who praised its "pleasant, if generally disposable songs, bold primary colors and vacation atmosphere" before concluding: "For a change Elvis doesn't seem totally embarrassed

Presley and Fabares teamed up for the first time in this musical comedy. She was his favorite leading lady.

by the screenplay handed him." He is right to suggest that Rusty Wells is a "sanitized approximation of the real Elvis: a popular entertainer who uses his charisma to pick up chicks for a little no-obligation lovin' back at the motel."

The formula certainly worked commercially. *Girl Happy* made over $22 million in today's money at the U.S. box office, and even the inadequate, badly produced soundtrack album sold over 400,000 copies. Yet the movie marked the end of the formula's golden age. None of his subsequent movies would make as much money at the American box office. Elvis had told Sagal: "I'm looking forward to doing a picture where I can finally act and not just sing." Despite the diminishing returns from his travelogues, he would have to wait three years to fulfill that hope—in *Charro!*, his last western.

Even in this most efficient of productions, there is a scene that uncannily reflects one aspect of Presley's life. As Jerry Hopkins notes in his biography, during the making of the 1968 comeback TV special, Parker entertained himself by playing a game called "Honesty," in which he thought of a number that NBC producer Bob Finkel had to guess right or lose $20. Finkel invariably lost, and the bets cost him hundreds of dollars throughout the making of the show.

In *Girl Happy*, when Elvis and his combo are arguing over who's going to mind Fabares, he invites the boys to guess what number between one in ten he's thinking of. They all guess wrong, meaning that Presley, as he had intended, gets to look after Mr. Frank's girl. Coincidence? Or was Parker already playing Honesty in the summer of 1964 when this film was shot?

Tickle Me, Allied Artists, 1965

Director, Norman Taurog; Writers, Elwood Ullmann, Edward Bernds, and (uncredited) Michael A. Hoey; Music, Walter Scharf; Producer, Ben Schwalb

Cast: Elvis (Lonnie Beale), Jocelyn Lane (Pamela Merritt), Julie Adams (Vera Radford), Jack Mullaney (Stanley Potter), Edward Faulkner (Brad Bentley)

Conceived in haste to save Allied Artists from bankruptcy, with a plot so loopy it could, as one fan has suggested, have been written to suit sets the studio already owned, and no original songs, it's easy to see why this quirky musical-comedy thriller was dismissed by Howard Thompson in the *New York Times* as "the silliest, feeblest, and dullest vehicle for the Memphis Wonder in a long time." Yet *Tickle Me* isn't quite what it seems, simultaneously celebrating and satirizing the finely honed formula the Elvis Presley movie had become.

The premise is simple enough. Elvis's singing, swinging, rodeo-ridin', bronco-bustin' Lonnie Beale arrives in a small western town, finds a job on the Circle Z dude ranch, and sings a bit. Lusted after by his luscious boss, Vera (played by the lovely Julie Adams, who sprang to prominence in 1954 in the cult classic *The Creature from the Black Lagoon*), he falls instead for sexy teacher Pam (Jocelyn Lane, a young actress known as the British Bardot—drafted in, so

Tickle Me was an exotic blend of Presley's music and Three Stooges' style comedy.

rumor has it, after the French Bardot turned down the part). Just as Lane stepped in for Bardot, Jack Mullaney (as Lonnie's sidekick Stanley Potter) provides some genuine comic relief as an ersatz Jerry Lewis.

Our hero soon realizes Pam is being terrorized by mysterious villains determined to ensure she doesn't find the cache of gold hidden by her grandfather in the ghost town of Silverado. Suspicion falls on swimming instructor Brad (Edward Faulkner), who looks shifty but turns out to be merely miffed because he thinks Lonnie has replaced him in the ranch owner's arms. All eventually ends well, but not before Lonnie becomes the Panhandle Kid in a dream sequence set in a ghost-town saloon that feels like the precursor of a host of similar sequences in the cartoon *Scooby Doo*. Indeed, Lonnie and Pam are the pesky meddling kids who unwittingly unmask the nefarious antics of the local deputy sheriff (Bill Williams) and his henchmen. Which may explain why one fan, intending to pay the movie a compliment, hailed it as "one of the best children's pictures ever."

The screenplay was originally written by Elwood Ullman (who was born in Memphis) and Edward Bernds, best known for their work with the legendary Three Stooges. Even after some on-set polishing by Michael A. Hoey, some of the film's slapstick routines seem right out of the Moe, Larry, and Curly playbook. Hoey also admitted that the haunted-house gags were "inspired by two wonderful old Bob Hope comedies, *The Cat and the Canary* and *The Ghost Breakers*." In the development process, *Tickle Me* came to include so many of the staple ingredients in the Presley movie recipe it seems sensible to conclude that Hoey, Taurog, and indeed Elvis are gently sending the formula up.

One of the great virtues of the dude-ranch setting is that it provides the perfect excuse for the bevy of beauties to be much bigger than usual. There is more eye candy on display than in any other Elvis movie, with the possible exception of *Spinout.*

The sound of Elvis bursting into song is usually the cue for every adoring female in the vicinity—be they guests or staff—to run after him shouting, "Lonnie, wait for me!" When he sings "Dirty Dirty Feeling" in the stables, there is so much cavorting by so many women, he is spoiled for choice; the constant back and forth of his glances seems a sly nod both toward his onscreen image as a "sagebrush Lothario" (as Pam puts it) and his offscreen reputation as one of Hollywood's great ladykillers. Before bursting into "It Feels So Right," there is another self-referential gag when, wondering how he will make ends meet, he tells the bartender: "Don't tell me I know" before swinging into action with his guitar. One female spectator's uninhibited response to Presley's swaggering, if slightly synthetic version of this blues-tinged pop song inevitably sparks a fight—with Elvis's buddy Red West starting the first of six brawls in the movie. During the obligatory romantic estrangement between Lonnie and Pam, Elvis even complains his loved one has sent his letter back "return to sender."

Wisely, Taurog keeps up the tempo: a song, fight, gag or slapstick routine is always just around the corner. The movie was shot in six weeks and the ambience on screen suggests the cast enjoyed making it. Adams brings a welcome touch of class as the inevitable older woman. Mullaney is a watchable goofball and Elvis, once again, is a reasonably adept straight man. Although not to everyone's taste, Lane is pert, smart and sexy, especially when, in the flashback/dream sequence inspired by a famous scene from the comedy Western *Destry Rides Again*, she is cast as Jenny Lind, the Swedish Nightingale, teasing and flirting with Elvis's Panhandle Kid. Elvis looks in pretty good nick—after this film his weight would fluctuate noticeably in the next four movies—and seems to be relishing the comedy, the dance routines (as odd as some of them are) and the better than average songs. The standout number is his reprise of "Put the Blame On Me," the best track on his 1961 studio album *Something for Everybody.*

Although most reviewers agreed *Tickle Me* was, to quote one critic, "a skimpy little nothing," it did well enough commercially, generating $3.4 million on release at the U.S. box office, to become the third highest-grossing movie in Allied Artists' history. The movie remains a firm favorite with many fans. For all the absurdities and clichés—there are times where you can predict the next line or stunt—*Tickle Me* has a kind of comic energy, never takes itself too seriously and Presley's engaging turn won him a Laurel Award from Motion Picture

Exhibitor magazine for best male performance in a musical film, the only official recognition he ever received for his acting. Elvis may have left this celluloid Circle Z dude ranch with fond memories because a few years later, when he acquired his own ranch in Mississippi, he gave it the rhyming name "Circle G."

Harum Scarum, MGM, 1965

Director, Gene Nelson; Writer, Gerald Drayson Adams; Music, Fred Karger; Producer, Sam Katzman; Running time, 95 minutes

Cast: Elvis (Johnny Tyrone), Mary Ann Mobley (Princes Shalimar), Fran Jeffries (Aishah), Michael Ansara (Prince Dragna), Jay Novello (Zacha), Philip Reed (King Toranshah)

Rudolf Valentino had long fascinated Elvis. Tony Curtis liked to claim that he had inspired the King's jet-black hair style, but Presley's friend Marty Lacker said: "I don't know, because he liked Valentino, too." After watching one of the silent screen legend's films, Elvis told his cousin Billy Smith he was fascinated by the way "Valentino projected a lot out of his eyes." Yet Curtis had thrilled the young Elvis in such adventure stories as *Sons of Ali Baba*. So when the idea of making a movie that drew on such Arabian adventures—especially Valentino's box office smash *The Sheikh*—was first mooted, Presley was enthusiastic, even if he knew the film was bound to be tongue-in-cheek. And then he read the script.

Worse still, in February 1965 he went to Nashville to record the songs. In the finished movie there is—and thanks to Bad Movie Planet's Chad Plambeck for doing the math—a song every seven minutes. One of those numbers—with the catchy chorus "Shake that tambourine [*pause*] that tambourine [*pause*], that tambourine"—required thirty-six takes to finish.

No wonder it took all of Parker's wiles and threats to persuade Presley to drive from Memphis to Hollywood to make the movie. Before he left, the singer gave a rare and thoughtful interview to journalist James Kingsley in which, shedding some insight into his troubled state of mind, he denied rumors that he had become a recluse, saying: "I withdraw not from my fans but from myself."

On the way to Los Angeles, when the motor home stopped in the middle of the desert, Elvis looked up and saw a cloud formation that resembled the face of Joseph Stalin and that turned into the face of Jesus. Whether you blame the uppers, the downers, the diet pills, or whatever else he was taking, Presley was obviously experiencing some kind of crisis. During the filming of *Harum Scarum*, he began visiting Sri Daya Mata, the spiritual leader of the Self-Realization Fellowship, and was talking of entering a monastery.

The quest for meaning would haunt Elvis for the rest of his life, but it seemed especially acute as he turned up to shoot what looked certain to be his worst movie yet. Seeing the faces of Stalin and Jesus in the sky must have seemed a damn sight more plausible than anything in Adams's screenplay. When the

The market scene in *Harum Scarum* (1965). Shaking that tambourine, that tambourine, Elvis does his best to lift *Harum Scarum.*

movie was released, *New York Times* critic Vincent Canby said Presley showed "the animation of a man under deep sedation, but then he had read the script."

The one thing you can say in *Harum Scarum*'s favor is that it exerts a kind of weird fascination. It has the distinction of being the only Elvis film to open with the star karate chopping a leopard (albeit in a movie within the movie) and in which an American ambassador leans over to our hero and confides: "Your goodwill tour of this part of the world is most helpful to the State Department." Even the makeup has gone awry. Mary Ann Mobley and Fran Jeffries, who were twenty-six and twenty-eight respectively when the movie was shot, are shot so unflatteringly at times that they look like fortysomethings trying to pass themselves off as much younger women. The inherent absurdities are captured rather well by the slogan on the trailer: "It's Elvis, doing what comes naturally, where the sultans and slave girls are swingers!" As Hampton notes in his *Hollywood Rock: A Guide to Rock 'n' Roll in the Movies*: "The movie offers one delirious interlude after another" and, for that reason alone, is probably not as debilitating to watch as the utterly predictable *Paradise, Hawaiian Style.*

Elvis is Johnny Tyrone, a matinee idol who, on a tour of the fictional Middle Eastern kingdom of Lunarkand, is kidnapped by a gang of assassins plotting to kill King Toranshah (Philip Reed) who were unduly impressed by the singer's leopard-killing antics on the silver screen. Though intrigued by the seductive Aishah (Jeffries), who is merely the most striking of the beautiful women in the harem in the Garden of Paradise, Johnny escapes with the aid of market thief and comic relief Zacha (Jay Novello), whose solicitation "O noble client!" recurs throughout the rest of the movie. After arranging to meet his accomplice at the Pool of Omar, Elvis falls for a lovely handmaiden (Mobley) who, like Goodwin's heiress in *Girls! Girls! Girls!* and Presley's oil heir in *Clambake*, turns out not to be what she seems. She is actually Toranshah's daughter, Princess Shalimar, a revelation that convinces Johnny not to commit regicide.

Rocking the casbah with such numbers as "Hey Little Girl" (sung to a slave girl so young that even Jerry Lee Lewis wouldn't marry her), and ignoring the advice from assassin-in-chief Sinan (Theo Marcuse) that "Nothing is true, everything is permitted," he thwarts the gang's evil designs and, after a climactic fight scene in which the action innovatively shifts back and forth between daylight and torch-lit darkness, invites everyone back to Las Vegas, where, backed by a new Middle Eastern dancing troupe, he sings "Harem Holiday." As strange as this all may sound, it doesn't really capture how odd this film is. Hampton sums it up when he says: "It's almost as though the entire movie has been made in code, with each moment of blissful obliviousness concealing a separate impenetrable double meaning of its own."

To be fair to Elvis, there are moments during the picture when he seems to be enjoying himself, as if even an eighteen-day shooting schedule, mediocre songs, an incomprehensible storyline, and borrowed props and costumes (his dagger had been used in the 1939 Hedy Lamarr drama *Lady in the Tropics*) couldn't quite obliterate his pleasure at playing Valentino. (He had initially been so keen on the movie that he wore the costume and makeup at home.) In the compulsory jail scene, as Elvis pours his heart into the theatrical ballad "So Close, Yet So Far," it's as if he has blocked out the surrounding mediocrity in an attempt to yearn like the silent-screen legend. And yet, at other moments, he seems so detached that *Variety* suggested: "If Presley were any more relaxed, Bing Crosby and Perry Como would have to retire."

The rest of the cast do their best but seem to be acting in different movie genres. Novello plays everything for laughs, while Ansara and Reed act as if this is a dramatic adventure. Only Mobley and Jeffries distinguish themselves, probably because the confusion has less impact on their roles. It doesn't really matter because, with the relentlessness of a pop video, the action pauses so Elvis can sing a desert song, be it "Golden Coins," "My Desert Serenade," "Mirage," or "Kismet." Most of the songs are impressive mainly for the writers' resolute determination to leave no Middle Eastern cliché unused, yet some of them are infuriatingly, almost subliminally, catchy. Elvis sings most of them stoically, seeming to find "Kismet" and "So Close, Yet So Far" the easiest to work with.

Even Nelson, who had filmed *Kissin' Cousins*, found the pace tough, especially as he strived to stage the songs as effectively as possible. He was touched when, one lunch break, Elvis offered to feign sickness to give the director time to shoot scenes as he wanted. The offer was never taken up, and the final product horrified Parker, who complained that it would take a "55th cousin of PT Barnum" to sell this movie. His trailblazing suggestion that the movie be narrated by a talking camel represents the Colonel's only known attempt at postmodern irony.

Not renowned for second thoughts, he cursed himself for agreeing with Katzman that the movie could be made so quickly. Though Presley would make six more movies with MGM, he would never work with Katzman or Nelson again. Even Parker could see that unless certain minimal standards were maintained, he might end up killing his golden goose.

The only consolation for the Colonel was that *Harum Scarum* still reached number 11 on *Variety*'s weekly box-office chart and grossed around $2 million in the United States. It was also, mysteriously, very popular in India. The soundtrack album peaked at number 8 but was the last of its kind to make the Top 10. In the official tome *The MGM Story*, John Douglas Eames characterized the movie as "produced by mistake and Sam Katzman." The fact that it was still the fortieth most successful movie of the year in the *Variety* charts is testament to Elvis's enduring charisma and the fact that 1965 was not a vintage year for Hollywood.

Some critics, like the usually forthright Judith Crist, almost felt sorry for Elvis, saying: "Miss Mobley is pretty (but Yvonne DeCarlo she's not), Elvis wears a burnoose (but Valentino he's not). Decent, wholesome stuff." That might just be the most merciful review Crist ever wrote.

For Elvis, the highlight of this not-so-riotous rock-and-rollin' spoof was meeting Terry Southern, who wrote *Dr. Strangelove*. Southern's girlfriend, Gail Gilmore, was in the film playing the beautiful slave girl Sapphire. Writer and star met outside her trailer. After Southern had recovered from his astonishment that Presley had watched *Dr. Strangelove* sixteen times, these shy men hit it off, enjoying what Gilmore called a "nice mutual respect."

Frankie and Johnny, United Artists, 1966

Director, Frederick de Cordova; Screenplay, Alex Gottlieb; Music, Fred Karger; Producer, Edward Small; Running time, 87 minutes

Cast: Elvis (Johnny), Donna Douglas (Frankie), Harry Morgan (Cully), Sue Anne Langdon (Mitzi), Nancy Kovack (Nellie Bly), Audrey Christie (Peg), Robert Strauss (Blackie), Anthony Eisley (Clint Braden)

"How can I get Johnny to give up gamblin'?" Frankie (Donna Douglas) asks her friend Peg (Audrey Christie) in this riverboat musical comedy. "It's easy," Peg assures her. "Shoot a hole in his head, poison his coffee, a fatal knife wound. Nothin' to it."

Having started out writing gags for Al Jolson and Eddie Cantor and been nominated for a Writers Guild award for Frank Tashlin's witty romantic comedy *Susan Slept Here* (1954), Alex Gottlieb ensured the script for *Frankie and Johnny* had more pep than some of the screenplays Elvis had recently been handed.

The front cover of the *New Musical Express*. The gags were slicker in *Frankie and Johnny* but the film still disappointed at the box office.

The period setting was an intriguing change of pace too. Although staging the story on a Mississippi steamboat in the nineteenth century posed a challenge for Fred Karger, who could hardly incorporate any anachronistic rock into the movie, it seemed a worthwhile gamble. This is probably as close as Presley ever came to an old-school Hollywood musical.

The repartee among Peg, her songwriting husband Cully (Harry Morgan), and unlucky riverboat gambler Johnny (Elvis) is brighter than usual. The costumes are colorful, and Douglas is always easy on the eye. All of which makes it hard to explain why *Frankie and Johnny*—loosely based on the tragic American popular song written by Hughie Cannon in 1904—doesn't quite click.

Johnny tries to change his luck at roulette with the help of beautiful redhead Nellie Bly (Nancy Kovack), an old flame of riverboat boss Clint Braden (Anthony Eisley). The boss's new flame Mitzi (Sue Anne Langdon, in a broadly comedic turn as a drunken, ditzy blonde) plays on Frankie's suspicions about Johnny, and, after the boss's loyal henchman Blackie (Robert Strauss) puts real bullets in the gun with which Frankie "shoots" Johnny in the big production number, the stage is set for an unusually tragic denouement for an Elvis musical. Luckily, our singing gambler is saved when the bullet lodges in a lucky charm given to him previously by his beloved. At this point, apparently overcome with remorse and relief, Frankie tells Johnny: "I want you any way you are."

Obviously, if she had decided this at the beginning of the story, there would have been no need for a movie. The fact that Nellie is just as forgiving, agreeing to marry the riverboat boss without bothering to suggest he modify his philandering ways, makes proceedings feel a tad inconsequential.

Elvis often looks uncomfortable in a dazzling array of costumes, uniforms, and three-piece suits (probably aware that he fills them out more than he ought to) and not always at ease with the period. Though he sparks well with Morgan, at other times he seems visibly to lose interest.

The music probably didn't do much to rouse his spirits. The score lacks energy—only "Shout It Out" and "Hard Luck" are performed with any great fervor—and some of the numbers ("Come Along," "Look Out Broadway," and "Down by the Riverside / When the Saints Go Marching In") feel like fillers. "Chesay" and "Petunia the Gardener's Daughter" are novelty numbers that work better onscreen than on record. The smooth ballads are best, especially "Please Don't Stop Loving Me," the entertainingly chauvinist "What Every Woman Lives For," and the beautiful, oddly overlooked "Beginner's Luck" (sung over a flashback in which Johnny reimagines his romance with Frankie at a Rhett Butler and Scarlett O'Hara picnic).

Presley may have concluded, as many critics did, that his twentieth movie was essentially the same formula as before but in different costumes and with slightly better gags. It doesn't help that, although Douglas's despairing love for him seems sincere, the star-crossed lovers don't have that much chemistry. There was no meeting of bodies onscreen, but there was a meeting of minds on set, with Douglas (who sprang to fame on *Beverley Hillbillies*) being the latest young actress to be invited to join in what his friend, guru, and hairdresser Geller called "heavy spiritual conversations."

The fact that Presley and Douglas don't really spark makes it easier for Morgan and Christie, who have the best lines, considerable talent, and vast experience, to steal the movie, and they do so with aplomb. No one else in the film—although Langdon has her moments—really shines. Kovack is a particular disappointment. She has the talent, cheekbones, and presence to make more of her part, but her detached interpretation makes her character less interesting than it ought to be.

The movie begins to lose momentum at about the point where the Mardi Gras masked ball sparks further romantic confusion—and a few too many drunk gags—and never quite regains its grip. Yet the movie's standout scene is still to come, when Elvis, after his winnings flutter away, teams up with a harmonica-playing black shoeshine boy to bemoan his hard luck with a passionate bluesy number. If anything, Presley overdoes the vocal pyrotechnics, but this rare sin is probably a sign of his relief at having something different to perform.

Critical opinion varied, with the *New York Times* dismissing *Frankie and Johnny* as a "turkey," and another suggesting that it "returned somewhat to the primitive quality of his earlier films." Still, the riverboat romance did reasonably well commercially, recovering some of the ground lost by *Harum Scarum* with takings at the North American box office of $2.7 million.

Paradise, Hawaiian Style, Paramount, 1966

Director, Michael D. Moore: Writers, Anthony Lawrence, Allan Weiss; Music, Joseph J. Lilley; Producer, Hal B. Wallis; Running time, 91 minutes

Cast: Elvis (Rick Richards), Suzanna Leigh (Judy Hudson), James Shigeta (Danny Kohana), Donna Butterworth (Jan Kohana), Mariana Hill (Lani Kaimana)

"Purgatory Hawaiian Style" might have been a more accurate title. Internal memos suggest that Wallis and his associates felt that the star had only one more good movie in him. This isn't that good movie but, instead, a disappointing retread of *Blue Hawaii.*

The lack of effort is symbolized by the name of Presley's character: Rick Richards. Was that really the best writers Weiss and Lawrence could come up with? Judging from the script, it probably was. Writing on autopilot, they cast Elvis as an irresponsible helicopter pilot, a handsome hedonist pursued by almost every pretty woman in Hawaii. The selection of Michael Moore, an experienced second-unit director, to helm his first movie may have been a money-saving exercise. The concern for costs was so great—and the schedule so tight—that even the production numbers suffered. As the Chinese American actress Irene Tsiu told Lisandi: "I picked the part of Pua because she was featured in one of the most lavish production numbers. Elvis and I come down a river in a canoe as he's singing "Drums of the Island" but this turned out to be difficult because we never rehearsed it. All they told me was where to get on the boat and that it would float down the river."

Sacked by his airline for getting to grips with a smoldering stewardess, Rick returns to Hawaii looking for work and suggests to his old buddy Danny Kohana (James Shigeta) that they go into business together, flying tourists around the islands in their helicopters. The idea is that Rick's many old flames—with Lani Kaimana (Marianna Hill), Pua (Tsu), and Joanna (Julie Parrish) being the most notable—will recommend their services. Overcoming what initially seem to be profound, perfectly understandable misgivings, Kohana mysteriously changes his mind, goes into partnership, and hires Judy Hudson (Suzanna Leigh) as an office girl Friday, persuading her to pretend to be married to deter rapacious Rick. The new business is so desperate for cashflow that Hudson agrees they will fly some dogs to a show. Funnily enough, this doesn't go too well, and as the dogs run riot, Richards nearly causes an accident and is grounded. He ultimately redeems himself by risking everything to rescue Kohana, who is stranded on a beach, with daughter Jan (Donna Butterworth), after breaking a leg.

That is the plot, such as it is. The movie starts brightly enough with a few predictably amusing gags about Presley's skirt-chasing ways and some eccentric minor characters (a comic crocodile salesman is played by Grady Sutton, once a favorite foil for W. C. Fields). Unfortunately, our hero is pursued by so many women—Leigh, Tsu, Parrish, Linda Wong, and Hill—it's hard to keep track. Although Presley and Hill didn't gel on set—of which more later—their romance has more resonance onscreen than Elvis's with Leigh. The office girl Friday looks very sexy in a skimpy bikini for a photo shoot, yet for most of the movie Leigh is allowed to reveal her growing love for Rick only by casting lingering glances in his direction as he leaves the office.

The songs aren't great. The prettiest, "Sand Castles," was cut and the best number recorded for the film, "This Is My Heaven," is interrupted so the movie can end with an eye-catching reprise of "Drums of the Islands." Two songs, "Datin'" and "Scratch My Back (Then I'll Scratch Yours)," are performed as duets. Both "Stop Where You Are" and "Drums of the Island" are lavishly staged but more memorable visually than on record.

The biggest flaw is lack of direction. Literally, in the sense that Moore didn't give Elvis or his co-stars much useful advice on how to play their parts. Moore would later return to second-unit directing and stage some of the most famous sequences in the Indiana Jones films. In *Paradise, Hawaiian Style*, he seems more at home with spectacle (the big production numbers with a huge cast of colorful extras) and the landscape than with the cast.

This may be why Elvis hides behind his "tough way to make a living, boys" grin. He looks livelier in his scenes with Shigeta, who probably gives the best performance in the film, albeit in a pretty one-dimensional role. Leigh does her best but isn't given much to work with. The same could be said for Hill, Parrish, Tsu—and Presley.

The film's failure to recapture the sparkle of *Blue Hawaii* is unintentionally symbolized by one scene in which Elvis, happy to show off his physique in 1961, does his best to keep his chest out of sight as he leaves the beach. This was especially odd given that Nathan, at Wallis's behest, had ordered Moore: "As often as possible we should try to get clothes off our cast—in the water, on the surfboards, even in the helicopter landing on the beach." The trouble was that Elvis was paunchy when he turned up on set. (You can almost follow the shooting schedule through the film: the thinner Elvis looks, the later the scene was filmed.) He looks tired, too, which may account for the scarcity of close-ups.

The other great blight on *Paradise, Hawaiian Style* is Butterworth, one of those child actors deemed adorable in Hollywood but nowhere else. Her presence appalled Presley biographer Dundy, who complained: "The depths were plumbed in *Paradise, Hawaiian Style* by a little nine-year-old horror in a grass skirt, bumping and grinding her way through the great ragtime classic "Bill Bailey, Won't You Please Come Home" while Elvis, who could have turned it into gold, remained seated at the nightclub table (grinding his teeth, one imagines)."

Sounds harsh, but when you watch the scene again, you realize that, yep, it really is that grim.

Presley's detached performance reflects his strange mood on set. He was a week late and out of shape when he turned up for shooting. Though most of his female costars describe him as the perfect gentleman, Hill complained that he didn't introduce himself and once, in a prank that went wrong, jumped on her on the beach, breaking her sunglasses. The actress claimed that Elvis kissed "like a frightened child," "was not a particularly accomplished actor," and had a Rolls Royce only because he felt he ought to as a big star. (The last charge seems wide of the mark: one thing Presley was not at all self-conscious about was his choice of cars.) More pertinently, she recalled his embarrassment during some scenes (when he was playing to the Memphis Mafia, not the cameras) and the "apathy on the set" and concluded: "Underneath it all there seems to be a lot of resentment, defensiveness and hostility."

That last point has the ring of truth. He was fed up of these movies, unsure of his appeal in an era dominated by British acts, and searching for some meaning in his life. Some of that mood infused his sardonic on-set interview with

Peter Noone, the lead singer of the Herman's Hermits. Yet which thirty-year-old rock star wouldn't be embarrassed, resentful, and defensive about starring in movies as indifferent as *Paradise, Hawaiian Style*?

The film got an inexplicably kind review in *Variety*. The movie's sense of landscape was rightly praised, but the scene in which six dogs almost crashed Elvis's helicopter was bizarrely hailed as if it was a comic masterpiece. Most critics have subsequently followed *Time Out*'s reviewer, who deemed it: "Irredeemably awful." The film did well enough at the box office—a gross of $2.5 million in the United States was more than its movie-making-by-numbers approach deserved—but the soundtrack album sold only around 225,000 copies.

By the mid-1960s, Presley was increasingly reclusive.

There was talk, as there had been around the time of *Roustabout*, of persuading the Beatles to do a number at the end of *Paradise, Hawaiian Style*. Mercifully, contractual obligations prevented such a stunt and spared Presley even greater embarrassment.

Spinout, MGM, 1966

Director, Norman Taurog; Screenplay, Theodore J. Flicker, George Kirgo; Music, George Stoll; Producer, Joe Pasternak; Running time 93 minutes

Cast: Elvis (Mike McCoy), Shelley Fabares (Cynthia Foxhugh), Diane McBain (Diana St. Clair), Deborah Walley (Les), Will Hutchins (Lt. Tracy Richards), Warren Berlinger (Philip Short), Carl Betz (Howard Foxhugh), Jack Mullaney (Curly), Jimmy Hawkins (Larry), Dodie Marshall (Susan)

You can tell that the Elvis movie-making machine is beginning to fall apart just from the King's appearance in his second singing race-car-driver movie. At the finale, as he rips into "I'll Be Back" with more gusto than it probably deserves, he is wearing a polo-necked jumper, under a jacket, waistcoat, and open-necked shirt—in a California nightclub in the middle of summer.

By the time Elvis filmed Spinout, his look had become so stylized it was almost weird. As Jane and Michael Stern put it in *Elvis World*: "His skin has the texture of a nylon stocking; his hair looks liked poured tar." This synthetic Elvis perplexed *Time* magazine's reviewer, who complained: "His cheeks are now so plump he looks like a kid chewing gum . . . What's more, he now sports a glossy something on his summit that adds at least five inches to his altitude and looks like a swatch of hot-buttered yak wool." Worst of all, he doesn't even move like Elvis. At times, it's as if he's lost the rhythmic instincts that made him such an explosive performer onstage.

Spinout started out as a romantic farce, which writers George Kirgo and Theodore J. Flicker loosely based on what they knew of Elvis's life. This was too autobiographical for Parker, so the writers revamped it, after being given the mysterious command "Put a dog in it." Then MGM, studying the grosses for *Viva Las Vegas*, told them to put a racing car in it. This tortuous development process is reflected in the number of working titles—*Jim Dandy, After Midnight, Always At Midnight, Never Say No, Never Say Yes*, and *Clambake* (that one was saved for later)—it went through before *Spinout* was chosen. (Even then, concerned that fans outside the United States wouldn't understand the racing terminology, the movie was renamed as *California Holiday* in the UK and *Le Tombeur de ces demoiselles—The Ladies' Man*—in France.) One of the studio taglines for the movie effectively sums up proceedings: "Swinging! . . . Chasing . . . ! Racing! . . . Romancing! . . . Swinging!"

Betsy Bozdech captures Elvis's character Mike McCoy rather well in her DVD Journal review: "a free-spirited, vaguely rebellious fella who never passes up a chance to flirt or play the guitar." A racing driver, singer, and nomad, McCoy is allergic to marriage, a chronic affliction that becomes a problem when he finds himself in Santa Barbara being pursued by three women: Diana St. Clair (Diane McBain), bestselling author of such classics as *The Mating Habits of the Single Male*; rich girl Cynthia Foxhugh (Shelley Fabares), whose father Howard (Carl Betz, who played Fabares's father in *The Donna Reed Show*), designs and drives racing cars; and tomboyish Les (Deborah Walley), the drummer in Mike's band, 1 Plus 2 + 1/2. The web of romance becomes even more tangled when each girl acquires a suitor of her own: Fabares is pursued by her father's dizzy, ditzy assistant Philip (Warren Berlinger), McBain by Howard Foxhugh, and Les by policeman and gourmet chef Lt. Tracy Richards (Will Hutchins).

Just to prove they can't be pushed around, Elvis and his band move into the mansion next door to the Foxhughs, after persuading the elderly couple who live there (beautifully played by Una Merkel and Cecil Kellaway) to refresh their marriage with a second honeymoon.

Cynthia's father wants Elvis to drive his fabulous Fox Five car in the Santa Fe road race. The contest, rather strangely paced by Taurog, who never seems sure whether to play it for laughs or thrills, sets up the issue-resolving climax as Philip stops fainting long enough to almost win. Yet Mike triumphs and, pressured by the women and their suitors to reveal which one he intends to marry, shouts out: "Uh, I'm going to marry all of them!" This seems a bit much even for one of Elvis's romantic comedies, but he does as he says: marrying each of the girls off to their suitors so he can stay free and single with Susan (Dodie Marshall), who dances and drums with a passionate, sexy intensity not matched by anyone else in the movie.

Occasionally, *Spinout* looks like an advert for mod fashion. The focus on Cordon Bleu cuisine that nurtures the budding romance between Walley's enthusiastic drummer and Hutchins's clumsy cop is curious, as it fulfills no obvious function in the film. There can't be many musical comedies where love starts blooming with a cop saying to a drummer: "That's not a béarnaise sauce, is it, fella?" Later on, they bond when discussing a cantaloupe glacé dessert.

The songs are slightly better than average. The rockers ("Adam and Evil," "I'll Be Back," "Never Say Yes," "Spinout," and "Stop, Look and Listen," which had been recorded by Ricky Nelson in 1964) are certainly listenable, though none swing with the kind of authenticity Elvis brought to "Down in the Alley," the Clovers classic he cut in May 1966, released as a bonus track on the soundtrack album. The Tepper/Bennett ballads have held up better. "Am I Ready" is smooth, sincere, and seductive, while "All That I Am" (which peaked at number 40 in the U.S. charts) is sweet and fluent, if a tad bland. As a party number, "Beach Shack" works in the film even if Elvis does invite a bevy of girls into his shack to see his etchings. "Smorgasbord" seems crassly sexist even for this kind of movie in this era of Hollywood, with its vow: "I'll take the dish I please and please the dish I take."

Spinout was the second—but not the last—singing race driver movie.

The cast is slightly above average too. McBain is not especially interesting as the author/temptress, but Fabares, Betz, Berlinger, Hutchins, Marshall, and Walley all hit the right note. Fabares is at her most entertaining as the spoiled but intrinsically decent heiress, while Walley, perhaps glad to have escaped such bombs as *Dr. G. and the Bikini Machine* and *Beach Blanket Bingo*, sparks well with Elvis. (On set, the two were seldom apart. Sensing that his young co-star was struggling to find her niche in Hollywood, Presley shared his journey into mystic philosophy with her and, she said later, changed her life.) One of the many beauties pressed into action in this film is Rita Wilson, who later married Tom Hanks. If you ignore the hair and curious clothing, Elvis proves himself a talented farceur.

Spinout's humor owes a lot to the Three Stooges—heck, two of Elvis's band are even called Larry (Jimmy Hawkins) and Curly (Jack Mullaney)—and the Martin and Lewis comedies, many of which were directed by Taurog (who presumably encouraged Mullaney to reprise the Jerry Lewis character he had used in *Tickle Me*). Most of the laughs are intentional. (Not always the case in an Elvis movie.)

Spinout did reasonably well at the box office, grossing nearly $3 million in the United States, but the iffy contemporary critical response was typified by one review: "It does him no good nor us either." If anything, *Spinout*'s reputation has risen since, though few would go so far as Bill Treadway, who, on DVD Verdict, rates it as almost as good as *King Creole*. The plots and subplots and one-liners are less predictable than in some Elvis musical comedies—there's a hint here of the kind of comic and romantic complexities that characterized the screwball comedies—and the scattergun approach to humor means that even when some of the running gags—Philip's fainting fits and Curly's failure to recognize that Les is "not a guy"—are overused, it doesn't matter too much. *Spinout* has more than its share of flaws, but by placing Elvis at the heart of a larger ensemble cast, and incorporating the songs into the flow of the story, Taurog keeps this ticking along. Elvis's twenty-second movie is no classic but, taken on its own terms, there aren't too many excruciating moments—apart from Elvis's multilayered costume in the finale.

Easy Come, Easy Go, Paramount, 1967

Director, John Rich; Screenplay, Allan Weiss, Anthony Lawrence; Music, Joseph J. Lilley; Producer, Hal B. Wallis; Running time, 95 minutes

Cast: Elvis (Ted Jackson), Dodie Marshall (Jo Symington), Pat Priest (Dina Bishop), Pat Harrington Jr. (Judd Whitman), Skip Ward (Gil)

"Just put them through their paces." That was Wallis's instruction to director Rich for *Easy Come, Easy Go*, the legendary producer's ninth and last movie with Elvis. The ruthless economizing, which even extended to the music, is evident in several studio memos published as an appendix to Bill Bram's book. Associate producer Nathan, advising Wallis on casting suggestions, noted: "Dodie Marshall. Asked $1,000 (per week)—would now probably take $650 (per week)."

This money-saving approach didn't stop them from fretting about Elvis's appearance. After all, in a slight change of pace, Elvis wasn't cast as a singing race-car driver, singing pilot, or singing trapeze artist, but as a singing frogman who had just got out of the U.S. Navy. Nathan noted: "Navy men aren't supposed to be fat." Rich agreed, noting after a viewing of *Paradise, Hawaiian Style*: "The clothes keep getting tighter and tighter and our hero fatter and fatter." Alarmed by the yak-wool hairdo in *Spinout*, Wallis wrote to Parker that Elvis's hero was "a rugged type of character who dives for the navy, deactivates bombs and mines, etc, and if he comes up from underwater and takes his helmet off and discloses the perfectly combed pompadour haircut, the whole picture will be ridiculous."

The weight problem that really sank *Easy Come, Easy Go* was the lightness of the plot. As Ted Jackson (surely the least appropriate character name in any of Elvis's films), he is a demolition expert on a quest to find a chest of Spanish pieces of eight in a sunken wreck called the *Port of Call*. Yet again, as he did in *G.I. Blues, Blue Hawaii*, and *Kid Galahad*, he plays a character leaving—or about to leave—the military.

Ted calls on Judd (Pat Harrington Jr., better known as the building super-intendent Schneider in the sitcom *One Day at a Time*), his old partner from the Easy Go-Go Club; a Jane Fonda–esque independent spirit, Jo Symington (Dodie Marshall), whose grandfather skippered the *Port of Call*, and Captain Jack (Frank McHugh, a veteran who made his name in James Cagney movies, in his last film role), a salvage equipment dealer and former children's TV host. Searching for the same treasure are unscrupulous playgirl Dina Bishop (Pat Priest, in a role originally earmarked for Suzanna Leigh to play in her second Presley film), who "collects excitement like most people collect stamps," and her mercenary boyfriend Gil (Skip Ward). Ted wins, of course, but the treasure turns out to be worthless copper coins. Even though our selfish hero has spent most of the film focused on the sunken treasure, this disastrous denouement provokes a seismic shift in attitude. As the movie closes, he consoles himself with Jo, helps her starts an arts center, and sings that "Ounce for ounce / Love is all that really counts."

Easy Come, Easy Go does have its ridiculous moments, but they have less to do with Elvis's hair than its bizarre take on the 1960s counterculture, in which hippies are called "kooks" and "beatniks" (the latter term, even in 1967, must have been long out of date), body painting is celebrated as far out, and a yoga class given by the redoubtable Elsa Lanchester—in her last movie—is inter-rupted by Elvis singing about a pain in his "posterior" in "Yoga Is as Yoga Does." Elvis fumed that this song was inserted to make fun of his new hobby, yoga. As paranoid as that sounds, it's hard to think of any other reason for its inclusion. Since the Beatles, Elvis's producers had normally done their utmost to make him seem up-to-date. For most of this movie, he comes across as old-fashioned, materialist, and a bit square.

Director and star had clashed on the set of *Roustabout*, and when Elvis and Memphis Mafioso Red West had a fit of giggles during one scene, Rich barred Elvis's bodyguards from the set. Presley wasn't happy and nor was Rich, but the director had, at least, come to understand—and sympathize with—his star's frustrations. In a rare interview with Elvis Infonet in 2001, Rich described this movie as a "throwaway," complaining: "Because the contract was at an end, Hal wanted to spend no money on it. It was done with very little music, which drove me crazy. By that time what was selling was the music, so why are we cutting out all the songs?"

Among the songs that didn't make the cut for this movie were the Ray Charles gem "Leave My Woman Alone," the gospel ballad "We Call on Him," "She's a Machine" (banned as too licentious by the Motion Picture Association of America), and "Saved," the rousing spiritual Elvis sang on the NBC TV special. Any of these would have been better than the songs that were recorded, although their quality might only have highlighted the mediocrity of the other numbers, which Elvis, using a technical term popular with musicians through the ages, described as "shit." The title track starts promisingly enough but soon tails off. Elvis does not disguise his boredom on "The Love Machine" (the first Elvis single to make no impression on the British charts) or his incredulity on "Yoga Is as Yoga Does." On film, "I'll Take Love" is a pleasant finale. On record, it sounds like a children's song. Only the gospel-flavored "Sing You Children" and the accusatory "You Gotta Stop," Elvis's favorite song in the film, which he liked so much he sang around the house, carry any conviction. No wonder the six-song EP sold only 30,000 copies. In a movie with so many "lasts" attached to it, this was to be the final Presley EP record.

The money saved on songs was certainly not spent on the script. To take just one small example: Elvis's old pal Judd is supposed to be a gas—and looks like he probably is—but we have to take this on trust because he doesn't have a single funny line. What could have been a reasonably amusing spoof of California hippie culture provides few laughs or thrills. When good confronts evil on the high sea, there's a moment when Priest (who made her name in *The Munsters* and is one of the most effective bad girls in an Elvis film) looks like she might turn genuinely nasty, but the script quickly lurches back into shallower waters.

It's not clear how much of this is Rich's fault. He was not an action director, so the underwater sequences vary from dull to competent but never really tense. Yet for the most part, he keeps the story moving, sidesteps some potential disasters, and sensibly clads Elvis in black civvies to make him look trimmer. He coaxes some decent turns out of the actors.

Marshall is especially lively, although, bizarrely, there is much less sexual chemistry between her and Elvis in *Easy Come, Easy Go* than in the scene when she's dancing next to him in a poolside party in *Spinout*. She sports so many outfits in the movie, she is virtually a walking fashion show. Even though *Variety* called her an "excellent young actress with appealing warmth and looks for meatier sympathetic roles"—and Nathan assured her this "would do a great deal for your career"—this would be Marshall's last film.

Presley played his part of the cheery star so well that co-star Priest felt he loved the movie. His real feelings were probably disclosed when he told Lanchester that he had once wanted to be a "proper actor." The veteran actress assured him: "Oh, but you are my dear, you are. Your performances always have a touch of magic even in the most trying circumstances."

Easy Come, Easy Go may have lost money initially, costing $2 million but raking back just $1.95 million at the U.S. box office by the end of 1967. It probably didn't help that it was released on a double bill with Marlon Brando's Western *The Appaloosa*. (It's hard to imagine any cinemagoer who went to see one of these films enjoying the other.) *Variety* was surprisingly effusive, commending the "good balance of script and songs," while Crist felt Elvis managed to "rise a teensy bit above his mediocre material."

Roger Ebert was much less impressed. Like Wallis, he found the star's appearance troubling: "Elvis looks about the same as he always has, with his chubby face, petulant scowl and absolutely characterless features. Here is one guy the wax museums will have no trouble getting right." He rounded off his damning review saying: "After two dozen movies he should have learned to talk by now. But it's still the same old slur we heard all those years ago on *The Ed Sullivan Show*."

In fairness to Elvis, the slur might have been sheer embarrassment. As eloquent as Ebert was, the best verdict on *Easy Come, Easy Go* came from the star himself. Asked what the movie was about by his friend George Klein, Presley snapped: "Same story, different location."

Double Trouble, MGM, 1967

Director, Norman Taurog; Screenplay, Jo Heims (based on a story by Marc Brandel); Music, Jeff Alexander; Producers, Judd Bernard, Irwin Winkler; Running time, 90 minutes

Cast: Elvis (Guy Lambert), Annette Day (Jill Conway), John Williams (Gerald Waverly), Yvonne Romain (Claire Dunham), Chips Rafferty (Archie Brown), Norman Rossington (Arthur Babcock), Monty Landis (Georgie), Michael Murphy (Mr. Morley), Leon Askin (Inspector de Groote), the Wiere Brothers (Detectives)

As Tony Pellum noted on the Flickdom Dictum website, "Norman Taurog, the workhorse, was perhaps the only Elvis director who could have shot "Old MacDonald" as if it actually meant something." The notorious scene in which Elvis, as roving troubadour Guy Lambert, sings the children's song while sitting on the back of a truck with his teenage love interest Jill (Annette Day) has been reason enough for many fans to shun this zany musical-comedy thriller.

Presley probably summed up *Double Trouble* best when he said: "I wasn't exactly a James Bond in this movie, but then no one ever asked Sean Connery to sing while dodging bullets!"

Yet Taurog got the job only under duress. First-time producers Judd Bernard and Irwin Winkler were desperate to use Rod Amateu, who had made sitcoms such as *The Many Loves of Dobie Gillis* for U.S. TV. They were so vehement they even walked off the lot in protest, but Bernard recalled: "MGM said either Taurog does it or there's no movie."

Even by the standards established by Presley's other movies, the title is mysterious. The original title—*You're Killing Me*—might have worked better. Though twin Elvises appear on the poster, separated by a promise that he "takes mad mod Europe by song as he swings into a brand new adventure filled with dames, diamonds and discotheques," the only double helping of trouble on show is that, once again, he is torn between two women: seventeen-year-old Jill, usually innocent though she occasionally turns into Lolita, and alluring older woman Claire Dunham (Yvonne Romain). As hard as Romain tries to convey romantic intrigue, the movie fails to suggest that Elvis's interest in her is anything but perfunctory, so, through no real fault of her own, she is far less effective as a femme fatale than Carolyn Jones (*King Creole*) or Tuesday Weld (*Wild in the Country*).

Jill brings Elvis plenty of trouble, because she is in love with him and because her shifty aristocratic uncle Gerald (John Williams, best known as the chief inspector in *Dial M for Murder*) has eaten into her trust fund and must kill her before her eighteenth birthday to conceal his crime. So singer and girl travel from London to Antwerp (without actually leaving the MGM lot), not realizing that comically ineffectual smugglers Archie Brown (Chips Rafferty) and Arthur Babcock (Norman Rossington) have stashed some diamonds in Guy's luggage. One of Robert Altman's favorite actors, Michael Murphy, is creepily effective in his movie debut as Morley, a suavely sinister assassin, with a manner that recalls Roddy McDowall, hired to strangle Jill.

The faux swinging-London setting is yet another attempt by MGM to market Elvis as either the fifth Beatle or the original Beatle, paradoxically presenting this quintessentially American icon in a European setting that suits his rivals far better than him. The fact that Rossington, one of the jewel thieves, was the road manager in *A Hard Day's Night* might be a coincidence. The fact that Elvis's backing band, the G Men, all have mop-top haircuts certainly isn't. The diamond-smuggling subplot seems an obvious nod to the valuable ring sent to Ringo in *Help!* Even Jill's age—Elvis's footloose hero is shocked to discover she is just seventeen—plays off the Beatles song "I Saw Her Standing There," with its famous line "She was just seventeen, you know what I mean," a snatch of lyric that Elvis later sang in Las Vegas.

Presley may have stayed on the MGM lot, but a pan-European cast surrounds him. Bernard discovered his leading lady when she was working in her parents' antique shop in London. She had no previous acting experience, but Bernard was convinced she was right for the part. Some of her English expressions—"biccies" (cookies)—were even woven into the script. Her fresh-ness works in her favor as the tension mounts. Her fear is almost palpable as her would-be killers close in. But at times, it's hard to understand what Guy sees in this heiress (who looks, in some scenes, to be worried by a propensity to show too much gum when she smiles) and easy to understand why her acting career began and ended with this movie. (She did, at least, get a white Mustang convertible off her co-star, which she left in her brother's care.)

Jill's age may have been designed to make romance with the King seem a tantalizingly realistic aspiration to younger female fans—at one point he even muses, "Seventeen will get you twenty"—but the scene in which Elvis sees her in her school uniform—is still something of a shock, giving the film a strange autobiographical subtext. A month after *Double Trouble* was released, the King would marry Priscilla, whom he had started dating when she was just fourteen. (Writer Jo Heims would explore the May–September romance again in 1973 with *Breezy*, in which a seventeen-year-old free spirit falls for William Holden, so this may have been a favorite theme.) There is also a gratuitous allusion to Elvis's stillborn twin when he bumps into identical twin girls in a London nightclub.

Perhaps to please Presley, who could quote Peter Sellers's Pink Panther movies verbatim, Leon Askin was drafted in to emulate Herbert Lom's exasper-ated police chief, and the Wiere Brothers, three comic siblings who had made their names in vaudeville, were cast as a trio of bumbling Clouseaus. Their unsubtle slapstick, intended to be painfully funny but usually merely painful, completely unbalances a movie that is already struggling to juggle music, sus-pense and comedy. In his memoirs, Michael A. Hoey, who helped rewrite the script, noted: "I was beginning to realize that Norman's love for slapstick comedy was out of touch with the modern audience's taste."

The script by Heims, who later wrote *Play Misty for Me*, was adapted from a story by the novelist Marc Brandel. From that working title *You're Killing Me*, you get a sense that this started out as a much darker story upon which, for obvious commercial reasons, seventeen minutes of songs, a whole lotta slapstick, mod fashion (with Elvis wearing a white jacket so often he occasionally looks like a waiter who's eaten too many leftovers), and a talking parrot were overlaid. The pity is that the suspense—especially the attempted murder at a masked carnival in Antwerp—works better than the comedy.

The songs aren't all as bad as "Old MacDonald." The eponymous title track is a crushing disappointment, especially as it was written by the great Doc Pomus and Mort Shuman. The Tepper/Bennett production number "I Love Only One Girl" has a cheerful momentum in the film, even if the lyrics are daft, and "There's So Much World to See" has a certain swing. The standouts are the delicious, if scandalously brief, rocker "Long Legged Girl (With the Short Dress On)," the pretty ballad "Could I Fall in Love," and "City by Night," a rare, jazzy paean to a city that never seems to sleep. Elvis relishes the song—and the unusual lyrics—right down to the final "Yeah." The quality of the soundtrack might have improved if Romain had asked her husband Leslie Bricusse, author of such classics as "Goldfinger" and "What Kind of Fool Am I?," to pen a few numbers.

For the most part, Elvis's performance is charming enough to keep the absurdities at bay. Faced with such horrors as a "moo moo here," a scene in which he sleeps on the very spot on the floor where he has been knocked out, and such dialogue as "I think I just sat on the tea service," even his enthusiasm occasionally wilts. He may also have wondered how the oldest well in Antwerp, where his beloved is nearly slain, happens to have corrugated-steel sides. Throughout all this, Taurog never gives up behind the camera. His dedication is even more impressive considering that, by 1967, he was blind in one eye.

Double Trouble was filmed before *Easy Come, Easy Go* but released just fifteen days after, a bizarre timing that smacked of desperation or incompetence. In such circumstances, a return of around $1.6 million at the U.S. box office was pretty decent. While some critics thought the movie "better than average," the British Film Institute's *Monthly Film Bulletin* observed: "All is brisk, painless and rather dull." That is unduly harsh. *Double Trouble* remains one of Elvis's most intriguing, if occasionally infuriating, entertainments of the 1960s—and a rare Presley musical comedy in which characters actually die.

Clambake, United Artists, 1967

Director, Arthur H. Nadel; Screenplay, Arthur Browne Jr.: Music, Jeff Alexander; Producers Arthur Gardner, Arnold Laven, Jules Levy; Running time, 100 minutes

Cast: Elvis (Scott Heyward), Shelley Fabares (Dianne Carter), Will Hutchins (Tom Wilson), Bill Bixby (James J. Jamison III), James Gregory (Duster Heyward), Gary Merrill (Sam Burton)

"A silly tired little frolic that could have used a few clams" was Howard Thompson's damning verdict, in the *New York Times*, on a musical comedy that Elvis later referred to as his "wedding cake movie," because it paid for his upcoming nuptials. Thompson can't be accused of making a snap judgment, because he was alert enough at the romantic finale to note: "And what do we see over his shoulder when the star drives Miss Fabares to the Miami airport and professes true love? Mountains, real Florida mountains."

Thompson was interested enough to complain. One critic restricted himself to "Oh dear!." It's easy to see why Elvis didn't want to make this movie, staying on his Circle G ranch for two weeks as shooting was supposed to start. Given an ultimatum by Parker, he also had to shed the pounds fast—although his weight fluctuates noticeably throughout the film. This may be one reason why he never bares his chest even when water skiing. Singing *Clambake* at the beach-party barbecue he wears a pullover and blouson.

The star and his cronies signaled their discontent by setting off firecrackers at will and shoving a birthday cake in director Arthur Nadel's face. The pranks annoyed studio bosses, although some of the cast—notably Bill Bixby and Hutchins—happily joined in. Perhaps they could understand the rationale behind the jokes. Hutchins noted: "Behind the mischievous eyes, I sensed an abiding melancholy. I figured he'd grown weary of making the same flick over and over again."

In *Clambake*, Presley's hero rebelled against his father—and fashion.

Parker had originally suggested *Clambake* as the title for *Spinout*, but there wasn't enough beach action in that movie to justify the name. So for this production it replaced another of Parker's suggestions, *Too Big for Texas* (an allusion to the fact that Elvis's character was an oil heir from the Lone Star state), which would have made it sound like a comedy western.

Writer Arthur Browne Jr., who had cut his teeth on such TV westerns as *The Rifleman*, was an unusual choice to craft a musical comedy, but he had worked with the producers Gardner, Laven, and Levy (who effectively stepped in to make this film on United Artists' behalf). He adapted Mark Twain's classic *The Prince and the Pauper* plot in such a way that he could incorporate the compulsory elements of previous Presley pictures. So Elvis is a rich heir who wants to make it on his own terms (like Chad Gates in *Blue Hawaii*), must prove his mettle by fixing a machine and winning a race (as he did in *Viva Las Vegas* and *Spinout* and would do in *Speedway*), and has a dysfunctional relationship with his father (*King Creole*, *Blue Hawaii*) and a goofy buddy (like Jack Mullaney in *Tickle Me*).

Browne does tweak the formula. For a start, he finds a reasonably believable excuse for Flipper, the dolphin who starred in his own TV series, to make a cameo appearance. As oil heir Scott Heyward, Elvis swaps identities with country bumpkin Tom Wilson (Hutchins), a ploy that means that although beautiful gold digger Dianne Carter (Fabares) is attracted to him, she holds back and tries to entice sleazy rich boy James Jamison (Bixby) up the altar. Jamison has other ideas—until Scott karate chops them out of him. This makes a refreshing change from the usual Elvis onscreen romances, with their relentless rhythm of rows and makeup kissing. Despite the inappropriate mountain scenery, the finale—when Fabares faints after discovering her true love is fabulously wealthy, after all—is genuinely funny.

Clambake is also the only Elvis movie in which he is cast as a hero who can sing and race powerboats and is a prodigiously talented chemist. He dares to challenge Bixby in the Orange Bowl Regatta boat race even though GOOP, the exciting new formula he uses to treat the hull of his boat, hasn't been tested properly. Though the racing scenes looked reasonable at the time, they haven't aged well, and the cuts to close-ups of spectators dissipate the tension, rather than adding to it. The outcome of the race is as predictable as Fabares's choice of suitor.

Fabares sparks Elvis into life. When she's not onscreen, he occasionally sleepwalks. Although he doesn't have a lot of screen time, James Gregory gives an amusing turn as Elvis's overbearing father who must learn from his son's mentor, powerboat designer Sam Burton (sympathetically played by Bette Davis's ex-husband Gary Merrill), before he can be reconciled with Scott. Bixby hits the right note, making his villain just light enough. The big letdown is Hutchins, who hams it up something rotten as the rural doofus. He was significantly more effective as the chef-cop in *Spinout* and as the cowboy in Monte Hellman's existential western *The Shooting* (1966).

The songs are a mixed bunch. "Confidence" is a poor man's "High Hopes," and the title track is certainly no classic—as Elvis acknowledges by laughing in the studio after one take ends. The best that can be said of "Who Needs Money?" and "Hey! Hey! Hey!" is that they move the plot along. For the latter number, longtime Elvis choreographer Alex Romero rouses the star with a neatly plotted dance in which a bevy of colorfully clad beauties get elbow greasy with pails and brushes before getting a grateful, swoon-inducing kiss from the King. The standouts are the lovelorn ballads "You Don't Know Me," "The Girl I Never Loved," and the delightful "A House That Has Everything."

Clambake does shed an intriguing light on a peculiar time and place in a certain stratum of American society. Elvis's souped-up red convertible has its own car phone. The lounge of the Shores Hotel, where he works as an instructor, is decorated as luridly as a bordello and is almost as flamboyant as the white cowboy outfit (which reputedly cost $10,000 to make) Presley wears at the start of the picture. When Elvis warns Fabares about Bixby's seductive intentions, he accurately predicts that she will be wooed with pheasant under glass, wine, and cherries jubilee, obviously regarded in this milieu as the perfect dinner.

Biscayne Bay in Florida in the 1960s is depicted as a millionaire's playground where nice girls like Fabares dip into their savings to come and live, find a job, and try to snare a rich husband. The bevy of beauties that constantly surround Hutchins's goofball at the hotel bar underscores the charisma of money. This game proves especially galling for Scott when he reluctantly agrees to tow Dianne behind the boat so she can impress Jamison with her water-skiing prowess. The name of Jamison's boat—*Scarlet Lady*—makes it pretty obvious what kind of women he is hoping to attract.

With this strange setting and promising initial premise, *Clambake* could have been a darker, more substantial movie. Nadel and Browne Jr. steer clear of such murky waters to create a musical comedy that isn't as bad as Thompson's damning review suggests but lacks the vigor and style of *Viva Las Vegas* and *Girl Happy*. The editing could have been more ruthless: it is ten minutes longer than *Viva Las Vegas.*

This was Nadel's first movie. He only made one more, *Underground,* in which Robert Goulet, the singer whose appearance on TV often prompted the King to reach for the nearest gun, is hilariously miscast as an action-hero spy trying to kidnap a Nazi general. If Elvis ever saw this film, he would have laughed louder than he did when Nadel's face was shoved into a birthday cake on the *Clambake* set.

5

I Want to Be Free

Stay Away, Joe to Change of Habit

Presley's movie career might have ended considerably sooner if MGM hadn't had the misfortune to decide, in January 1967, to extend Presley's contract, committing to four more movies: *Speedway*, *Stay Away, Joe*, *Live a Little, Love a Little*, and *The Trouble with Girls*. Young producer Douglas Laurence, who made the 1967 Sandra Dee comedy *Doctor, You've Got to Be Kidding*, was promised he would be given free rein to choose his projects if he agreed to make three Elvis films. Fearing for his reputation, he agreed to make *Stay Away, Joe*, *Speedway*, and *Live a Little, Love a Little*. Though he later said working with Elvis was one of the highlights of his career, his forebodings were justified. He never made another movie after his third Presley film.

Having decided to persevere with their star, MGM did at least decide to heed Parker's plea for meatier, more challenging roles. After *Clambake*, Presley made only one more formula musical, the charming *Speedway*. In his last three years as an actor, Presley would play a roguish Native American and part-time rodeo rider (*Stay Away, Joe*), a photographer (*Live a Little, Love a Little*), a wronged cowboy (*Charro!*), the manager of a traveling show (*The Trouble with Girls*), and a doctor in a New York ghetto (*Change of Habit*).

Commercially unsuccessful and, for the large part, critically ignored, these movies represented a belated, largely unsuccessful attempt to change the King's image onscreen. Freed from the constraints of a business model that shoe-horned ten songs into every picture, Presley was finally allowed to act his age and gave fluid, committed performances in *Stay Away, Joe*, *The Trouble with Girls*, and *Change of Habit*. Quality control was still a bit hit and miss—the studios weren't making enough profits by this point to justify too much care and attention—but he was better than the material deserved in *Charro!* and *Stay Away, Joe*. In *Live a Little, Love a Little*, he is entertaining, if miscast. Artistically, if not financially, the finale of Presley's film career would be more rewarding than much of what had gone before.

Ed Asner, who had worked with Presley on *Kid Galahad* and *Change of Habit*, said: "In *Kid Galahad*, he was a delightful young man to be around, never offensive, and worked hard. Then in *Change of Habit* he was a different young man and seeming to be concentrating very seriously on being an actor." Perhaps the resurrection of his career, inspired by the magical 1968 NBC TV special, had given him a new confidence and focus as an actor.

His renewed engagement went unrewarded at the time. *The Trouble with Girls* had fifteen minutes cut before its UK release, and *Change of Habit* wasn't even shown in British cinemas. Studios, exhibitors, and fans had largely lost patience with Elvis's movies by 1968. The quality of the music he was making between 1968 and 1970 made his films look irrelevant. When the movie contracts ran out in 1970, Parker wasn't interested in negotiating anymore. Hollywood was out, Las Vegas was in. The only films Presley made in the 1970s were the concert documentaries: *Elvis: That's the Way It Is* and *Elvis on Tour*. Parker never seems to have seriously considered the idea that, as Siegel suggested, Presley could prosper if he worked as a singer and an actor.

Presley publicly admitted he had got tired of singing to the guy he had just beaten up in a movie and pined for contact with a live audience. He was probably also glad to escape Hollywood, where, Siegel sadly noted, he had become almost a joke. Yet he enjoyed making most of his last few movies and remained open to the possibility of returning to acting, even if, in retrospect, it seems inevitable that he would never return to Hollywood.

Presley never completely abandoned his acting ambitions and was infuriated by Parker's inability to strike a deal with Barbra Streisand and Jon Peters to make *A Star Is Born* (1976). His investment in the karate movie *The New Gladiators* was another attempt to escape the trap of perpetual touring. In his final years, Elvis's disenchantment with the industrial treadmill of live performances became increasingly obvious. As he told an audience in December 1976: "I hate Las Vegas. I ain't gonna do it, you know. 'Cause this is my living, folks, my life."

It needn't have been. This is a minority view, but Elvis shows far more genuine creative spark singing "Clean Up Your Own Backyard" in the criminally underrated *The Trouble with Girls* than he does in the blockbusting kabuki theater of *Aloha from Hawaii*, even if that TV special was watched by more people than saw Neil Armstrong take one giant step on the moon. The comparison becomes even more poignant when you consider Schilling's verdict on his friend's death at the age of forty-two: "The pills were just a band aid. What killed Elvis was creative disappointment."

Stay Away, Joe, MGM, 1968

Director, Peter Tewksbury; Screenplay, Michael A. Hoey, from the eponymous novel by Dan Cushman; Music, Jack Marshall; Producer, Douglas Laurence; Running time, 102 minutes

Cast: Elvis (Joe Lightcloud), Burgess Meredith (Charlie Lightcloud), Joan Blondell (Glenda Callaghan), Katy Jurado (Annie), Thomas Gomez (Grandpa Lightcloud), Quentin Dean (Mamie Callaghan), L. Q. Jones (Bronc Hoverty), Henry Jones (Hy Slager), Douglas Henderson (Congressman Morrissey), Susan Trustman (Mary Lightcloud), Anne Seymour (Mrs. Hawkins), Angus Duncan (Lorne Hawkins)

When Elvis reported for shooting of his twenty-sixth movie in Sedona, Arizona, on October 8, 1967, even MGM's executives had realized that they needed to do something different and stop trying to replicate the success of *Viva Las Vegas*.

The premise of *Stay Away, Joe* was certainly unusual. Dan Cushman's 1953 novel, inspired by the author's experiences growing up near the Rocky Boy Reservation in Montana, dwelled on the comic misadventures of a Native American family who squander the golden opportunity presented by a congressman who offers them a small herd of cattle to tend. A book-of-the-month selection, *Stay Away, Joe* was praised by *Kirkus Reviews* for its "native vitality," yet others—notably the Native American novelist James Welch—were profoundly offended by its cast of feckless, irresponsible, yet rambunctious Native Americans. Rather than addressing these concerns, the movie tries to sidestep them by playing for laughs.

As Joe Lightcloud, Presley plays a hell-raising, rodeo-riding, womanizing Navajo who is charming and eloquent enough to convince Congressman Morrissey (Douglas Henderson) that it would be politically astute to give the Lightclouds nineteen heifers and one cattle to manage. With comic inevitability, the bull gets barbecued at the riotous party the Lightclouds' prodigal son throws to celebrate his triumphant return. Joe's efforts to salvage the situation, while having as much fun with as many women as possible, provides what narrative thrust this comedy-western possesses.

There are plenty of diversions before Elvis saves the day by going on the rodeo circuit, miraculously earning enough money to buy one hundred cows. The Lightcloud family is entertainingly dysfunctional. Katy Jurado, who made her reputation as Gary Cooper's mistress in *High Noon*, fulminates to great effect as Joe's stepmother, Annie. Her stepdaughter Mary (Susan Trustman) is engaged to newspaper owner Lorne Hawkins (Angus Duncan), and, desperate to make the best impression on the rather proper Mrs. Hawkins (Anne Seymour), Annie starts selling off members of the herd to redecorate the Lightclouds' shambolic residence in preparation for Mrs. Hawkins's visit. Joe's ineffectual father, Charlie (Burgess Meredith, wearing the least convincing makeup in the entire film), is too weak to argue, while curmudgeonly grandfather Chief Lightcloud (Thomas Gomez) yearns for the old ways and delivers such one-liners as "Scorpion squaw should work more, talk less" with deadpan humor.

In his essay, Nazareth contends that Elvis plays his character a classic trickster figure. There are some similarities between Joe and the Trickster, the roguish, shape-changing, hero of many Native American myths. Nazareth's subsequent contention that "the movie is about neo-colonialism and the bourgeois dreams of Third World People, dreams that turn out to be risky fantasies" surely gives the writers far too much credit, although the movie does underline, in a ham-fisted way, the risks of Annie's hunger for modernization.

Inevitably, Joe's womanizing ways get him into trouble, provoking several fights (all staged with great relish by director Peter Tewksbury) and enraging his old flame Glenda Callaghan (Joan Blondell), who points a shotgun at his groin after realizes he has been wooing her nineteen-year-old daughter, Mamie (Quentin Dean). Although the movie opens with Elvis's heartfelt, homesick ballad "Stay Away," it ends with him and his buddies demolishing the family home in a rumpus that he aptly describes as "one hell of a fight."

Sadly, it wasn't only moviegoers called Joe who stayed away when this film was released.

Elvis described his character as "part Alfie and part Hud, a wheeler dealer who's always promoting something"—and Paul Newman's antihero provided the template for writer Michael A. Hoey's script, which Burt Kennedy, who later directed the entertaining western parody *Support Your Local Gunfighter*, had a hand in. Yet Hoey said later that Tewksbury "basically threw my script away and had the actors ad-libbing." Sadly, the improv in *Stay Away, Joe* would not have impressed the great Konstantin Stanislavski, and some scenes did, as Hoey said, come across as "just a drunken brawl."

Yet Tewksbury was reportedly dismayed by the quality of material he was working with. So, given the hackneyed nature of the central plot—and the quality of the actors playing the film's memorably eccentric cast of supporting characters—he may have decided his best strategy was to give as much of the limelight as possible to the likes of Jurado, Gomez, and Blondell.

Jurado makes the most of her first comedy role, telling producer Laurence that her limp (actually caused by broken bones in her foot) was part of her characterization. She gives her all without quite chewing the set, sparring brilliantly with Gomez. Pitted against two such strong actors, Meredith looks lost. Blondell is feisty and funny, interacting nicely with Dean, her beautifully dumb daughter, and Elvis. She raises a laugh or two with her intimidation of the clergyman in an aborted shotgun wedding.

Even the minor roles are ably played—with Seymour subtly comic as the blue-blooded Mrs. Hawkins and Jones and Henderson surprisingly believable as the political fixer and the congressman.

As Joe, Elvis is at the center of the action, fighting, kissing, and singing. The songs aren't shoehorned into the story but, apart from "Stay Away" and the wistful faux blues of "All I Needed Was the Rain," they aren't that good either. As a party song, "Stay Away Joe," with its line about lips being ripe for the picking, builds the mood. The nadir is undoubtedly "Dominic," which Elvis sings to a dozy bull whose impotent inability to be a stud like Joe endangers the Lightcloud family's fortunes.

Although he made his record producer Felton Jarvis promise never to release the song, Elvis carries this challenging scene off with reasonable aplomb in the movie. But then he seems in irrepressibly good spirits throughout *Stay Away, Joe*, looking trimmer and more handsome than in any film since *Girl Happy*. He certainly enjoyed the fact that, as he put it, "there isn't a guitar in the whole picture." It's possible that he had, by this point in his celluloid career, given up and decided to play it for laughs. His mood was probably also buoyed by the fact that his wife Priscilla was due to give birth in five months.

Though Elvis's great-great-great grandmother on his mother's side was a full-blooded Cherokee, he hardly goes out of way to get inside his Navajo character in *Stay Away, Joe*. His character certainly isn't as well defined as, say, the half-breed Pacer in *Flaming Star* and has few serious lines. Yet he is better than his material. His natural performance embodies the general air of genial good humor that goes some way to redeeming the film's many flaws.

The plot is bedeviled by the familiar absurdities, and there is one unintentionally hilarious scene in which he wakes up after sleeping on the ground with his black hair as shiny and smooth as ever, but the biggest flaw is Tewksbury's editing. In his second and last Elvis film, *The Trouble with Girls*, he captures the milieu of 1920s America in a sprawling style that recalls Robert Altman. That may have been his goal in *Stay Away, Joe*, but the parties and fights, resembling the kind of horsing around made famous by his Memphis Mafia, last so long you begin to feel you are watching them in real time. It doesn't help that much of the slapstick is terribly predictable. The one aspect of the film that has stood the test of time is the gorgeous use of landscape by cinematographer Fred J. Koenekamp, later an Oscar winner for his work on *The Towering Inferno*.

In the right hands—such as Burt Kennedy's—this bizarre comedy-western might have come off. When *Stay Away, Joe* was released in April 1968, the *New York Times* complained that the movie "could scarcely seem more embarrassingly tasteless or ill-timed than right now." One critic declared: "Stay whatever your name is." The movie wasn't a great commercial success either, though it was the top grosser for two weekends in March 1968, only reaching 65 on *Variety*'s list of the top-selling movies of 1968.

Since its release, the film's reputation has risen slightly. Elvis's biographer W. A. Harbinson, who lambasted many Presley movies, regarded this as a "healthily bizarre curio," while Peter Guttmacher, in his book *Elvis! Elvis! Elvis!: The King and His Movies*, hails this as a "wonderful change of pace for the frequently squeaky-clean Elvis."

In a sympathetic essay in the book *American Indians and Popular Culture*, Michael Snyder notes: "The problem was, no one involved, except Elvis Presley, actually cared about making a good movie about American Indians. Like others involved with the film, Meredith refused to take it seriously . . . 'The reason I took the role was to get financial backing to do the Chayefsky play [*The Latent Heterosexual*],' he admitted."

It's hard to be dispassionate about *Stay Away, Joe*. In some ways, the change of approach makes matters worse, because the scale of the missed opportunity is all the more obvious. Yet Elvis did at least seem to enjoy making this movie, and for that reason alone it is easier to watch than his worst travelogues.

The contributors who did best out of *Stay Away, Joe* were the 140 Native Americans hired as extras and Cushman. The movie may have bombed, but his novel enjoyed a new lease of life. As he told a reporter: "By golly, Elvis Presley sold books."

Speedway, MGM, 1968

Director, Norman Taurog; Writer, Phil Shuken; Music, Jeff Alexander; Producer, Douglas Laurence; Running time, 95 minutes

Cast: Elvis (Steve Grayson), Nancy Sinatra (Susan Jacks), Bill Bixby (Kenny Donford), Gale Gordon (R. W. Hepworth), William Schallert (Abel Esterlake), Carl Ballantine (Birdie Kebner)

"Pleasant, kind, polite, sweet and noble" was how Ebert characterized *Speedway*. The last Presley musical-comedy travelogue, the last to spawn its own largely ignored soundtrack album, and his final outing as a singing racing driver, looks now like a fond farewell to a formula that critics and the star had come to detest.

Speedway is that rarest of celluloid creations: a movie that combines stock-car racing, rock and roll, and tax evasion. Shuken's screenplay was originally intended for Sonny and Cher, but after their musical *Good Times* (directed by William Freidkin, who later made *The Exorcist*) flopped, the story was adapted for Presley. Steve Grayson (Elvis) is accustomed to winning the girl, the race, and compliments from everyone who knows him. Yet as the film opens, he is being tracked by a mysterious beauty who seems inordinately interested in his prize money. The woman turns out to be Susan Jacks (Nancy Sinatra), a miniskirted agent for the Internal Revenue Service who is tracking him at the behest of her boss Mr. Hepworth (Gale Gordon).

Grayson's only interest in money is spending it. So he lets his manager and friend Kenny Donford (Bill Bixby) manage all his accounts. Such trust soon proves tragicomically misplaced after Hepworth's inspection of Grayson's returns reveals that he owes the government $145,000. To make matters worse, Grayson is so impulsively generous he has just bought a new station wagon for the destitute Esterlake family (led by genial patriarch William Schallert) and some furniture to cheer up a tearful waitress (Charlotte Stewart, most famous for her role as Betty Briggs in *Twin Peaks*), who can't afford to marry her fiancé. Shaken, but confident they have a few thousand put away, Steve turns to Kenny, only for his friend and agent to reluctantly admit that he has gambled away all the winnings.

The parallels with Elvis's own life are obvious and intriguing. He was free with money, liking to spend it on himself and others—sometimes random strangers who happened to be in the same car showroom—with an intense generosity that startled his father and led some biographers to diagnose bipolar depression. His disinterest in financial details was certainly convenient for Parker, who manipulated Presley's finances for his own gain. In the early 1970s, Parker's own gambling habit would prove almost as disastrous as Bixby's in *Speedway*. Alex Shoofey, president of the International Hilton (where Elvis performed), once estimated that Parker was good for losses of $1 million a year.

In *Speedway*, Kenny's addiction is the cue for comedy, not tragedy, as Grayson and his entourage lose their furniture, station wagon, trailer, and even a spare engine. The plight of the adorable Esterlake girls thaws Susan's heart, and she renegotiates the hero's repayment deal so he can keep some of his next winnings to get everyone's lives back on track. By the time the final race comes around, driver and IRS agent are truly in love. In *Spinout*, Elvis had to borrow a car to win the race. In *Speedway*, he has to dispose of a sleeping passenger and skids off the track into third place, just as victory seems inevitable. Luckily, he has won enough to settle some of his debts—even if he still owes Uncle Sam $137,000—and retire to the Hangout, a racing-car-themed club, for the inevitable dance, song, and embrace.

Shuken's screenplay has a lot of sport with Presley's playboy lifestyle. The trailer he shares with his manager has tape-recorded animals to convince visiting girls it is the only safe haven in the vicinity. When racing driver and Internal Revenue agent first meet, Bixby locks them into the trailer, making our chaste heroine so nervous she duly escapes from a window.

Sinatra looks hip in the go-go boots that became a trademark after the promo for her biggest hit "These Boots Are Made for Walking." She suits the milieu so well it's hard to believe she was cast only after Petula Clark opted out (under orders from her vigilant husband, publicist Jean-Claude Wolff). She had caught the eye in—of all films—Roger Corman's outlaw biker movie *The Wild Angels* (1966)—and topped the U.S. singles charts in 1966, more recently than Elvis. Her cool persona makes a pleasant change from some of Elvis's more monotonous leading ladies, especially when she's allowed to strut her stuff and sing the Lee Hazlewood number "Your Groovy Self."

Yet *Speedway* is as much of a buddy movie as it is a romance. The banter between Presley and Bixby—the two had previously sparred in *Clambake*—has its funny moments. Bixby has a telltale habit of looking someone straight in the eye when he's lying to them. At one point, Elvis's hero shouts: "I'd like to break you in half!" To which Bixby replies, with impeccable timing: "If you did, you'd have two very short friends."

The races are better filmed than, say, the climactic powerboat contest in *Clambake*, although it is not really clear why it was necessary to draft in a cast of famous stock-car racers (Richard Petty, Gale Yarborough, and Tiny Lund being merely the best known). *Speedway* is, as Ebert suggests, a very southern movie, so their presence may have had some promotional appeal.

Most of the songs are performed in the Hangout, a club with a memorably colorful Pop Art decor, so beautifully shot by Oscar-winning cinematographer Joseph Ruttenberg it inspired the retro look of Jack Rabbit Slim's, the 1950s-themed restaurant in Quentin Tarantino's *Pulp Fiction*. The big production number—"He's Your Uncle, Not Your Dad"—is set in a tax office and can be seen as a comic counterpoint to George Harrison's much angrier "Taxman." As Elvis and Bixby salute the screen, their plaintive cry of "Oh say can you see, if there's anything left for me?" is almost endearing.

The best song in the movie is Elvis's opener "Let Yourself Go," a seductive rocker that features in the NBC TV Special. Presley had to sing to a few too many few children in his movie career, but he brings all his warmth to "Your Time Hasn't Come Yet, Baby," a charming ballad sung to the oldest Esterlake girl (Victoria Meyerink). The smooth "Who Are You?" is bland but inoffensive, enhanced onscreen by Sinatra's adroit reacting. "There Ain't Nothing Like a Song" is so poor it feels like a leftover from *Easy Come, Easy Go*. The biggest musical disappointment is that "Suppose," a poignant ballad Elvis had become fascinated by, didn't make the cut.

For fans, the most enjoyable aspect of this movie is how lithe, cool, and at ease their idol looks. Whether it was the thrill of some heavy flirting on set with Sinatra, his joy about becoming a father during shooting, or the relief that this particular treadmill was finally coming to an end (or a combination of all three), Presley seems in tremendous humor, using what *Variety*'s reviewer called "his own particular brand of lightness" to sell the film.

Speedway doesn't demand a lot of its audience—apart from the ability to overlook the odd changes in the style and color of Bixby's hair—and the plot is as absurd as ever, but there is something, as Ebert said, sweet, polite, and noble about this innocent comedy musical. Perhaps *Speedway*'s biggest flaw has little to do with the film itself but the waste of talent it symbolized. As Renata Adler, in a mildly favorable *New York Times* review, put it: "And this is, after all, just another Presley movie—which makes no great use of one of the most talented, important and durable performers of our time."

The movie was no smash, barely covering its costs on initial release—although it certainly resonated with Tarantino. When he sat down with the husband-and-wife team of production designer David Wasco and set director Sandy Reynolds to make *Pulp Fiction*, one of the first assignments he gave them was to watch *Speedway*. In a scene deleted from Tarantino's most famous movie, Uma Thurman asks John Travolta if he's a Beatles fan or an Elvis fan. In 2007, the director himself declared: "Now I'm an Elvis fan over the Beatles man any day of the week." Only Tarantino knows how significantly movies like *Speedway* influenced that preference.

Live a Little, Love a Little, MGM, 1968

Director, Norman Taurog; Writer, Michael A. Hoey, Dan Greenburg, from Greenburg's novel *Kiss My Firm but Pliant Lips*; Music, Billy Strange; Producer, Douglas Laurence; Running time, 90 minutes

Cast: Elvis (Greg Nolan), Michele Carey (Bernice), Dick Sargent (Harry), Don Porter (Mike Lansdown), Rudy Vallee (Penlow), Sterling Holloway (Milkman), Celeste Yarnall (Ellen)

Bernice (Michele Carey) is such a free spirit she has a name for each mood. In the course of Elvis's twenty-eighth movie, she reveals so many different facets of her personality she must have more aliases than the FBI's 100 most wanted. It's not especially Carey's fault, but her part is so profoundly ill conceived that she comes across, to quote Steve Werner's description in his satirical novel *Elvis and the Apocalypse*, as "an obsessed dingbat out to get Elvis." This serious miscalculation—and a plot that doesn't make a great deal of sense even on its own terms—foils Taurog's brave attempt to change Presley's image by reviving the screwball comedy, a microgenre that enjoyed a glorious heyday in the 1930s and 1940s.

Greg Nolan (Elvis) is a photographer whose life takes an incomprehensible turn after he ends up on the beach next to Bernice and her Great Dane Albert. He catches pneumonia, is knocked out with drugs, is fired from the newspaper, and loses his apartment after Bernice—who may or may not be married to the put-upon, inoffensive Harry (Dick Sargent, who had a bit part in Elvis's first movie, *Love Me Tender*)—moves him and his belongings into her house. In a laudable bid for freedom, Greg gets two jobs: one taking glamour photos for Hugh Hefner–style entrepreneur Mike Lansdown (Don Porter), the other for a very formal ad-agency tycoon known as Mr. Penlow (played by 1930s singing icon Rudy Vallee). Yet with Bernice in pursuit, frustrating a budding romance with Ellen (Celeste Yarnall) by hoovering, Greg is doomed to be domesticated. He does, though, uniquely in an Elvis film, go all the way with Carey, prompting her to run off in confusion before they joyfully reunite on the beach where they met at the beginning of the film.

Hoey and Greenburg get quite a lot of things right. For once, Elvis is not a superannuated beach boy. It's a refreshing change to see Elvis as prey, not predator—the twist subverts many of the certainties that characterized most of his musical comedies. Yet the central flaw in this movie is that Presley doesn't really suit the role. Greenburg had assumed an actor like Woody Allen would play his hero. Presley was just too handsome and had too much presence to play a character the novelist described as a "sensitive, Jewish, nerdy kind of guy." Hoey admitted as much, saying: "Part of this guy has 'Jewish guilt' and I can't give Elvis Jewish guilt." Unsure of himself, Presley plays his character as angry—understandable, really, as Carey's brand of kookiness becomes increasingly wearing—and, though he does his best, it doesn't really come off. He might have been better off playing it straighter, quieter, in the vein of Cary Grant in *Bringing Up Baby*, the screwball comedy this film bears the most resemblance to.

The writers extract much mirth out of Elvis's twin occupations. Although Taurog rather overdoes the scenes where the star has to change on the stairs as he hurtles from magazine to ad agency, this subplot is so effective that *Variety*'s reviewer found it more interesting than Carey and Presley's on–off–on romance.

Greenburg had once edited *Eros* magazine, and the script lets Porter revel in such chauvinistic lines as "It's a man's world, and I plan to keep it that way because that's the way the birdies like to nest." Vallee, probably the only one of the King's co-stars to have seriously considered running for president (in 1940), is almost as entertaining onscreen as he was on set. He usually drove from his home on Rudy Vallee Lane to the set in a station wagon with his name emblazoned on it and contrived to ensure that MGM paid for every item of clothing he owned to be dry-cleaned. The former crooner entertainingly reprises the priggish ad-agency president J. B. Biggley he had played in *How to Succeed in Business Without Really Trying* (1967).

Poster for *Live a Little, Love a Little* (1968). Presley and Taurog tried to revive the screwball comedy—in a part written for Woody Allen.   *MGM/Photofest*

There are some intriguing running gags—such as the recurring visits by the milkman (Sterling Holloway), who calls Carey's character Betty, and impudent delivery boy (Eddie Hodges)—and some of the dialogue has a kind of wacky appeal, notably when Elvis sets up meetings with his prospective bosses by telling the receptionists: "Tell him Nolan is here, with the truth."

Presley and Carey have the right chemistry too, it's just a pity that, unlike Katharine Hepburn in *Bringing Up Baby*, her character seems merely meretricious rather than charmingly capricious. In a scathing review of the movie, Scott Huffman comments on the scene where Elvis rebuffs her advances, after she's dropped her mink coat to reveal she is naked: "Apparently it's not her body he's interested in, but rather her stupid, dishonest, psychotic, convoluted mind." Even if you like the movie more than Huffman does—not difficult—it's hard not to agree that there's some truth in this assessment of her character. All of which makes it harder to swallow Greg's refusal to, as Harry tells him, "Run for the hills."

Variety suggested the duo's incompatibility was underscored by their makeup. "For some reason, Presley's makeup tones resemble the American Indian character he played in *Stay Away, Joe*, while Miss Carey's flesh tones are unnaturally pink. Makes for some unusual two-shots.

The script has a few clunkers, with Carey proclaiming in the very first scene: "The sand is grainy." Later on, Presley is obliged to say that "I never liked egg rolls and hot dogs before, and now . . . I hate them."

Yet the journey to the inevitable romantic bliss is less predictable than in most Elvis movies, there are some genuine laughs, and the story does at least feel contemporary—as does the music. "Edge of Reality," which Elvis sings in a dream sequence with a dancing dog, sounds like no other record he's ever made. (And that is a compliment.) Cameron Crowe later hailed this sequence as "seismically funny and unintentionally profound." It was, as the writer/director noted, the star's "only true foray into psychedelia," so trippy "you can't quite believe it exists." The ballad "Almost in Love" has a jazzy/cocktail feel. Mac Davis's uptempo "A Little Less Conversation" is so good it's possible not to be distracted by the bizarre shapes the party guests are making as they dance around the pool.

It's been said that Elvis didn't much like the movie, but he gives it his all onscreen swapping wisecracks with Porter, shows appropriate exasperation at Carey's antics, and, for all his discomfort, looking significantly cooler, trimmer, and hipper than he had in any film since *Viva Las Vegas*. He may also have felt an obligation to the nearly blind Taurog, who was directing his last movie.

Urban myth has it that the dog that imprisons Elvis in the sea at the start of the film is his own dog Brutus. Priscilla has since refuted this rumor, saying the Great Dane was a studio-trained canine. Elvis trivia buffs like to point out that Susan Henning (who is dressed up as a mermaid in one of the movie's photo sessions) would reappear in the comeback TV special as the innocent girl who tempts him when he walks into a bordello. (She obviously tempted him offscreen too, because he had a fling with her.)

By the time *Live a Little, Love a Little* was released in October 1968, most critics and cinemagoers had given up on Elvis. The movie did about as poorly as *Speedway* and was hardly distributed at all in the UK. Crist complained: "Only the most devout Presleyites will be enchanted . . . it shortchanges him and them with only a couple of songs and a completely incoherent plot." *Variety* wasn't much more impressed by what it called "one of Presley's dimmest vehicles," asking: "Story peg—why has Michelle Carey effectively kidnapped him?"

Yet some writers, notably Sheila O'Malley and Jeremy Richey, author of the blog the *Moon in the Gutter*, have acclaimed this as if it were some kind of lost masterpiece. For Richey, it is a pleasure to see Presley playing a character who is recognizably human, harassed by "demanding bosses, impatient clients, chilly secretaries, a ditzy-eyed dame and a giant slobbering dog." He has a point. *Live a Little, Love a Little* is a welcome departure from the norm, but it would be more satisfying if the central characters in this madcap romance were better conceived.

In retrospect, Greensburg was glad the film got made. Yet the member of the crew who enjoyed it most was probably Marvin Robinson, a singer in the film. Elvis spotted Robinson eyeing his ring during a get-acquainted session with the singers and dancers and, hours later, returned to give it to the singer. Robinson was so overcome, he locked himself in the bathroom screaming.

Charro! National General, 1969

Director, Charles Marquis Warren; Screenplay, Warren, based on a story by Frederick Louis Fox; Music, Hugo Montenegro; Producer, Warren; Executive producer, Harry Caplan; Running time, 98 minutes

Cast: Elvis (Jess Wade), Ina Balin (Tracey Winters), Victor French (Vince Hackett), Solomon Sturges (Billy Roy Hackett), Barbara Werle (Sara Ramsey), Lynn Kellogg (Marcie), James Almanzar (Sheriff Ramsey)

"A different kind of role, a different kind of man." That was how National General tried to interest cinemagoers in Elvis's dwindling movie career in the trailer. The role certainly was different. There were no songs in the film itself— just the atmospheric title track sung over the credits—and for the first and only time in his movie career, Elvis, playing reformed outlaw Jess Wade, wears a beard, which, alas, does shrink and grow in such a fashion that it all but constitutes a continuity error.

Lured into a Mexican cantina by the promise of a rendezvous with old flame Tracey Winters (Ina Balin, who is beautiful and, as the story unfolds, increasingly superfluous), Jess is seized by his old outlaw gang, led by stolid Vince Hackett (Victor French) and featuring Vince's deranged brother Billy Roy (Solomon Sturges, son of the great director Preston Sturges) and artillery expert Gunner (James Sikking). Hackett's gang has stolen a gold and silver cannon that fired the last shot against Emperor Maximilian in the Mexican revolution. Vince has Jess branded on the neck and let loose to act as a decoy for the forces of law and order on both sides of the border. To clear his name, Jess meets up with old friend Sheriff Ramsey (James Almanzar), but they bump into Billy Roy, who has ridden into this dusty little town in search of women and booze. After a violent confrontation in which Ramsey is wounded, Jess imprisons Billy Roy and becomes stand-in sheriff. Enraged, Vince directs Gunner to point the cannon at the town and threatens to blow it to smithereens unless his brother is released.

Having economically orchestrated this intriguing buildup, writer/director/producer Charles Marquis Warren lets the story lose impetus—prompting many viewers to lose patience. Jess's only plan to save the town from being blasted into oblivion seems to be to keep Billy locked up and hope for a miracle. As law-and-order policies go, this is a tad unconvincing, and, after the desperate townsfolk turn their anger on him, he heads up to the hills with his prisoner for a showdown. The rationale for his change of heart isn't entirely clear. Maybe he

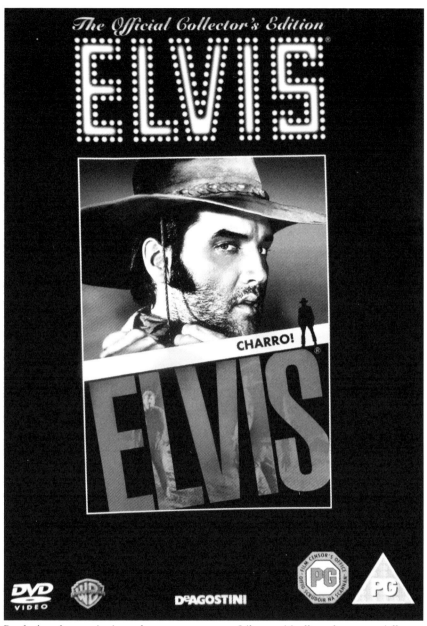

Presley's only non-singing role was a courageous failure, critically and commercially.

fancies his chances in the dark. If he'd taken the same course of action a few hours earlier, his old friend Ramsey might not have been killed in his sick bed, a point that is not lost on grieving widow Sarah Ramsey (Barbara Werle, who gets more chance to emote here than she did as Leilah, Mary Ann Mobley's servant, in *Harum Scarum*).

Jess triumphs in an unorthodox shootout, aided by the stupidity and coward-ice of Vince's gang, and rides off with villain and cannon in his custody. A tad ungallantly, he doesn't even kiss Tracey as he leaves (though he gets a forgiving peck on the cheek from the widow Ramsey). The poor woman has to run after him before he assures her that he will send for her—a scene that just about sums up their relationship in the film.

Presley must have had high hopes when he saw the script. He even went to see Clint Eastwood in *Hang 'Em High* days before shooting started in Apacheland, Arizona. He seems to have quickly realized that his western was not going to match that standard, although it has its moments, stays true to genre, and convincingly depicts the central friendship between Jess and Sheriff Ramsey.

One of the difficulties in judging *Charro!* is that, as Amazon reviewer Charles Jannuzi has pointed out, it's a Hollywood imitation of a genre, spaghetti west-erns, which were originally imitations of Hollywood westerns! Even though the best Italian westerns directed by Sergio Leone and Sergio Corbucci surpassed the Hollywood originals, this cycle of imitation goes to the heart of much that is wrong with *Charro!*

Making a Hollywood version of a spaghetti western with Elvis in the title role was always a mission implausible. It became a mission impossible when Warren and Frederick Louis Fox (who wrote the story for *Charro!*) were drafted in. Warren had not directed a movie since 1958 (the Foreign Legion adventure *Desert Hell*) and had done little of note as a writer since leaving the TV horse opera *Rawhide* in 1960. Fox had written some recent episodes of *Bonanza* and *Branded* but hadn't penned a western for the big screen since *Dakota Incident* (1956). So the fate of this attempt to cash in on the popularity of such movies as *A Fistful of Dollars* was in the hands of two men whose careers had peaked long before Leone's *The Man with No Name* had laconically revolutionized the genre. The only aspect of the production that seems genuinely inspired by Leone is Hugo Montenegro's dramatic score. Even here, the effect is marred by the insistent manner in which Warren uses it to underline dramatic moments and even, on occasion, to suggest tension where none exists.

That isn't Warren's biggest mistake as director. As Susan Doll wrote in a perceptive review for TCM, "He relied heavily on fades to black, which were typical for episodic television at the time, particularly before commercial breaks. Warren tended to fade between key scenes that were supposed to occur in rapid succession instead of cutting between them, which destroyed the sense that one event followed immediately after the other." Lacking the technique or vision to match Leone, Warren gives us a movie that, at its worst, feels like an overlong episode of a TV western.

To be fair to Fox, the original story for a project that was to be called *Come Hell, Come Sundown* did feature violent gunfights and several bare-breasted ladies of the night. But by the time filming started, these elements had been toned down. The gunfights were mainly predictable—more *Gunsmoke* than *The Good, the Bad and the Ugly*—and the explicit sex disappeared, although the scene in which Elvis talks to Balin while she is having a bath mysteriously survived. You get a glimpse of what might have been in the saloon scenes: the casual lechery on display suggests how sordid the saloon girls' lives would have been on the real frontier. The one authentically grisly scene—in which Elvis is branded as a traitor with a hot iron—isn't especially convincing. Warren doesn't seem to know whether to revel in the agony or allude to it. At least, as Elvis said in a rare interview promoting the movie, he wasn't asked to play a singing gunfighter.

Elvis's performance has divided opinion. At the time, most reviewers agreed with the *New York Times*'s Roger Greenspun, who suggested he "treats his part rather as a minor embarrassment." *Variety* was kinder to the star, saying, "He strolls through a tedious role that would have driven many another actor up the wall." Some, notably Doll, have suggested he is subdued by his disappointment at the story's evisceration. This doesn't quite square with reports of a relatively good atmosphere on set, where the Memphis Mafia grew beards but staged fewer practical jokes than usual. Presley's relationship with Warren blossomed after the star accidentally shot his director with a blank charge early on! Other reviewers have suggested Elvis tries too hard, mumbling every line too seriously.

Most of the few plaudits that greeted *Charro!*'s release went to French's villain and Balin's saloon madam. Solomon Sturges's giggling sociopath earned more praise than it deserved—the performance starts well enough but becomes excruciating through repetition and histrionic exaggeration. Having to share so much screen time with such a scenery chewer, Elvis has little choice but to underplay. They do, though, share the best scene in the movie, when Elvis bangs his prisoner's head against the bars of his cell to good effect.

The unconvincing branding scene ironically reflects the movie's difficulty in branding its eponymous hero. As a man trying to reform and clear his name, he is intended to be the bad-good hero, one of the western genre's enduring archetypes. Yet, as Greenspun noted, "not even the rudiments of conflict or suppressed doubt exist within the central character. Although he brands Presley with a red-hot poker, it is Vince who bears the real scar: a gun-happy kid brother to whom he remains loyal . . . even to his own undoing." Greenspun even likened French's performance to William Holden's Pike in *The Wild Bunch*, a comparison that now seems absurd.

French's villainy now seems too small for the big screen. He may be more accomplished than Elvis, but he has none of Presley's mystery. There are times in this intriguing failure when you see Elvis consciously trying to look enigmatic, perhaps under the influence of Clint's *Man with No Name*. At such moments, Elvis really is trying too hard because, as Nick Tosches pointed out years later, he came by his air of mystery naturally, and, decades after it was made, he remains the most intriguing thing in the movie.

Westerns suited Elvis, and, at his best in this film, he seems utterly at ease. Watched without prejudice, *Charro!* doesn't really deserve the mauling it received on release. Hollywood made many worse westerns in the 1960s, a decade when the studios started to lose faith in this quintessentially American genre. For an Elvis movie, this is an honorable failure in which, for the most part, Presley seems engaged by a story that, for all its corny touches, gives him the chance to act. Still, as the hero rides off triumphantly into the sunset, it's hard not to wonder what Siegel or Sam Peckinpah might have made of this.

The Trouble with Girls, MGM, 1969

Director, Peter Tewksbury; Writer, Arnold and Lois Peyser, adapted from the novel by Day Keene and Dwight Babcock, based on a story by Mauri Grashin; Music, Billy Strange; Producer, Lester Welch; Running time, 97 minutes

Cast: Elvis (Walter Hale), Marlyn Mason (Charlene), Sheree North (Nita Bix), Nicole Jaffe (Betty), Edward Andrews (Johnny)

When Elvis's thirtieth movie was released in September 1969, the King had just completed his sensational monthlong engagement at the International Hotel in Las Vegas. One of his favorite jokes was to describe his new record as "my latest escape, er, release," and escape is pretty much what *The Trouble with Girls* did. In some parts of the United States, it was on a double bill with *The Green Slime*, a witless sci-fi flick listed by Golden Raspberry Award founder John Wilson as one of the 100 Most Amusingly Bad Movies Ever Made. In the UK, twenty-five minutes was cut in a forlorn attempt to liven up the box office. The assumption that the film was a mere relic of the King's discredited past meant some fans even ignored the film.

Such neglect was especially sad because this is one of Elvis's best movies. The *New York Times*, which almost had an official policy of loathing Presley's films, enthused, in a review by Roger Greenspun: "Peter Tewksbury's *The Trouble with Girls* is a charming though ineptly titled comedy with one fortunate murder, several pleasant songs, Elvis Presley, and a huge cast all of whom, down to the last extra, seem willing to act their fool heads off."

Presley stars as Walter Hale, the young manager of a chautaqua (a traveling school that provided education and entertainment in the 1920s) who has several challenges to resolve when his troupe stop in Radford Center, Iowa. His deputy, Johnny (Edgar Andrews), wants him to use the mayor's talentless daughter as the lead in the pageant. The troupe's union leader, Charlie (Marlyn Mason), always on the alert for any infringement of employees' rights and regarding herself as a champion of talent, isn't so keen. The chautaqua's wise-cracking card shark Clarence (Anthony Teague) is arrested on suspicion of murdering Harrison Wilby (Dabney Coleman), a sleazy, two-timing chemist who, in Charlie's words, "liked picking the wings off people." Walter intuitively realizes that the real killer is Nita Bix (Sheree North), who had the misfortune to work for—and be forced into having an affair with—Wilby. At the finale of the last show in

Radford Center, Walter manages to reveal the killer's identity in such a way that the woman isn't penalized. He has one last mission before the chautaqua—trick the local sheriff into forcing Charlie, who has quit in all the excitement, to get on the train with the rest of the troupe.

That summary doesn't do justice to the quirky charm of Tewksbury's movie. As Greenspun noted in his review: "The evocation of 1920's Americana is exceptionally even-handed, detailed, affectionate without sentimentality, funny without condescension." The ensemble cast features Joyce Van Patten (a channel swimmer who lectures on the virtues of axle grease), Vincent Price (lecturer Mr. Morality), and John Carradine (snobbish Shakespearean actor Mr. Drewcolt, who, when asked if Romeo and Juliet ever had premarital relations, snaps back: "Only in the Des Moines company"). Flirtatious hotel receptionist Betty (Nicola Jaffe) is so keen to help out, she volunteers to play the piano for nothing. A group of clean-cut college boys prove of general assistance, one even killing time onstage with a (slightly anachronistic) Donald Duck impersonation.

This is so far from the usual Presley formula it is a wonder the film ever got made. The idea had been kicking around the MGM and Columbia lots since 1959 with both Glenn Ford and Dick Van Dyke inked in for the Walter Hale role. In 1968, MGM bought it back and the Peysers adapted it for Elvis. This was Tewksbury's second Elvis movie, and, more confident in this story than *Stay Away, Joe*, he lets the camera roam in a way that would later come to be called Altmanesque. In an interview with *Elvis: The Man and His Music* magazine, Elvis's leading lady Mason said: "Peter would let us improvise. If it was a close-up of Elvis—and he wanted a particular visual reaction—he would say to me: 'Marlyn, I don't care what you do but I need this reaction from him.'"

Tewksbury's style is perfect for establishing milieu, character, and story. There are enough set pieces too—notably the fireworks that go off as Walter and Charlie argue about the pageant—to keep everyone entertained. There are fewer songs, but they suit the story, with Elvis looking at ease and uninhibited as he sings "Swing Down, Sweet Chariot" with three-quarters of a gospel quartet. This had been his boyhood ambition, never fulfilled, and his delight is obvious here. The soulful "Clean Up Your Own Backyard" and the wistful "Almost" are both seriously underrated songs with lyrics that actually relate to the plot!

The pacing begins to go awry when the murderess gets drunk before appearing onstage to confess. North does, as *Variety* complains, overact, but the main problem is that the sobering-up process (even with slaps in the face and buckets of water) takes far too long. Yet when all is resolved, as the chautaqua pulls out of Radford Center, and an affectionately nostalgic voiceover reflects on the demise of this phenomenon, the movie does leave a glow.

Unlike many period movies, *The Trouble with Girls* really does feel as if it inhabits the style, culture, and language of its time. An unpretentious small-town movie, which makes a quiet plea for tolerance (even the mayor says: "No Klan feeling here"), *The Trouble with Girls* is, as Greenspun says, "a film that succeeds so amiably in its many parts that the relative weakness of the whole doesn't matter too desperately."

For once, Elvis's character actually drives the plot. He is—and this probably amused him—playing the Parker/Svengali figure that recurs throughout his movies. Though we are convinced of his intrinsic decency, he is not afraid to be Machiavellian, prompting his right-hand man Johnny (Andrews), who bears some physical resemblance to Parker, to exult: "He's a louse! He'll use anything!" While Elvis doesn't quite act his fool head off, he quietly makes the most of the opportunity to create a character that isn't a stranger's cartoon version of himself.

His most memorable scenes are with Andrews and Mason. Andrews's seasoned chautaqua veteran is a perfect foil for Elvis, and their rapport produces some delightful moments, notably when Johnny decides that things are going so badly he might as well play American football. The fiery romance between Presley and Mason is even better. (For once, Elvis has the audacity to suggest they go to bed.) Mason gives as good as she gets, accusing him of looking like a caricature of a capitalist, berating him for hiring a pianist for nothing, and warning him: "Don't bedroom-eye me, boss man." She wasn't a unanimous choice for the part—Parker wanted a buxom blonde—but Tewksbury put his foot down, and she has the charisma and wit to make the inevitable romantic complications a pleasure rather than a chore.

Most of the performers make a difference, especially Anissa Jones (as gifted girl entertainer Carol Bix) and Pepe Brown as her friend Willy. Jaffe is brilliantly daffy as Betty, Teague is suitably superior as "the snotty nosed" card shark, and Coleman is so slimy as the lecherous druggist you wouldn't be surprised if he leaves a trail. Apart from her long drunken scene, North is effective too. Presley used to discuss acting with her and ask for tips between scenes. She later said of his role: "He was a sort of a con-guy but if you're going to be a con-guy, you better be charming or likeable or we're in trouble. I thought it was a fine character for him and he upheld that character beautifully."

The ridiculous title was foisted on Tewksbury by a new studio head. The director objected so strongly he asked for his name to be taken off the picture before ultimately relenting. Though *The Trouble with Girls* does make this drama sound like a formula musical like *Girls! Girls! Girls!* or *Girl Happy*, it could have been worse: one of the other suggestions was *Love in a Tent*.

Mason said that Elvis told her wanted to make one decent film before he left Hollywood because "I know the whole town is laughing at me." He had already made several, but he ought to have realized, as he watched the rushes, that *The Trouble with Girls* was pretty decent too. As Sheila O'Malley says on her website devoted to rehabilitating Elvis as an actor, "In movies where Presley does NOT sing a lot, something very interesting starts to happen. A space starts to open up for him as an actor." That's precisely what happens in *The Trouble with Girls*, and Elvis makes the most of that space.

Change of Habit, Universal Pictures, 1969

Director, William A. Graham; Screenplay, James Lee, S. S. Schweitzer, and Eric Bercovici; Story, John Joseph, Richard Morris; Music, William Goldenberg; Producer, Joe Connelly; Running time, 89 minutes

Cast: Elvis (Dr. John Carpenter), Mary Tyler Moore (Sister Michelle Gallagher), Barbara McNair (Sister Irene Hawkins), Jane Elliot (Sister Barbara Bennett), Robert Emhardt (The Banker), Regis Toomey (Father Gibbons)

Change of Habit draws on the real-life story of Sister Mary Olivia Gibson, whose pioneering work with children with speech disorders in Syracuse, New York, involved some theatrical techniques. Opinions differ on how much of her story made it to screen, but her life did inspire a script that was unlike any Elvis had acted in before. The movie was produced at Universal under the deal to make the 1968 NBC TV special, and one of the pleasures of Presley's last feature film is that some of that renewed optimism, vigor, and self-confidence infuses his performance.

Presley is Dr. John Carpenter, a groovy doctor who runs a clinic in a New York ghetto. He has requested assistance but is surprised when three smart, attractive young women turn up. Unbeknownst to him they are all nuns, taking part in an experimental scheme to help the Catholic Church reach out to the community: Sister Michelle (Mary Tyler Moore), Sister Irene (Barbara McNair), and Sister Barbara (Jane Elliot). They all find their mission difficult for different reasons. Michelle is trying to focus on her cases—autistic child Amanda (Lorena) and troubled stuttering teen Julio (Nefti Miller)—but is falling in love with the doctor. Barbara discovers her role is incompatible with her political beliefs, as she combats profiteering at a local supermarket (her protest provokes an amusing confrontation with Ed Asner's socially aware cop). Irene is appalled by the havoc wrought by money-lending crime boss the Banker (Robert Emhardt), whose thugs provide the clinic with many badly beaten patients. To make life even more challenging, local priest Father Gibbons (Regis Toomey) is an autocratic arch-traditionalist who is appalled by "brides of Christ in flapper skirts."

The budding romance between Carpenter and Sister Michelle, deepened by the emotional bond they develop after the doctor's rage-reduction therapy cures Amanda, comes to an abrupt halt when the church leaders decide the nuns must wear their habits. After provoking the Banker to violence at an event to celebrate the feast of Puerto Rican saint Juan de Cheguez, Irene returns to the peace of the convent. So does Michelle—after the doctor has saved her from being raped by Julio—but, haunted by her experiences, she seeks divine guidance in Father Gibbons's church, where she finds Carpenter leading the congregation in a rousing performance of "Let Us Pray Together." The movie ends ambiguously with a shocking hint of blasphemy as Michelle is torn between images of Christ and the doctor.

Is director William A. Graham implying that Elvis—not the Beatles—is really bigger than Jesus? Or merely pointing at the godlike myth surrounding the star? The closing ambiguity certainly resonated with Universal's orders to writer Eric Bercovici to present Elvis as "pure and good." He chose the name John Carpenter to match the JC in Jesus Christ. The finale has prompted such speculation that Graham eventually admitted he thought Sister Michelle would choose Presley. Either way, it is an unusual ending to a very different kind of Elvis film.

Change of Habit is an easy movie to ridicule. On Jabutoo's Mad Movie Dimension website, Ken Begg takes seven pages to dissect every flaw, discovering "how really awful this film is, moment by moment, scene by scene, actor by actor, line by line." It's hard to dispute a lot of Begg's analysis. The blend of comedy and drama doesn't always work. In ninety-three minutes, it tries to raise every significant social issue afflicting the ghetto. Many of the characters are simplistically either wholly good or completely bad—and it is almost always the white characters who create and solve the problems. Father Gibbons's ultimate conversion to a groovy new style of church service is convenient but wholly unconvincing. The presentation of rage-reduction therapy as an instant cure for Amanda's problems is unrealistic . . . it's easy to go on—as Begg does—but, after a certain point, all such dissections prove is that a critic, to allude to the title of one of Ebert's anthologies of reviews, really, really hated the movie.

In *Change of Habit*, Presley's ghetto doctor fell in love—emphatically but inconclusively—with Tyler Moore's nun.

Universal Pictures/Photofest)

Many viewers, while acknowledging some—or all—of the flaws Begg has highlighted, still find *Change of Habit* easy to watch. One of its pleasures is that, rather like *In the Ghetto*, it plays to what Guralnick called "the liberal hero complex we grafted onto Elvis." In a role that essentially allows him to play a version of himself, Presley looks more contemporary, charismatic, and interesting than in most of the musical comedies he had made in the last decade.

His warmth makes the rage-reduction scene, where he grabs the autistic girl to cure her, repeatedly telling her, "Love you Amanda," genuinely moving. Lorena Kirk, who played the afflicted girl, was terribly shy in real life and began screaming, crying, and kicking for real until Tyler Moore stopped the filming and walked off the set.

Elvis had a great rapport with Graham, who called the star "one of the nicest men I have ever met." The director gave Presley some acting exercises and was generally impressed with his star's dedication and craft, although he did say: "His line readings could be conventional." Presley's co-star Jane Elliot recalled catching the movie years later on late-night TV and was impressed by his performance, telling Bill Bram: "At the time he seemed too reserved, too close to the vest, like he wasn't giving enough of himself. As the decades go on, his work is now dead on the money. His work was very honest and very simple. That is what people do now. Me, Barbara and Mary were acting, we had capital A's, all three of us. Elvis was just present, simple and authentic."

Graham took the unprecedented step, for an Elvis director, of encouraging the star to learn the basic principles of Method Acting. At Presley's house, Graham would give his star what are known, in acting classes, as "simple action problems"—for example, how to steal a watch from a bedside table. They progressed to improvising situations. Inevitably, Parker got wind of this and, after a couple of weeks, called the director over and admonished him not to get any ideas about winning awards. Graham understood the warning but persisted. It seems absurd, and ironic, that the only acting class Presley was given in a fourteen-year movie career was on his final film.

Although Elvis's stepbrother David Stanley said Tyler Moore was the leading lady the King most disliked, they didn't really come into conflict. Their relationship was cordial, though not deep. Accounts by cast and crew suggest that Elvis was at his most gregarious on set, whereas Tyler Moore was, in the director's words, "a little bit on the prissy side but that was okay because she was playing a nun." Naturally reserved—and worried about her skin (which could look wrinkled on camera because she had diabetes)—she was also not quite sure what she was doing in an Elvis movie. She had her own entourage and resented the occasions when Presley was slightly late for shooting. His remark to Stanley may have been prompted by his suspicion that, as Elliott put it, "Mary neither liked nor understood him."

The movie was slammed on release, derided as a ghost from Presley's past. In the *New York Times*, A. H. Weile condemned Elvis as "mostly the somewhat subdued, callow, slightly unconvincing and largely mystified Pasteur to the poor throughout most of the proceedings." Yet *Variety* was impressed by the sensitive handling of the romance between Presley and Moore, which progresses in a much less clichéd manner than most of the King's previous relationships with his leading ladies.

There aren't many songs—the action is disturbed only by "Rubberneckin'," "Have a Happy," and "Let Us Pray"—but they are not at all bad and suit the movie's ambience. "Rubberneckin'" has a passionate urgency that is impossible to resist, and "Have a Happy," although the scene itself isn't especially convincing, is catchy and charming, one of the best songs Elvis ever crooned to a kid.

On set, Presley's propensity to break into song with the Blossoms (who accompany him during "Rubberneckin'") prompted McNair to sing with him as a dozen elderly extras took the floor and started dancing. Caitlin Wyles, who had a minor role in the film, said: "The set was bedlam. Elvis and the dancers just wouldn't quit. I wondered why the director didn't film it. It would have been the best part of the picture. It was Elvis at his best, spontaneous and alive. I only wish the motion picture screen could capture him that way."

If you accept *Change of Habit* on its own terms—neither Graham nor the writers were seriously suggesting they were going to resolve all the ghetto's ills in one film—it is reasonably entertaining and a welcome change of place for the star. Although the social commentary is sugar coated, the story does at least take place in a space that has some relevance to the real world. After some of the indignities Elvis endured in other movies, it is a pleasure to see him so obviously enjoying his work.

Elvis: That's the Way It Is, MGM, 1970

Director, Denis Sanders; Director of photography, Lucien Ballard; Producer, Herbert F. Solow; Running time, 108 minutes

"What does Elvis really think? And what is he really like?" These were the questions that struck Vincent Canby when he reviewed Denis Sanders's concert documentary for the *New York Times*. The clue really is in the title: this is *That's the Way It Is*, not *That's the Way He Is*.

Sanders is trying to explain the phenomenon—and to do that you have to show the man himself at work—not unlock Presley's personality. So wife Priscilla, daughter Lisa Marie, and manager Parker are mostly conspicuous by their absence. Unlike two famous rock documentaries also released in 1970—*Let It Be* and *Woodstock*—this film has a pretty conventional purpose: in its eccentric way, it is essentially trying to prove Cary Grant's proposition that Elvis was the greatest entertainer since Jolson.

As compelling as Sanders's movie is—it is a must have for every genuine Presley fan—it falls into a gray zone. It isn't an out-and-out record of the King in concert in Vegas in 1970, but neither is it a documentary packed with stunning revelations about its star, his milieu, or his celebrity. The interviews with fans (who generally come across as weirdos) and hotel staff (none of whom have a great deal to say) don't tell us much. The occasional cuts to Vegas's skyline at night or the odd glimpse into the Hilton's inner workings are almost as pointless. In one very strange scene, Sanders fills half the screen with Presley rehearsing while steaks are hauled into the kitchens in the other half. It's not clear if the director is implying that, in Vegas, at least, Elvis is just another piece of meat or, indeed, if he means to imply anything at all.

There was a certain amount of tweaking before the movie was released. Parker wrote a stiff three-page memo to Jim Aubrey, head of MGM, complaining that there were "too many cut-ins on the songs . . . which tend to distort real life performance," that the movie condescended to the fans, insulted other entertainers such as Frank Sinatra and Dean Martin, and cast aspersions on the quality of *Blue Hawaii* and *G.I. Blues*. He also cautioned that the interviews "be thoroughly checked [so that it] doesn't become monotonous and take away from the performance." The "slurs," as Parker called them, against Presley's movies were cut. You wonder what else was cut too.

For example, in the film there is a scene in which Elvis reads congratulatory telegrams. Sanders filmed the singer reading one out: "Dear Elvis, after fourteen years we have finally learned to understand what you say on record—yours sincerely RCA." As released later in *This Is Elvis*, the moment is genuinely funny, with Presley pausing at just the right moment before he bursts into laughter, but it was obviously deemed too controversial for release at the time. (A similar gag, in which he pretends to have received a telegram, saying: "My God why hast thou forsaken me?" from the Pope, also never made the original release.) So what we have in Sanders's print is a sanitized, yet still immensely charismatic, Elvis.

Such caveats aside—and they reflect what, in retrospect, seems such an enormous missed opportunity—*That's the Way It Is* remains utterly compelling, especially when Presley is in rehearsal or onstage. He is the orchestrator of an enormous enterprise and makes it happen with his artistic direction, charm, and humor. At one point, he quips: "If the songs don't go over, we can do a medley of costumes." He also occasionally lays down the law, such as admonishing over-enthusiastic guitarist James Burton, "They don't tell you when to start, man."

Though the Vegas Elvis might now seem overly familiar, the jams and the performances repay reviewing. Onstage, he seems utterly in command and, although his show has a defined structure, it is clear Elvis might take it anywhere, mumbling a joke, mocking one of his old hits, drawing out "Suspicious Minds" with exquisite precision, or alluding to the Beatles with a snatch of "Get Back." This is the Elvis who, as Jon Landau said in *Rolling Stone* in 1971, "sings like an angel and moves like a ballerina."

The greatest performance in this documentary may just be his driving, passionate rendition of Tony Joe White's swamp-rock classic "Polk Salad Annie." This showstopper starts with a lazy, Dean Martin drawl of a monologue ("Some of you never been down south too much"), gains momentum as soon as he belts out "Down in Louisiana," and runs through crescendo after crescendo, with his flailing arms driving the band on, until he, the musicians, and the audience can take no more. So effective is his showmanship, the tension isn't even dissipated when he turns his back to the audience, reads a small note, and hands it to a sidekick. That demonic intensity contrasts superbly with his tender, soulful version of "I Just Can't Help Believin'," where he is beautifully cast as the helpless romantic who can't help believin' that each new romance will last forever.

Cinematographer Lucien Ballard captures every twitching leg muscle and every drop of sweat, showing us how, amid all the crash-boom-bang orchestration and sumptuous vocal backing on "Bridge Over Troubled Waters," Elvis sings most of this iconic ballad to himself, standing still and looking upward like a boy singing a hymn in church.

Sanders's movie is not to be missed. There was so much footage that could have been included that in 2000, Ernst Jorgensen and archivist Rick Schmidlin released a remade version that focuses on Elvis in rehearsal and performance but, oddly, cuts "I Just Can't Help Believin'" and "Bridge Over Troubled Water" to squeeze in some oldies. Schmidlin's recut makes for good viewing, though it has none of the artistic ambition of Sanders's original. Yet, given the quality of some of the footage which has resurfaced elsewhere—for example, the rehearsals of "Don't" and "Baby Let's Play House" on the video *The Lost Performances*—it is clear that neither version is definitive.

That's the Way It Is did reasonably well at the box office—reaching number 22 on *Variety*'s box-office survey—and remains a landmark in pop-cultural history. Sanders and Schmidlin have done Elvis, his fans, and popular culture the great service of proving that, on his return to live performance, Presley was not a joke or a parody but a cool, handsome, humorous performer, blessed with soul, spontaneity, and showmanship.

If there is sadness in the movie, it is sparked by the final scene, as the credits roll, that shows Elvis joking with Sammy Davis Jr. and Cary Grant at a party after one of his concerts. The scene has particular poignancy; they are all enjoying themselves so much, it offers a glimpse of what might have been if Vegas had remained an event rather than a biannual contractual obligation. At this point in his life, the world is once again at his feet. Everything seems possible. The failure to seize this opportunity would prove fatal for Presley.

Elvis on Tour, MGM, 1972

Directors, Pierre Adidge, Robert Abel; Music, Elvis Presley; Producer, Abel; Running time, 93 minutes

"I want to shoot you, but the trade-off is you've got to be open with me," Robert Abel told Elvis. "If I feel like you're posing, I'll just turn the camera off. And then MGM will just be out of a lot of money." Elvis replied: "I like your honesty. When do we start?"

Adidge and Robert Abel had established themselves with the innovative *Mad Dogs and Englishmen* (1971), a fascinating documentary account of Joe Cocker's 1970 U.S. tour. If Adidge had lived up to the promise of that first conversation with Elvis, this concert documentary might have been a revelation. Yet somewhere along the way, the filmmakers settled for something much more conventional.

They set out to present Elvis as an authentic American folk hero—and in that they succeeded brilliantly—but that goal did mean that some of the most revealing material, from an interview in which Presley reflected on the failure of his film career and such episodes as being forced to sing to a dog on the Steve Allen show, never made it into the final cut. Schilling, who helped in the editing and sat in on the interview, felt that Presley's review of his career was almost too candid for Adidge and Abel. It could have provided the heart of the film—after all, Elvis rarely said anything in public beyond "Thank you very much, you're a beautiful audience"—but it would have been a very different movie than the one Adidge and Abel wanted to make and MGM and Parker hoped to sell.

That doesn't make *Elvis on Tour* a bad movie, but it does, as *Time* suggested in its review, present a "a movie of missed opportunities: something very shrewd, pointed and telling could have been made about the man who began as a hard-driving rock star and became a sort of star spangled mascot of Middle America." Canby was even less impressed in the *New York Times*, complaining: "The camera never catches him in a truly candid moment."

Canby has a point, but there are revelations if you know where to look. The scene that haunts many fans, especially in the light of the tragic decline that followed, is the shot of Elvis gazing out of the limo window, lost in his thoughts, utterly alone though the car is full, oblivious to sycophants and schedules. The expression on his face, as Schilling has pointed out, is very close to the look he had in the famous Alfred Wertheimer photo of him gazing out of the train in 1956.

Adidge realized the significance of this moment and used it at the end of the movie, where it almost seems to ask the question: who is Elvis? The implied answer is that we don't know and nor, despite their time on the road with him, do the filmmakers. You then wonder, at this stage of his life, did Elvis know who he is anymore?

The other truly insightful scene is the gospel singalong after a concert. In the film, Elvis says: "A lotta times we'll go upstairs and sing until daylight—gospel songs. We grew up with it. It more or less puts your mind at ease." And he looks utterly natural, around the piano with J. D. Sumner and the Stamps, singing "Lead Me, Guide Me" and then swooping into the infectious "Bosom of Abraham." It's one of those rare moments in an Elvis film that leaves you with a sense of roads not taken.

His entourage don't all seem to be enjoying the jam session as much as he is, but he is entranced as the Stamps power through "Sweet Sweet Spirit" and "The Lighthouse," and when he strolls over to the piano to join in, he sings with a joy, tenderness, and passion that you seldom see in the onstage numbers, where, in jumpsuits designed to resemble superhero costumes, he offers the songs he knows the audience want to hear with grace, gusto, and self-deprecatory humor.

One of the highlights of this movie is that it lets Burton's invigorating guitar playing and Ronnie Tutt's relentless drumming share the limelight.

Though Presley performs such hits as "Polk Salad Annie," "A Big Hunk of Love," and "Never Been to Spain," the experience is more about theater—the moves, the costumes, and the audience reaction—than about the music. The exception is "You Gave Me a Mountain," a powerful performance of a song that reflected the breakup of his own family. The footage of Elvis singing the autobiographical "Separate Ways" in the studio also hints at the private grief behind the public face.

The clip of the Madison Square Garden press conference shows Elvis at his most charming. The moment where he refutes the suggestion that he's a shy country boy at heart by standing up to reveal the gold belt given to him by the Las Vegas Hilton is priceless. Once more, the frustration is that Adige and Abel didn't do more with this material, especially the wonderful moment where a reporter says they are reminded of *The Ed Sullivan Show* (on which the singer was filmed from the waist up) and Presley fires back: "So am I, that's why I'm sitting down."

Although *Elvis on Tour* eventually succumbs to the temptation to be just another concert movie—albeit with an incredibly charismatic star at its heart—it does give a flavor of the industrialized insanity of life on the road. The glimpses of Elvis backstage, greeting a dignitary, charming the press, give us a sense of what it must have been like to be there.

One of the intriguing contrasts between the two concert documentaries is their sense of scale. In *That's the Way It Is*, Elvis is conquering Vegas and hence, so the film implies, the world. In *Elvis on Tour*, he is presented as, to quote the *New York Times* review of his 1972 Madison Square Garden concert, like "a prince from another planet," landing in various interchangeable towns and cities across America. In this way, *Elvis on Tour* says more about the intensity of Presley's bond with his fans than do any of the interviews in *That's the Way It Is* and gives a firmer sense of how important this incarnation of the King became to America's popular culture in the 1970s.

Adidge and Abel present us with very different Elvises. He can seem remote, almost like one of his own impersonators in a red jumpsuit, big hair, and bigger glasses, and intimate, as when he grins at a hidden camera he has just discovered while singing the slow verse in "Suspicious Minds." In retrospect, *Elvis on Tour* captures the moment where the dynamic optimism of *That's the Way It Is* has mellowed into something less intense but still enjoyable.

Although the star's itinerary is so packed as to be almost presidential, the movie leaves you with an underlying sense that Presley had begun to suspect that, after escaping from those Hollywood contracts, he had ended up on a different kind of treadmill. When you watch this film, it is still shocking to remember that within five years of its release, Presley would be dead.

The splitscreen montaging, a trademark of *Mad Dogs and Englishmen*, doesn't always work but, at its best, makes the impact of Presley's performance almost viscerally clear. Martin Scorsese did some of the editing on this film. He wasn't very talkative while at work, so Schilling was surprised when Scorsese turned to

In *Elvis on Tour*, the theater was almost as important as the music Presley was performing.

him in the booth one night and said: "You know what I've got, Jerry?" Fearing the editor might have discovered he had some incurable disease, Schilling said, "No, what?" Scorsese replied: "'That's All Right Mama,'78, Sun Records."

Though the movie recouped its cost of $600,000—not including Elvis's $1 million salary—in days, it wasn't a massive hit, appearing on *Variety*'s box office survey for just two weeks and peaking at number 13. The movie could have done significantly better if Parker hadn't decided to scrap a planned soundtrack album, *Standing Room Only*, because it would come too soon after the release of the *Live at Madison Square Garden* live album (which was, in itself, a dry run for the grandiose bid for world domination that was *Aloha from Hawaii*). *Standing Room Only* could have sold well, especially if it had featured "Burning Love," Presley's biggest hit since 1969, and helped promote the movie. Instead, Parker released the smash on an appalling budget compilation, *Burning Love and Hits from His Movies*, probably because—as the revenue from those albums was split 50/50 between manager and artist—he would make more money than from a regular RCA release.

Unlike most previous Presley movies, *Elvis on Tour* impressed most critics and gave its star genuine artistic satisfaction. Adidge and Abel's film was nominated for a Golden Globe for Best Documentary. Elvis watched the award ceremony live in his suite at the Las Vegas Hilton in January 1973. His entourage was startled by a cry of: "My God! Son of a bitch! We won! We've won the Golden Globe." His movie was co-winner with *Walls of Fire*, a documentary about the history of Mexican murals.

This Is the Story: *This Is Elvis* and Beyond

Nineteen eighty-one was a pivotal year in Elvis's posthumous career. Four years after the singer's mysterious death in Graceland, Albert Goldman's sensational biography *Elvis* tried to reduce the singer to a tabloid caricature. Goldman's Elvis was a dumb, racist hillbilly who had lucked his way to unprecedented success. As absurd as this now sounds, the critique was surprisingly influential at the time, although one critic complained that this muckraking biography, which claimed to tell readers everything they needed to know about Presley had nothing original, profound, or relevant to say about the one aspect of his life that made him so fascinating and important: his music. Charles Hamm, one of America's most influential musicologists, said the publishers should withdraw the book and reclassify it as fiction.

The biography's reputation has sunk since, with even Lamar Fike (who talked to the author) disowning some of its claims, revelations that Goldman edited some quotes misleadingly to make his point, and its central contention—that Elvis was culturally irrelevant—comprehensively rebutted by Guralnick's seminal two-biography series: *Last Train to Memphis* (1994) and *Careless Love* (1999).

In the same year as Goldman's biographical assassination, Warner Brothers released *This Is Elvis*, an odd fusion of real footage and dramatic reconstruction that, as uneven as it is, proved he could say more with someone else's song than Goldman could say in a book. Panned by many critics, *This Is Elvis* doesn't have the dramatic coherence of John Carpenter's *Elvis* (the 1979 TV movie in which Kurt Russell did a reasonable job as the icon he had once kicked in *It Happened at the World's Fair*), but by putting the singer center stage, it paved the way for the resurrection of the King's reputation. In 1985, the release of *One Night with You*, Steve Binder's compilation of live performances from the mesmerizing NBC TV Special, offered proof—if it were needed—that Goldman had utterly underestimated the man *Mojo* magazine once hailed as "rock's one true star."

Andrew Solt, one of the directors of *This Is Elvis*, would later make *The Great Performances Center Stage Volume 1* and *The Great Performances Volume 2: The Man and His Music* (1990), both decent showcases of Presley's talent. Yet *He Touched Me* (2000), focusing on his love for gospel, got much closer to his musical soul. Two years later, the King's comeback was complete when a slew of documentaries were released in *The Definitive Elvis*, his music inspired Walt Disney's animated smash *Lilo and Stitch*, and Junkie XL's remix of his *A Little Less Conversation* topped charts across the world. The DVD releases have kept on coming, but only *Elvis by the Presleys* (2005) is really essential viewing.

Astonishingly, for a star whom Leonard Bernstein hailed as "the greatest cultural force of the twentieth century," Presley has never enjoyed the definitive documentary treatment that, for example, Scorsese gave the Rolling Stones or Bob Dylan, both of whom were inspired by the King.

The rehabilitation of Presley has even embraced some of his films, especially *Loving You, Jailhouse Rock, King Creole, Flaming Star, Blue Hawaii, Viva Las Vegas*, and, to a lesser extent, *The Trouble with Girls* and *Wild in the Country*. Much as Elvis loathed making many of them, the better pictures—even the musical comedies—are now regarded as slightly better than many of the movies Hollywood made in the 1950s and 1960s to exploit the appeal of rock stars and teen idols. And some of the scenes—especially when he performs numbers like *Jailhouse Rock* or *Trouble*—still feel, with every passing Elvisless year, as exciting as when he filmed them and serve as enduring proof of his greatness.

This Is Elvis, Warner Brothers, 1981

Directors, Malcolm Leo, Andrew Solt; Screenplay, Leo, Solt; Producer, David L. Wolper; Running time, 144 minutes

Having previously collaborated on the critically acclaimed documentary *Heroes of Rock and Roll*, Malcolm Leo and Andrew Solt seemed a safe pair of hands to helm this biopic. They probably didn't intend this to be, as Pauline Kael dubbed it, "a pop-culture horror movie" in which "we witness the transformation of a young whirlwind performer into a bloated druggie with dead eyes," but then, as the critic rightly pointed out, they were asking for trouble the moment some-one—presumably in the Warner Brothers marketing department—chose to bill this as "the first theatrical movie to tell a story by blending existing footage with historically accurate re-creation." In practice this means we get the real Elvis, four impersonators onscreen, Ral Donner (who had a hit in 1961 with a cover of "Girl of My Best Friend") narrating as Elvis, and Ronnie McDowell providing the singing voice of Elvis in high school. Other casting oddities included Knox Philips playing his dad Sam Phillips and Cheryl Needham, who made such an impression as El's longtime girlfriend Linda Thompson that her next movie role came four years later as the woman in a bar in *What Comes Around*, directed by—and starring—Jerry "Guitar Man" Reed.

This Is Elvis is still worth watching if you're prepared to fast-forward through the "historically accurate re-creations" and watch the footage of the King, much of which had never been seen before. The clips—and the interviews—are inspiring and ultimately heartbreaking, much like Presley's life. It is hard to watch the joyous magnetism of the young star (on the Dorsey Brothers, Ed Sullivan's show, and Frank Sinatra's *Welcome Home* special in 1960) and the harrowing footage of his final years, where he looks, as Ebert sympathetically put it, like a man who has lost his mind but not his heart or voice. *This Is Elvis* is far from definitive but it does, for all its inadequacies, reveal why he still matters.

6

How Good an Actor Was Elvis?

The Views from Critics, Co-Stars, Directors, and Others

lthough he made thirty-one feature films, opinion remains divided over Presley's quality as an actor. Writer Joe Queenan entertainingly summed up the traditional view when he wrote:

> Unlike Frank Sinatra, a shorter, tougher man with a colossal ego, Elvis was probably not temperamentally suited to be an actor. He seemed nervous and embarrassed in *Love Me Tender* and did not show much more range in films like *King Creole* and *Flaming Star*, by far his best "serious" pictures. His phrasing was mechanical: he tended to snarl and brood a lot. Of course, most people would snarl and brood a lot if they were trapped in a film where they had to play a hip-swiveling pharmacist's son who is being courted by a local gangster who wants him to come back and do his nightclub act in the lounge where he used to work as an underpaid busboy even though his father wants him to finish high school and enter a profession like, well, pharmacy.

That is pretty much the view that guided Presley's movie career. Parker was never convinced that his boy had the ability to act, and his verdict seems to have influenced Hal B. Wallis, who produced nine Elvis movies, and the Hollywood community as a whole, with Joe Pasternak, who produced *Girl Happy* and *Spinout*, flatly saying: "He hasn't got it." Wallis's best biographer, Bernard F. Dick, wrote: "Wallis knew the public would never accept Elvis in straight roles. They wanted the singer; if they could have the actor too, all the better."

This view is backed by some rock critics and biographers, like Peter Guralnick, who essentially regard Elvis's movies as a colossal distraction from the serious business of creating the kind of authentic, innovative music that makes Presley's Sun recordings sound fresh today, nearly sixty years after they were cut. The star's own disgust at making some of these movies has colored many critics' views. Yet in the years since his death, his acting has been

Blue Hawaii (1961). Elvis's movies didn't always give him the meaty roles he needed to show off his acting.   *Paramount Pictures/Photofest*

reevaluated, with writer Sheila O'Malley campaigning through her website, The Sheila Variations, to ensure that Presley's acting gets the credit she thinks it deserves.

What did the actors and directors who worked with him think? A minority agree with Queenan. Marianna Hill, who loathed appearing alongside him in *Paradise, Hawaiian Style*, never rated him as an actor. Millie Perkins, one of Presley's love interests in *Wild in the Country*, complained that he was joking around between scenes, while she was thinking about her character. This kind of holier-than-thou attitude does seem to ignore the fact that different actors have different styles. Spencer Tracy liked to have a laugh between scenes, but that didn't make him a bad actor.

Of all Presley's co-stars, Walter Matthau (who played the villain in *King Creole*) has probably been the most generous in his appraisal of the King's thespianship. He told the BBC: "I creep up to the sentence, he was an instinctive actor. Because that almost is a derogation of his talents. That's saying, 'Well, you know, he's just a dumb animal who does it well by instinct.' No, he was quite bright, too. He was intelligent enough to understand what a character was and how to play the character simply by being himself through the means of the story. He

Nancy Sinatra and Elvis. Presley's writers seemed to feel he was most at ease with musical comedies.

didn't overact. He was not a punk. He was very elegant, sedate . . . refined and sophisticated."

Most of his directors who have put their verdict on record agree that he could act and could have become a good actor. In this camp are Michael Curtiz, Philip Dunne, William A. Graham, Hal Kanter, Gene Nelson, John Rich, Don Siegel, and Norman Taurog. Two directors who never worked with him but watched him—George Cukor and Sidney Lumet—were as impressed. Kanter said Presley "had very good instincts. Philip Dunne and I were comparing notes several years later and he said that Elvis had a natural ability to perform in front of a camera. He could have been an excellent movie star, and not a freak attraction, if he hadn't limited himself, and had done things like a drama or a light comedy."

With Parker deciding the real money lay in using the movies to promote the music, that career path never opened up. In most of Presley's films, he was cast in a bigger-budget version of the classic teen musical, in which the characters focus on an attainable, concrete goal—such as winning a race—in a story set in an exotic backdrop, a flavor of which might infuse the music, in which the hero invariably, but not always, relinquishes his girl-chasing ways to settle down with, and sometimes marry, his true love.

The inevitable result was that, after too many interchangeable musical comedies, the star himself gave up. Allan Weiss, who wrote most of the Wallis/Presley pictures, said, "When he realized it wasn't going to happen, he just started walking through the movies. All that natural gift, that extraordinary ability, squandered." Edward Anhalt, who scripted *Girls! Girls! Girls!*, said, "I thought he was very good, but of course no one gave him much of a chance."

Graham, who directed *Change of Habit* in 1970, had been less impressed, fearing that Elvis was very "limited in his acting ability" after watching the other films. On set, he engaged Presley in the Actors Studio Method Acting exercises, mentioned earlier in discussion of that film. After a few sessions, he concluded, "Elvis was looser when it came to comedy than drama. He was a little self-conscious in dramatic scenes but he could handle comedy very well." Ultimately, although he thought Presley's line readings weren't always as interesting as they could be, he felt the star had more talent than he had suspected.

Michael A. Hoey, who worked as a writer and dialogue coach on five Presley movies, echoed Graham's observations about the actor's dramatic skill, recalling one scene opposite Nancy Sinatra in *Speedway*: "The scene was basically an argument, but since they found each other attractive, it was supposed to have a sexual undercurrent. This was the kind of scene Elvis had difficulty playing: he didn't deal well with subtext, preferring more straightforward emotions like anger and mockery." After Elvis had giggled his way through countless takes, Taurog angrily dismissed the company. The next morning, Presley apologized and did the scene in one take.

The shame is that he was given acting lessons only on his final feature film. Although initially Elvis had agreed with producer David Weisbart's suggestion that the best way to act was to rely on your natural ability, he seems to have been open to—but never seriously pursued—the idea of learning his craft at an institution like the Actors Studio. He did tell *TV Guide* in 1956, "I don't think you learn to be an actor. If you learn to be an actor—in other words, you're not the real actor. You're not a real actor. You're false." Yet he greeted Graham's beginners' class in Method Acting with enthusiasm and he did his best to improve by watching his co-stars, quizzing them about the craft ("He was always asking a lot of questions," recalled Carolyn Jones, who starred in *King Creole*) and, back in Memphis, watching countless movies during which he made mental notes about the actors' performances. His minute study of Peter Sellers may explain why Graham found him more comfortable with comedy.

So how good an actor was Elvis? At times, very good. Watch him leer at Judy Tyler in *Jailhouse Rock*, flirt with Carolyn Jones in *King Creole*, mourn Dolores Del Rio in *Flaming Star*, show sensitivity and vulnerability as he falls for Hope Lange in *Wild in the Country*, quarrel with Angela Lansbury in *Blue Hawaii*, innocently unnerve the gangsters in *Follow That Dream*, stroll moodily through a nightclub in *Viva Las Vegas*, argue with Barbara Stanwyck in *Viva Las Vegas*, and debate the chautauqua's prospects with Edward Andrews in *The Trouble with Girls* and you see an actor who has the ability to transcend his own image. And that, for someone as famous as Presley, is no mean feat.

There are little moments too—the way he plays with a comb in *King Creole*, walks away after a fight in *Flaming Star*, asks Hope Lange, "Do you think this is art?" in *Wild in the Country*—that creates a rare intimacy between him and us that still works even today, so long after his death.

Wardrobe test photo for *Flaming Star* (1960). For some critics, Presley's performance in *Flaming Star* was the most powerful of his career.   *20th Century Fox/Photofest*

Elvis was not an actor who reinvented himself in the vein of Dustin Hoffman or Robert de Niro at his peak. Yet given the scope in *King Creole* and *Flaming Star*, he commands the screen, hinting at inner complexities, emotions, and intelligence that belie the cliché that he was just a dumb country boy who got lucky. In the best Presley travelogues such as *Blue Hawaii* and *Viva Las Vegas*, he judges the material shrewdly, creating a charming, charismatic representation of his own personality in the manner of such actors as Cary Grant and John Wayne, who proved so adept at playing different versions of themselves.

There are other movies where his disenchantment or disinterest is all too apparent, and there are too many moments where you can see him thinking about the next scene instead of losing himself in this one. Even by 1964, by the time he was making *Roustabout*, Rich felt the star had lost his passion for acting. "There was a kind of laziness, initially, that it was good enough," the director told Bill Bram. "I said 'You can do better this. He rose to the bait and I said: 'You are working with very keen professionals, the likes of Barbara Stanwyck, it is like playing tennis with a better partner, you've got to come up." When challenged, Presley responded, as Rich said: "He never fought it, he drove himself and he did the work."

In a few clunkers like *Paradise, Hawaiian Style*, he tried to distance himself from the mediocrity with smiling disbelief. Given some of the scripts he had to work with, the wonder is that not that his morale flagged but that he maintained it for so long.

One of Rich's recollections, discussed above, of working with Presley on *Roustabout*; it has particular poignancy. "One day he showed an interest in the editing process and said 'Could I come and watch?' I said 'My God . . . absolutely!' I had him up in the editing room and I was showing him things and he was fascinated. I'd have been happy to go a long way down that road but the group around came in and they said: 'C'mon, this is boring' and they took him away. He was crestfallen. I think he wanted to stay but they took him away and I never saw him again in the editing room. It bothered me, because I saw an awakening there."

In a way, that memory sums up Elvis's acting career. There was an awakening there—you can see it in his best films and even in some moments in his worst—but he never fulfilled his immense promise. Much of the blame for that lies with Hollywood, his producers, and the Colonel, but some of it lies with the star himself. As Nelson, who directed him in *Kissin' Cousins* and *Harum Scarum*, said: "He could have been a very good actor but mostly he would just be his charming self—and get away with it."

7

Big Boss Man

What Kind of Technical Advice Did Parker Provide for Elvis Movies?

As "technical advisor," Colonel Parker was hailed by showbiz bible *Variety* as an "expert property developer." Though some of the movie properties Elvis's manager helped develop were incredibly slapdash, that observation does raise one of the most puzzling aspects of the star's movie career. How much control did Parker have over Presley's films, and what kind of technical advice did he provide between 1956 and 1972?

Although many aspects of Presley's life are open to debate, there is no doubt that Parker orchestrated the star's move to Hollywood, negotiated all the movie contracts on his client's behalf with input from the William Morris agency, and expressed the view that "all Elvis's films are good for is making money." As the easiest way to make money was to sell music, Presley would sing at least once in thirty of his thirty-one feature films.

So the Colonel developed the strategy—and ensured that it was executed. Though his client often complained that he was "tired of these damn movies" in which he was fighting in one scene and singing to a dog in the next, he never decisively rebelled, preferring to signify his distaste by hiding out in Memphis for as long as possible until the next shooting schedule beckoned. Presley proved especially reluctant to turn up for the making of *Harum Scarum* and *Clambake*, almost reducing his manager to apoplexy. Yet Presley was usually, as Hoey has noted, "very conscientious about his work, and always arrived on the set on time, knowing his dialogue and ready for business." Parker had repeatedly threatened him that if he offended the studios he would return to oblivion, cleverly playing on one of the star's recurring nightmares.

It is much harder to say how much interest Parker took in the movies themselves. Hoey concluded: "The Colonel had absolutely no interest in the quality of the projects, only the size of the check. His only consideration was with the music selection and a quick read of the script to see where the songs would fit." Once, when Hoey and Taurog discussed a different kind of movie with Elvis, the star told them to consult his manager. Parker refused to read the script, saying, "Give me a million dollars and you can have him and shoot the phone book, if you're crazy enough."

Elvis's manager certainly liked to suggest that he only cared about money, telling *Variety* in 1964: "Look, you got a product, you sell it. As long as the studios come up with the loot, we'll make the deal." Michael Fessier Jr., who interviewed Parker for *Variety*, explicitly points out in the story: "Once a deal is made, the studio takes complete control of a film, the Presley camp having no say-so on cast, script or production costs." Parker justified this laissez-faire attitude by saying, "We start telling people what to do and they blame us if the picture

Colonel Tom Parker and Elvis on the set of *Change of Habit* (1969).   *Photofest*

doesn't go. As it is, we both take bows and if it doesn't hit, maybe they get more blame than us. We don't have approval on scripts—only money. Anyway, what's Elvis need? A couple of songs, a little story and some nice people with him."

As usual with Parker, the reality wasn't as straightforward as his observations suggest. For a start, there were rarely just a "couple of songs." Only seven—*Change of Habit*; *Charro!*; *Flaming Star*; *Live a Little, Love a Little*; *Love Me Tender*; *Stay Away, Joe*; and *Wild in the Country*—had fewer than five songs. In his memoirs, *Elvis, Sherlock and Me*, Hoey says Parker and Presley both took an interest in the songs: "Their choices differed greatly and the Colonel, looking out for his album tie-ins, frequently prevailed."

That interview fails to reflect how Parker's contractual antics shaped how and what films were made. For a start, his insistence on a large fee upfront for his "boy" made it significantly less likely that a studio would take a risk on a more artistic picture. Parker actually acknowledged as much in the *Variety* interview when he claimed he had turned down one producer who had asked to reduce Elvis's fee so he could pay for a better script and rebuffed another who insisted he had an Oscar-winning story: "I told him pay us our regular fee and if Elvis gets the Oscar, we'll give his money back. We never saw him again."

While Presley may have been dreaming of an Oscar nod—not an absurd aspiration after *King Creole* and *Flaming Star*—Parker was in pursuit of a very different kind of holy grail: getting a fee of $1 million a picture for his star. He achieved it in 1966 at the very point the formula was wearing thin. He was perplexed when Elvis, who understood the impact this would have on budgets and co-stars, greeted his new status as Hollywood's highest-paid star rather coolly. Needing to recoup such hefty fees, the studios were bound to play it safe and give the people more of what the box-office receipts had proved they wanted.

Such fees also encouraged them to cut costs, although even Parker had, after watching *Harum Scarum* and complaining that it would take a "55th cousin of P. T. Barnum" to sell that movie, decided never to work with quickie producer Sam Katzman again and wrote to MGM suggesting they spend more time on the next film to get a better result. By that point, with box-office revenues shrinking, the studios were saving money wherever they could.

Though Hoey insists that the Colonel never had any input into the stories on the Elvis movies he worked on, Parker didn't always just stand idly by, counting the money, thinking up promotional stunts, and writing to the studio with title suggestions. (*Clambake* was one of his. He also helped persuade MGM to retitle *Chautaqua* as *The Trouble with Girls (and How to Get Into It.)*)

Right from their first meeting, Wallis and his partner Hazen had known Parker would need careful management. Making *Roustabout* was partly designed to flatter the Colonel, honoring his carnival past, a point Wallis made explicit in a letter: "Of course, we want you to be associated with the project, as I know how close this type of life is to you." This wasn't mere rhetoric: the producer ended up paying Parker $25,000 for a weekend's consulting on carny lore with scriptwriter Weiss. The notes from that meeting are incredibly detailed and specific, and three of Parker's suggestions made it into the final print.

Parker often didn't look at scripts, telling Katzman it would cost $10,000 to appraise a draft for *Kissin' Cousins*, but he certainly read others, including those for *Spinout* and *Kid Galahad*.

Theodore J. Flicker once recalled the making of *Spinout*: "Pasternak had given us the line for the story: the daughter of the richest man in the world wants her father to invite the biggest singing star in the country to sing for her Sweet Sixteen Party. So we sat down, we tried to imagine what Elvis' life was like. And we wrote that—as if we were writing a real movie. The next thing we knew, the head of the studio called us in and said: 'The Colonel read the script and said 'When I want to do Elvis' life story, I'll get a hell of a lot more than a million dollars for it.'" A new script was submitted, and Parker turned up in the writers' offices, threw the script on the desk, and said: "This is great. Just one thing: put a dog in it." Later a senior suit at MGM told Flicker and co-writer George Kirgo, "We can't accept this script. There's no racing in it." Having added a dog, they were hardly likely to balk at incorporating racing. Fortunately, all the debate and revisions were done quickly enough for the script to be ready when Elvis turned up at the lot for pre-production in February 1966.

Spinout was merely one significant departure from Parker's stated policy of never interfering. John Flynn, assistant director on *Kid Galahad*, told Bill Bram, author of *Elvis Frame by Frame*: "The writer asked: 'Colonel, how did you like the script?' The writer was wondering how the Colonel liked the dramatic flow but the Colonel couldn't give a shit. He just said 'It needs two more songs.'" When the writer queried this, the Colonel explained: "Boy, there's ten songs on an album and you got eight. It needs two more songs." In the event, the released version contained six songs, but here, once again, we find Parker having his say, sending out a message not just to the makers of that film but to the producers of other Presley pictures. As Michael Moore, assistant director on six Presley pictures and the director of *Paradise, Hawaiian Style*, put it, the star, the crew, and the studio knew that the best way to keep Parker happy was to include a dozen songs.

The idea that Parker didn't approve anything in Elvis's films but the money was a convenient fiction and, like many great fictions, all the more convincing because it contained an element of truth. The Colonel was obsessed by money, but he also kept close, if not claustrophobic, tabs on Presley, monitoring shooting, turning up to offer his own brand of comic relief when nerves got frayed (striding around the set of *Kissin' Cousins* wearing Elvis's blond wig), and stopping the cameras rolling one morning during the filming of *The Trouble with Girls* because the star's eyes were puffy. He also acted as the conduit for producers' instructions regarding his star's appearance—Wallis was particularly vocal about Elvis's weight, facial appearance, and hair as the 1960s wore on. Before the release of *That's the Way It Is* in 1970, Wallis spelled out his objections to certain scenes in a three-page letter to MGM boss Jim Aubrey. Needless to say, his concerns were addressed.

The Colonel's influence on casting is hard to gauge. Marlyn Mason, Elvis's leading lady in *The Trouble with Girls*, was chosen over his objections. Parker, the actress recalled, "wanted some buxom blonde; and Peter Tewksbury said 'I'll walk if you don't cast Marlyn.'" It sounds plausible, although there's little other evidence of Parker trying to have his say on casting, apart, perhaps, from noting that Elvis enjoyed working with particular actors, like Shelley Fabares.

The clinching evidence that Parker did not hand over complete control to the studios once filming had started is *Viva Las Vegas*. Realizing that the movie was soaring over budget—and that Ann-Margret was getting as much of the limelight as Elvis—Parker protested so vehemently that the stars' duet on "You're the Boss" was cut. He complained that director George Sidney's camera angles favored Ann-Margret and threatened to drop his usual promotional campaign. Though he couldn't prevent the film busting its budget, Parker won most of the other battles and, enraged, made the disastrous decision to make two pictures with budget-conscious Katzman. Ironically, *Viva Las Vegas* is one of nine Presley movies in which the Colonel is not credited as technical advisor.

The true relationship between Presley and Parker is one of the most mysterious in popular culture. The most likely explanation for the Colonel's dominance—that, offstage, Presley lacked the confidence to confront such a

Colonel Tom Parker and Elvis on the set of *Love Me Tender* (1956). Parker soon made it emphatically clear how he saw his relationship with his client.   *Photofest*

powerful character and was also reluctant to do so because of his morbid fear that he would fall back into the poverty of his youth—is too prosaic for many, who prefer to speculate about blackmail and other dark arts. Depending on whom you believe, Parker may have threatened to reveal the family secret (Vernon Presley's conviction for fraud), compromising photographs of the star, or the terrible details of a stunt involving three midgets, a human cannonball, and the roof of Ellis Auditorium in Memphis. Others—notably Steve Binder, the producer of the 1968 TV special, have a simpler explanation: "I swear the Colonel hypnotized Elvis."

Although their partnership endured for more than twenty-one years, it did so, in part, because they kept out of each other's way as much as possible. Cast and crew on Presley's movies didn't see Parker that often, but many have testified that a visit from his larger-than-life, cigar-chomping manager usually didn't improve the star's mood.

Every eccentricity, flaw, and mistake in Presley's life has been chronicled, dissected, and often overhyped. Parker remained relatively unscathed—even in the Steve Dunleavy tabloid hatchet job *Elvis: What Happened?*—until Nash's 2002 biography depicted him as an obsessive-compulsive tyrannical genius with a serious gambling addiction who had been certified as psychopathic by a military doctor and, according to his onetime aide Byron Raphael, was obsessed by his own feces.

After Presley's death, Parker declared: "Yes, I did love him"—an enigmatic statement that tacitly admitted the issue was, publicly at least, in some doubt. Yet *love* is too simple a word for what Parker felt for Presley. There was resentment, obsession, jealousy, exasperation, and anguish in there too. Raphael recalls Parker's reaction when Elvis forgot his birthday on June 26, 1957. After a party to mark the event, Raphael stayed over with the Parkers and was woken by, as he put it to Nash: "These horrible sounds . . . like an animal wailing, the strangest sound I ever heard in my life." The crying lasted all night long and when the aide raised the issue with Parker's wife Marie, she shrugged: "Oh I don't know, Elvis forgot the Colonel's birthday." Stunned by the reaction to the oversight, Raphael got word to Elvis, who have him a ring and instructions to say he just hadn't been able to deliver a gift in time. As a supreme con artist, Parker wasn't deceived.

Whatever kind of technical advice Parker provided for Presley's movies, it is clear that he was hardly a disinterested professional. Maybe the answer to the mystery of how rock's most charismatic star came to sleepwalk his way through such fluff as *Paradise, Hawaiian Style* lies in his extraordinarily complex relationship with his manager.

8

Roads Not Taken

Although Al Jolson's success in *The Jazz Singer* (1927) triumphantly established that popular vocalists could sell cinema tickets, Bing Crosby (1903–1977) made a career proving the point, starring in fifty-five full-length pictures between 1932 and 1971, and became the fourth-most-popular box-office draw of all time. From 1944 to 1948, he was voted the top box-office attraction in Quigley's annual poll of exhibitors.

In many of these films—from his first major feature *The Big Broadcast* (1932) to *Mississippi* (1935) and *White Christmas* (1954)—he played an idealized version of himself, an easygoing, self-mocking crooner in feel-good fare that helped lift America's spirits in the 1930s and 1940s as the nation struggled with the Great Depression and World War II. Elvis was one of the millions who flocked to the cinemas to watch Crosby and set aside, for a while, the worries of everyday life. Yet Bing broke with the formula often enough to win an Oscar as genial Father O'Malley in *Going My Way* (1944). He was nominated for reprising the role in *The Bells of St. Mary's* (1945), but the performance that really merited recognition from the Academy was his turn as the broken-down actor in Clifford Odets's poignant drama *The Country Girl* (1954). He also made sure to showcase himself alongside other stars (notably Bob Hope in the Road series) to maintain his broad appeal. In 1956, he teamed up with Frank Sinatra, Grace Kelly, and Louis Armstrong in *High Society*. Four years later, he was starring alongside teen idol Fabian and Tuesday Weld, Presley's co-star in *Wild in the Country*, in Blake Edwards's college comedy *High Time*. In 1964, he had a movie-stealing turn in the Rat Pack musical comedy *Robin and the 7 Hoods*. His last major film was a remake of *Stagecoach* (1966) in which he elicited better notices as the drunken doctor than the movie itself garnered.

Crosby proved that, if you picked the right roles more often than not—and you made enough musicals with decent songs—you could dominate both the box-office charts and the record charts. His films popularized many of his most famous songs, such as his biggest hit, "White Christmas" (which sold an all-time record 50 million units as a single), "Swing on a Star" (in *Going My Way*), "Sweet Leilani" (a lilting ballad in *Waikiki Wedding*), and "True Love" (a duet with Grace

Kelly from *High Society* that was his last big hit). No actor-singer has enjoyed as much artistic—and commercial—success in the movie industry as Crosby.

That was the model Frank Sinatra (1915–1998) aspired to. He wasn't quite as successful but probably enjoyed his movie career more than Presley did. In his first proper role, in the enjoyable musical *Higher and Higher* (1943), he played himself. When Michele Morgan hears a knock on the door and asks who's there, he answers, "Frank Sinatra," in the Hoboken-tinged tones that would become famous around the world. Ten years later, his portrayal of Private Angelo Maggio in *From Here to Eternity* earned him an Oscar for Best Supporting Actor. He was nominated again for his convincing portrayal of a card dealer struggling to conquer drug addiction in *The Man with the Golden Arm* (1955).

For Sinatra, *From Here to Eternity* wasn't just an Oscar-winning role, it was a career-saving piece of casting. A run of musicals in which Sinatra often played the man who wasn't quite as interesting as Gene Kelly had exhausted his box-office appeal. After an operation on his vocal cords, he wasn't even sure he would sing again. After hearing that original choice Eli Wallach couldn't get out of an obligation to play on Broadway, Sinatra inundated Harry Cohn, who ran Columbia Studios, with letters and telegrams pleading for the role. The fact that he accepted a fee of just $8,000 to play Maggio is a mark of Ol' Blue Eyes' determination and desperation. The move paid off. Learning more about acting from co-star Montgomery Clift than any of his previous directors, Sinatra excelled as the Italian G.I., giving what the *New York Times* praised as a "characterization rich in comic vitality and genuine pathos."

Emboldened by that success, Sinatra recorded a string of classic, commercially successful albums with such arrangers as Nelson Riddle and Billy May, reinventing himself as a singer, perfecting his phrasing, and becoming an icon of late-night cool on such albums as *In the Wee Small Hours* (1955), his best-selling album in eight years and acclaimed by *Rolling Stone* as one of the greatest albums of all time.

There is a popular misconception that Sinatra spent most of his Hollywood career starring in Rat Pack buddy pictures with his pals Dean Martin and Sammy Davis Jr. Yet in the 1950s, that was far from the case. Inspired by Clift's example, he made a string of impressive dramas—*Suddenly* (1954), *Not as a Stranger* (1955), *The Man with the Golden Arm*, *Pal Joey* (1957, winning a Golden Globe for his role as a charming womanizer), and Vincente Minnelli's ambitious, if flawed, *Some Came Running* (1958). Even after Sinatra made his first Rat Pack movie, *Ocean's Eleven*, in 1960, he was utterly believable in a difficult straight role in John Frankenheimer's political psychodrama *The Manchurian Candidate* (1962). Sadly, that was probably the last truly noteworthy film Sinatra ever appeared in. After that, he made some more Rat Pack films (the worst being the pointless *4 For Texas* in 1963) and, by the end of the decade, looked even more out of touch than Elvis in the below-par detective movie *Lady in Cement* (1968). After the misunderstood semi-serious western *Dirty Dingus Magee* (1970), his Hollywood career was effectively over.

One aspect of his movie career directly inspired Presley. The star was rather taken with the crooner's debonair suits, designed especially for him by "tailor to the stars" Sy Devore. He was dressed by Devore in *It Happened at the World's Fair* and regularly dropped into the tailor's store on Vine Street, near Sunset Boulevard, ordering fifteen suits at a time—all size regular 42—when he was working in Hollywood.

Something else Sinatra and Presley had in common was their awed idolization of Dean Martin (1917–1995). The crooner was as laid-back as he appeared, often distant to friends, family, and co-stars, never caring what anyone thought of him. His movie career offers an intriguing parallel to Elvis's, because he started out with the same producer, Wallis, as an underrated straight man to Jerry Lewis. The duo were the top box-office attraction in 1952, and, although their appeal began to wane as their partnership soured, they remained among the top ten box-office acts between 1951 and 1956. Sensing his duo was drifting apart, Wallis was on the lookout for a new celebrity by 1956 and, after seeing the King on TV, decided to invest in Presley.

When Martin and Lewis split, everyone expected the manic comedian to flourish. Dino's prospects were less rosy. He looked affable but lost in the flimsy romantic comedy *Ten Thousand Bedrooms* (1957), produced by Pasternak and directed by Richard Thorpe, who worked with Elvis that same year on *Jailhouse Rock*. Like Sinatra with *From Here to Eternity*, Dino decided to gamble and accepted the part of a Broadway showman pulled into the army against his will in Edward Dmytryk's adaptation of Irwin Shaw's *The Young Lions*. Although Bosley Crowther sniffed that Dino played his role as if "he was lonesome for Jerry Lewis and didn't know exactly what to do," most critics were impressed. Though Dino played down his performance—"I just played myself, a likeable coward"—the part changed Hollywood's perceptions of him.

Though Sinatra's movie career is better known—and he won Oscars and Golden Globes, which Martin was never even nominated for—Dino was the bigger all-time box-office attraction. He dutifully appeared in the Rat Pack films, but he also impressed in *Some Came Running* (1958) and found his true genre, the western, with a fine turn opposite John Wayne in *Rio Bravo* (1958). Although he publicly conveyed the impression that he spent every waking leisure hour partying in Las Vegas, Martin liked nothing better than to retire to his apartment and watch a few horse operas.

In the 1960s, he was best known for the Matt Helm spy-spoof series (an obvious influence on Mike Myers's Austin Powers) but gave his best performance in Billy Wilder's *Kiss Me Stupid* (1964), sending himself up superbly as a drunken, arrogant, lecherous crooner. That same year, he knocked the Beatles off the number 1 spot in the United States with "Everybody Loves Somebody," a song that became one of his musical trademarks. (Elvis even sang a few lines when his idol came to see him in Vegas.)

By 1967, Martin was one of the top ten box-office attractions, a ranking Presley and Sinatra had slipped out of. He had learned to act with what Roger

Sinatra, Crosby, and Dino got more fun—and plaudits—out of their movies than Elvis.

Ebert characterized as "smooth confidence," gently underplaying in such westerns as *5 Card Stud* (1968), although, in a nod to his offscreen image, he invariably seemed to have a glass of whisky in his hand. His last big success was as the pilot in the disaster movie *Airport* (1970). Although he returned for the Burt Reynolds capers *Cannonball Run* and *Cannonball Run II*, in 1980–81, he had lost interest in movies by then—and the cinemagoing audience had lost interest in him. Although, like Sinatra, Martin played opposite Montgomery Clift (in *The Young Lions*), he was no Method actor, observing once: "Motivation is a lot of crap."

In 1956, Presley emerged as a potent challenger to the showbiz status quo, as epitomized by Crosby, Sinatra, and, to a lesser degree, Martin. His success made it harder for their music to find an audience, a development Crosby gracefully acknowledged, saying: "He helped to kill off the influence of me and my contemporaries, but I respect him for that. Music has to progress and no one could have opened the door to the future like he did."

Yet when Elvis came to Hollywood, the precedents set by Crosby, Sinatra, and Martin would influence his career. Queenan has insisted: "Elvis was never in a class with crossover artists like Sinatra and Dean Martin; they knew how to lighten up and enjoy themselves on the big screen." There is some merit in Queenan's claim, although Presley does—perhaps because he realizes the game is up—look relaxed in his later work, notably *Stay Away, Joe* and *The Trouble with Girls*. In his best films—*King Creole* and *Flaming Star*—lightening up probably wouldn't have helped his performance or the movies. And given the right care, Elvis could have perfected the kind of nonchalant reliability that made Martin, who had a modest talent for acting, so successful.

Though he aspired to be the new Brando, it was always more likely, given Hollywood's eye for golden opportunities, that Presley would have to sing. The initial idea that he might star alongside Burt Lancaster and Katharine Hepburn in *The Rainmaker*—a move that might have immediately introduced him to a much broader audience—fell through and he was cast in *Love Me Tender*. That set the tone for most of the next thirty-two films. Apart from *King Creole, Flaming Star*, and *Wild in the Country*, the studios and producers would make no real attempt to establish Presley as a true movie star who could carry a movie even if he didn't carry a tune. To the powers that be, the obvious question was probably: why bother? He was already the fourth-biggest box-office draw in 1957, so why fix a formula that wasn't broken?

Presley never enjoyed the same kind of control of his movie career as any of the crooners. So, although he worked with some of the same directors (George Sidney, Gordon Douglas) and producers (Crosby, Martin, and Presley all made films for Wallis), his roles were far less diverse and, with a few significant exceptions, he worked with less talented actors and writers. Parker's insistence on top billing for his boy scuppered some promising projects—notably a part in Robert Mitchum's moonshine movie *Thunder Road*—and ensured he would never be tested/inspired by working in a stellar ensemble cast.

When Wallis made *The Sons of Katie Elder*, the John Wayne western, the only way he could persuade Dino to star was to give him script approval and delay production for four months. The crooner proved a much tougher negotiator than Parker, who didn't always exert the right to approve scripts on Elvis's behalf. It may be that in Hollywood, even more than in the music industry, Presley needed to be more forceful and open, as Sinatra and Martin had been, to truly fulfill his dream. Hiding behind the Memphis Mafia didn't always help. Though they helped assuage his insecurity, they screened him from the movie business and alienated many Hollywood insiders. A more direct engagement on set with co-stars and directors might have helped him integrate in Hollywood, attract a different kind of part, and boost his self-confidence. That wasn't his way, and he paid the price.

After a promising start, Presley's films soon settled into a musical-comedy rut where every movie had to promote a soundtrack album. He was unlucky that he was drafted as soon as *King Creole* had been filmed. The creative momentum behind that movie—and his acting career—had dissipated by the time he returned in 1960 and made the innocuous but entertaining *G.I. Blues*.

Presley tried to escape the trap, but, unlike with Sinatra and Martin, his gambles on dramatic roles didn't pay off. The problem was not so much the movies themselves—*Flaming Star* was especially good—but with the way they were marketed and cast. In neither *Flaming Star* nor *Wild in the Country* did he play alongside the kind of star name that might have signaled to non-Presley fans that these were different kinds of pictures. That was a blow to Elvis, who grew as an actor when working with Don Siegel on *Flaming Star*. The western genre seemed to suit him too—if not quite as snugly as it did Dino. The mere fact that Presley was transposed to a different time and place, putting a distance between his performance and his rock-star persona, seemed to help him grow as an actor. The relative commercial failure condemned him to make films as mindless as *4 For Texas*. By the time he was given more interesting roles—from 1968 onward—his fans, the studios, and sometimes even the star himself had lost interest.

Sinatra, as his signature song put it, did it his way in Hollywood. So, to differing degrees, had Crosby and Martin. Although Elvis later adopted Paul Anka's self-glorifying ballad, the truth is that in Hollywood he didn't do it his way. For the most part, he did it the Colonel's way. Interestingly, the one time Presley did rebel he was inspired by Crosby. In February 1957, recording the *Loving You* soundtrack at Radio Recorders in Hollywood, Elvis was asked to record a children's song, "Here Comes Peter Cottontail." Spotting the lyrics on his music stand, Presley said, "Who brought that Brer Rabbit shit in here?" Insisting he wasn't going to sing it, he burst into a chorus of "True Love," recently a big hit for Bing. Presley's beautifully chilled rendition of the Cole Porter classic was later released on EP. If he had been inspired to exert such influence more often, he might have enjoyed as productive a film career as his idols.

9

Directing Elvis

The Twenty-two Men Who Shouted, "Lights, Camera, Action," on a Presley Movie

There we no auteurs in the director's chair when Elvis was on set. Only a few of his directors—notably Michael Curtiz, George Sidney, Don Siegel, and possibly Peter Tewksbury—could be said to have a recognizable artistic vision or a trademark style. Most of them were chosen because—like Norman Taurog and Richard "One Take" Thorpe—they could be relied to do a job. And a job is what they did, albeit with dramatically different levels of satisfaction.

Robert D. Webb (1903–1990)

Elvis's first director faced the toughest challenge. When he sat down on the set of *Love Me Tender* in August 1956, he didn't know if Presley could act. Yet he did his best to put his star at ease, running through key scenes between takes, breaking down the lines to give his star breathing points, and helping the young tyro to visualize the action ahead. The work paid off in the sense that, whatever the critics said, Presley's debut was no disaster. Teri Garr, who later appeared in nine of his movies, said of his performance: "He was on the edge there and did some acting that was quite great."

Almost forgotten today, Webb was not a flashy director, but he was seldom without an assignment between 1953 and 1961, his golden era. Immediately before *Love Me Tender*, he had made *The Proud Ones*, a creditable psychological western starring Robert Ryan as a lawman struggling with villains and bouts of blindness that is probably his best feature film. His sea-sponge-diving yarn *Beneath the 12-Mile Reef* (1953) was nominated for the Cannes prize primarily on the strength of Bernard Herrmann's magnificent score and the beautiful cinematography.

Webb never quite made it to the top in Hollywood. He was second-unit director on such prestige pictures as *The Agony and the Ecstasy* (1965) and won an Oscar as Best Assistant Director for *In Old Chicago* (1937), in which Don Ameche and Tyrone Power are feuding brothers on the eve of the city's great fire. Yet Elvis could probably have asked for no better director on his first film.

Hal Kanter (1918–2011)

Though he had never directed a movie before *Loving You*, Kanter was no novice. He had written dialogue for *Road to Bali* (1952), adapted Tennessee Williams for the screenplay for the Oscar-winning *The Rose Tattoo* (1955), and, like almost everyone else who knew Wallis, been conscripted into helping him promote Dean Martin and Jerry Lewis, writing the script for *Artists and Models* (1955).

So when Wallis made his first Presley picture, Kanter seemed a reasonably safe bet—and the fact that he could write and direct would save the producer a bit of money. (Bear in mind that, at this point, Hollywood still wasn't sure if Presley's popularity was a fad.) Kanter cheerfully accepted his mission. Compared to many of Presley's other directors, he was granted unprecedented access to the star, following him on tour so he could craft a movie that reflected, albeit in a distorted, sentimentalized fashion, the singer's rise. Humor was one of Kanter's strengths, and he leavened the music and the sentiment with enough comedy to make *Loving You* one of Presley's most enjoyable movies. He even pulled off the difficult feat of celebrating his star, using a lot of shadows to emphasize his iconic status, while gently exposing some of the ploys used to sell such acts to the masses.

Kanter liked Elvis, although he found their relationship very ephemeral. Many years later he recalled an incident when he gave the King a black suede shirt. When they next met in Hollywood and Elvis was wearing the shirt, Kanter said to him, "Hey, that's a great-looking shirt. Where'd you get that?" To which Elvis replied: "Oh, some fan gave it to me." Kanter saw this as proof of the star's superficiality—it didn't even occur to him that Presley might have been teasing him.

After *Loving You*, Kanter was back in the exploitation trade, directing TV stars George Gobel in *I Married a Woman* (1958) and Rowan and Martin in *Once upon a Horse* (1958). He never directed another movie after that, but he did keep writing screenplays, with *Pocketful of Miracles* (1961) and *Move Over Darling* (1964) probably being the standouts. In 1961, Wallis called him in to rewrite the *Blue Hawaii* script. He met Elvis again and couldn't believe how his personality had changed. To Kanter, Elvis looked like a man who was ashamed of the songs he was singing and the movies he was making but had begun to realize he was trapped.

Richard Thorpe (1896–1991)

Loved by moguls like MGM boss Louis B. Mayer, "One Take" Thorpe was one of the most prolific directors in Hollywood. He stopped the cameras only if an actor fluffed his lines (which he usually took as the cue for a close-up reaction shot), prided himself on bringing pictures in under budget, and could turn his hand to anything: Tarzan, Elvis, or historical romps like *Ivanhoe*.

With a real name like Rollo Smolt Thorpe, some kind of alias was a professional necessity, especially if you were going to make westerns in Hollywood in the 1920s. Style was not something he never thought about, so, although the likes of Mayer would always keep him busy, he was not often trusted with the big blockbusters. Even when he was asked to remake *The Prisoner of Zenda* (1952), he created what was virtually a shot-for-shot re-creation of John Cromwell's 1937 original.

So the choice of Thorpe for *Jailhouse Rock* does suggest that producer Pandro Berman's initial priority was to stick to the budget. On set, Thorpe gave his star little guidance, and Presley began asking assistant director Bob Relyea for suggestions. Thorpe's brand of remote cordiality did the trick, however, as Elvis gave one of his best performances. (At this point in his movie career, he was still keen enough to study the daily rushes.) The end result isn't exactly stylish in any aesthetic sense, but it is certainly compelling. The same, alas, cannot always be said for Thorpe's next Elvis film, *Fun in Acapulco*.

The fun there is to be had in the musical—apart from spotting the amateurish use of blue screen—comes from Larry Domasin's boyish manager and Elvis's sharp performance of "Bossa Nova Baby." The choice of Thorpe, instead of Wallis's usual Presley director Taurog, may indicate that the producer had already begun looking to save money after *Girls! Girls! Girls!* failed to deliver the same boffo box office as Blue Hawaii. Four years later, Thorpe made his 185th—and last—film, the decent western *The Pistolero of Red River*.

Today he is probably best known for *Jailhouse Rock* and for his brief reign in the director's chair on *The Wizard of Oz*. His vision for Dorothy included a blond wig and cutesy baby-doll makeup. Luckily, George Cukor talked him out of it.

Michael Curtiz (1886–1962)

"Where ees he? Where the hell ees that son-of-a-bitch motherfucker?" This was certainly not how Presley hoped to be greeted when he reported for duty on *King Creole*. Yet for Curtiz, a wayward genius who had entered the entertainment industry by running away to the circus in his native Hungary, this was par for the course. When the director put the megaphone down, he was disarmed by a polite young Presley who stuck out his hand and said, "Pleased to meet you, sir!"

Curtiz had a long, storied, and successful career in Hollywood, winning the Best Director Oscar for *Casablanca* and trying his hand at virtually every genre. He almost invented the sitcom with William Powell in *Life with Father* (1947) and made such indispensable Hollywood classics as *Angels with Dirty Faces* (1938), *Mildred Pierce* (1945), *The Adventures of Robin Hood* (1938), and *Yankee Doodle Dandy* (1942). Throughout all those films, there was one constant: he didn't usually get along with his actors. Yet he loved Presley—they had similar libidos, although Elvis was more discreet—and, after he had showed the star he was boss, they got along famously. Curtiz shrewdly boosted Presley's morale when he was shooting scenes with such gifted, experienced actors as Matthau and Jones. By the time *King Creole* had finished, Curtiz had grown quite proud of "Elvy" and his development as an actor. For an actor who could be so reticent, uncertain of his worth, Presley flourished under the director's tuition.

Curtiz was criticized for not worrying about plot—not always a disadvantage in Hollywood—and caring only about the visuals, yet he often used his style to highlight the way his characters were trapped by fate and their environment. Like Danny Fisher, many of Curtiz's protagonists were morally divided and their choice, as it is in *King Creole,* was at the heart of those movies. And unlike in many of Presley's later films, Curtiz's passion ensured that *King Creole* never lacked energy. He liked to say: "Who cares about character? I go so fast nobody notices," which was funny but not really true. Think of the simplicity with which he tells a complex story in *Casablanca.*

Presley was sorry to see Curtiz go and could have worked with the director again on *G.I. Blues.* Yet by 1960, the filmmaker was obviously ill and he died in 1962.

Curtiz and Wallis worked closely with Elvis on *King Creole* (1958)—with inspiring results.

Paramount Pictures/Photofest

Norman Taurog (1899–1981)

"Mr. Taurog doesn't watch the clock, is a hard worker and knows what he's doing." That's how Parker recommended that the veteran filmmaker, who had made *G.I. Blues*, should return for *Blue Hawaii*. The clinching argument, for Parker, was that "Taurog . . . works very well with Elvis. Elvis has great respect for him." And that is how it probably came to pass that a former successful child actor, who had made his first movie (a short called *The Fly Cop*) in the silent era—and won his Best Director Oscar in 1931 for *Skippy*, an adaptation of the comic strip about a mischievous but well-intentioned boy—came to direct nine Presley pictures, more than any other director.

In Peter Buskin's *Easy Riders, Raging Bulls*, there is a fascinating vignette of Taurog at the time he was making *Double Trouble*. Producer Irwin Winkler shocked Parker by asking to meet the director and was ordered to be in front of the Thalberg Building the next day at 11:00 a.m. Winkler did as he was told and was astonished to see an elderly gentleman totter out of a car. When Winkler congratulated him on having a chauffeur, Taurog replied: "I'd like to drive myself, but I can't see in one eye and the other one's going real fast." (At this point, he still had three Presley movies to complete: *Double Trouble*, *Speedway*, and *Live a Little, Love a Little*.) There is an agenda behind the anecdote—Biskind wanted young turks like Coppola and Scorsese to sweep out Hollywood's old guard—but the story does suggest how far Presley's stock had fallen.

The image of the doddery old gentleman is slightly deceptive too. Taurog had always known when to be tough on set. On *Skippy*, when his nephew Jackie Coogan couldn't cry on demand, he threatened to take the boy's pooch to the dog pound. He wasn't as threatening on Presley's movies, but he still knew when to lay down the law, often insisting that Presley could try one more take.

Despite his antics on the set of *Skippy*, Taurog was regarded as a competent craftsman who worked well with animals and children. The archetypal contract studio director, Taurog made over 180 pictures, yet only 4 stand out: *Skippy*, *Boys Town* (starring Spencer Tracy as a priest building a home for orphaned boys and earning the director an Oscar nomination), *The Adventures of Tom Sawyer*, and *Jumping Jacks* (his first Martin and Lewis vehicle, widely considered their best film). *Room for One More* (1952), his family comedy starring Cary Grant, is ripe for reevaluation.

To Presley's movies, he brought a professional focus, a work ethic, and a preference for sight gags that, by the late 1960s, began to feel incredibly dated. His involvement with Presley probably extended his career, and he killed time between Elvis pics with such ephemera as *Sergeant Deadhead* and *Dr. Goldfoot and the Bikini Machine* (both 1965).

Though Hoey had his reservations about Taurog's comedy, he defended him as a "talented director with a marvelous sense of story." Others were less impressed. Gene De Ruelle, the second assistant director on *Double Trouble*, said the director reminded him of golfer Lee Trevino's quote: "The older I get, the better I used to be." In his view, "He was engrossed in himself. By and large, if the actors didn't mis-take and the camera was okay, he printed."

That doesn't seem entirely fair. You may not like what Taurog is doing, but usually it's hard to fault him for effort. His best Presley films—*Blue Hawaii, It Happened at the World's Fair, G.I. Blues*—have an easy momentum that's hard to resist. Even on *Tickle Me, Spinout,* and *Double Trouble,* you never get the sense that he's phoning in his direction. To see what those nine films could have been without Taurog's involvement, just watch *Paradise, Hawaiian Style.*

By the time Winkler met him on *Double Trouble,* even he was beginning to chafe at the absurdities involved in obliging his star to play the same carefree, twentysomething bachelor in movie after movie. He even suggested new kinds

Elvis, Robert Ivers, and director Norman Taurog on the set of *G. I. Blues* (1960). Taurog directed nine Elvis movies but never felt he got the most out of the star.   *Paramount Pictures/Photofest*

of scripts to Presley, and his last film, *Live a Little, Love a Little*, as uneven as it is, is a commendable attempt to update the King's image. He retired in 1968 and became a director of the Braille Institute in Los Angeles.

Don Siegel (1912–1991)

For a director with a reputation for being difficult, Siegel quickly came to terms with the bombshell that his next western would be starring Presley, not Brando. Yet in his memoirs he makes it clear that this was a challenging shoot. Once he had staved off the studio's demands for ten songs, his main challenge was his star, as he admitted he "had a problem communicating with Elvis."

Siegel found it difficult to separate the star from his entourage. He didn't know that Presley, whose insecurity often flared up on movie sets, became convinced that the director was looking down on him, his karate, his cars, and his friends. The rare times when director and star were alone, Siegel felt they clicked, but that happened so infrequently that he decided never to do another Presley picture. That was a shame, because as the hypercritical David Thomson acknowledges in his *Biographical Dictionary of Film*, Elvis "gives a genuine performance in *Flaming Star.*"

Siegel had entered the movie business in the 1930s, initially as a librarian. He then worked as assistant editor, created a montage department, and directed his first full-length movie, *The Verdict* (1946). By learning all these trades, Siegel became an extremely effective director—he could manage fifty-five single-camera setups in a day—and this helped him overcome budget constraints and lack of shooting time as he sought to create films that suited his vision. Soon after that, he took the risky step of going freelance. He couldn't always find work, but when he did it could be as good, as in *Riot in Cell Block 11* (1954), *Invasion of the Bodysnatchers* (1956), *The Killers* (1964), *Dirty Harry* (1971), *The Beguiled* (1971), and *Charley Varrick* (1973).

Flaming Star isn't quite in that class, but Elvis's Pacer Burton is another fine example of Siegel's predilection for protagonists who are, as Richard Combs notes, "an unarguably consistent line of defiant loners, outside whatever system may be operating," who may move, interchangeably, between one side and the other.

After the comparative commercial failure of *Flaming Star*, Siegel's star waned, and it took a collaboration over four movies with Clint Eastwood—the best being the least commercially successful, the Gothic horror *The Beguiled*—to reestablish himself in Hollywood. He returned to the western to make John Wayne's final movie, *The Shootist* (1976), but his last great film was the amoral thriller *Charley Varrick*, in which the eponymous laconic antihero (played by Walter Matthau) robs a bank that turns out to have been holding Mafia drug money.

Philip Dunne (1908–1992)

"I hope Elvis Presley realized before he died that he took full advantage of Clifford Odets' poetic material," Dunn wrote in his memoirs, *Take Two*, recalling the making of *Wild in the Country*. In the same book, he claimed the credit for persuading Presley to appreciate the music of Johann Sebastian Bach.

Those claims give the measure of the man. A good filmmaker, though not as good as he liked to think he was, Dunne was never short of an opinion about movies or politics—and his outspoken liberal views made him a likely candidate for the blacklist at the height of the McCarthy era. Yet Dunne kept working, writing one or two movies a year for much of the 1950s and directing his first film, *Prince of Players*, in 1955, in which Richard Burton was intriguingly cast as the brother of Lincoln's assassin, John Wilkes Booth.

Wild in the Country was his eighth film and arguably his toughest assignment. The studio couldn't decide whether Elvis would sing or not, Odets had been fired after failing to complete a three-hundred-page script, and budgets were impinging on casting. Faced with such a mess, Dunne did a pretty decent salvage operation, coaxing some strong performances out of Lange and Weld. He had been apprehensive about working with Presley but soon decided the star had a flair for Odets's inimitable dialogue. "I began to dream that between us we were creating a new dramatic star," he said. The performance he draws out of Presley isn't as consistent as the star's turn in *King Creole*, but it looks better with each passing year. What Dunne lacked was a sense of pace, and, at 114 minutes, the picture came in 10 minutes too long for its own good.

Dunne didn't create a new dramatic star, but he did give Elvis one of his most satisfying roles of the 1960s. He made only two more movies. His next film, *The Inspector* (1962), in which Dolores Hart starred as a Jew wanting to be smuggled into Palestine, was nominated for a Golden Globe as best drama. His finale was the classy light thriller *Blindfold* (1965). That same year, he wrote *The Agony and the Ecstasy*, his last screenplay, after being told to make Michelangelo fit Charlton Heston, who was, so studio boss Darryl Zanuck maintained, "the only American actor who can wear a toga." That may have been the final straw, as Dunne gradually drifted out of the movie business and became a syndicated columnist.

Gordon Douglas (1907–1993)

"Don't try to watch all the movies I have directed. It would turn you off movies forever." Douglas was being unduly modest when he said that—he did, after all, make the sci-fi masterpiece *Them!* (1954)—but that was his style.

A child actor, a gag writer for Hal Roach, a director of budget films for RKO, Douglas only really found his niche at Warner Brothers, where between 1950 and 1965, he directed some of the most entertaining American movies of the era. Some of them—like *Follow That Dream*—were made for other studios. The other highpoints of this era were the Frank Sinatra/Doris Day drama *Young at Heart* (1954) and *Come Fill the Cup* (1951), a memorable drama about alcoholism in which James Cagney, Gig Young, and James Gleason all shone. The low point was the hysterical red-baiting *I Was a Communist for the FBI* (1951), on the poster for which the star said: "I had to sell out my own girl . . . so would you."

Douglas accommodated Sinatra on *Young at Heart*, allowing him not to die (as John Garfield had in the original, *Four Daughters*), to replace the cinematographer, and to sing the same number of songs as Day. Placated, Sinatra would later invite the director to make four other pictures, most notably *Robin and the Seven Hoods* (1964) and *The Detective* (1968).

Perhaps trying to suss out if Presley had similar demands, he caused consternation on the set of *Follow That Dream*, by inviting Elvis out for dinner. A horrified Parker quickly explained that Presley was not comfortable having dinner one-to-one, so Douglas invited the whole entourage. This is another of those moments where it is hard not to wish that Presley had had the nerve to get out of his comfort zone. That misunderstanding over, director and star got on reasonably well. Presley played his role straight as "Gordie" directed him to. The end result is one of the few Elvis films from the 1960s that nonfans can watch without wincing.

Douglas was in reasonable demand until the mid-1970s, signing off in 1977 with the appalling biopic *Viva Knievel*, in which the stuntman shares the screen with a thoroughly unlikely cast that includes Gene Kelly, Leslie Nielsen, and Red Button and an even more unlikely plot in which the motorcycling hero takes on drug dealers who threaten truth, apple pie, and the American way. If you watch that film, it really will put you off movies for life.

Phil Karlson (1908–1985)

The Phenix City Story (1955) was good enough to change Karlson's life. Shooting in semi-documentary style in the quarter that had earned this burg in Alabama the tabloid label "Sin City," Karlson overcomes his meager budget to create a classic noir with Edward Andrews (Elvis's handyman in *The Trouble with Girls*) strolling the streets blithely as the crime boss. Yet mysteriously, that didn't lift Karlson out of the B-movie ranks. Nor did *Kansas City Confidential* (1952), *99 River Street* (1953), or *Scandal Sheet* (1952), which were almost as good in the same gritty, tough, realistic vein.

Yet Karlson, who had started out as an assistant director on the Abbot and Costello movies, kept plugging away. He was a reliable filmmaker, easy to get on with, and seemed—to studio boss Walter Mirisch—the ideal choice to direct Presley in a remake of *Kid Galahad*. The star didn't agree, preferring Curtiz, who had directed the original, but once the choice was confirmed, he threw himself into the role, the boxing, and countless on-set karate contests. Karlson encouraged his star to ad-lib and was delighted when Presley and his sparring partners started trading real punches in some fight scenes. The end result doesn't quite hang together, but it is entertaining enough. The director and star had one thing in common. Unit production manager Bob Relyea insisted they were two of the sweetest people in Hollywood.

After *Kid Galahad*, Karlson made a couple of Matt Helm flicks with Dino but really hit the jackpot with *Walking Tall* (1973), in which Joe Don Baker excels as the not-so-nice guy who decides he has to clear the crooks out of his Tennessee town. The picture was a surprise hit and, as he owned a large slice of it, made Karlson suddenly wealthy. He retired a couple of years later. Crime had always been his forte—he had studied law before coming to Hollywood—and it paid off spectacularly in the end.

Gene Nelson (1920–1996)

"I didn't become the star I wanted to be," was Nelson's honest verdict on a career that would have seemed remarkable to most. He played Will Parker, the high-stepping lasso dancer in *Oklahoma* (1955), won a Tony award for an acrobatic 1930s-style dance solo in the 1971 Broadway production of *Follies*, and worked with Doris Day in *Tea for Two* (1950). Yet all was not was as triumphant as it seemed: in musicals, he usually lost the girl to Gordon MacRae, and when he did turn to directing, he made two of Elvis's most ridiculed movies: *Kissin' Cousins* and *Harum Scarum*.

The dismal reception of *Harum Scarum* was especially painful because Nelson loved directing. "I was happier directing than I've ever been doing anything else. That form of creativity is very rewarding and I liked it a lot," he said once, admitting that that aspect of his career was "incomplete."

Nelson's first movie in the director's chair was a low-budget horror called *Hand of Death* (1962). His first film for Katzman, *Hootenanny Hoot* (1963), though a thinly disguised excuse for the likes of Johnny Cash and Sheb Wooley to strut their stuff, was significantly better. His Hank Williams biopic, *Your Cheatin' Heart* (1964), with George Hamilton—not Elvis—as the doomed country singer was Nelson's first really good movie. Some critics insist it was his last.

On *Kissin' Cousins* and *Harum Scarum*, he was hampered by ridiculously tight shooting schedules, absurd stories, and below-par songs. Though Presley empathized with him, he was distracted by the pressure and, on *Kissin' Cousins*, the sense that this was the first movie he would be genuinely ashamed of. By the time Nelson and Presley teamed up again for *Harum Scarum*, the star looked resigned to his fate, sensing that the movie was so bad it was pointless to argue.

Two years later, Nelson redeemed himself with *The Cool Ones*, an amusing sendup of the music industry and TV shows like *Shindig* and *Hullabaloo*. It isn't great, but it is competent and it has Roddy McDowall playing an egotistical record tycoon (modeled on Phil Spector) and lots of songs. Sadly, it wasn't enough to save Nelson's reputation as a film director.

George Sidney (1916–2002)

One of the greatest exponents of the Hollywood musical, Sidney was the man behind such classics as *Anchors Aweigh* (in which he pioneered the pairing of live actors and cartoon characters), *Show Boat*, *Pal Joey*, and *Kiss Me Kate*. He also helped his good friends William Hanna and Joseph Barbera launch their company after MGM closed its animation studio in 1957. In the 1940s, he launched the career of Hollywood's favorite mermaid Esther Williams and, in the early 1960s, did more than anyone—apart from the actress herself—to make Ann-Margret a star, investing $60,000 of his own money to commission a title song for *Bye Bye Birdie* and to film her sensational rendition of it.

Hired to direct an Elvis film, Sidney almost turned *Viva Las Vegas* into an Ann-Margret film. He certainly succeeded in, as Tony Pellum noted on the blog Flickdom Dictum, "fleshing out one of the most complete female characters in the Elvis oeuvre—one who can hold her own scenes and musical numbers with Elvis nowhere in sight." Of course, the fact that such a spirited, sexy creature eventually succumbs to Elvis only underlines the presentation of the King as an unstoppable force.

Sidney's craft means that some moments—notably the title song and the moody "I Need Somebody to Lean On"—are a class above the presentation of such material in any other Presley film. Some of the scenes—like the "What'd I Say" sequence, added at the last minute by Sidney—don't really have any purpose other than to celebrate Ann-Margret, Presley, and the growing chemistry between them. As Sidney was obsessed by the actress, you wonder how he viewed his co-stars' romance. At one point, according to the *Las Vegas Sun*, the publicists even sought to capitalize on this development by changing the title to *The Lady Loves Me*. The end result of Sidney's art and craft is Presley's greatest musical comedy, but the director's cavalier attitude to the budget—at least that's how the Colonel saw it—meant that such a success was unlikely to be repeated.

Sidney's next big-screen movie, *The Swinger* (1966), is best understood as a rather tawdry exploration of the director's fascination for Ann-Margret. After that he bowed out with one last musical, directing Tommy Steele in *Half a Sixpence* (1967). By that time, the genre he had made his name in—and helped invent—had fallen out of favor. He once said: "Once I make a picture I never look back at it again." Millions of Elvis fans keep looking back at *Viva Las Vegas* and wondering what might have been if their hero had worked more often with such talented directors from Hollywood's golden age.

John Rich (1925–2012)

The most famous scene Rich ever directed was a kiss between bigoted Archie Bunker and Sammy Davis Jr. (playing himself) on the sitcom *All in the Family*. As he recalled later: "The roar from the live audience went on for about 30 to 40 seconds and we had to dial the audio down because it was far too big a laugh for the home viewer." Comedy—and TV—suited Rich. Dick Van Dyke, who had worked with him on his show between 1961 and 1966, described him as "the best comedy director I ever met." Yet Rich didn't just want to be the king of TV comedy, he wanted to make movies and, working for Wallis, directed the King in *Roustabout* and *Easy Come, Easy Go.* His most critically rated film is the Van Johnson/Janet Leigh family comedy *Wives and Lovers* (1963).

Just three Roustabouts: Barbara Stanwyck, director John Rich, and Elvis share a moment on the set of *Roustabout*, an above average circus movie.

Paramount Pictures/Photofest

Rich wasn't the obvious choice to direct Presley: "I didn't know too much about the musical theatre and I knew nothing about Elvis." He took an unusual approach to directing Presley: he challenged him. Various accounts by the Memphis Mafia suggest this didn't go down too well with the King—already uncertain, on *Roustabout*, about playing alongside such a gifted actress as Barbara Stanwyck—yet the director himself recalled no tantrums or even a hint of dissent from his star. "We talked a lot about acting," Rich said, "because he knew that I was pushing him to be better and he was better. But the group around him got involved and took him out of that notion."

The director intrigued his star by shooting some of the sequences—when Elvis sings "Wheels on My Heels" on his Honda and "It's a Wonderful World" on the Ferris wheel—live. The latter scene was particularly technically demanding, as it had to be done in a single take and couldn't be shot too often because six grips had to be waiting on their knees to bring the wheel to a gentle stop. That kind of meticulous invention—shot beautifully by Lucien Ballard—made *Roustabout* look and feel like a step up from the normal travelogue. It was one of the few Presley movies from this era that the star enjoyed watching.

Rich went on to direct Wallis's other principal attraction, Jerry Lewis, in *Boeing (707) Boeing (707)* before returning to make *Easy Come, Easy Go* with Presley. With a much tighter budget, a wayward script, less gifted co-stars, and a handful of mediocre songs, Rich couldn't do a lot with the material. The movie was made in a spirit of contractual obligation, and there are times—especially during the underwater action scenes—when Rich seems to lose interest. By the end of this film, he had acquired a greater understanding of his star's tribulations and decided to focus on the small screen.

Boris Sagal (1923–1981)

If anybody recalls Sagal these days, it is probably because of the way he died: of severe head and shoulder injuries after turning the wrong way after getting out of a helicopter and walking directly into the rear rotor blade. He was making the TV film *World War III*—astonishingly, a new director, David Greene, turned up on set the next day so shooting could continue—and it was TV where this Russian immigrant seemed most comfortable. His best work is probably either the wrenching TV movie *A Case of Rape* (1974) or *The Omega Man* (1971), an entertaining, if slightly tacky, postapocalyptic sci-fi starring Charlton Heston.

Sagal worked with Presley once, directing him in *Girl Happy*. Not a firm fan favorite on release, this musical comedy about spring fever among college girls and boys in Fort Lauderdale has worn reasonably well. Sagal brings up the situational comedy in the mix, throws in one of his trademark set-piece stunts (when the lothario's boat is miraculously dragged from the front and dumped in the hotel swimming pool), manages to get Elvis in drag, bathes the proceedings in some vivid Pop Art colors (with a little help from director of photography Philip

Lathrop), and seldom lets the pace flag. He sensed his star's discomfort with the material, suggesting he get off the treadmill and take acting classes.

Girl Happy was an unusual film for Sagal. Many of his movies seem preoccupied by tension and violence, neither of which were required in a Presley musical comedy. After the film wrapped, Sagal was back on his own kind of treadmill, making TV movies, some indifferent films (the comedy *Made in Paris* with Ann-Margret), and leaving the big screen in some style with *The Omega Man.*

Frederick de Cordova (1910–2001)

Far better known for being Johnny Carson's "chief traffic cop, talent scout, number 1 fan and critic" than a film director, De Cordova's most famous movie is undoubtedly *Bedtime for Bonzo* (1951), an innocuous comedy starring a chimpanzee that came back to haunt Ronald Reagan during his political career.

Between 1947 and 1953, de Cordova made films at a punishing rate, including the sequel *Bonzo Goes to College* (1952), but his focus shifted to TV. In 1965, he returned with the Bob Hope sex comedy *I'll Take Sweden*, in which two slightly out-of-date teen idols—Frankie Avalon and Tuesday Weld—are pressed into service to appeal to a younger audience. That was no great smash, but De Cordova returned in 1966 with Presley's period musical *Frankie and Johnny*, which he directed in pleasant style, presiding over a convivial set and delivering a film that may be inconsequential but doesn't take itself too seriously.

After that it was back to TV and to far more significant things, like producing Carson's *Tonight Show* from 1970 to 1992. When he died in 2001, in all the eulogies, the fact that he had once directed Presley was regarded as a mere footnote.

Michael D. Moore (1914–2013)

A child actor in the silent-screen era (contracted to Famous Players–Lasky), Moore became a director after a long apprenticeship. He starred in his first film, Tod Browning's *The Unpainted Woman*, in 1919, was assistant director on the Bing Crosby comedy *Welcome Stranger* in 1947, and in 1966 directed *Paradise, Hawaiian Style*, the first of three movies he made before vacating the director's chair and making a name for himself as a second-unit director coordinating the action sequences in such blockbusters as *Butch Cassidy and the Sundance Kid* and the *Indiana Jones* movies, applying some of the advice he had been given by his old mentor Cecil B. DeMille.

Giving up directing was probably a wise move. It seemed the one role Moore wasn't suited for. Though no great shakes, his directorial debut *Paradise, Hawaiian Style* was probably his best. Various accounts suggest he didn't control the set as Taurog would have done and he certainly didn't interest his disenchanted star in the part. As there was no budget to rehearse, he staged the big production numbers—especially *Drums of the Island, Stop Where You Are*, and *This*

Is My Heaven—pretty well. He has an eye for the landscape, although sometimes this leads him astray, slowing the pace with too many scenic views.

Moore followed this with the budget western *An Eye for an Eye* (1966) and *The Fastest Guitar Alive* (1967), which is remembered today only as a curio—a Civil War western cum musical comedy that stars Roy Orbison and Sam the Sham. (The latter's "Woolly Bully" was *Billboard*'s best-selling single of 1965.) The kindest review, in the *New York Times*, called it "an old-fashioned, good-natured bad movie." That was enough for Moore to discover his true vocation, as the man who arranged some of the most thrilling action scenes in Hollywood.

Arthur H. Nadel (1921–1990)

At first sight, Nadel seemed an odd choice to direct *Clambake*. Though he started out editing in the late 1940s, he had established himself as a director of such TV westerns as *The Rifleman*, *The Virginian*, and *The Big Valley*, but he was a close friend of the producers—Arnold Laven, Jules Levy, and Arthur Gardner—who had been asked to make the movie for United Artists on a tight budget. As Laven recalled to Bram: "Arthur was a very knowledgeable guy and he had a much better sense of Elvis Presley's music, and his appeal to his audience, than any of us did."

Nadel didn't do a bad job, though the script from Arthur H. Browne, who had also worked on *The Rifleman*, wasn't one of the strongest Presley had to work with and some of the musical numbers—a clambake without clams and the kitsch "Confidence"—were downright odd. Though shooting started late, because of Presley's concussion, Nadel found his star a delight. "Elvis is a director's dream because it takes an Act of Congress for him to suggest changes," he said once. The film seems at its most confident when exploring the relationships between its central characters and at its dullest in the speedboat race, which could have been cut heavily.

The film is affectionately regarded by many Presley fans, but it did little for Nadel's career. After one more film—an unintentionally hilarious, badly lit World War II spy movie, *Underground* (starring Robert Goulet)—Nadel returned to television, where his credits ranged from episodes of *The Streets of San Francisco* to the cartoon *He-Man and the Masters of the Universe* (1983–1985), for which he is probably best known.

Peter Tewksbury (1923–2003)

When Tewksbury died, in the small Vermont town of Brattleboro, he was known as "Henry the Cheeseman," as he had managed the cheese department at the local cooperative store for the past eight years. A year before his death, he had published a gourmet's guide to the state's "artisanal cheesemakers."

You couldn't get much further away from Hollywood, and that, for Tewksbury, was the whole point. He quit Hollywood in the 1970s, disillusioned with the film industry. He was so keen to put the past behind him that he once told his sons: "Peter Tewksbury the director is dead."

It is quite possible that he never intended to be a director. After serving in the Pacific in the U.S. Army in World War II, he became a jack of all trades at a radio station in Porterville, Tulare County, California. He founded a community theater there in 1947 and produced 270 plays, attracting Hollywood's attention.

Self-trained as a director, he was asked to direct—and won an Emmy for—the Robert Young series *Father Knows Best*. Yet the most satisfying work of his TV career was probably *It's a Man's World* (1962), an hour-long show about two orphaned brothers, a rich kid from Chicago and an itinerant folk singer, that dared to raise all kinds of subjects—premarital sex, the generation gap, feminism—that were barely featured on any other TV show. It was, one critic declared, such a tender, tearing portrait it was "almost painful to watch." Tewksbury had high hopes—the series even earned him a Directors Guild nomination—but advertisers shunned it and it was canned after nineteen episodes.

Though he did not know it then, that may have been the most creative leeway Tewksbury was to enjoy. He bounced back with his first movie, the charming sex farce *Sunday in New York* (1963), based on Norman Krasna's play. With a talented cast—Cliff Robertson, Rod Taylor, and Jane Fonda were among the leads—Tewksbury extracted every possible laugh from the twin themes of mistaken identity and sexual double standards. He followed that with the above-average Disney family comedy drama *Emil and the Detectives* (1964) and the Sandra Dee comedy *Doctor, You've Got to Be Kidding* (1967), which is just as predictable as the title suggests.

He was then given the MGM lot's equivalent of the poisoned chalice and asked to direct Presley in *Stay Away, Joe*. Ditching Michael Hoey's script and letting his actors improvise, Tewksbury produced a film that was unlike any other Presley movie ever made—and not always in a good way. Critics were vitriolic, but fans have been more tolerant, largely on the grounds that Elvis does at least look engaged.

The omens were not good when Tewksbury reunited with Presley to film *The Trouble with Girls*. The script had been hanging around Hollywood for slightly longer than the director. Yet with a varied, talented cast, Tewksbury created the best Elvis movie of the late 1960s and drew a lovely performance from his star. He was happy to try anything to get his point across. He had a different eye, and a feeling for milieu and ensemble that, if it wasn't as sure as Altman's, certainly pointed in that direction.

Sadly, interest in Presley's movies was so sluggish by then that the quality was largely irrelevant. And with the film's commercial failure, Tewksbury's film career was over. He kept his hand in with a few TV series, but Vermont—and cheese—beckoned.

Charles Marquis Warren (1912–1990)

"I haven't believed in anybody so strongly since Ernest Hemingway." That's how F. Scott Fitzgerald recommended his godson Warren to MGM. Such eulogizing would stagger anyone who watched *Charro!* all the way through, but the producer/writer/director of Presley's ersatz spaghetti western was out of practice by 1969.

Warren's name will forever be associated with *Rawhide*, the enduring TV western on which he had performed the same triple role. From his very first directorial assignment—*Little Big Horn* (1951)—he seldom strayed too far from the West, though in 1957 he made two so-so horror movies: *Back from the Dead* and *The Unknown Terror*. His brainchild *Rawhide*, a televisual riff on *Red River*, was more satisfying and made Clint Eastwood a star, though the actor disliked his role as Rowdy Yates, calling him the "idiot of the plains." Long hours, punishing schedules, and Warren's autocratic style all took their toll, and the director/writer/producer left after eighty-four episodes in 1961.

His stock waned after that, but he must have seemed a safe pair of hands for *Charro!* Although Presley loved making the movie, he soon realized it was not going to match anything Eastwood had done. Warren's methods were eccentric, his technique old-fashioned (too many TV-style fadeouts), his pacing haphazard, and his plotting clumsy. The end result wasn't in the same class as the visceral westerns then being made by Sergio Leone and Sam Peckinpah. *Charro!* is easier to enjoy today, accepted on its own terms, and not compared to any of the westerns it was likened to at the time. It wasn't the kind of ending to his career Warren would have scripted, but, although he was only fifty-seven, he never wrote, directed, or produced another film or TV show again.

William A. Graham (1933–)

Graham has the strange distinction of being the last man alive to direct Elvis. A TV director who had worked his way up the ranks with such shows as *Naked City*, *The FBI*, *Dr. Kildare*, and *The Fugitive* and moved into movies with the comedy western *Waterhole Three* (1967) with James Coburn. This latter fare was good enough for the *New York Times* to praise its "bursts of comical business and exchanges of surprising dialogue" but has left fewer traces than his next movie, *Change of Habit*, Elvis's final feature film.

Universal had asked Graham to direct—he was contracted to make a number of films a year for them—and, after looking at the script and realizing that it was a little more taxing than some of the travelogues his star had walked through, he encouraged Elvis to do some acting exercises at his home in California. He was realistic about his mission, telling Bram: "It was not exactly an art masterpiece. It was a commercial film that was made because Elvis had a contract with Universal that he had to fulfill." Yet he got on well enough with his principal star to go forward and have the script rewritten.

Apart from the controversial rage-reduction scene—which had many veteran crew members in tears and prompted Mary Tyler Moore to storm out—*Change of Habit* was a happy shoot. Presley enjoyed the acting exercises and discussions with Graham, and his joy at his career renaissance established the mood on the set. The film was derided by many critics—and wasn't even released in the UK—but Graham wasn't surprised: "He had lot of respect as a performer. He was an extraordinarily popular guy, an icon, but I don't think people took him too seriously as an actor."

Graham then returned to his contractual duties, making movies and TV movies almost like clockwork until the late 1990s. His most satisfying work is probably *Where the Lilies Bloom* (1974), a beautiful, honest movie about growing up in the Appalachians based on a novel by Vera and Bill Cleaver. He unwisely returned to the Presley myth with a mediocre TV movie about Elvis and the Colonel in 1993. That same year, Graham touched on another of the great popular-culture phenoms of the late twentieth century, directing three episodes of *The X Files*.

Denis Sanders (1929–1987)

Nothing fazed Sanders. He won an Oscar for Best Short Documentary with *Czechoslovakia 1918–1968*, his compelling history of the troubled east European nation. He made a biopic of the preacher Norman Vincent Peale (*One Man's Way*, 1964). He made the cult sci-fi flick *Invasion of the Bee Girls* (1973), in which women become queen bees who kill men by sexually exhausting them. And he filmed Elvis in Las Vegas for *Elvis: That's the Way It Is*.

Sanders had always been his own man. Studying film at the University of California, he won an Oscar in 1954 for Best Short Subject for his student project *A Time Out of War*, a story about soldiers agreeing to an hour's peace in the American Civil War. In 1962, he gave Robert Redford his screen debut in *War Story*. Two years later he made the powerful but neglected drama *Shock Treatment*, a kind of companion piece to Samuel Fuller's *Shock Corridor*, in which Stuart Whitman pretends to be insane to locate $1 million in loot.

For a director of an Elvis movie, this was hardly the usual CV. And in Parker's eyes, the gamble didn't work. He fired off a furious letter to MGM boss Jim Aubrey demanding a host of changes, most of which were made, but underlying his anger was, as Guralnick has suggested, what he saw as the director's implicit contempt for his subject. This wasn't just Parker's view: Pierre Adidge and Robert Abel, who made *Elvis on Tour*, felt that Sanders had "done a job" on Elvis. Yet, paradoxically, the movie remains one of the most powerful testaments to Presley's charisma we have today.

Sanders continued to follow his own drum, making the acclaimed documentary *Soul to Soul* (1971), reflecting on John Ford's America for TV and making his cult classic about nymphomaniac bees. Yet by the 1980s, he was more interested in his academic work, as a professor at San Diego University.

Robert Abel (1937–2001) and Pierre Adidge (1939–1974)

For Abel, *Elvis on Tour* was an inspirational experience yet far from his greatest achievement. Today, his fame rests not on the pioneering rockumentaries he made with Adidge but on his record as a pioneering visionary in the development of visual effects. He accidentally discovered the slit scan effect used in *2001: A Space Odyssey* (1969), but there was nothing accidental about the TV commercials—most notably a man in jeans walking a Levi's label that had been refashioned to look like a dog—that, according to New York's Museum of Modern Art, "changed television forever."

Abel had grabbed the industry's attention as the writer/director of the TV documentary *The Making of the President 1968* (1969). Two years later, working with Adidge for the first time, he made *Mad Dogs and Englishmen*, a candid account of the American tour by British blues singer Joe Cocker, which, Roger Ebert concluded, "had an instinctive feel for the Cocker personality, on stage and off."

Adidge's expertise was sound recording. He had formed a company with Jim Webb, whose innovative use of sound had made a significant impact on Altman's *M*A*S*H*. Together they approached *Elvis on Tour* with some caution. After one Vegas concert, they were unconvinced, but Presley charmed them into accepting. Abel said later: "He had incredible native intelligence, the ability to read a human being, to watch someone's eyes and look inside their soul." When they followed him on tour across America and saw the passionate response he generated from the audience—and the depth of his commitment to his fans—they knew the job was much easier than anticipated. They used a complicated eleven-camera setup—and the latest lightweight equipment—to bring the audience closer to Elvis than they had ever been. Though not as revelatory as *That's the Way It Is*, the Abel/Adidge documentary is much more personal.

The documentary did reasonably well commercially, and the shared Golden Globe did its co-producers no harm. They went on to make the rollicking rockumentary *Let the Good Times Roll* (1973), the last of their films to be released before Adidge died of a heart attack at the age of thirty-five. In his biography of Presley, Guralnick suggests Adidge was addicted to Demerol. Abel then changed careers, focusing on his visual-effects studio in Hollywood.

10

Hal B. Wallis

Starmaker or Starbreaker?

O ne of the biggest mistakes Elvis made in his relationship with Hal B. Wallis (1899–1986) was to keep snubbing his long-term producer's frequent invitations to dinner. Wallis never quite realized that Presley's reluctance was primarily down to his shyness and assumed he was being snubbed. The chill prevented producer and star from developing a strong relationship independent of the man who manipulated them both: Colonel Parker. That kind of connection might have helped give Elvis the confidence to stand up to Wallis and request better parts, as Charlton Heston and Burt Lancaster both did when they worked with the producer.

It is important not to make too much of yet another road not taken in Presley's sojourn in Hollywood, but Wallis certainly had a high regard for his star—he found his politeness a welcome relief from Jerry Lewis's megalomania—and talking about movies (a subject about which Presley's curiosity was endless) over dinner might have changed the producer's perceptions and broadened Elvis's horizons.

The title of Wallis's autobiography—*Starmaker*—tells us all we need to know about how the producer saw himself. That perception was certainly partly true. Film historian David Thomson says of Wallis's career at Warner Brothers, between 1922 and 1944: "A case can be made that no head of production at any studio put his name (and his imprint of care, smarts and taste) on so many outstanding pictures. In those years he was in charge of such best picture winners as *The Life of Emile Zola* and *Casablanca*, as well as contenders like *The Adventures of Robin Hood, Four Daughters, Jezebel, Dark Victory, The Letter, The Maltese Falcon* and many more." He joined Warners when he was twenty-four, working his way up from production executive to head of production and promoting the studio's hardboiled macho male stars while nurturing such talents as Errol Flynn and Bette Davis. Then in 1944, Wallis jumped ship, setting himself up as an independent who, with Joseph Hazen looking after the money, made movies for Paramount. As Thomson notes: "Paramount was not the same, but that was hardly Wallis' fault."

As a movie producer, Wallis was hard to categorize. He always had a shrewd eye for the commercial impact of movies, once quipping as Warner Brothers head: "Every time Paul Muni parts his beard and looks down a microscope, this company loses two million dollars." Michael Moore, an assistant director of many of the producer's movies—and director of *Paradise, Hawaiian Style*—once said of his boss, "The thing I liked about Hal Wallis: he could make a Jerry Lewis picture, he could make an Elvis Presley picture, which were not the highest quality, and he could make big pictures like *Becket*. He was very versatile, he knew where the money should be spent and where the money should not be spent."

That last gift came in very handy if your movies benefitted from Wallis's largesse, but it was harder to admire when, as happened on *Easy Come, Easy Go*, he decided your movie was not worth spending more money on.

Wallis's nine movies with Elvis—*Loving You*; *King Creole*; *G.I. Blues*; *Blue Hawaii*; *Girls! Girls! Girls!*; *Fun in Acapulco*; *Roustabout*; *Paradise, Hawaiian Style*; and *Easy Come, Easy Go*—effectively sum up the narrative of Presley's movie career. Early promise (*Loving You*) comes close to being fulfilled (*King Creole*) before commercial considerations step in (*G.I. Blues, Blue Hawaii, Girls! Girls! Girls!, Fun in Acapulco*, and *Roustabout*), becoming so all-important that the star, the audience, and the producer himself lose interest.

Deciding how much of this decline can be fairly blamed on Wallis is no easy task. Though he always resolutely defended the musical-comedy formula he perfected—the Presley travelogues, as the star called them—on the grounds that they made money and that they suited the star's limited range as an actor, he also made *King Creole*, which many critics regard as Elvis's best film. While Curtiz's movie does deliver enough songs for a soundtrack album, it is—if you apply that ruthless philosophy that Moore so admired—burdened with unnecessary investments.

Curtiz, Wallis, and Nathan all pored over the script in some detail, polishing, redeveloping, and rewriting to get the mechanics of plot and character just right. The casting was lavish: Jagger, Jones, Matthau, and Morrow were some of the best character actors in American movies at that time. No expense was spared on the music, and the final movie risked mixing more genres than the audience might know what to do with. The result was an artistic triumph yet no commercial smash. Appearing on *Variety*'s box-office survey for four weeks, peaking at number 5, was respectable but not as good as hoped. Wallis later said, "I don't have all the figures but I believe that one of the least successful of Elvis's films was *King Creole*. But that was my favorite."

Did that comparative failure change Wallis's strategy? Did he sift through the takings and decide that, in future, it would make more sense to make an Elvis film that appealed more strongly to the hardcore fans? If he made that calculation, Parker would have supported him. The star's aspirations to become a "proper actor" might not, at this point, have been too high on the producer's list of priorities. It's as if, creatively, he had given up on Elvis. He would do his best for a star he seemed to be genuinely fond of though he was primarily, as far as he and Parker were concerned, a cash cow.

So when Presley was available again after his U.S. Army service, Wallis reverted to a safer variation of the all-around family entertainments he had been making with Martin and Lewis, often calling on the same directors (Taurog), writers (Anhalt), and actors. Commercially, the new appeal-broadening strategy looked extremely shrewd between 1960 and 1963, with *G.I. Blues* and *Blue Hawaii* being spectacularly successful. The less inspired applications of the formula—*Girls! Girls! Girls! Girls!* and *Fun in Acapulco*—still made money—and *Roustabout*, released after the Beatles had started their conquest of America, did pretty well. Yet 1965 was the tipping point for Presley at the box office, and when Wallis returned to make *Paradise, Hawaiian Style*, he was not impressed by the returns. His disastrous interview, in which he basically suggested that the Presley pictures existed primarily so he could make artistically significant movies like *Becket*, had not endeared him to the star, who challenged him on the set of *Roustabout*.

Elvis's dissatisfaction was already apparent on *Blue Hawaii*. Wallis was soon beginning to wonder how long he could make money out of a teenage idol in his late twenties whose appearance—from 1961 onward—caused him enough concern for him to write to Parker before each movie and order him to get his client in shape. Before *Roustabout* he warned, "I hope he will have trimmed down as it could have a detrimental effect on his entire career."

Wallis's concerns with Presley's appearance were often couched in talk of realism—a ludicrous concept when applied to such movies as *Paradise, Hawaiian Style* and *Easy Come, Easy Go*—but they also reflected his recognition that it would be increasingly hard to sell a star who looked overweight or jaded and ceased to project the sly sensuality that made him so compelling in *Loving You*.

Yet the care, smarts, and taste that Thomson cited as hallmarks of Wallis's heyday were inconsistently applied to other aspects of Presley's movies. The crew were often top-notch: Edith Head on costumes, Lucien Ballard as cinematographer, Hal Pereira in the editing suite—so that even the worst of his Presley vehicles had more gloss than many teen movies of the time.

The producer's focus seemed to be on finding the right story—substantial enough to set up a situation that had to be resolved, but not so heavy it impeded the songs—and selecting a co-star who might inspire Presley (Angela Lansbury, Barbara Stanwyck). By this time, Taurog had become the default choice of director with John Rich (*Roustabout*; *Easy Come, Easy Go*) and even Moore stepping in when it was appropriate or necessary. After *Roustabout*, Wallis realized a more rebellious Elvis might sell better, but, for whatever reason, he never acted on that impulse.

Relations with Parker, which had once been cordial, had become increasingly prickly. The last round of negotiations that preceded *Easy Come, Easy Go* had been especially laborious. And when the cash cow stopped delivering cash, Wallis decided the game was up. He had to consider the opportunity cost. He could make only two or three movies a year, so when the money stopped rolling in there was no incentive for him to devote a third of his resources to a Presley picture. His other franchise—Jerry Lewis movies—was also running out of steam. Having pulled the plug on Presley and Lewis—and perhaps realizing that it was pointless for him to try to understand the nuances of an increasingly unpredictable youth culture—he retreated to the past: westerns like *True Grit* and historical dramas like *Anne of a Thousand Days*.

In truth, Wallis had long ceased to be an innovative producer. As Thomson suggests, you can't blame him entirely, but he was more creative at Warner Brothers, where, apart from those already mentioned in the 1930s, his successes included *Little Caesar, Captain Blood, I Am a Fugitive from a Chain Gang*, and *Jezebel*. As an independent, he had a good eye for the next big thing (Martin and Lewis, Elvis) but he often played safe with westerns, material that had already been a smash elsewhere (like the plays of Tennessee Williams or Neil Simon's *Barefoot in the Park*), and in 1975 he wisely retired. He died in 1986, nine years after Elvis, at the age of eighty-seven.

So how much responsibility does he bear for the failure of Presley's movie career? He produced one of Elvis's best pictures (*King Creole*), one of his most successful (*Blue Hawaii*), and one of his worst (*Paradise, Hawaiian Style*). His other six varied from the superior jollity of *Roustabout* to the weird, almost-so-bad-it's-good foray into hippie culture that is *Easy Come, Easy Go*.

Yet in partnership with Parker, he helped steer Presley's movie career into a dead end. His subsequent insistence that there was no sense in stretching Elvis as an actor—and that he only ever wanted to star him as an actor who sang—is slightly contradicted by the artistic ambition evident in *King Creole*. In the 1960s, his instinctive preference for the travelogues, justified in part by a change in the cultural mood, set a dismal precedent for Presley, and he seemed to either willfully ignore or conveniently overlook his star's growing disenchantment. Rather than challenge Parker, or find the kind of story that would inspire his star—whom he had genuine affection for—Wallis made his excuses and left.

It's easy to blame Wallis for that, but, given what we now know about how the Presley machine operated, most producers would have made the same call. As those snubbed dinner invitations made evident, even if he wanted to challenge the status quo he knew he could not rely on Presley's wholehearted support.

The King's Consorts

Elvis's Leading Ladies and the Part They Played in His Life

Elvis was not one of the great screen lovers, although he could have been. A sexual liberator onstage, he grew increasingly chaste on celluloid. Only in *Jailhouse Rock* ("That ain't tactics, honey, that's just the beast in me") and *King Creole* do we get a glimpse of the animal magnetism that had women screaming at his concerts. He was often depicted as a womanizer—*Girl Happy*; *Paradise, Hawaiian Style*; *Roustabout*; *Speedway*; *Tickle Me*, and others—but equally he often spent as much time singing to children as to the women he was wooing. Though it was once said he slept with all but one of his leading ladies, that sounds increasingly unlikely, as this rundown shows.

Debra Paget (1933–): *Love Me Tender*

Presley was so bowled over by Paget he proposed to her, not realizing that she was seeing reclusive billionaire Howard Hughes at the time. Nineteen fifty-six was a big year for Paget, who starred in Elvis's debut as Cathy Reno and won the part of Lilla in *The Ten Commandments* without auditioning because director Cecil B. DeMille felt the "hand of God was on her."

She found Presley a "sincere, obliging young man" and recalled: "Had anyone told me he'd never done a dramatic lesson, never stood in front of a movie camera, I wouldn't have believed it." The only time she was irritated by her co-star was when a stray football pass flew inches past her head. Her subsequent career did not suggest any divine destiny. After a slew of movies that underwhelmed audiences and critics, her last picture was Roger Corman's creepy horror film *The Haunted Palace* (1963). Within two years, after some guest spots on TV, her screen career was over. She was only thirty-two. She made a surprise return to showbiz in the 1990s as the host of a talk show for born-again Christians.

Lizabeth Scott (1922–): *Loving You*

A protégé of Wallis's, Scott had a voice that the producer's biographer Bernard F. Dick described as a "baritonal purr with a creamy huskiness." The choice of the word *baritonal* may not be accidental. In 1955, *Confidential* magazine accused her of belonging to Hollywood's "weird society of baritone babes"—then a favorite code for closeted lesbians. The publicity—and a suggestion that her name had been found in a call girl's book—could have wrecked her career. Luckily, having realized that she was regarded in Hollywood as a poor man's Lauren Bacall, Scott had returned to the theater. Although she was suing the magazine, the furor was dying down when Wallis asked her to play manipulative agent Glenda Markle in *Loving You.*

Lizabeth Scott's career was hurt by insinuations that she was a "baritone babe"—code for lesbian in 1950s scandal sheets.

Onscreen, her rapport with Presley is one of the strongest aspects of *Loving You*. They even make their brief May–September romance convincing. The mawkish scene in the cemetery, where Presley fesses up that he stole the name Deke Rivers from a gravestone, could have been lachrymose but is quite affecting.

Sadly for Scott, that was almost her swan song in Hollywood. She would have to wait fifteen years to make her next movie, Mike Hodges's *Pulp*, a satire of detective movies starring Michael Caine that has acquired a cult following. Scott isn't bad in that either. Apart from *Loving You*, she is best known for her role as Toni, a blonde from the wrong side of the tracks, in Lewis Milestone's classic noir *The Strange Love of Martha Ivers* (1946).

Judy Tyler (1932–1957): *Jailhouse Rock*

Just the kind of petite brunette that appealed to Elvis in real life, Tyler sparks off the King so well in as record plugger Peggy Van Alden, it's hard to believe this was only her second feature-film. Tyler had showbiz in her blood—her father was a trumpeter for Paul Whiteman and Benny Goodman—and came to prominence on the *Howdy Doody* series as Princess Summerfall Winterspring.

Presley was infatuated with her and was so stricken by her shocking death three weeks after the shoot finished, he couldn't bear to watch the film. She died in a terrible road accident—police reports suggest her body was virtually cut in half—alongside her second husband, actor Gregory LaFayette. Singer/actor Kenny Baker recorded a tribute song in her memory titled "Goodbye Little Star" (1959).

Dolores Hart (1938–): *King Creole*

A young actress who always gave off an innocent glow, even when the King was inviting her to enter a seedy hotel room in *King Creole*, Hart is now known, in tabloid shorthand, as the nun who kissed Elvis.

Another of Wallis's discoveries, Hart co-starred with Elvis in *Loving You* (1957) and *King Creole* (1958). As Susan Jessup, she had little to do but look pure and sweet in her first Presley movie, but in *King Creole* she is quietly, unshowily impressive in the challenging role of Nellie, an innocent awakened by love. She and Presley blushed so much during one scene that they required extra makeup. In 2003, she said of her famous co-star: "If there is anything I am most grateful for it is the privilege of being one of the few people left to acknowledge he was an innocent."

She later starred in the college comedy *Where the Boys Are* (1960), a precursor to the King's *Girl Happy*, and Michael Curtiz's biopic *Francis of Assisi* (1961). She retired two years later, saying, "I'd done two movies with Elvis Presley. I'd been around Hollywood for a while—and saw how needlessly competitive and negative it could be. It never held my interest." She joined a convent and is now the Reverend Mother Dolores Hart, prioress of Regina Laudis (Queen of Praise) Abbey in Bethlehem, Connecticut. She holds the unique position of being the only nun to be a voting member of the Academy of Motion Picture Arts and Sciences. When asked how she could go from kissing Elvis to joining a convent she said, "How much closer to Heaven can you get?"

Juliet Prowse (1936–1996): *G.I. Blues*

Rejected by the London ballet scene because of her height—six feet tall—Prowse danced at the London Palladium and various European nightclubs, where she was spotted by choreographer Hermes Pan, who signed her up for his movie *Can-Can* (1960). That film made her world-famous after Soviet Premier Nikita Khruschev, watching the dancers rehearse, denounced their routine as immoral. When Khruschev's denunciation was reported in the press, her picture accompanied the story around the world. She soon generated even more publicity by becoming engaged to Frank Sinatra. They never got married. As Prowse explained once: "Frank's a nice guy but he can get a bit difficult after a couple of drinks." During *G.I. Blues*, she had a fling with Elvis.

Born in India to South African parents, Prowse may have the most distinctive persona of all of the King's leading ladies. As nightclub dancer Lili, she steals *G.I. Blues* with a stunning dance routine that still oozes sex appeal. Yet in other scenes, she can look like an attractive hausfrau who is organizing her boyfriend's life. She said of Presley, "He would make a damn fine dancer—he's got fabulous rhythm." Unfortunately, he never got to look rhythmically fabulous in the movie.

Prowse was due to return for *Blue Hawaii*, but Wallis was so incensed by her salary demands and her request for her own makeup man and secretary that he replaced her with Joan Blackman. Prowse didn't figure she was missing much—complaining that her character "just sort of hulas all the way through"—but her Hollywood career never really recovered. Her last film, *Who Killed Teddy Bear* (1965), a lurid B movie in which she plays an aspiring dancer and DJ who is plagued by obscene phone calls and decapitated teddy bears, may be her most interesting.

Like Elvis, Prowse had a successful career onstage in Vegas. One of the highlights of her nightclub act was a spot-on impersonation of Presley. She may have based on this her own research: she is one of the celebrities who turns up to see Elvis in *That's the Way It Is*. She learned the old adage about never working with animals the hard way. When rehearsing for the show *Circus of the Stars* (1987), she was mauled by a leopard and needed five stitches. A few months later while promoting the show on Johnny Carson, she was mauled by the same leopard and needed to have forty stitches and part of her ear reattached.

Barbara Eden (1934–): *Flaming Star*

Best known as the genie in the bottle in the sitcom *I Dream of Jeannie*, Eden was drafted into *Flaming Star* by Siegel after shooting had started when British actress Barbara Steele's western accent was found wanting.

A former cheerleader and pop singer, Eden broke through as a movie actress in 1960. She impressed in Edward L. Cahn's *Twelve Hours to Kill* (1960), even if the movie was noir by rote, did well in the Paul Newman/Joan Woodward drama *From the Terrace*, and justified Siegel's faith with a memorable performance as Roslyn, the unwitting object of Pacer's unrequited love, in *Flaming Star*.

She was impressed by Presley's ease in the saddle, his manners, and his dedication to his work: "He cared so much about doing a good job, and knowing his craft. He followed direction, he listened, and he was no problem. There wasn't a huge ego. He wanted to please." Eden would star in other significant movies—notably alongside Tony Randall in George Pal's *7 Faces of Dr. Lao* (1964)—but is still best known for not being able to show her navel as Jeannie.

Hope Lange (1931–2003): *Wild in the Country*

Making her stage debut when she was just nine, Lange had trained as a dancer, made her movie debut opposite Marilyn Monroe in *Bus Stop* (1956), and became nationally famous in the pioneering soap opera *Peyton Place* (1957). She was a last-minute choice for the role of Irene Sperry after the studio decided they couldn't afford Simone Signore, but, even though she was only four years older than Presley, she handled the role well. Her rapport with her co-star—she even persuaded him to drink vodka for the duration of the shoot—makes their scenes stand out. The stars' relationship might have deepened, but Lange was embroiled in a bitter divorce from Don Murray, one of her costars in *Bus Stop*. Director Philip Dunne hailed her performance as the best of her career.

Though Lange never gave a bad performance, she fell out of fashion as cinema changed in the 1960s and began working almost exclusively in TV. She won two Emmys for her role as Mrs. Muir in the sitcom *The Ghost and Mrs. Muir*. Her rare forays into film were often memorable—as Charles Bronson's dying wife in the original *Death Wish* (1974) and Laura Dern's mother in David Lynch's *Blue Velvet* (1986).

Joan Blackman (1938–): *Blue Hawaii, Kid Galahad*

Darlene Tompkins, one of the beautiful girls Elvis has to chaperone in *Blue Hawaii*, was always profoundly grateful to Blackman for one particular bit of tradecraft. "She didn't want to blink into the camera so she would look—she has the most beautiful pale eyes you ever saw—into the sunlight so she could practice not blinking when looking at the production lights." Blackman shows the same unblinking gaze as Rose in *Kid Galahad*: the ease with which she focuses on Elvis as he croons "Home Is Where the Heart Is" is almost unnerving.

Blackman made her movie debut in the Fred MacMurray western *Good Day for a Hanging* (1958). She was more impressive alongside Anthony Franciosa, Shirley Maclaine, and Dean Martin in *Career* (1959), a grim low-key drama, produced by Wallis. After the obligatory stint opposite Jerry Lewis in *Visit to a Small Planet* (1960), she was asked to replace Prowse as Maile Duvall, Elvis's half-Hawaiian girlfriend, in *Blue Hawaii*.

As Prowse had suggested, the part didn't give Blackman a lot to do, but she did it prettily and effectively, even if there isn't a great deal of chemistry between her and Elvis. This was odd because they had a romance on set. As Blackman later recalled: "We had rooms next to each other in the hotel and for weeks we just about lived together." They had dated in 1957, but on set, as often as not, the actress was happy to get an early night so she would look the part each morning. Her husband Joby Baker later starred alongside Presley in *Girl Happy*.

Blackman was more memorable as Rose, the kid sister of wheeler-dealer Willie (Gig Young), looking more striking in her yellow dress than she ever did in a one-piece bikini in *Blue Hawaii* and generating more romantic chemistry with Elvis.

Her movie career became more sporadic after her successive Presley movies. She co-starred with Nick Adams in *Twilight of Honor* (1963), for which Elvis's friend won his only Oscar nomination. But by 1964, she was more in demand on the small screen. One of her oddest roles was as a domineering lesbian painter in Raphael Nussbaum's *Submission* (1974), a film that *TV Guide* summed up in three words: "Vile misogynist trash."

Anne Helm (1938–): *Follow That Dream*

Born in Toronto, Helm made her name as Sleeping Beauty in *The Shirley Temple Storybook* (1958), and was given her big break opposite Presley in one of his funniest comedies, yet is still best known for her role as Mary Briggs, the nurse who was married to a convict, in *General Hospital* (1971–73).

Follow That Dream was the then twenty-three-year-old actress's third movie of 1962. She had significant roles in Owen Crump's serial-killer movie *The Couch* and Bert I. Gordon's compellingly strange fantasy *The Magic Sword*. Holly, the girl adopted by the feckless Kwimpers, was her first leading role, and she enjoyed the experience immensely, sharing the King's bed and playing poker with him and his entourage. "I really fell for Elvis, I mean who wouldn't?," she admitted later. She grew accustomed to the practical jokes but also to the pressures on her co-star, recalling: "I did see a lot of things that brought him down." Their relationship ended after she brought the piano top down on his fingers when he said something to upset her. Presley apologized, but they never met again.

Helm was an astute choice for the part, fleshing out a character that could have been a cipher, and playing her scenes with Presley with a natural ease that builds the story. She was nominated for a gold medal by *Photoplay* as most promising new female star. Her career soured after she had the misfortune to be fired from the schlock horror flick *Strait-Jacket* (1964) by Joan Crawford, who had approval of cast and script. Her other 1960s movies were ho-hum. In producer/director/screenwriter Jack H. Harris's *Unkissed Bride* (1966), she played the virginal bride of a husband who needs an LSD spray to perform his conjugal duties. Helm's last movie, *Nightmare in Wax* (1969), must have felt like a nightmare to make. She was thirty-one, a difficult age for an actress who wasn't an established megastar in that Hollywood era, and her movie career was over.

Ursula Andress (1936–): *Fun in Acapulco*

The stunning Swiss actress was considered for Prowse's part in *G.I. Blues* but was overlooked and made arguably the most stunning entrance in movie history, emerging from the ocean, as the original Bond girl Honey Ryder, in a clinging white bikini in *Dr. No*. She made such an impression that 007 creator Ian Fleming even name-checked her as a "beautiful movie star" in his novel *On Her Majesty's Secret Service*.

Because of her thick Swiss-German accent, Andress's lines in *Dr. No* were dubbed by Nikki van der Zyl, and though her diction had improved by the time she made *Fun in Acapulco*, her line readings sometimes make it hard to figure out which European aristocracy her character Marguerita Dauphin is supposed to come from. She felt stymied by the producers' scrutiny of her costumes—they couldn't be too sexy—and doesn't come across brilliantly in the film. She did love working with Elvis, saying, "He's a very well-mannered and sensitive person—just like me." There doesn't seem to have been any great on-set romance, but two met once or twice a year for a while after the movie wrapped. She found Presley a "troubled person."

Andress's beauty was almost too startling, too exotic, for directors to know what to make of her. So she often ended up providing the eye candy in such mediocre films as *4 For Texas* (1963). She was more effective as the countess seduced by George Peppard in John Guillermin's World War I drama *The Blue Max* (1966), giving what was probably the best performance of her career. As absurd as it may sound, she was the original choice for Meryl Streep's role in *Sophie's Choice* (1982).

Joan O'Brien (1936–): *It Happened at the World's Fair*

In 1957, O'Brien gave up a steady income as a singer on TV to try to make it as an actress. The gamble paid off swiftly when she was cast as the female lead in Blake Edwards's hit comedy *Operation Petticoat* (1959) opposite Cary Grant and Tony Curtis. That role set a precedent, as, for some mysterious reason, she was often cast as a nurse in her later films, as she was opposite Jerry Lewis in *It's Only Money* and Elvis in *It Happened at the World's Fair*.

Ursula Andress showing off the kind of curves she couldn't display in *Fun In Acapulco.*

Playing hard to get as Nurse Diane Warren, O'Brien invested the romance with just enough emotional depth to give *World's Fair* more heart than some of the other musical comedies. She enjoyed the relative simplicity of the story and Presley's professionalism but struggled with the difficult task of being sung at by the King. Her class eluded the critics, with *Variety* remarking that "Miss O'Brien is easy to look at," and made only one more movie, *Get Yourself a College Girl* (1964), although she did feature in TV shows including *The Man from U.N.C.L.E.* She left acting to concentrate on her singing and raising her children, whom she fought to regain custody of after a bitter court battle with two ex-husbands.

Laurel Goodwin (1942–): *Girls! Girls! Girls!*

Goodwin's role as Laurel Dodge was one of two moments where her acting career threatened to take off. Four years after romancing the King, she was cast in *The Cage*, the unaired pilot for *Star Trek*, but her role as Ensign Colt was written out of the series.

A child model from Wichita, Kansas, Goodwin made her debut in *Girls! Girls! Girls!*, attracting good notices and comparisons to Doris Day for a spirited performance in one of the King's breezier lightweight vehicles. She said later, "I look back at my performance now and think, hot damn, for a kid who had never done a motion picture before, I was pretty good."

Of Presley she said: "I had no romance with him but we became good friends. I learned an attitude of relaxation from him, and not to take the stardom bit too seriously. It helped me keep my balance. I owe a great deal to that alone." Rarely for an Elvis co-star, Goodwin persuaded him to leave the cocoon of the Memphis Mafia and go out for dinner with her in the Hawaiian city Hilo. They had three nights out, eating, drinking, and dancing and, she recalled, "it was one of the few times after he became popular that he enjoyed a really laid back evening."

Yvonne Craig as Batgirl. Craig's best role wasn't in an Elvis movie.

She couldn't have known it, but this musical comedy was to be as good as it got for her as a movie actress. By 1964, she was getting smaller parts in B westerns like *Stage to Thunder Rock*. After some guest spots on TV, Goodwin married businessman Walter Wood in 1971 and settled in Palm Springs. She occasionally attends Elvis and Star Trek events.

Yvonne Craig (1937–): *Kissin' Cousins*

Now best known for her recurring performance as Batgirl—a role she took so seriously she complained to DC Comics when the caped crusader was shot and paralyzed in 1988—Craig didn't know who Elvis was before she was given a cameo in *It Happened at the World's Fair*. "'My sister Meridel had to tell me who he was," the actress has said, "but only because I had lived such an insular life as a dancer. I didn't know he was hot stuff."

Craig is the first woman Presley tries to seduce in *World's Fair*—while singing the feverish number "Relax"—and looks far more alluring in that cameo than as Azalea Tatum, who falls for Josh (the brunette Elvis) in the hillbilly comedy *Kissin' Cousins*. She was close to Elvis but says of the relationship, "It wasn't the love of your life or the love of his life. It was just kinda hanging out." She found the Presley films perplexing—"the philosophy seemed to be don't say it if you can sing it"—but enjoyed making them.

They didn't do a lot for her movie career. Before her Presley films, she had been racking up significant parts in some decent movies, notably *The Gene Krupa Story* (1959). Afterward, she found such parts harder to come by. She did get a starring role in *Ski Party* (1965), a beach-party movie with snow instead of sand, but was probably relieved to be asked to play Barbara Gordon, aka Batgirl, on the cult TV series in 1967. After that, Craig focused on the small screen, appearing in various series and TV movies. *Kissin' Cousins* wasn't the low point of her career: that has to be Larry Buchanan's *Mars Needs Women* (1967), regularly cited as one of the worst films ever made.

Ann-Margret (1941–): *Viva Las Vegas*

Ann-Margret Olsson is the co-star who almost changed the course of Elvis's life. With Priscilla waiting impatiently at Graceland, where she had been ensconced since 1963, Presley and his *Viva Las Vegas* co-star simply fell in love. They fell so deeply that Elvis started behaving in unprecedented ways, ditching the Memphis Mafia to ride off into the desert with Ann-Margret. "We felt a current, an electricity that went straight through us," the actress wrote later. "It would become a force we couldn't control."

The force stunned Presley's cronies, worried his manager, delighted the movie's publicists, and enraged Priscilla, who at one point shouted at Elvis: "Why doesn't she keep her ass in Sweden where she belongs?," a sentiment the Colonel might have echoed before the filming of *Viva Las Vegas* was done. So overwhelmed by his feelings he even suggested Parker manage his co-star, Presley was genuinely in a quandary while the film was being shot and for a time afterward. Yet as besotted as he was, he also knew, as he told Priscilla, that "her career meant a lot to her," and that proved to be the stumbling block. As Fike said: "Elvis would have married her in a second but he made it clear she would have to quit the business." That was not something she was ever going to do. The romance fizzled out, but there was still enough feeling left that when Presley decided to marry Priscilla in December 1966, he couldn't face telling the actress himself. The Presleys were married at the Aladdin Hotel in Las Vegas on May 1, 1967. Ann-Margret married Roger Smith a week later, in the same city, at the Riviera Hotel.

Ann-Margret was known as "the female Elvis."

Being an entertainer was a dream the actress had cherished since, at the age of five, on her first day in America, her father took her to Radio City Music Hall in New York. She danced on a Vegas stage with George Burns in 1962, and by then she had already broken into the movies. Her third movie, the high-school-musical and rock-and-roll spoof *Bye Bye Birdie*, made her a star. That film's director Sidney wanted her to play in *Viva Las Vegas* and, given that she had already been billed as "the female Elvis," the idea seemed a no-brainer.

She was fiery, sexy, charming, and, very occasionally, irritating, in *Viva Las Vegas*. Her presence lifted Presley out of his torpor, and their combined power ensured that, even if the plot was as light as a handkerchief, this was Elvis's best musical comedy.

After the stars parted, Ann-Margret had a surprisingly varied—and intriguing—movie career, earning an Oscar nomination in Mike Nichols's *Carnal Knowledge* (1971) for seriously overacting and cavorting in detergent foam, baked beans, and chocolate. *Empire* magazine ranked her as the tenth-sexiest star in movie history in 1995. Elvis would probably have ranked her higher. Until the end of his life, he sent a guitar-shaped flower arrangement for all of her Vegas opening performances.

Joan Freeman (1942–): *Roustabout*

Freeman had been playing bit parts in movies and TV for years before landing the role of Cathy in *Roustabout*. She was far from the obvious choice: her previous most prominent role was as Lady Margaret in Corman's *Tower of London* (1962), where she was completely overshadowed by Vincent Price's evil Richard of Gloucester. On set, she had to play third fiddle to Presley and Stanwyck, a point that was made explicit when Wallis ignored her outstretched hand and greeting at the photo shoot for the movie's PR.

Freeman didn't especially bond with Elvis ("His background was so different to everyone else on the set," she told Bram), and onscreen they lack a certain something. To be fair to Freeman, her part wasn't especially well written, with *Variety* noting: "Miss Freeman doesn't have much to do except wring her hands when her father and boyfriend get in fights but she does it prettily."

Although *Roustabout* was one of Presley's biggest earners, Freeman didn't get much traction from its success. After a decent part in the comedy western *The Rounders*, she bowed out from the big screen with *The Fastest Guitar Alive*, a Civil War musical western that killed Roy Orbison's movie career instantly.

Shelley Fabares (1944–): *Girl Happy, Spinout, Clambake*

"They weren't great pictures, but they were great fun to make," is how Fabares, the only actress to play the leading lady in three Presley movies, recalls *Girl Happy*, *Spinout*, and *Clambake*.

Fabares and Presley were never romantically involved—she was married to record producer Lou Adler when they worked together—but he was certainly smitten and, whatever is going on around them in their three films together, they seem to connect. In *Girl Happy*, as a mobster's daughter, she is lucky enough to have Presley as her eager chaperone and exerts a charm so powerful that the King ditches the beautiful Mary Ann Mobley. In *Spinout*, she is the spoiled rich girl who forces Presley to sing at her birthday party, although, because Fabares is so pretty, perky, and innocent, no one really seems to mind. The denouement is a bit odd because she has far too much vigor for wimpy Philip, who would almost certainly have needed a dose of liver salts to survive his wedding night. In *Clambake*, she has a far more interesting role as a gold digger with a heart of gold and makes the implausible revamp of *The Prince and the Pauper* ring vaguely true at times.

One of a pack of teen queens who shot to fame in America in the early 1960s, Fabares was a stalwart of *The Donna Reed Show* and had a number 1 hit with "Johnny Angel" in 1962. Her first major movie role was in the Hawaiian beach-party movie *Ride the Wild Surf* (1964), alongside Fabian. Having starred with one of the pretenders to Presley's throne, she was cast alongside the King himself in *Girl Happy*. Her summary of the films—not great but great fun to make—is pretty accurate. She didn't take any of it too seriously and emerged relatively unscathed from *Clambake*. She later found a new audience as the altruistic wife of dying footballer James Caan in the TV movie *Brian's Song* (1971) and then as resourceful anchorwoman Christine Armstrong—and the titular hero's girlfriend—in *Coach*, which ran from 1989 to 1997 and won her two Emmy award nominations.

Jocelyn Lane (1937–): *Tickle Me*

Before Lane played Pam, the curvaceous fitness instructor in this spoof musical-comedy western, Lane had been billed as the "British Bardot." This was a tad misleading, as she was born in Vienna and her mother was Russian, but she had been appearing in British films since 1955 under the stage name Jackie Lane. When she moved to Hollywood in 1964, she became Jocelyn to avoid confusion with another actress who shared her old stage name. It didn't take her long to land the female lead in *Tickle Me*, and she has more presence than many of

One of many British leading ladies in Presley movies, Jocelyn Lane's presence brightened up *Tickle Me* (1965).   *Allied Artists/Photofest*

Presley's other leading ladies, bringing a refreshing sharpness to the role. She certainly shows why such the playboy and actor George Hamilton described her as "the most beautiful woman in the world" in 1965.

Tickle Me wasn't a great film, but it made money. Sadly, after this promising start, Lane's career stalled. She appeared in other films—most notably in the biker exploitation movie *Hell's Belles* (1969), in which she starred with Jeremy Slate (the villainous boat owner in *Girls! Girls! Girls!*)—but she retired in 1971, marrying Prince Alfonso of Hohenlohe-Langenburg. They divorced in 1984, and Lane dismissed her million-dollar settlement as "not fitting for a princess."

Mary Ann Mobley (1939–): *Harum Scarum*

In 1965, former Miss America Mobley was the vamp in *Girl Happy* and the princess in disguise in *Harum Scarum*. Incredibly, those roles helped her share the Golden Globe for Most Promising Newcomer with Mia Farrow and Celia Kaye. Yet in 1966, she married TV host Gary Collins and, as she focused on her daughter, found film roles harder to come by. She lost out to Stefanie Powers (as *The Girl from U.N.C.L.E.*) and saw Yvonne Craig cast over her as Batgirl. Her last film, *For Singles Only* (1968), was another Sam Katzman outing and derided as an "impotent fantasy about the sex lives of the young" by the *New York Times*. She made something of a comeback in the 1970s and 1980s with parts in such series as *Diff'rent Strokes* and *Falcon Crest.*

Luckily, Mobley enjoyed working on both Elvis films. She recalled, "Elvis and I felt a common bond, coming from Mississippi. He thought I understood him. He didn't have to put on airs with me, and I wasn't after anything. This is an odd thing to say about Elvis Presley, but it was like I was working with my brother." She appreciated his humor too. At one point during the shooting of *Harum Scarum*, he turned to her, his lip curling, and said, "*Harum Scarum*. This isn't going to change history, is it?"

Mobley does what she can with a weak part, silly script, and dodgy makeup in *Harum Scarum* but is far more effective as Deena, the temptress who almost entices Presley away from Fabares in *Girl Happy*. Her reacting as Elvis sings "Cross My Heart and Hope to Die" to her is one of the funnier moments in the movie.

Donna Douglas (1939–): *Frankie and Johnny*

As Elly May Clampet in *The Beverly Hillbillies* (1962–1971), Douglas was already a star when she was cast opposite Elvis in *Frankie and Johnny*. Although the riverboat musical was her only lead film role, she remained one of the most popular TV icons of the 1960s, with dolls and toys modeled after her character in the series.

Douglas had left Louisiana when she was seventeen to make it in showbiz in New York. After winning a local beauty contest, she appeared on *The Ed Sullivan Show* and was spotted by Wallis, who gave her a small part in *Career* (1959).

Douglas and Presley had many heavy spiritual conversations on the set of *Frankie and Johnny* and onscreen, as gorgeous as she looks, they relate more like siblings than lovers. *Variety* wasn't overly impressed, making passing reference to her beauty, and Douglas returned to *Beverly Hillbillies* until 1971. Like Buddy Ebsen, one of her costars in that show, she developed a second career singing gospel, Elvis's favorite music.

Presley and Donna Douglas bonded over religion on the *Frankie and Johnny* set.

United Artists/Photofest

Suzanna Leigh (1945–): *Paradise, Hawaiian Style*

The goddaughter of Vivian Leigh, whom she took her surname from, the English actress did her best with the underdeveloped role of Judy, the office girl Friday, in *Paradise, Hawaiian Style* (1966). Immigration difficulties may have prevented her from returning for *Easy Come, Easy Go* (1967). She insists Parker nixed her casting because he didn't like her introducing Elvis to new people and thinking about new movies. This might sound paranoid, but Schilling liked to say, "I had the feeling that, as far as the management around Elvis was concerned, the dumber you were around Elvis the longer you lasted."

She didn't get much action with the King onscreen but later declared, "Elvis' kisses held an intensity that melted my very being. I slipped my arms around his neck and our bodies entwined. This was all madness, but we didn't stop. A person could go to the gallows with such a kiss lingering on their lips, knowing life had been good."

Leigh went on to play frail heroine roles in a couple of Hammer movies: *The Lost Continent* (1968) and *Lust for a Vampire* (1971). She has recently achieved notoriety with her public insistence that "the mafia killed my soulmate Elvis."

Dodie Marshall (1945–): *Easy Come, Easy Go*

After beating off over two hundred other actresses to play the part of wild-child drummer Susan in *Spinout*, Marshall must have thought her time had come. Being asked to return as Jo Symington, the romantic lead, in *Easy Come, Easy Go* seemed to confirm that she was a rising star. Unfortunately for Marshall, she never made another movie again. That final scene in *Easy Come, Easy Go*, in which the sunken treasure turns out not to be worth very much at all, seems symbolic of her career—or what starring alongside Elvis did to it.

Born in Great Britain but raised in Philadelphia, Marshall never made any secret of her acting ambitions. After winning a part in a Broadway production of *Oliver!*, she moved to Hollywood in 1964, winning a guest role opposite Bill Bixby in the sitcom *My Favorite Martian*. A few more guest spots earned her a chance to compete for the part in *Spinout*, where she drums with an abandon that makes Presley's singing race-car driver look a bit tame.

In *Easy Come, Easy Go*, she is energetic as a free-spirited beatnik, who loves dancing, yoga, and, eventually, Elvis. Though she didn't seem to enjoy making the movie—she got injured during one scene and seemed to have felt out of her depth on set—*Variety* loved her performance, others admired her vast array of colorful outfits, and associate producer Nathan assured her it would do wonders for her career. It didn't.

Annette Day (1947–): *Double Trouble*

Having failed with attempts to sign Hayley Mills, Susan George, Judy Gleeson, and just about every other actress in London, *Double Trouble* producer Bernard was relieved when he spotted the seventeen-year-old Day working in an antique store in Portobello Road. Making her an offer he knew she wouldn't refuse, he talked her into the role of mysterious heiress Jill and took her off to Carnaby Street so he could buy her the right clothes to make the movie (which was supposed to be partly set in Swinging London) look authentic.

Day handled the transition from antique shop to film studio pretty well and quickly found Presley a helpful co-star. "I thought 'My goodness, what have I let myself in for here,' but he had tremendous patience with me," she said. "He very kindly took me through it. He said 'It's no problem, just take it easy.'" The reviews for her performance weren't especially glowing and she was soon back in London. The King gave her a white Mustang to show his appreciation (which she left in her brother's safekeeping).

Quentin Dean (1944–2003): *Stay Away, Joe*

In 1967, the twenty-three-year-old Dean won a Golden Globe nomination for Best Supporting Actress in her big-screen debut in *In the Heat of the Night*. That same year she had a minor role in Tom Gries's underrated western *Will Penny*.

Her star certainly seemed to be on the ascendant when she was cast as wannabe teenage nymphet Mamie Callaghan in *Stay Away, Joe*. Yet within a year, she left the entertainment industry, bowing out with a few roles in such TV westerns as *The High Chaparral*. She kept such a low profile after her exit that, for years, the very question of whether she was still alive was debated in various Internet forums. It has since been confirmed that she died in 2003.

Her retirement looks even odder because she is one of the best things in *Stay Away, Joe*. Her pursuit of Joe Lightcloud (Elvis) provided a welcome relief to the parties and fights that so frequently punctuate this good-humored comedy-western. She earned backhanded praise from *Variety*: "If Miss Dean wants to become stereotyped as a teenybopper dumb dora she can certainly do it."

Nancy Sinatra (1940–): *Speedway*

Nancy first met Elvis when she was sent to greet him on March 3, 1960, after his discharge from the U.S. Army, to promote her father's *Welcome Home Party for Elvis Presley* show.

As she recalled: "I got married and basically forgot about Elvis. Then *Speedway* came." Not first choice for the part of IRS agent Susan Jacks, she was still the King's most famous female lead since Ann-Margret, having had two U.S. number 1 hits with "These Boots Are Made for Walking" and "Somethin' Stupid" (a duet with her father), sung a Bond theme ("You Only Live Twice"), and played alongside other Presley leading ladies Mobley and O'Brien in *Get Yourself a College Girl* (1964).

Debate still rages over her performance, with the *New York Times*'s Renata Adler saying, "Miss Sinatra is far better singing than dancing or acting." She certainly looks good belting out Lee Hazelwood's "Your Groovy Self," the first number by another singer to appear on an Elvis soundtrack album. Others have been kinder, though she doesn't—and this was presumably the intention—generate the sparks with Elvis that Ann-Margret did in *Viva Las Vegas*. They were certainly close enough on set, fooling around but never having a full-blown affair. At one point, with Sinatra clad only in tight jeans and bra, he grabbed her and started kissing her. She remembers, "I started to melt," but then he pulled away and apologized. They parted on good terms: Sinatra even organized Priscilla's baby shower when Presley revealed she was pregnant.

Sinatra never made another movie, focusing instead on an intermittently successful recording career that has made her a cult heroine and an inspiration to directors like Tarantino, giving her a cachet that has nothing to do with her famous father.

Michele Carey (1943–): *Live a Little, Love a Little*

A model before she made an impression with a small role in *The Man from U.N.C.L.E.* movie *The Spy with My Face* (1965), Carey was really discovered by

Howard Hawks, who gave her a breakthrough part in *El Dorado*, a retread of *Rio Bravo* that is funnier, and tauter, than the original. Whether she is wrestling with James Caan or shooting John Wayne (don't worry, she doesn't kill him), Carey makes the western feel livelier and, crucially, younger.

That star quality impressed Douglas Laurence, the producer of *Live a Little, Love a Little*. He told Bram: "I saw many girls before Michele. One meeting and the contest was over as far as I was concerned. She had all the requirements to be a star."

On set she was focused and reserved, and she felt close to Elvis (though they probably didn't have an affair). She may have been struggling to think how she could make the kooky heroine Bernice, who virtually kidnaps Elvis for no apparent reason, appealing to the audience. She doesn't quite succeed, but it's hard to imagine anyone doing it better, and she may irritate but she never bores.

After this foray into screwball comedy, Carey rode back to the range starring in the below-par feminist revenge tale *Five Savage Men*, the Sinatra comedy–horse opera *Dirty Dingus Magee* (both in 1970), and Robert Butler's quixotic *Scandalous John* (1971). After that, she did not make another movie for six years until she had a minor role, as the punningly named Ora Lee Tingle, in *The Choirboys*. Carey had the beauty and talent but not the drive to claw her way to the top. Laurence concluded, "She didn't make a big splash because she didn't want to."

Ina Balin (1937–1990)—*Charro!*

You would never really know it from her underwritten part as Tracey in *Charro!* but Balin was an accomplished actress who had shown in such films as *From the Terrace* (1960) and *The Comancheros* (1961) that she could hold her own onscreen with such heavyweights as Paul Newman and John Wayne. She was nominated for a Golden Globe for her role as Newman's love interest.

Balin had always wanted to be an actress and, after studying with some of the Actors Studio's leading lights, got her big break as Anthony Quinn's sensitive daughter in *The Black Orchid* (1958). Called upon to play a variety of ethnicities, Balin never really found the part that could transform her career. She is seen to best advantage as the beautiful girl in *The Projectionist* (1971), the first Rodney Dangerfield movie, a whimsical wish-fulfillment showbiz fantasy that now looks like a harbinger of Woody Allen's *Purple Rose of Cairo*. Soon after that, she gave up acting to focus on the children she had adopted from Vietnam.

In *Charro!* she makes the most of her part, injecting more passion into her clinches with Presley than did many of his other leading ladies. The scene in which she talks to him while having a bath looks as if it has mysteriously survived the cuts that took much of the raunch and violence out of the story. Her role seems to have been significantly curtailed in the rewrite, as she starts off as a point of contention between the hero and villain but gradually becomes peripheral to the story. Though the part didn't do much for her career, she relished working with Presley.

Marlyn Mason (1945–): *The Trouble with Girls*

"Two seconds after we were introduced I was in love." That's how Mason recalls her first meeting with Elvis. Although Presley often named Fabares as his favorite co-star, he had a lot of fun with Mason. As she recalled: "We worked alike, never late, loved rehearsing, loved singing, liked playing pranks, loved to entertain. It was one hilarious ten-week ride working with The Man." The crew got used to hearing Elvis shout, "Cap!," his nickname for her, whenever he felt the set needed livening up.

Mason enjoyed a lot of small-screen time in the 1960s, most notably on the medical dramas *Ben Casey* and *Dr. Kildare*, but her role as Charlene, the militant, feisty entertainments boss of the chautaqua in *The Trouble with Girls*, was her first proper movie role. Buoyed by her director's faith—and her rapport with her leading man—Mason makes her heroine likeable, entertaining, and believable. She fires out the one-liners with panache yet is almost as impressive in the more reflective scenes. Her performance was generally liked, but after one more movie—John Erman's uneven coming-of-age comedy-drama *Making It* (1971)—it was back to television, where she played alongside Bruce Lee, one of Elvis's idols, in a drama about a blind insurance investigator. She has kept busy over the years, usually being called upon to provide what she self-deprecatingly calls "feisty energy."

Mary Tyler Moore (1936–): *Change of Habit*

Moore was an old hand by the time she appeared in Elvis's last feature, having starred in the *Dick Van Dyke Show* for eight years and held her own alongside Julie Andrews in the musical *Thoroughly Modern Millie* (1967).

Slightly surprised to find herself in an Elvis film, Tyler Moore was very focused on set, only occasionally joining in the bonhomie and laughingly complaining when Elvis tried to tickle her when they shot the football game in the park. Although they were, at best, cordial while shooting, Presley and Moore interact well onscreen, making the slightly less clichéd than usual romantic storyline all the more effective. As an actress, Moore has always had a formal, almost prissy quality, and that served her well as Sister Michelle, the nun torn between God and Elvis.

For once, appearing in an Elvis movie did an actress no harm whatsoever. In 1971, *The Mary Tyler Moore Show* began, becoming one of the cornerstones of CBS's unbeatable Saturday-night lineup. The show ended on a high in 1977, but Moore found it difficult initially to shake off that familiar persona until she played the bitter mother in Robert Redford's Oscar-winning *Ordinary People*. Since then she featured in the cult movie *Flirting with Disaster* and popular TV programs *That 70s Show* and *King of the Hill*.

12

"Son of a Bitch, We've Won!"

Those Elvis Awards and Nominations in Full

T hough some movies—like *Jailhouse Rock*—have been recognized as cultural landmarks since Presley's death, in his lifetime they got scant recognition. Which is why he was so overjoyed when *Elvis on Tour* shared the Golden Globe for Best Documentary in 1973. Here are the other nominations his films earned on release. The Laurels were awards created by *Motion Picture Exhibitor Magazine.*

G.I. Blues

1961   Elvis nominated for Grammy, Best Soundtrack Album or recording of original cast for motion picture or television
1961   Second place, Golden Laurels, Top Musical
1961   Edmund Beloin and Henry Garson nominated for a Writers Guild Award (Screen) as Best-written American Musical

Blue Hawaii

1962   Elvis nominated, Grammy, Best Soundtrack Album or recording of original cast for motion picture or television
1962   Came fourth in Golden Laurels, Top Musical
1962   Hal Kanter nominated for a WGA Award (Screen) for Best-written American Musical

Girls! Girls! Girls!

1963   Nominated for a Golden Globe, Best Motion Picture, Musical
1963   Elvis came second in Golden Laurels' Top Male Musical Performance category
1963   Third place, Golden Laurels, Top Musical category

Kissin' Cousins

1965   Gerald Drayson Adams and Gene Nelson nominated for a WGA Award (Screen) for Best-written American Musical

Viva Las Vegas

1965   Second place, Golden Laurels, Musical
1965   Elvis came third in Golden Laurels for Male Musical Performance
1965   Ann-Margaret took third place in Golden Laurels for female musical performance

Roustabout

1965   Anthony Lawrence and Allan Weiss nominated for a WGA Award (Screen) for Best-written American Musical

Girl Happy

1965   Fourth in Golden Laurels for Musicals

Tickle Me

1966   Elvis won a Golden Laurel for Best Male Musical Performance

Frankie and Johnny

1966   Fourth in Golden Laurels for Musicals

13

The Last Farewell

Proof That Elvis's Movies Could Damage Careers

I want to be a star and I see no reason to conceal it. I want to get to the top of my profession and that's more than just an expression of ego. I have the desire and some of the qualifications and I hope I can acquire the others."

That was fighting talk from Dodie Marshall after the 1967 release of *Easy Come, Easy Go*, in which she had played Presley's hippy, trippy leading lady. The twenty-two-year-old actress had been praised by *Variety* as "an excellent young actress." Yet after two Presley movies—she had impressed as a sexy drummer in *Spinout*—her big-screen career was over. She was last seen, that same year, as a woman trying to save a wounded white rhino in the barely remembered Chuck Connors series *Cowboy in Africa*.

Stella Stevens could have warned Marshall about her fate. After she read the first script for *Girls! Girls! Girls!* she went on strike. As a fellow Memphian, she had been intrigued by the idea of working with Elvis, but after reading the script, as she told *Bright Lights Film Journal*, "I went back to Paramount and said, 'I'm sorry I'm not going to be in this. You're not going to put me in this junk and make me the girl Elvis Presley dumps for another girl.' And they said: 'Young lady you are going to do this picture or be put on suspension and you will not be able to work here or anywhere.'"

Eventually, after being promised a role opposite Montgomery Clift, she relented. Stevens did her duty in *Girls! Girls! Girls!* but never got to play alongside Clift—though she later worked with Jerry Lewis and Dean Martin and shone as the heroine of Sam Peckinpah's neglected poetic western *The Ballad of Cable Hogue* (1970). Stevens's disgust—this was 1962, remember, when Elvis's movies were still generally pretty good—was strengthened by her conviction that the role of Robin, the sexy shoulder to cry on, would damage her career. It's easy to dismiss Stevens's fears as the predictable professional paranoia of an insecure actress, but when you study the credits of Elvis's movies—especially those made in the 1960s—it's hard not to be struck by how many careers these films ended or sabotaged.

Some ends were neither untimely nor unexpected. Norman Taurog left the director's chair for the last time after wrapping *Live a Little, Love a Little* in the summer of 1968. He was sixty-nine by then—he'd made his directorial debut in 1920—and almost blind. The last four movies he directed were all Presley musical comedies, and with his last star leaving Hollywood, there was no work for Taurog. Equally, it was no great shock when Philip Reed (King Toranshan in *Harum Scarum*), who hadn't made a movie since 1957, bowed out after his appearance in Elvis's quickie musical comedy. Or when veteran thespians Frank McHugh and Una Merkel (who had started as a stand-in for silent movie queen Lillian Gish) quit after *Easy Come, Easy Go* and *Spinout*, respectively.

Yet for many others, working on an Elvis movie proved strangely toxic, as if their mere participation put them professionally beyond the pale. Few suffered as swiftly or as tragically as poor Judy Tyler, who died in a road accident when she was twenty-five, just three weeks after filming had completed on *Jailhouse Rock*.

Elvis's leading ladies were in almost as much peril as King Henry VIII's wives. Like Marshall, Annette Day (*Double Trouble*), Quentin Dean (*Stay Away, Joe*), Donna Douglas (*Frankie and Johnny*), and Nancy Sinatra (*Speedway*) never played in another Hollywood movie after being romanced by Presley.

The toxin worked more slowly for Joan O'Brien (who made one more major film after *It Happened at the World's Fair*) and Jocelyn Lane (the *Tickle Me* star bowed out of Hollywood in 1970, playing opposite Fabian, comically miscast as gangster Pretty Boy Floyd in the dismal *A Bullet for Pretty Boy*). No wonder Lane gave up movies to marry into the aristocracy and design feather necklaces.

After an eye-catching role in Burt Kennedy's entertaining comedy western *The Rounders* (1965), *Roustabout* star Joan Freeman's career petered out with the oddity that was *The Fastest Guitar Alive* (1967). She made a fleeting, cultish comeback in *Friday the 13th: The Final Chapter* (1984).

Suzanna Leigh lasted longer after *Paradise, Hawaiian Style*, but only because she was willing to play an exhausted pop star terrorized by bees (in *The Deadly Bees*) and be stranded on an island populated by giant monster crabs and Spanish conquistadors in *The Lost Continent* (representative sample of dialogue: "I'll not pray to any man! Let alone a child who is hardly enough to wipe his own bottom") before bowing out in *Son of Dracula*, a bizarre genre-straddling comedy/horror/musical in which she is pursued by Harry Nilsson, playing Count Dracula's son. Maybe Dolores Hart, the star of *Loving You* and *King Creole*, foresaw such indignities and therefore decided to become a nun. Even the villainesses weren't immune: Pat Priest, one of the more charismatic bad girls in an Elvis film, played her last significant role in *The Incredible 2-Headed Transplant* (1971), which is every bit as dire as the title makes it sound.

Even a cursory glance through Tom Lisandi's books on 1960s movie bombshells—*Drive-In Dream Girls* and *Fantasy Femmes of Sixties Cinema*—reveals how ruthlessly Hollywood recruited, used, and discarded actresses in this period. Yet the casualty rate among Presley's female co-stars was high, even for this turbulent era in Hollywood history. The problem for actresses like Fabares was that, when the fashion changed, and Hollywood began making more rebellious, youth-oriented films like *Easy Rider*, they had already been typecast and were deemed too cute, nice, or square for these more challenging roles.

Elvis's movies exacted a similar toll on the men who wrote the screenplays, although, as these were the often the most glaringly inept aspect of his movies, fans might feel that in this case, as least, justice was done.

Sinatra bowed out of the movies after being romanced by Presley in *Speedway*.

MGM/Photofest

Allan Weiss wrote seven pictures—six for Elvis and the tolerable western *The Sons of Katie Elder* (1965). Weiss's first draft for his debut *Blue Hawaii* was polished by Hal Kanter, who had written and directed *Loving You*. By the time Weiss had written his last Presley script—*Easy Come, Easy Go*—even he had realized the formula was beyond polishing.

Into the breach stepped Michael A. Hoey, dialogue coach on *Tickle Me*, whose greatest contribution to the cinema to date had been to co-write and direct the Mamie van Doren sci-fi horror B movie *The Navy vs. The Night Monsters* (1966). Hoey was hardly the ideal candidate to write the quirky comedy-western *Stay Away, Joe* or the screwball throwback *Live a Little, Love a Little*, but budgets were budgets. After that, Hoey retired to the small screen, where he was briefly notable as one of the producers of *Fame*, a smash TV series about young showbiz talent that prefigured *Glee*.

Apart from Arthur Browne Jr. (*Clambake*), Weiss, and Hoey, other writers whose last movie credit was an Elvis film include Gerald Drayson Adams (*Harum Scarum*), Edward Bernds (*Tickle Me*), William Fay (*Kid Galahad*), Henry Garson (*G.I. Blues*), Michael V. Gazzo (*King Creole*), James Lee (*Change of Habit*), Arnold and Lois Peyser (*The Trouble with Girls*), Philip Shuken (*Speedway*), and Charles Marquis Warren (*Charro!*). *Wild in the Country* was also the last Clifford Odets script filmed before the playwright's death.

So why did Elvis's movies derail so many careers apart from his own? It's partly sheer professional snobbery—as Sue Anna Langdon (who appeared in *Roustabout* and *Frankie and Johnny*) put it: "For an actress, appearing in an Elvis movie was either a step down or a take the money and run kind of thing."

Everyone in Hollywood in the 1960s—even the stars—was deeply insecure about their status role and power. Industry lore was full of cautionary tales about an apparently minor misstep that had proved professionally fatal. Such insecurity was exacerbated in the 1960s because, although everyone knew the old studio system was dying, no one really knew what would replace it. As Elvis's movies deteriorated artistically and commercially, there was less percentage in any decent performer, writer, or director risking guilt by association. Failure begat failure. With lesser co-stars, there was less incentive for Elvis to raise his game as a performer—compare his scenes with Barbara Stanwyck in *Roustabout* or Charles Bronson in *Kid Galahad* to the bemused, smiling acquiescence with which he endures *Paradise, Hawaiian Style*. By 1967, Elvis's disinterest had spread to cast, crew, and many fans—the magazine *Elvis Monthly* even referred to them as "animated puppet shows for not over bright children."

As budgets plunged after Katzman made *Kissin' Cousins*, it was increasingly hard for a co-star to even take the money and run.

The most toxic Elvis movie of all is probably *The Trouble with Girls*. Feisty co-star Marlyn Mason would make only one more movie, although she enjoyed a durable acting career on TV. Nicole Jaffe, who plays the hotel owner's zany daughter, never won another credited film role but earned lasting fame as the voice of Velma in the *Scooby-Doo* cartoons. Child star Anissa Jones (the sparky, talented dancing girl Carol) became a household favorite in the sitcom *Family Affair* but, after it was canceled in 1971, struggled to find good parts and died of a massive, accidental drug overdose in August 1976. She was just nineteen.

Producer Lester Welch quit after *The Trouble with Girls*. The film was also the last bow for director Peter Tewksbury. After eight years in television, Tewksbury quit the industry to run the cheese department in a Vermont food co-op. That made him the sixth director to sign off with an Elvis movie. The others are Nadel, Taurog, Charles Marquis Warren (*Charro*), John Rich (*Easy Come, Easy Go*), and Gene Nelson (*Harum Scarum*).

The curse of the Presley movie isn't quite up there with the *Superman* curse—the Man of Steel films were associated with more unlucky, mysterious, or untimely deaths—but it was powerful enough to blight acting careers. Especially Presley's.

The Rules of the Game

How to Get Cast in an Elvis Movie

The casting of Presley's movies has often perplexed cineastes, with some accomplished performers (Lola Albright, Charles Bronson, Dolores Del Rio, Hope Lange, John McIntire, Carolyn Jones, Angela Lansbury, Walter Matthau, Barbara Stanwyck, and Gig Young) standing out among a throng of thespians of variable gifts, some of whom were making distinctly inauspicious movie debuts. The most random casting for any Elvis film was surely *The Trouble with Girls*, in which he shares the limelight with such talents as John Carradine, Dabney Coleman, and Vincent Price. For the travelogues, the casting was usually more predictable, with producers putting the most effort into finding the right leading lady. Their definition of *right* could be idiosyncratic—as their choices for *Double Trouble* and *Live a Little, Love a Little* testify—but their record wasn't all bad.

Casting has always been a mysterious process, and budgets and tinseltown snobbery made it even more challenging on Presley's movies. Yet if you pore over the cast lists, it is possible to discern a few rules. Here they are, in no particular order of importance.

I. When in doubt, find someone who's worked with Jerry Lewis.

The movie careers of Presley and the king of hyperactive comedy ran almost in parallel. Both got their start with Hal Wallis, were directed by Norman Taurog and John Rich, and worked with scripts written by Edward Anhalt, Herbert Baker, Edmond Beloin, Hal Kanter, and Elwood Ullmann. Lewis started earlier—with partner Dean Martin he was a box-office smash in the early 1950s—but his movie career ran into the ground at roughly the same time as Presley's. Though he made a comeback in the acclaimed *King of Comedy*, Lewis's reign in Hollywood ended with the flop *Which Way to the Front*, released in 1970, the same year as Presley's last feature film, *Change of Habit*.

Although Lewis's career nosedived after he succumbed, as Dino put it once, to the delusion that he was the new Charlie Chaplin (a delusion many French movie fans share), he and Presley were exploited rather than developed by Hollywood, condemned to keep remaking the same movie at a similarly relentless pace. Indeed, Wallis had explicitly recruited Elvis as insurance, in case the split between Martin and Lewis led to them falling from favor. This exploitative strategy is revealed, in part, by the number of performers their films had in common. Most of the time, the performers would appear in Lewis's films first, but occasionally it would be the other way around. Stella Stevens's reward for knuckling under on *Girls! Girls! Girls!* was a leading role opposite Lewis in the cult classic *The Nutty Professor*, in which Julie Parrish—later one of El's love interests in *Paradise, Hawaiian Style*—had a minor role.

Running through Lewis's movies and counting the actors who would later star with Presley is a repetitive yet bizarrely engrossing exercise. Five of the King's leading ladies—Ina Balin, Joan Blackman, Suzanna Leigh, Joan O'Brien, and Lizabeth Scott—played opposite Lewis first. Both stars' films drew on a similar pool of character actors, as they shared screen time with the likes of Stanley Adams, Michael Ansara, Leif Erickson, Glenda Farrell, Milton Frome, James Gleason, Gale Gordon, Robert Ivers, Jack Kruschen, Elsa Lanchester, John McIntire, Howard McNear, Frank Puglia, Sheree North, Mickey Shaughnessy, Robert Strauss, and John Williams. Lewis's comedy *The Family Jewels* (1965) also marked the screen debut of child star Donna Butterworth, who would run amok in *Paradise, Hawaiian Style*.

For Elvis fans, the galling aspect of this crossover is that Lewis, certainly when he had Martin as a straight man and in his heyday in the late 1950s and early 1960s, consistently worked with better actors. Tony Curtis, who had inspired Elvis to act, was in *Boeing (707), Boeing (707)* (1965), and Janet Leigh, who consistently refused to appear in a Presley film despite frequent overtures from Wallis and his associates, starred in two Lewis comedies: *Living It Up* (1954) and *Three on a Couch* (1966)—the latter also featured Mary Ann Mobley, who had starred in *Girl Happy* and *Harum Scarum*.

Lewis and Presley had so many collaborators in common, but the comedian had more say in his career—and, unfortunately, more responsibility for its ignominious end. As bad as some of Elvis's films are, none sink to the depths of *The Day the Clown Cried* (1972), Lewis's ill-advised mawkish Holocaust movie, which was described by actor Harry Shearer as so perfectly, awe-inspiringly bad it could not be improved in any significant way.

2. If that fails, call Batman.

For two years and 120 episodes between 1966 and 1968, the kitsch Adam West version of the *Batman* comics was a huge, self-parodying hit. Elvis was one of the show's biggest fans. He must have been tickled to see his old co-star Yvonne Craig as Batgirl. So many actors in the series appeared in his films, you suspect that Elvis—or his directors—was using the caped crusader's capers as a talent pool.

Presley specifically requested that Burgess Meredith star in *Stay Away, Joe* because he enjoyed his villainous Penguin. Other actors from the series to star opposite Elvis include Rudy Vallee (Lord Marmaduke Ffogg in *Batman* and Presley's boss in *Live a Little, Love a Little*), Vincent Price (a cookery book writer in *Batman* and Mr. Morality in *The Trouble with Girls*), Stanley Adams (Captain Courageous in *Batman* and Captain Roach in *Double Trouble*), Monte Landis (Basil in *Batman*, Presley's manager in *Double Trouble*), and Diane McBain (Lisa/Pinky Pinkston in *Batman* and one of the women pursuing Elvis in *Spinout*).

3. Be big on the small screen.

This ploy worked for Shelley Fabares, a stalwart on *The Donna Reed Show* between 1958 and 1965, who starred in three Elvis movies. In her second outing, *Spinout*, her father was played by Carl Betz, who also played her pa in the TV series. (The role didn't do much for his career: he wouldn't make another movie for nine years.) Tyler was cast in *Jailhouse Rock* after making her name in the *Howdy Doody* TV series, Douglas parlayed her success in *The Beverley Hillbillies* into the role of Frankie in *Frankie and Johnny*, and Priest, having made her name on *The Munsters*, was cast at the last moment in *Easy Come, Easy Go*. This casting strategy even applied to supporting roles: Howard McNear, the absent-minded travel agent in *Blue Hawaii*, had made his name as Floyd the barber on *The Andy Griffith Show*.

4. Join the stock company.

If you had been cast in one Elvis movie, the odds were pretty high that you would be asked to return. The Presley movie began to acquire its own stock company. Repeat performers include Fabares (*Girl Happy, Spinout*, and *Clambake*), Pamela Austin (*Blue Hawaii, Kissin' Cousins*), Bill Bixby (*Clambake, Speedway*), Joan Blackman (*Blue Hawaii, Kid Galahad*), Yvonne Craig (*It Happened at the World's Fair, Kissin' Cousins*), Edward Faulkner (*G.I. Blues, Tickle Me*), Gail Gilmore (*Girl Happy, Harum Scarum*), Norman Grabowski (*Roustabout, Girl Happy*), Dolores Hart (*Loving You, King Creole*), Jimmy Hawkins (*Girl Happy, Spinout*), Will Hutchins (*Spinout, Clambake*), L. Q. Jones (*Love Me Tender, Flaming Star, Stay Away Joe*), Gary Lockwood (*Wild in the Country, It Happened at the World's Fair*), Dodie Marshall (*Spinout, Easy Come, Easy Go*), Howard McNear (*Blue Hawaii, Follow That Dream*), Mary Ann Mobley (*Girl Happy, Harum Scarum*), Jack Mullaney (*Tickle Me, Spinout*), Arthur O'Connell (*Follow That Dream, Kissin' Cousins*), Jan Shepard (*King Creole, Paradise, Hawaiian Style*), Jeremy Slate (*G.I. Blues, Girls! Girls! Girls!*), and Roland Winters (*Blue Hawaii, Follow That Dream*). And then there's Billy Barty, who, presumably because of the Colonel's mysterious affection for midgets, turns up in *Roustabout* and *Harum Scarum*.

Sometimes the feeling of déjà vu must have been overwhelming for Presley. In *Blue Hawaii*, he ends up in jail after a fight with Steve Brodie, who, as obnoxious Tucker Garvey, flirts with one of the young girls Elvis is acting as a tour guide for. Fast-forward three years and the same actor, playing an even more obnoxious carnivalgoer, starts another fight, which—and here we find a slight change in the formula—ends up with grumpy Leif Erickson spending a night in the slammer. Yet Brodie is only following a curious precedent set by Ken Becker, who goads the King into his first screen fight in *Loving You* and was deemed so effective he returned to provoke another round of bar-demolishing fisticuffs by playing the jukebox as Elvis croons "Doin' the Best I Can."

The star who appeared in most Presley films apart from the King and Red West is dancer and actress Teri Garr, who can be seen in nine Elvis movies. Her presence is, at least, easy to explain. The King liked her. After talking to her during the making of *Viva Las Vegas*, he made sure that she got the call if dancing was required—as it invariably was in an Elvis movie in this period. As she said: "We were good but he gave us a boost in the right direction. And he was very loyal to his friends." So loyal that he prevented Rich from firing her after she had been out of step in a dance number in *Roustabout*. She was touched that he seemed to take pride in her success, spotting her on TV and saying: "That's our Teri Garr."

5. Be nice to Hal Wallis.

As the producer of nine Presley pictures, Hal Wallis probably had the greatest influence on the casting of the King's movies. He had his own kind of repertory company—from which he chose Wendell Corey, Dolores Hart, and Lizabeth Scott for *Loving You*—and he was responsible for casting some of Elvis's best co-stars, notably Carolyn Jones, Angela Lansbury, and Walter Matthau. Yet Julie Parrish, one of the King's co-stars in *Paradise, Hawaiian Style*, insisted that the producer was not averse to recruiting via the casting couch. "Mr. Wallis was an old lech," she told Lisanti. "I think he thought there was an unspoken premise that I would sleep with him since he allowed me to re-test for the part." After a kiss the day before shooting started, she avoided Wallis and his frequent warnings that "Little girl you better think again."

6. Join the Memphis Mafia.

Membership of this exclusive organization did wonders for Red West's movie career. He had roles—mostly uncredited—in seventeen Presley movies, not counting his appearance as himself in *Elvis on Tour*. His most demanding role was as Presley's no-good brother in *Wild in the Country*, but his main function was to start a fight with the King. His most famous punch-up is probably the extended rumble in the newspaper printing plant in *Live a Little, Love a Little*. He also wrote a few songs for Elvis movies, his composition "If You Think I Don't Need You" making the cut for *Viva Las Vegas*.

Although the Memphis Mafia were not universally popular on set, West did well enough to make a kind of living in Hollywood long after Presley had given up on acting. Even while Elvis was still in Hollywood, West branched out as a stuntman and bit-part player in the TV series *The Wild Wild West*, becoming great friends with Robert Conrad and appearing in two of the star's other series, *Flying Misfits* and *The Duke*.

None of Presley's other mafiosos made such productive use of their time in Hollywood. Charlie Hodge, best known as the man who gave Elvis his scarves onstage, had four minor roles, including as a Mexican in *Charro!* Memphis DJ George Klein had the same tally as Hodge. Lamar Fike had an uncredited role in *Jailhouse Rock*. Jerry Schilling played the deputy sheriff in *The Trouble with Girls* and, as Hoey recalls in his memoirs, decided to movie into editing after being stung by Presley's apparent indifference when he broke his arm on the set of *Live a Little, Love a Little*. Although Schilling was given a job as assistant to Hal Ashby, editing didn't really work out. Ironically, his biggest contribution may have been working with Martin Scorsese in the editing booth on *Elvis on Tour*.

7. Be cheap.

That must have been part of the rationale for casting Day as the lead in *Double Trouble*. Plucked from an antique shop in London, she was nice enough, but John Alderson, who played the menacing Iceman in the movie, summed it up nicely when he said: "She was a very sweet girl but they could've done a lot better finding an actress." In one casting memo for *Easy Come, Easy Go*, Wallis's associate producer Paul Nathan lists the options for Judd (the part of Presley's nightclub-owning buddy). Top of the list is actor Dick Martin, but Nathan notes: "Excellent choice but will cost $20 or $25,000." Ultimately, Pat Harrington got the part for a guaranteed minimum of $10,000.

Never Say Yes

Those Working Titles, from the Sublime to the Ridiculous

On movie exec said they could have been numbered, but some thought did go into naming Elvis movies, as this list shows:

Lonesome Cowboy, *Running Wild*, and *Something for the Girls* were all considered for *Loving You*.

Danny and *Sing, You Sinners* were passed over for *King Creole*.

Café Europa was deemed too sophisticated, so Presley's first post-army film became *G.I. Blues*. *Lonely Man* was too somber—and the song was cut anyway—so Clifford Odets's drama became *Wild in the Country*, which is, after all, a line from Walt Whitman's *Leaves of Grass*.

Hawaii Beach Boy. Not so much a title, more of a description of the plot or a marketing statement, this became *Blue Hawaii*.

A Girl in Every Port, *Welcome Aboard*, and the dire *Gumbo Ya-Ya* were possibilities before *Girls! Girls! Girls!* was decided on.

Vacation in Acapulco was the prosaic precursor of *Fun in Acapulco*. Sounds functional, but two later films would be billed as *Harem Holiday* and *California Holiday* in the UK.

Polynesian Paradise, *Hawaiian Paradise*, and, yep, *Polynesian Holiday* were options for Elvis's last Hawaiian movie.

Jim Dandy, *After Midnight*, *Always at Midnight*, *Raceway*, *Never Say No* (too saucy, said the Colonel), then *Never Say Yes*, and finally *Spinout*.

A Girl in Every Port (again) was an option for *Easy Come, Easy Go*.

You're Killing Me would have been better than *Double Trouble*.

Bumblebee, Oh Bumblebee and *Born Rich* would have been quite odd. Thankfully, they were bypassed in favor of *Stay Away, Joe*.

Pot Luck was mooted before *Speedway* got the vote. Was the original choice an attempt to cross-promote the 1962 studio album of the same name?

Something in the Way He Moves

Elvis the Dancer

A lthough Presley's pelvic disruption had helped make him the most successful recording artist in the world in the 1950s, his hip shaking would be circumscribed onscreen, especially in the 1960s when Hollywood sold him as an entertainer the whole family could enjoy. Even before that, some of the industry's most talented choreographers had tried to incorporate his moves into more stylized routines. The effects varied. He could look glorious—as he did in the numbers "Jailhouse Rock" and "Bossa Nova Baby"—yet he could also look slightly embarrassed, as he did in many of the faster numbers in such movies as *Spinout* and *Double Trouble*.

The dancers on his films recall him with particular affection. As Garr recalled in an interview with the Elvis Information Network, "Dancers on movie sets are treated like the lowest form of vegetable life." Presley never treated them like that, standing up for them against directors and choreographers. The tight schedules and budgets on his later films made their jobs particularly difficult. Often there wasn't time to rehearse the routines properly, so Elvis would ask his friend Lance LeGault to work the steps out with the choreographer. Patricia Casey, assistant to choreographer Alex Romero on *Double Trouble*, recalled: "I would work out the kinks with Lance to see if we thought it would be uncomfortable for Elvis to do. We'd work to get the kinks out and then I'd teach Elvis." The star may have had his own way of moving, and he was, as Romero put it, "great," but he "could only move his hips." Everything else had to be choreographed and staged by Romero or someone like him.

Most of the choreographers he worked often with—Romero, David Winter, and Jack Baker—came to the conclusion that Presley was more at ease when people were dancing around him. This is partly why, especially in his 1960s movies, he is invariably shown performing onstage or surrounded by a bevy of beautiful dancers around a swimming pool or in a nightclub. Charles O'Curran, who staged the songs in six of the Presley/Wallis movies, had tried a different tack. Aiming to build the King's moves into the numbers, he had jumped around offscreen to show the star how he wanted him to move. Usually a low-key actor, particularly in the musical comedies, Presley had to be encouraged to overplay when he was performing onscreen.

"Jailhouse Rock"

The standout number from Elvis's third film is Romero's finest contribution to the King's movies. The son of a Mexican general, Romero taught himself to tap dance by the time he was fifteen and started in Hollywood as a dancer in such musicals as *An American in Paris*. He soon began assisting such choreographers as Hermes Pan and Fred Astaire (on *The Barkleys of Broadway*), Michael Kidd (*Seven Brides for Seven Brothers*), and Gene Kelly (*An American in Paris*), developing a reputation as the go-to choreographer for producers needing clever, inventive dance pieces that used props.

His original choreography for the *Jailhouse Rock* number was more suited to a classically trained dancer. When Presley confessed he was struggling, Romero had a rethink, saying later: "I chose steps that were foreign to him, but that were also like him, so he could pick them up." The end result was glorious and, fittingly enough, was applauded by Romero's mentor Kelly.

"C'mon Everybody"

Recommended by Ann-Margret, David Winters did some fine work on *Viva Las Vegas*. A former child actor, Winters has always been a bit of a jack of all trades, directing two episodes of *The Monkees* and making the sci-fi movie *Space Mutiny* (described by one critic as the worst sci-fi adventure movie ever made) but also teaching such stars as Garr, Ann-Margret, and Raquel Welch how to dance. The pièce de résistance in *Viva Las Vegas* was this sizzling duet between the King and his co-star in which, perhaps galvanized by sexual attraction and the recognition that the actress is serious competition for the camera's attention, Presley wiggles his hips, snaps his fingers, and generally moves with a freedom not seen since "Trouble" in *King Creole*.

"He's Your Uncle, Not Your Dad"

Speedway was Romero's fourth and last Presley movie, and he bowed out with an entertaining production number that wouldn't have felt out of place in the kind of classic Hollywood musical he had cut his teeth in. The song may be absurd, but Presley handles the complex routine with aplomb, interacting with an office full of anxious businessmen, changing the tempo, taking a breather to light a cigarette for a shuddering fellow sufferer, and ending with a comically patriotic salute to Uncle Sam.

"Edge of Reality"

Baker had started out as an actor, and tried his hand at songwriting, before choreographing Taurog on *The Stars Are Singing* (1953). He later worked on the Lewis–Martin hit *The Caddy*, some beach-party movies, and Taurog's bizarre hybrid of beach-party comedy and spy spoof *Dr. Goldfoot and the Bikini Machine*. Baker had worked with an army of bikini-clad robots in that clunker, and the experience may have influenced his choreography on *Live a Little, Love a Little*. This comedy features the weirdest dance routine in any Presley movie, with the King singing in a dream sequence with a troupe of girls, Michelle Carey, and a man in a dog suit. Miraculously, it works. The King looks superb in an electric blue suit and is, for the most part, deployed in front of the troupe. The fact that this whole sequence is taking part in a drug-induced dream helps mask his occasional stiffness. It has been suggested that Jack Regas, who had staged some of the numbers in *Paradise, Hawaiian Style*, was responsible for creating this unique sequence. Either way, this number has to be seen to be believed, and it is, in its way, much less embarrassing than some of the concepts Steve Binder came up with for that year's NBC TV special.

17

"With His Foot on the Gas and No Brakes on the Fun!"

The Best of Those Tag Lines

Be amazed at what Hollywood's top wordsmiths came up with to promote Elvis's movies. Here are some of their finest.

"See How Youth Reacts When the Gates are Opened?"
How youth reacts, apparently, is captured in *Girl Happy*, a movie with no gates in sight.

"Them Kittyhawks Is Swoopin' Down on Poor, Unsuspecting Soldiers"
That's as good as it gets for *Kissin' Cousins*.

"With His Foot on the Gas and No Brakes on the Fun"
As fair a description of *Spinout* as you're ever likely to get.

"Mr. Rock 'n' Roll in the story he was born to play"
The slogan for *Love Me Tender* has a nice sense of history about it. Unlike . . .

"Elvis Presley back on the screen . . . for the first time in a year!"
The resistible slogan selling *Loving You*.

"Watch Elvis Click With All These Chicks"
Because in *Live a Little, Love a Little*, he's a photographer!

"On his neck he wore the brand of a killer. On his hip he wore vengeance"
The poster for *Charro!* Promises a mean, ornery West the movie doesn't deliver.

"Elvis goes West . . . and the West goes wild . . . And that's no Sitting Bull!
For once, the slogan does give you a pretty good idea of what to expect.

"ELVIS AS THE GAY, SINGING SENSATION . . . TOAST OF THE WORLD'S GIRLS . . . ENVY OF EVERY MAN IN THE ARMY!"
Some slogans—like this one for *G.I. Blues*—don't age too well.

"Elvis brings the big beat to Bagdad in this riotous rockin' rollin' adventure spoof!!!"
This one hasn't stood the test of time either. Three exclamation marks is a sure sign of desperation.

18

It's Only Words

Writing for the King

Anthony Lawrence (1928–)

M y agent called me up and said, 'Would you consider doing a movie for Elvis Presley?' And I said, 'Who's Elvis Presley?'" That is how Anthony Lawrence, who wrote *Roustabout*, recalled the start of his association with the King. A saloon singer and big-band enthusiast, Lawrence was a "bit overwhelmed" to be asked to rewrite Allan Weiss's script, but he did as he was asked. Put on a week-to-week contract, he wrote three Presley movies—the other two being the significantly less impressive *Paradise, Hawaiian Style* and *Easy Come, Easy Go*—but he recalled: "At the end of every week, I'd pick up my pencils and go home because I figured I was going to be fired."

Many Elvis fans might wish Lawrence had been fired before he could pen his last two Presley movies—although he partially redeemed himself by scripting John Carpenter's above-average biopic *Elvis* (1979)—but that would be to miss the point. Most of Presley's writers were working to a fairly specific brief, as Weiss said: "Wallis kept the screenplays pretty shallow." Most producers—especially Joe Pasternak—followed Wallis's lead.

Lawrence was better than some of the writers who scripted Elvis's films and worse than others. He had made his name as the writer who specialized in killing off the wives of Ben Cartwright (Lorne Greene) in *Bonanza*. Between 1969 and 1974, he was a regular writer on *Hawaii Five-0*, one of Presley's favorite shows. That kind of profile was not untypical for one of Elvis's screenwriters. Although their backgrounds varied, his scribes were, without exception, older than the star they were writing for. The most famous was playwright Clifford Odets, whose unfinished script for *Wild in the Country* was twice as long and three times as florid as it needed to be. Charles Lederer penned the classic screwball comedy *His Girl Friday* twenty-two years before he adapted Richard Powell's novel for Elvis's *Follow That Dream*.

Others did decent work for other producers or actors. Theodore J. Flicker, co-author of *Spinout*, is best known for the satire *The President's Analyst* (1967), which included a swipe at the FBI that so enraged director J. Edgar Hoover, the writer was escorted from the lot. Edward Anhalt, who co-wrote *Girls! Girls! Girls!*, was versatile enough to win an Oscar for *Becket* and pen Robert Redford's mountain-man western *Jeremiah Johnson*. A few—Philip Shuken (*Speedway*) and Weiss (who wrote many of Wallis's scripts for Elvis)—were tyros. And one—Gene Nelson—was pressed into service to save money, helping Gerald Drayson Adams on *Kissin' Cousins*.

Gerald Drayson Adams (1900–1988)

Watching *Harum Scarum*, it is almost impossible to believe it was written by a former literary agent who had studied at Oxford University. Yet Adams was not such an odd choice for the assignment. He had started in Hollywood in the 1940s, churning out stories for William "one shot" Beaudine, but by 1950, he was writing the very Arabian adventures, *The Prince Who Was a Thief* and *Son of Ali Baba*, that made Tony Curtis a star and enthralled millions of teenagers (including the young Presley). In the latter, he wrote what is probably, thanks to Curtis's pronunciation, his most famous line: "Yondah lies the castle of my faddah."

By the 1960s, Nelson spent most of his time writing TV westerns, and his movie work had become increasingly intermittent. After collaborating with Nelson on *Kissin' Cousins* and penning the incomprehensible *Harum Scarum*, he wisely retired. Ironically, he won the only award nomination of his twenty-five-year Hollywood career, for *Kissin' Cousins*, which was shortlisted by the Writers Guild of America for Best-written American Musical.

Sally Benson (1897–1972)

The author of *Meet Me in St Louis* was an unusual choice to write an Elvis movie. Starting out writing autobiographical stories for *The New Yorker* that inspired Vincente Minnelli's classic musical, Benson had range, sharing credits on Hitchcock's *Shadow of a Doubt* (1943), *Anna and the King of Siam* (1946), and the Barbara Stanwyck film noir *No Man of Her Own* (1950).

Truth be told, she was slightly behind the curve when she was assigned *Viva Las Vegas*, having written only one movie—the Hayley Mills/Disney drama *Summer Magic* (1963)—in the preceding decade, but her fast-moving, easy-on-the-ear screenplay for Sidney's musical comedy revived her fortunes for a while. She might well have written more but called it a day after sharing the credit on the Debbie Reynolds vehicle *The Singing Nun*. Retirement left her with more time for to indulge her favorite pastimes: playing the piano, reading, and visiting racetracks.

Edward Bernds (1905–2000) and Elwood Ullman (1903–1985)

Bernds and Ullman will always be remembered for two things: making us laugh as the writers of most of the Three Stooges' best work—and being nominated for an Academy Award by mistake. In 1955 they made a low-budget feature called *High Society* that was shortlisted for best script. Unfortunately for Bernds and

Ullman, the Academy had actually intended to honor the Frank Sinatra–Bing Crosby musical *High Society*. Informed of this case of mistaken identity, they graciously allowed their nomination to be withdrawn. They collaborated on only one Elvis film, *Tickle Me*, bringing a welcome, if slightly deranged, conviction to this musical comedy, harking back to the humor of the Stooges era and looking forward to the comic ghost stories that kept the pesky meddling kids so profitably occupied in *Scooby-Doo*. Slapstick, self-parody, women cavorting like excited horses as the King belts out "Dirty Dirty Feeling" . . . *Tickle Me* has all this and more. Bernds and Ullmann made sure that once seen, the film is never forgotten.

Clair Huffaker (1926–1990)

A respected author of western novels, who had learned the art of storytelling from a compulsive reading of Edgar Rice Burroughs's fiction as a boy, Huffaker drifted into Hollywood in the late 1950s, helping out on series like *The Rifleman*. His first movie script, from his own novel, was the superior Audie Murphy western *Seven Ways from Sundown* (1960). When Nunnally Johnson threw a tantrum and refused to tweak his *Flaming Star* screenplay for Presley, Huffaker rode to the rescue, agreeing to adapt his own story for Siegel.

For the next thirteen years, he would be one of the most sought-after writers on the celluloid range, with *The Comancheros* (1961), *Rio Conchos* (1964), *The War Wagon* (1967), and *100 Rifles* (1969), a feminist take on the western starring Raquel Welch, among his most notable credits. It's a shame he wasn't asked to write *Charro!*, as he would probably have done a much better job than Charles Marquis Warren. His work dried up only as the western genre fell out of fashion in the mid-1970s. His daughter, Samantha Clair Kirkeby, is one of the advisors on the Gore Verbinski–Johnny Depp version of *The Lone Ranger*.

George Kirgo (1926–2004)

Spinout, which Kirgo wrote with Flicker, was only his second script. His first was the Howard Hawks movie *Red Line 7000*. After chipping in on the pedestrian Tony Curtis comedy *Don't Make Waves*, which lived up to its title, Kirgo wrote *Voices* (1973), an arty horror that impressed some critics and bored others. He then retreated to television, where he made a living until the late 1980s and earned enough regard to be chosen as president of the Screen Writers Guild, which he led during the 1988 strike.

It would be fair to say that nothing in Kirgo's screenwriting career was as amusingly brilliant as his 1960 book *Become the First Author on Your Block Unless There's an Author Already Living on Your Block in Which Case You'll Become the Second Author on Your Block and That's Okay Too and Other Stories*. He was unlucky to be assigned *Spinout*, which started out as a completely different kind of comedy but, by the time Parker and MGM's bosses had intervened, had been remade into something that adhered much closer to the Presley formula. Still, at least Kirgo got some funny stories, a check, and an awful signed painting from Elvis out of the experience.

Michael A. Hoey (1934–)

A protégé of Taurog's, Hoey wrote the script for *Stay Away, Joe* (which director Tewksbury largely discarded) and helped adapt Dan Greenburg's novel *Kiss My Firm but Pliant Lips* into *Live a Little, Love a Little*. He also polished dialogue on *Tickle Me* and advised Taurog on *Double Trouble* and *Speedway*. The son of Dennis Hoey (who played Inspector Lestrade in the Universal Sherlock Holmes series), his greatest contribution to celluloid history is as the writer/director of the ludicrous Mamie Van Doren camp sci-fi extravaganza *The Navy vs. the Night Monsters* (1966). Although he and Presley were contemporaries, you sense from his memoirs that writer and star never really bonded. His verdict on Elvis's life and death, a tragedy "caused by overindulgence," is so crass and superficial, it's hard not to feel the King was right to keep his distance.

Charles Lederer (1911–1976)

A junior member of the Algonquin Round Table, a gathering of wits presided over by Dorothy Parker, Lederer is easily the most accomplished scriptwriter to work on an Elvis film, and, although *Follow That Dream* is not perfect, it remains one of the best-crafted screenplays in the Presley canon.

His most acclaimed screenplay is the seminal screwball comedy *His Girl Friday* (1934), which, like much of his best work, was the fruit of collaborating with Ben Hecht and Howard Hawks, but such was Lederer's versatility that he also won acclaim for the sci-fi horror *The Thing from Another World* (1951), *Kiss of Death* (1947, in which Richard Widmark, one of Presley's favorite actors, made his debut as a cackling psychopath), and the musical comedy *Gentlemen Prefer Blondes* (1953). He also wrote the first Rat Pack movie, *Ocean's 11* (1960), and the script for Brando's remake of *Mutiny on the Bounty* (1962).

Lederer had written a script for *Pioneer, Go Home!* from Richard Powell's novel, but it wasn't intended for Elvis until Walter Mirisch stepped in. The United Artists mogul said, "I thought it offered an ideal vehicle for Elvis and could easily be tailored to his talents." Lederer was asked to revise the story, which was then presented to Presley, who told Mirisch "it would work out just fine." And so it did.

Clifford Odets (1906–1963)

A founding member of the Method acting group alongside Lee Strasberg, Odets was one of the greatest American playwrights of the 1930s, specializing in socially conscious dramas like *Golden Boy*. Yet today he is probably best known as the likely inspiration for Barton Fink, the confused, eponymous hero in the Coen brothers' comedy.

Odets went to Hollywood to subsidize his theater production of *Paradise Lost* and wrote his first screenplay for the Gary Cooper movie *The General Died at Dawn* (1936). He tried his hand at directing, making the criminally neglected Cary Grant drama *None but the Lonely Heart* (1944). Briefly a member of the Communist Party in 1934, he was caught up in the McCarthyist red scare in the early 1950s, evading a blacklist by going to the House Un-American Activities Committee and naming names (although he only revealed the identities of people

Playwright Clifford Odets. *Wild in the Country* was his last film.

already known to be Communists). Such a harsh education in the vicissitudes of American public life, politics, and the ways of the media infused the brilliant, bitter screenplay, which Odets reconstructed after Ernest Lehman's draft, for the dark masterpiece *Sweet Smell of Success* (1957).

Four years later, Odets was assigned to write *Wild in the Country* but was fired before shooting even started. His friend Oscar Levante said in his memoirs: "Only Odets would write a story for Elvis in which he committed suicide. Actually, it was humiliating that Odets had to write that kind of picture at all, but he needed the money. Everything he was against, in the beginning of his career, he wound up doing himself." In the event, nobody died in the final film, but Odets, exhausted, did die two years after the film was made, killed by, as he said of Marilyn Monroe, "a slow bleeding of the soul." If you want to know how much he despised working in Hollywood—and having to write scripts like *Wild in the Country*—watch the compelling, if overblown, *The Big Knife* (1955).

Allan Weiss

Of all of Presley's screenwriters, Weiss probably had the strangest career. He wrote only six movies, five of them for Elvis (*Girls! Girls! Girls!; Fun in Acapulco; Paradise, Hawaiian Style;* and *Easy Come, Easy Go*) and six for Wallis. His only non-Elvis screenplay was John Wayne's western *The Sons of Katie Elder* (1965), directed by one of Wallis's stalwarts, Henry Hathaway. And when shooting wrapped on *Easy Come, Easy Go*, Weiss's screenwriting career ended with it. Many of his scripts and stories were also heavily rewritten by more seasoned hacks: Hal Kanter was called in to give *Blue Hawaii* a drastic polish, while Lawrence performed a similar service on *Roustabout; Paradise, Hawaiian Style;* and *Easy Come, Easy Go*. The only Weiss screenplay on which he retained sole credit was for *Fun in Acapulco*.

Yet as one of Wallis's protégés, Weiss was there right at the start of the King's movie career, watching the screen test and admiring his boss's shrewdness.

"Wallis had an eye," the writer recalled later. "He signed people before they got famous. Signed them to a long contract and then he wouldn't have to pay them very much. But what an eye." As Presley's movie career developed, Weiss began to be less impressed by his boss's ear, despairing of the rigidity of the formula he was asked to write ("You had to make room for 12 songs and they had to be integrated") and depressed by the effect his work was having on Presley.

19

Not as a Stranger

The Actors Elvis Befriended—From Nick Adams to Sammy Davis Jr.

E lvis's intrinsic shyness and insecurity meant that, as time went by, he kept increasingly to himself in Hollywood. The encounter that meant most to him may have been shaking hands with Marlon Brando in the studio commissary during the making of *King Creole*. Yet when he arrived, buoyed by his sudden fame, he was more open and was especially keen to meet those who knew and worked with his idol James Dean, quickly joining a social circle of actors linked to Dean, Brando, and The Actors Studio and making new friends elsewhere. As Dundy recalls in her biography: "More mature actresses like Jean Simmons (who later named one of her horses after Elvis) and Shelley Winters were immediately struck by his sense of humor and his beauty."

Over the years, many entertainers, actors, and crew—notably Robert Conrad, Ty Hardin, and Ricky Nelson—would take part in Presley's Hollywood football games (including Pat Boone, who was usually carefully watched by his wife). He would sometimes emerge from his shell with cast and crew—for example, he socialized with Hope Lange and Tuesday Weld freely during the making of *Wild in the Country*. Though he dated and slept with many starlets, there weren't many people in Hollywood Elvis grew really close to. In a way, he didn't need to, because his entourage was always on hand to cater to every whim.

Hollywood could be pretty corrosive when it came to relationships. He was friendly with Ty Hardin, the star of the TV horse opera *Bronco*, for a while, but the young actor couldn't control his jealousy. When Presley sang during a birthday party on the *King Creole* set, Hardin kept shouting, "Elvis is stealing all of my material." His closest Hollywood relationship, with Ann-Margret, was derailed by their careers, not jealousy, as we learned in chapter 11 on the King's leading ladies.

Yet his isolation only added to the image of Presley, in the film community, as some kind of joke. That wasn't the case on set. Most of his fellow actors found him easy to work with, and as Hank Moonjean, associate producer on *Spinout*, said, "The crews loved him." Yet in the wider community, he was understandably, if slightly unfairly, perceived as out of his depth in Hollywood.

Nick Adams (1931–1968)

Elvis's most controversial friend in Hollywood. A young actor who had co-starred with Dean in *Rebel Without a Cause* and dubbed dialogue so that *Giant* could be completed after the star's untimely demise, Adams was one of the few actors whose friendship with the King endured. This was especially remarkable because he used to write magazine articles about his showbiz friends. Such self-publicizing was normally anathema to Colonel Parker.

Dundy has credibly suggested Adams was one of the Colonel's paid informers, a view supported by June Juanico, Elvis's girlfriend, in her book *Elvis in the Twilight of Memory*. It has also been suggested—by another *Rebel* co-star, Sal Mineo, and in a book by Earl Greenwood—that Nick and Presley had an affair.

The Memphis Mafiosos are unconvinced on both counts. Elvis's cousin Billy Smith says if the singer had known Adams was gay, "He would have been torn about it because he liked Nick but he didn't like homosexuals." Marty Lacker was even blunter: "If he'd ever approached Elvis, he wouldn't have been around for very long."

In Smith's view, Adams was a "nice guy" who had a "pretty strong friendship" with Elvis that deteriorated, primarily because of their careers. Adams's star waned after a stint as Confederate soldier Johnny Yuma in the TV series *The Rebel*. Even an Oscar nomination for his role in *Twilight of Honor* (1963) couldn't revive his fortunes. With his career—and marriage to actress Carol Nuget Adams—on the skids, Adams died of a drug overdose on February 7, 1968. The cause of death was listed as homicide, then suicide, and finally undetermined.

Adams's memories of his friendship with Elvis have recently been published by the actor's daughter Allyson Adams (who also happens to be Parker's god-daughter). She has a succinct explanation for their deaths: "Elvis had too much fame and my father didn't have enough."

Sammy Davis Jr. (1925–1990)

One of the most inspiring sights in *Elvis: That's the Way It Is* is watching Sammy Davis Jr.'s arms pumping away in the Hilton showroom as he gets caught up in the rhythms of Presley's frenetic take on "Patch It Up." Davis was probably Presley's closest friend in the Rat Pack. Their relationship stretched back to the 1950s. In February 1958, *Jet* magazine caught Elvis roaring his approval as Sammy, doing one of his affectionate yet accurate parodies, hollered out the words to "Hound Dog."

The two were neighbors in Beverley Hills for years, and Schilling recalled, "They had a very personal bond." They would often visit each other at their respective shows in Vegas, with each impersonating the other. The two almost starred in a movie together, as escaped prisoners changed together, but Parker nixed the idea. Presley was weeping when he broke the bad news to his friend.

Sammy Davis Jr. was Presley's closest friend in the Rat Pack.

Asked once to explain his bond with Elvis, Davis said: "Somebody told me Elvis was black and I said no he's white but he's down-home and that's what it's all about. Not being black or white it's being 'down-home' and which part of down-home you come from."

Billy Murphy (1921–1989)

An eccentric character actor who walked around Hollywood dressed in black like a gunfighter, Murphy had a notable role in *The Sands of Iwo Jima*, one of Elvis's favorite films, and was rarely without a script for a *Billy the Kid* movie he wanted to make. As Elvis's friend George Klein put it, "When he spoke you always got the sense that he was letting you in on some dark mystery." Murphy was always welcome whenever Elvis or the Memphis Mafia were in Hollywood. The gang soon picked up on his habit of calling everyone "Mister." In 1967, Murphy turned up on the set of *Stay Away, Joe* in Arizona, explaining that he had got in his car "and followed the sun." Presley as so delighted he asked Tewksbury to get the new arrival a part. Watching Murphy cross the street in one scene, Elvis turned to his friend Schilling and said, "Watch that walk. I'm going to use that on the Singer [TV] special."

Patti Page (1927–)

One of Gladys Presley's favorite singers, Patti Page was married to Charles O'Curran, who choreographed some of the King's best movies. The two singers first met when she was performing in Vegas at the Sands Hotel, probably in 1956, when he introduced her to his mother. Page loved watching him on the set of *King Creole* and relished their nightly singalongs in the hotel bar when they filmed *Blue Hawaii*. Her husband later said that was one of the happiest times of his life. Page even appears in a canoe as an extra in one beach scene and was invited to watch Elvis record the songs. That was O'Curran's last Presley film, and it is a pity because, at that very point, Presley could done with some disinterested advice from someone who knew the ropes like Page. She observed later, "I think the Colonel guided Elvis's career the way he would have liked his career to be. I think Parker thought he was Elvis. I had the same situation with my manager. He booked me to all the places he wanted to go because he wanted to play golf or tennis or something." If Elvis had been able to integrate friends like the O'Currans into his social life, he might have felt more secure in Hollywood and found the experience more professionally and intellectually rewarding.

Russ Tamblyn (1934–)

Born nine days before Elvis, Tamblyn is still best known for his lead role in *Tom Thumb* (1958) and as Riff, the leader of the Jets in *West Side Story* (1961). Adams introduced Tamblyn to Elvis and the two became reasonably good friends for a while. During the shooting of *Jailhouse Rock*, Presley rehearsed the title song at Tamblyn's beach house, asking his host for a few dance tips. Their rapport was never the same after Tamblyn sublet that beach house to Presley for a month and came back to find it "a snake pit, with an eviction notice on the door."

Tuesday Weld (1943–)

"He was funny, charming and complicated but he didn't wear it on his sleeve." That was Tuesday Weld's appraisal of her *Wild in the Country* co-star and former lover. The actress, only seventeen when filming on Elvis's seventh movie started, had a reputation as a Hollywood wild child—indeed, her tantrum in the foyer of the Beverley Wilshire when staff wouldn't admit her to Elvis's suite was one of the incidents that persuaded management the King and his entourage ought to move on—and she certainly had, as Lamar Fike noted, "an edge to her."

Danny Kaye famously described her as "fourteen going on twenty-seven." Yet she was one of the people who, Fortas says, "could come over to Elvis's house in Hollywood anytime she wanted, even after they stopped dating. Their romance was never a big one. Mostly they were just good friends." Although she won good reviews for her superb performance in *Wild in the Country*, such roles made it harder for her to convince Hollywood she deserved a shot at serious fare.

Natalie Wood (1938–1981)

The first Hollywood actress Elvis dated properly was Dean's co-star Natalie Wood. He even took her to Memphis, to meet Gladys, where she complained later to friends she was "constantly hiding from Mama Presley." Their romance didn't last long, although there is no consensus on why it failed.

The orthodox view is that she lost interest because, as she told her sister, he was just a voice, yet there are enough stories about their romance—some thoroughly scurrilous—to suggest that was a rationalization with 20/20 hindsight. Presley may have been equally relieved to see it end, as he found her attention-seeking ways a bit tiresome. Once when she ran out onto a hotel balcony and threatened to jump off, he told everyone to ignore her and that she would soon crawl back in. She did just as he had predicted. Shelley Winters, who knew them both, insisted: "I knew them both very well at the time. They were deeply in love. And if they'd been allowed to marry, none of the rest of it would have happened." "It," presumably, being the untimely deaths of Elvis (aged forty-two, in 1977) and Wood (aged forty-three, in 1981). The assumption being that the people behind both stars feared a marriage would damage their careers. Wood was certainly not the kind of bride Parker would have envisaged for his star. When she did marry Robert Wagner in 1957, Wood's mother protested vehemently.

20

Return to Sender

The Scripts, Ideas, and Movies Elvis Never Made

Y ou could argue that the acting career Presley could have had is more interesting than the one he actually pursued. Hollywood lore is full of roles Presley might have had. Some of them were unlikely—playing Sundance in *Butch Cassidy and the Sundance Kid* with Roman Polanski expected to direct—while with many others, it's hard to be certain how serious the suggestions were. If Wallis had really wanted Elvis, not Glen Campbell, in *True Grit*, surely he—of all the producers in Hollywood—knew how to close the deal. After a promising start, Presley became a victim of his films' inadequacies, with many producers, directors, and writers deciding it would be too risky to cast the Memphis wonder in anything other than the usual fare. Parker's approach to fees and billing deterred many others.

So, sifting through the chaff, here are some of the most intriguing roads not taken in Presley's time in Hollywood.

The True Story of Jesse James

Nicholas Ray had directed *Rebel Without a Cause*, one of the movies Elvis cherished, and in 1957, when he was asked to make a biopic of the western outlaw, his thoughts turned to Presley. He wanted to cast James as a pre-twentieth-century sexy symbol, and who better than to play a country boy turned superstar than Elvis? The director had met Presley, who had recounted much of the script to *Rebel Without a Cause*, and been fascinated by him. Yet 20th Century Fox insisted he use one of their contract players, Robert Wagner. Either out of disillusionment, or because of his other personal problems, Ray's direction was erratic and Wagner merely bland. Though the director insisted he was satisfied with the film, he later regretted not casting Elvis, who had more charisma than Wagner and, as Ray acidly observed, did not spend so much of his time onscreen wondering if he looked good in a scene.

Even Robert Mitchum's charisma couldn't persuade Elvis to defy the Colonel.

Thunder Road

In 1957, Robert Mitchum turned up at Presley's hotel suite with a script in one hand and a fifth of scotch in the other. Ushered in, the actor regaled the star-struck Presley with a few of his favorite stories, before getting down to business: "Here's the fuckin' script. Let's get together and do it." The script for Mitchum's movie about moonshining in Tennessee impressed Presley, but he insisted he couldn't do it without his manager's say-so. Mitchum shot back: "Fuck, I'm talking to you, I don't need to talk to your manager. Let's do the picture." As much as he admired Mitchum, Presley insisted he couldn't go ahead "unless the

Colonel says I can." Inevitably, Parker asked for a fee that accounted for most of the movie budget and the deal was off. A pity, because *Thunder Road* acquired an enduring cult following, is considerably better than many of Presley's movies, and even generated a title song that (sung by Mitchum) reached number 61 on the Billboard charts. Presley's behavior during this discussion with Mitchum chimes with director Rich's description of Elvis's attitude on set, which he described as "extreme compliance with respect."

Midnight Cowboy

The mere thought of Presley playing Jon Voight's cowboy gigolo in the X-rated *Midnight Cowboy* now sounds absurd, but in 1969 director John Schlesinger was deadly serious. Actor Kevin O'Neal, who knew Schlesinger, told Bram for his book *Elvis Frame by Frame*: "He thought Elvis would've been a great Joe Buck and he would've. But Schlesinger only got as far as the Colonel." Parker inquired how many songs were involved, and when the director said they were looking to give Elvis a new look, Parker replied: "We're not interested in a new look, we're interested in more money."

A Star Is Born

In March 1975, Barbra Streisand and producer Jon Peters visited Elvis backstage in Vegas and offered him the role of Norman Maine, the fading star, in their forthcoming remake of *A Star Is Born*. Schilling, who was present when discussions took place, said: "He was very excited. He said he'd do it." When Streisand and Peters left, Presley was still invigorated, but you could tell, Schilling said, that he was already starting to realize how many battles he would have to fight to seal the deal. Parker wanted top billing for his star, $1 million in advance and demanded that Peters, whom he regarded as a former hairdresser short of producing experience, be barred from the set. Peters had sold Streisand on the casting as a historic opportunity and couldn't accede to all those demands. Streisand later recalled: "Elvis Presley really wanted to do it, but the Colonel talked him out of it." Peters was haunted by the missed opportunity for years. He had planned, as he put it, "to get to the beauty of his soul" and believed "we could have got the best performance out of him than anyone." Presley's loss was Kris Kristofferson's gain. Yet it's hard not to watch the film now and think of what might have been. As Streisand said: "Elvis would have been monumental. It was a great pairing."

Being There

Hank Moonjean, associate producer on *Spinout*, had promised Elvis he would keep an eye out for different material. The star had told him how much he had enjoyed making *Charro!*, a radical, if ill-fated, departure from his usual fare. In

1971, Moonjean read Jerzy Kosinski's satirical novel *Being There*, in which a good-looking, mysterious gardener rises to power when his simple sayings are taken for sage-like wisdom and thought: "God, this is written for Elvis!" He rang Kosinski, who agreed and then called George Cukor, who agreed to direct. Yet by the time the idea was presented to Presley's go-to man, Joe Esposito, Presley was in poor health and died before the idea could progress. In 1979, *Being There* was made as a film, starring Peter Sellers, one of Elvis's acting idols.

Presley studied Peter Seller's movies—and could have had his hero's part in *Being There*..

21

They Were Contenders

The Co-stars Who Could Have Been

C asting can always be a complex, cumbersome process, and it is often hard to say why certain actors did appear in Elvis's movies and others didn't. How seriously Elke Sommer and May Britt were considered for the Juliet Prowse part in *G.I. Blues* is something only the producers can really say. What is clear is that, as the formula for the films became increasingly refined, the people casting them became much more conservative. Dreamcasting trivia nuts may enjoy this selection of the actors who could have starred with the King.

Petula Clark: *Paradise, Hawaiian Style, Speedway*

The English pop starlet turned down the chance to play opposite Presley twice, in *Paradise, Hawaiian Style* (a wise move) and *Speedway*. In subsequent interviews, she has claimed that her husband Claude Wolff was against her taking either part because of Presley's reputation for sleeping with his co-stars. Instead, she landed parts in *Finian's Rainbow* (1968) and *Goodbye, Mr. Chips* (1969). She and her friend Karen Carpenter visited Presley in Vegas, but they made, Clark insists, a strategic retreat when she realized that their host wanted to be "more than a friend."

Jean Hale: *The Trouble with Girls*

Best known as the icy, manipulative blonde Lisa in *Our Man Flint*, Hale was a classically trained actress who had tested for the Faye Dunaway role in *Bonnie and Clyde* and, two years later, missed out on *The Trouble with Girls*. "I was a very big Elvis fan," she said later, and was bitterly disappointed to hear, at the last moment, that she had lost out to Marlyn Mason. As a stunning blonde, Hale certainly fitted Parker's profile for the ideal Presley co-star, but she couldn't sing. Tewksbury preferred Mason and used the excuse that as she could dance and sing, she could save them the cost of dubbing Hale's vocals.

Hayley Mills: *Double Trouble*

When producer Judd Bernard flew to London to find an English actress to play opposite Elvis in *Double Trouble*, he was hoping to sign Hayley Mills. The actress had made her name as the heroine of *Pollyanna* (1960) and in a twin role in the Disney comedy *The Parent Trap* (1961) and was the fifth most popular actress at the U.S. box office in 1963. Just twenty when Bernard hoped to sign her up, Mills was looking to forge a new identity as an actress. When he landed in London, Bernard learned to his dismay that Mills had accepted a new part two days before he arrived. He then auditioned a host of other English actresses—including Judy Geeson—before signing newcomer Day.

Simone Signoret: *Wild in the Country*

In 1960, French actress Signoret was hot, having just won an Oscar for her warm, sexy portrayal of a married woman who mistakenly thinks she has found true love in *Room at the Top*. Signoret and her second husband Yves Montand were in Hollywood in March 1960 to collect her Oscar and so that he could play opposite Marilyn Monroe in *Let's Make Love* for 20th Century Fox. Before shooting started on *Wild in the Country*, there was talk of Signoret signing up for Hope Lange's part as the psychiatrist who falls for Presley. Nothing came of it because, as director Philip Dunne put it: "The studio refused to meet her justified salary demands."

Mae West: *Roustabout*

The role of hardbitten carnival owner Maggie Morgan could have gone to West. She was certainly offered a role in *Roustabout*—initially as Presley's screen mum, a suggestion she rejected out of hand—but there are conflicting explanations for her failure to play Maggie. One theory is that West wanted to turn it into a vehicle for her, with Presley in a smaller role, singing the odd song in between her famous one-liners. This is probably what Parker feared and told Wallis that he didn't want his star to be a stooge. A more lurid account by entertainment writer Darwin Porter has West trying to "audition" Presley in bed, claiming: "I have the body of a 26-year-old gal." As she was seventy at the time, that would have been some boast. She did actually admire Presley, whom she described as a "real sex personality" but the account of her attempt to seduce Presley sounds too gloriously amusing to be true. Mercifully, the part went to Stanwyck, who interacts brilliantly with Elvis.

22

The King's Oscars

The Movies Elvis Really Loved

Elvis loved movies even more than he liked guns and collecting police badges. He watched them all his life, as a boy, as a teenage cinema usher, as an actor looking for tips, and as an enthusiast who, when he came home to Memphis, would watch them in all-night sessions at the Memphian Theater, accompanied by his entourage, while the cinema employees and their guests looked on in awe. The day before he died, he asked a local cinema if they had a print of *MacArthur*, starring Gregory Peck. He also had a VCR, hooked into the trio of TV sets in the TV room, which weighed a ton and he didn't really know how to use. "He had one of us do it for him," said Lamar Fike.

His taste was broad and eclectic, embracing such forgotten masterpieces as Victor Fleming's tragic drama *The Way of All Flesh* (1927), and *Executive Action* (1973), Dalton Trumbo's chilling conspiratorial view of the JFK assassination, and more mainstream fare such as *The Godfather, A Streetcar Named Desire*, and *On the Waterfront*—the common factor there being the presence of Brando. As his friend Alan Fortas said: "He was a very avid movie fan." Here is a list of the King's favorites.

Across 110th Street (1972)

Barry Shear's gritty, violent American crime drama, starring Yaphet Kotto as a black cop who has to work with racist, streetwise captain Anthony Quinn, so impressed Presley that he once recounted the entire script, word for word, to his backing singers. The Bobby Womack soundtrack probably struck a chord too.

Dirty Harry (1971)

Clint Eastwood's seminal role as no-nonsense detective Harry Callaghan was bound to impress Presley, who liked .44 Magnums and cops. The film was also directed by Siegel, who had helmed *Flaming Star*. It's hard to see the King enjoying this quite as much if Sinatra, who was originally cast as Callaghan but broke a wrist just before production started, had played the part.

Dr. Strangelove (1964)

On the set of *Spinout*, second assistant director Gene De Ruelle asked Presley to name his favorite movie. Elvis said: *Dr. Strangelove*. After Brando and Dean, Peter Sellers may well have been the actor he admired most. When the Beatles came to visit in 1965, John Lennon and Elvis bonded by recounting their love for Sellers. During the shooting of *Spinout*, De Ruelle used to make Presley laugh by standing off camera, in the star's line of sight, and trying to strangle himself with his rogue right arm—just like Sellers as the mad doctor. When the Stanley Kubrick comedy was released, Presley watched it sixteen times.

Letter from an Unknown Woman (1948)

Max Ophüls's graceful tragic drama is an unusual film for Presley to have watched, but he was a sucker for a tearjerker. There's enough pathos in this movie—in which a young girl (Joan Fontaine) falls for a narcissistic pianist (Louis Jordan) in a romance that is doomed not to end well—to soften even the hardest heart. Fontaine all but retired from the movies in the 1960s—she was only fifty-one—because, she said in an interview years later, "I was asked to play Elvis Presley's mother." She had nothing against Presley, but being his screen mum was, she said, "not my cup of tea."

Patton (1970)

Elvis watched George C. Scott's portrayal of the controversial World War II general half a dozen times and memorized the hero's opening speech, which cast him as a patriotic lone wolf. This probably vied with *Dr. Strangelove* as his all-time favorite, and he quoted both of them more often than any other film. He was so taken with Franklin J. Schaffner's biopic that he often visited one of Patton's colleagues, General Omar Bradley (played by Karl Malden in the movie), a neighbor in Beverly Hills.

The Prince Who Was a Thief (1951)

"Son of a noseless mother! Maggot-brained child of a jackass!" With that reasonably representative sample of dialogue, it is a wonder the sixteen-year-old Presley bothered to memorize lines from this Arabian Nights–style nonsense. Yet he did, captivated by the sight of his boyhood idol Tony Curtis as the prince who is spared from death by a soft-hearted assassin and almost overlooks the considerable charms of Piper Laurie. The script was adapted from a Theodore Dreiser story by Gerald Drayson Adams, who bowed out from Hollywood with *Harum Scarum*. This escapist adventure isn't one of Presley's all-time favorites but a guilty pleasure he enjoyed as a teenager, along with *Son of Ali Baba* and *King Solomon's Mines*. Presley and Curtis met on the set of *Paradise, Hawaiian Style*. Elvis greeted his idol as "Mr. Curtis." "Call me Tony," said Curtis. "What shall I call you?" Presley grinned and shot back, "You can call me Mr. Presley."

Rebel Without a Cause (1955)

"I could watch James Dean's films 100 times over," Presley said once. He certainly watched Dean's breakthrough performance so often he could recite the entire script by heart and act out all the parts. When he moved to Hollywood, one of the first things he did was seek out actors like Nick Adams, Dennis Hopper, and Natalie Wood, who had starred in this film. Dean's influence on Presley is most obvious in his portrayals of the alienated heroes in *Jailhouse Rock* and *King Creole*.

Monty Python and the Holy Grail (1975)

One of the more surprising entries in the King's video collection at Graceland was *Monty Python and the Holy Grail*. Men of a certain age have irritated friends—and spouses—with their ability to parrot sketches such as the Dead Parrot sketch, and Presley pioneered that kind of behavior in the United States. He had the tapes on his plane and took to calling people "squire" from the Nudge Nudge sketch. Python member Eric Idle was astonished to hear, when he met Linda Thompson, that Elvis would watch Python all night. As she told Idle: "He'd make me learn these things and we'd laugh and laugh and laugh."

The Student Prince (1954)

Presley worshipped Mario Lanza. Onetime Memphis Mafia chief Marty Lacker says: "He would watch *The Student Prince* over and over again. He loved the power of big voices, big orchestras. He liked real dramatic things." Presley was so keen he played the soundtrack album until he wore the record out.

To Kill a Mockingbird (1962)

Presley was disappointed by the 1962 Oscars. In his view, a clear injustice had been done. As good as David Lean's *Lawrence of Arabia* was, he didn't think it deserved to overtake *To Kill a Mockingbird* as Best Picture. His understanding of the social, political, and geographical nuances in Robert Mulligan's film of Harper Lee's bestseller may have swayed him. Before the ceremony, he told the *Memphis Commercial Appeal*: "Lawrence will win because it's had more money spent on it but Mockingbird was really better—that was a wonderful movie."

23

On to Greater Things

From Bobby Kennedy's Bodyguard to Voices in *Scooby Doo*: The Remarkable Future Careers of Elvis's Supporting Actors

Ed Asner: *Kid Galahad*

Asner made his movie debut as an assistant district attorney in *Kid Galahad*—and later had an entertaining cameo as a socially savvy cop in *Change of Habit*—and was renowned as one of the hardest-working, most respected actors in Hollywood even if his liberal politics have not proved to everyone's taste. A former president of the Screen Actors Guild, Asner has been nominated for twenty Emmys and won seven, more than any other actor.

Jack Albertson: *Kissin' Cousins, Roustabout*

Albertson made an entertaining contribution to two Elvis movies, but this character actor's most iconic role was as Grandpa Joe in *Willy Wonka and the Chocolate Factory* (1971). Three years before that, he won an Oscar as the troubled father in the middle-class domestic drama *The Subject Was Roses*, based on Frank D. Gilroy's Pulitzer Prize–winning play.

Charles Bronson: *Kid Galahad*

Bronson was a bit-part TV regular and was moving into the big time with *The Magnificent Seven* by the time he starred in *Kid Galahad*. Despite his diminutive five-foot-eight-inch frame, he became the archetypal tight-lipped screen tough guy, second only to Clint Eastwood in the 1970s. Best known for his roles in *Once upon a Time in the West*, *Dirty Dozen*, and Michael Winner's Death Wish movies, the son of Lithuanian immigrants was likened by one critic to a "Clark Gable who had been left out in the sun too long."

Henry Corden: *Frankie and Johnny*

Corden had an uncredited part as a gypsy in Presley's 1966 riverboat musical, which rather summed up the kind of insignificant supporting roles he picked up in the movies. He raised his profile as Barbara Eden's father in *I Dream of Jeannie* before achieving the kind of fame that lives forever as the voice of Fred Flintstone in the enduring Hanna-Barbera classic.

Barbara Eden: *Flaming Star*

A rising star when she won the role of Roslyn Pierce in *Flaming Star*, Eden's performance as a genie in a bottle in *I Dream of Jeannie* won her a cult following and a unique place in pop-cultural history. When that sitcom premiered in 1965, censors ensured that her genie costume didn't expose her navel.

Nicole Jaffe: *The Trouble with Girls*

Having featured briefly in *The Love Bug* in 1968, Jaffe won the role of stand-in pianist Betty in *The Trouble with Girls* (1969). That same year she was also chosen to be the voice of Velma in the Scooby-Doo franchise. After four years as the voice of a pesky meddling kid, she became an agent. Coincidentally, Frank Welker, who plays a Rutgers college boy in the same film, voiced Fred in the same cartoon.

Rafer Johnson: *Wild in the Country*

By the time Johnson was cast as Davis, Phil Macy's capable assistant in *Wild in the Country*, he had already won an Olympic gold medal in the decathlon at the 1960 Games in Rome. A competitive long jumper and basketball player, he was chosen by the Los Angeles Rams in the 1959 NFL Draft. He is best known as one of the two men who apprehended Robert F. Kennedy's assassin Sirhan Sirhan in 1968. Part of Kennedy's campaign detail, he and football player Roosevelt Grier captured Sirhan.

Carolyn Jones: *King Creole*

Jones had already won rave reviews for her performances in *Invasion of the Body Snatchers* and *The Bachelor Party* before she starred as femme fatale Ronnie in *King Creole*. Her most famous role was as Morticia in *The Addams Family*, to which she brought the sultry sexiness she had shown opposite Presley. A huge hit, the show was still canceled after just two years in 1966, leaving Jones typecast but not wealthy.

Richard Kiel: *Roustabout*

The seven-foot-two-inch-tall Kiel featured as a strongman in *Roustabout* and went on to play Jaws in *The Spy Who Loved Me*. This steel-toothed hunk was so popular with audiences he was reprised for *Moonraker*, during which he changes sides and helps Roger Moore's 007 save the planet.

Lance LeGault: *Girls! Girls! Girls!, Kissin' Cousins, Viva Las Vegas, Roustabout, Clambake*

Elvis's stunt double, LeGault gets his own moment on the screen in the finale of *Kissin' Cousins*, thanks to a tight budget and some bad planning by director Nelson. He also worked as a singer—releasing his own album in 1970—and starred in many TV shows, most famously as Colonel Roderick Decker in *The A Team*.

Gary Lockwood: *Wild in the Country, It Happened at the World's Fair*

Having started out as a stuntman and a stand-in for actor Anthony Perkins, Lockwood—whose real name is John Gary Yurosek—starred in two Elvis movies. But his most famous role was as Dr. Frank Poole in Stanley Kubrick's *2001: A Space Odyssey* (1968). Between 1966 and 1974, he was Mr. Stefanie Powers.

Walter Matthau: *King Creole*

Matthau was already a familiar and distinctive face when he took the role of menacing mobster Maxie Fields in *King Creole*. In that movie, he showed the prowess as a character actor that would win him an Oscar for *Meet Whiplash Willie* (1966) and, in the late 1960s, make him the most unlikely of movie stars. Matthau collaborated regularly with Billy Wilder and Jack Lemmon, the trio working on such classics as *The Front Page* and *The Odd Couple*.

Raquel Welch: *Roustabout*

Welch was just an uncredited college girl in the opening scenes of *Roustabout*. On set, she upset the crew by insisting on doing her own makeup. As actress Lynn Borden out it: "She knew what she wanted to look like and wouldn't have it any other way." Welch won her first featured role in the beach-party flick *A Swingin' Summer* in 1965. (Sample tagline for the movie: "Spread out the beach towels, grab your gals, it's going to be a swingin' summer.") A year later, she emerged from the sea in a furry bikini in *One Million Years BC* and, even though she had only three lines in the film, a new sex symbol was born.

Rita Wilson: *Spinout*

An uncredited bit player in *Spinout*, Wilson and went on to wed Tom Hanks, star in *Sleepless in Seattle*, and produce *My Big Fat Greek Wedding* and *Mamma Mia!* As Forrest Gump, Hanks is shown teaching his young tenant Elvis how to wiggle.

Gig Young: *Kid Galahad*

Presley was so appalled by Young's behavior on set he vowed never to work with the actor again. When he wasn't mercilessly goading Bronson, Young spent much of the time drinking with actor Judson Pratt. Elvis didn't like the way the actor treated his wife Elizabeth Montgomery, the nose-twitching star of *Bewitched*. Nor, it turned out did Montgomery—she divorced him in 1963. Young won an Oscar as the slimy emcee in *They Shoot Horses, Don't They?* but, possibly because of his alcoholism, never quite got the billing his talent warranted. In 1978, after making *Game of Death*, Young shot himself and his fifth wife, Kim Schmidt.

24

"Your Time Hasn't Come Yet, Baby"

Child Stars in the King's Movies

lvis shared the screen with some of Hollywood's most adorable, precocious, and irritating child stars. Here's what became of some of them.

Vicky Tiu: *It Happened at the World's Fair*

Elvis's endearing World's Fair promo was Vicky Tiu's only film role, but the Hong Kong–born singer was one half of the popular musical revue the Ginny Tiu Revue with her sister. Producers originally wanted to cast her sister Ginny (who had starred in *Girls! Girls! Girls!*), but she was busy playing piano for President Kennedy at the White House, so six-year-old Vicky took the role of Little Sue Lin.

Vicky remembered Elvis as good with children. After thirty takes, Vicky was still struggling with a scene, so Presley told them to stop filming and told Taurog, "That's it, it's a wrap, the little lady and I are going to have something to eat." Elvis took her to dinner and put her at ease, and the next day she finished the scene quickly. "At that age, I didn't understand the magnitude of his fame and popularity," she recalled. "But he was a gentleman."

Vicky later became the First Lady of Hawaii. Now known as Vicky Cayetano, she married Ben Cayetano in 1997, when he was Governor of Hawaii. He left office in 2002. The couple have five children between them. One of her musical performances appeared as archive footage in Cameron's Crowe's 2011 Pearl Jam documentary *Twenty*.

Ginny Tiu: *Girls! Girls! Girls!*

Two years older than her sister Vicky, Ginny featured in several TV shows, including *Make Room for Daddy* (1959), *The Dinah Shore Chevy Show* (1959), and *Bachelor Father* (1961). She also starred in a Kellogg's Cornflakes ad and made her TV debut as a five-year-old piano-playing prodigy on *The Ed Sullivan Show*. She probably would have worked more if her father hadn't fallen afoul of California child labor laws.

She was eight when she appeared as Mai Ling in *Girls! Girls! Girls!* boasting her and her sister's trademark long braids. The movie also featured her brother Alexander and younger sister Elizabeth. Today Ginny has returned to her first love, the piano, releasing two albums and playing at the Sheraton Moana Surfrider Hotel in Honolulu.

Kurt Russell: *It Happened at the World's Fair*

One of those rare child actors to forge a successful acting career as an adult, Russell was signed by Walt Disney himself in 1960 to a ten-year contract. Russell had starred in three TV shows by the time he made his film debut in *It Happened at the World's Fair* at the age of ten as the boy Elvis paid to kick him in the shins. When he got too old to be cast in adolescent roles, Russell briefly left acting to play minor-league baseball. His father had been a baseball player, and Russell had a promising career with a .563 batting average until he was badly injured in the shoulder by a player running to second base.

With his focus back on acting, he starred in a slew of TV shows before giving a decent turn as Elvis in the John Carpenter TV movie *Elvis* (1979). Impressive performances in *Used Cars* (1980), *Escape from New York* (1981), and *Silkwood* (1983) followed, the latter earning him a Golden Globe nomination for Best Supporting Actor. He starred in many less impressive films in the late 1980s and 1990s, including *Swing Shift* (where he was reacquainted with Goldie Hawn, who became his long-term partner), *Tequila Sunrise*, and *Tango & Cash*. His acting career has been revitalized by his role as a psychopathic stunt man in Quentin Tarantino's *Death Proof*.

During his career, Russell narrowly missed out on many famous roles, including Han Solo in *Star Wars*. Yet losing out on the part of Crash Davies in *Bull Durham* is one of his biggest regrets. Ron Shelton wrote the role for him, but the studio insisted Kevin Costner be cast.

Donna Butterworth: *Paradise, Hawaiian Style*

Originally born in Pennsylvania, Butterworth moved with her family to Hawaii, where her father got a job in construction. A gifted performer of traditional Hawaiian music, Donna played concerts all around the islands. A producer of *Paradise, Hawaiian Style* watched one of them and she was instantly cast as Jan, the daughter of Elvis's friend and business partner Danny (James Shigeta). The first time she met Elvis on set, she was so in awe of him she couldn't speak. Luckily he—and the crew—laughed, breaking the ice.

Paradise wasn't her first movie. Butterworth had already starred opposite Jerry Lewis in *The Family Jewels* in 1965, earning a Golden Globe nomination. She also starred opposite Ron Howard in *A Boy Called Nuthin'*, a Walt Disney Presents production, and sang on a number of hit TV shows including *The Dean Martin Show*. She gave up acting in Hollywood and returned to Hawaii. When

Elvis played Hawaii in 1973, she went to see the concert but was too shy to ask to see him. Four years later, she wept when he died, running to her scrapbook to console herself with pictures of herself with the King.

Victoria Paige Meyerink: *Speedway*

The daughter of actress Jeanne Baird, Meyerink's career started when he was just three as the voice of toy manufacturer Mattel's Chatty Cathy. Within a year she was a regular on Danny Kaye's variety show. After roles in *Brainstorm* (1965) and *The Night of the Grizzly* (1966), she was cast opposite Elvis in *Speedway*. Only eight, she proved one of the King's more endearing child co-stars as Ellie Esterlake, the sweet daughter in a family of ne'er-do-wells. Though she always called him "Mr. Presley," they grew close enough on set for him to smuggle food for her to ensure the kitten she had concealed in her trailer wouldn't starve.

Meyerink went on to star in *Green Acres* and *My Three Sons* (both in 1970), yet eight years later, when she was just eighteen, she decided to move away from acting and turned to producing alongside her husband Lawrence David Foldes. She produced the budget movie *The Graduates of Malibu High* in 1983 when she was just twenty-two.

Anissa Jones: *The Trouble with Girls*

Aged eight, Anissa Jones first found fame when she won a starring role in *Family Affair*, the hit sitcom about a group of siblings sent to live with their uncle when their parents die in a car crash. The show became a hit, thrusting the young star into the spotlight and earning her an eye-catching role in *The Trouble with Girls*. She wanted to break into the movies but felt typecast as Buffy in *Family Affair* and struggled to find new roles, missing out on the part of Regan in *The Exorcist* and Iris in *Taxi Driver*.

Jones's personal life was similarly heading downhill. Her father was given custody of her after a bitter divorce battle, but he died suddenly of a heart attack shortly after. The young actress eventually dropped out of school and into drugs, dying of a severe overdose in 1976. The producers of Louis Malle's *Pretty Baby* were keen to cast her as Violet, the part that eventually made Brooke Shields famous, in Louis Malle's *Pretty Baby*, but she died before she could audition.

25

The King's New Clothes

Presley as a Fashion Icon

T ommy Hilfiger said: "Elvis was the first white boy to really bling it up. He was one of the first performers of any race to view himself as being very sexy and masculine but with a certain femininity."

Presley's look had always been distinctive. As a teenager starting out at Sun Studios, he used to peer in the window of Lansky's clothing store on Beale Street, which predominantly catered to the city's African-American community. He told the owner, Bernard Lansky, "When I get rich, I'm going to buy you out." To which Lansky replied, "Don't buy me out. Just buy from me." Which he did. He knew the look he wanted—as Phillips said once, "You know, Elvis didn't walk into Lansky Brothers because someone suggested, 'Why don't you buy a chartreuse fucking shirt?'" In the segregated Deep South of the 1950s, his choice outfits was so exotic—his favorite color combo was pink and black and he was not averse to the odd see-through shirt—that some of his family wondered, as his cousin Billy Smith put it: "Why doesn't he just go down on Beale Street and live with 'em!"

Although Jackie Gleason had dubbed Presley a "guitar-playing Brando," Presley's image was less macho than the mumbling Method actor's. As a teenager in the 1950s, Elvis was wearing mascara and royal blue eye shadow, even giving his girlfriends makeup tips. He learned from other actors too: Tony Curtis inspired the jet-black hair; the upturned collar was an homage to James Dean.

He said once: "My favorite hobby is collecting these real cool outfits. I'd almost rather wear them than eat." Whatever else it did, his movie career fed that habit, giving him the excuse to wear some bold, beautiful, and occasionally ugly outfits.

The saving grace of *Harum Scarum* was that he could take the Rudolph Valentino outfit home and wear it around the house. He was almost as enamored of the Latin outfits he wore in *Fun in Acapulco*. He enjoyed that kind of look far more than the denim he wore in *Loving You*, *Wild in the Country*, and *Follow That Dream*. Such plain threads reminded him too much of the poverty of his childhood. His producers often preferred to play it safe, giving him a uniform to wear for all—or some—of *G.I. Blues*; *Kid Galahad*; *Kissin' Cousins*; *Paradise, Hawaiian Style*; and *Easy Come, Easy Go*. In only one film, *Change of Habit*, where he strolls through a ghetto in an eye-catching, if impractical, combo of brown shirt and white trousers, do you get a sense of the flashy taste that he indulged at Lansky's.

Yet he looks sharp in *It Happened at the World's Fair* and *Viva Las Vegas*. One of the first items he had bought from Lansky's was a tailored bolero jacket, and he wore four of these one-button jackets (in black, yellow, blue, and red) in George Sidney's fast-paced musical. In *It Happened at the World's Fair*, he looks snappier still, having just discovered the Rat Pack gloss of the great Hollywood tailors Sy Devore and Jack Taylor. Returning from the U.S. Army in 1960, Presley agreed to guest in Frank Sinatra's TV show. Ol' Blue Eyes gave Elvis two Devore shirts as a welcome-home present. Smitten, Presley became such a regular customer that the tailor kept his suit patterns locked in a strongbox. For *It Happened at the World's Fair*, Presley spent $9,300 with Devore. The order included ten suits, two cashmere coats, and fifty-five ties. The tailor's assignment was even more challenging because in the early 1960s, Presley often didn't wear any underwear.

Yet as his movie career progressed—and his weight fluctuated—the outfits became more hit and miss. The departure of serial Oscar-winning costumier Edith Head, who left when Wallis gave up on Presley, may have had an effect on quality control, although some of the outfits designed under her aegis for Elvis to wear in *Paradise, Hawaiian Style* were unflattering, to say the least. In the early 1960s, in films like *Blue Hawaii, Kid Galahad,* and *Fun in Acapulco,* he was often barechested. But from 1966 onward, he seems to hide behind his costumes in such films as *Spinout, Frankie and Johnny, Double Trouble,* and *Clambake.* Watching him swing through "I'll Be Back" in the finale of *Spinout* while wearing four layers of clothing is especially bizarre because, by this point in his career, he was sweating so profusely the costumiers had to insert extra pads and shields into his clothes.

He had always taken extraordinary care of his hair. Even in 1956 he had, author Karal Ann Marling wrote, the kind of hair that "made decent men cringe and maidens yowl." Though he spent an age combing it, in photographs his hair often looked disheveled, to suggest, in Marling's words, "a moving body just barely come to rest." Yet in the 1960s, his pompadoured hair was more likely to make his fans cringe and enrage producers like Wallis, who berated Parker about it to little effect. If the star was going to convince as a singing sailor in *Easy Come, Easy Go*, the producer fretted, he couldn't emerge from a dive with his coiffed, pompadoured hair intact. Wallis had a point.

By this time in Presley's career, his hair could, as Jane and Michael Stern wrote in *Elvis World*, look like poured tar and his face had begun to disappear, becoming so smooth behind a mask of makeup that his skin seemed to be made of nylon. In publicity stills from this era, he can look remote, plump, and absurdly stylized. RCA tacitly admitted the problem by using a still from *Fun in Acapulco*, made in 1963, on the cover of the *Paradise, Hawaiian Style* soundtrack, released in 1966.

The first sign of the artistic renaissance to come was the reassertion of his own look as the lithe antihero in *Stay Away, Joe*, in which the hair, still inky black, looks much more natural. In *Speedway*, he was still treasonably trim and at ease in his red and blue jackets with white vertical stripes. The image kept improving in those final movies: he looks slick in a suit in *Live a Little, Love a Little*, stunning in an anachronistic white suit in *The Trouble with Girls*, and nonchalant in a kind of take-me-or-leave-me way in *Change of Habit*. By the time he made that feature film, he had resurrected his career and—presumably not coincidentally—looked like the man himself, not a plastic replica. That last feature was an intriguing prelude to the spectacle of Presley in some of the grooviest multicolored shirts ever glimpsed on celluloid, rehearsing with joy and purpose in *That's the Way It Is*.

26

"Real Florida Mountains!"

The Worst Goofs

Real Florida mountains": That was how one reviewer groaningly greeted the final scene in *Clambake*. Having mountain ranges in the wrong place was just one of the gaffes that marred the King's movie career. Here are the best/worst of the others.

Viva Las Vegas

The race is worth watching for connoisseurs of continuity errors, as is the dance routine in which Ann-Margret starts off wearing high-heeled shoes, switches to flat ballet shoes, and reverts to high-heeled shoes for the finale.

Fun in Acapulco

Just watch Presley's hair in the final diving scene and marvel at how, despite swimming across the inlet and diving from such a fearsome height, it still remains combed.

Kissin' Cousins

In the finale, you can clearly see that one of the twin characters played by Presley is not Elvis.

Easy Come, Easy Go

When Jo (Dodie Marshall) asks Ted (Elvis Presley) to drive her home from the club, she is clearly wearing a red dress, but when they arrive at her house she is in a striped top and white trousers.

Frankie and Johnny

When Johnny pulls down Cully's beard during the Mardi Gras party, Cully says something as he fixes his beard, but his lips never move.

Jailhouse Rock

When Vince and Peggy enter her parents' house, you can see the black "T" tape on the carpet where Elvis has to stand. This is more visible in the colorized version.

Love Me Tender

A Confederate soldier zips up the trousers that were taken off Northern soldiers, at least twenty-eight years before zippers were invented.

Clambake

Not only are the mountains in the wrong place, the movie can't spell the hero's name. The signs for the family-owned gas stations say "Heyward," and at the end of the movie, when the real Scott shows Diane his driver's license, the last name is spelled "Hayward."

27

Young Dreams

Elvis and the Teen Movie

Hollywood had been in the exploitation business since it became the world's preeminent dream factory in the 1920s. Just look at the careers of Elvis's directors. Norman Taurog made six movies with Dean Martin and Jerry Lewis (for Hal Wallis) in the 1940s and 1950s. One of Gene Nelson's first appearances on the big screen was an uncredited role as a skater in *Everything Happens at Night*, a 1939 comedy drama starring Norwegian ice-skating queen Sonja Henje. Among the more than 180 movies Richard "One Take" Thorpe directed were Tarzan films and two pictures starring Mario Lanza, one of the singers Elvis most admired.

Even before Presley revolutionized America's popular culture, Hollywood had proven that it could, for artistic and commercial profit, tailor movies to fit musical stars like Fred Astaire and Ginger Rogers so adroitly that their acting ability was largely irrelevant. In the 1950s, with TV persuading millions of older people to stay home, the studios turned to rock and roll as they desperately courted a younger audience who were escaping to drive-ins in search of thrills and privacy (by the late 1950s, there were over four thousand outdoor screens across the United States).

The studios succeeded by perfecting a genre known as teen movies and casting some of rock and roll's brightest talent—most notably Elvis Presley—in their movies. On December 30, 1953, six months after the man who would be King had walked into Sun Studios for the first time, the first modern teen movie, Lazlo Benedek's *The Wild One*, was released. Benedek's sadistic, iconic movie—a fictionalized version of a riot at a motorcycle rally in Hollister, California, in July 1947—established motorcycles and leather jackets as potent symbols of rebellion. The central antihero Johnny Strabler was played by Presley's idol Marlon Brando. When asked what he is rebelling against, Brando famously replies: "Whadda ya got?"

Although the movie was banned in Britain until 1968, it was such a smash it inspired the inevitable slew of imitations and convinced Hollywood that the teen audience could prove extremely lucrative. Brando was the big screen's first symbol of adolescent rebellion against authority, but he was soon challenged—if not superseded—by James Dean, the first American teen idol who, in the words of film writer Tim Dirks, "was the epitome of adolescent pain." Dean was, as his most famous movie indicated, a *Rebel Without a Cause*, who died when he was just twenty-four in a car crash on September 30, 1955.

On tour in Gladwater, Texas, Elvis wept in his hotel room when he heard the news. Seven months later, the singer signed for Paramount, having been hailed as the James Dean of rock and roll. It was not to be. Producer Hal Wallis insisted, "We didn't sign him as a second Brando or a second Dean. We signed him as number one Elvis Presley." Yet in *Jailhouse Rock* and *King Creole*, both creditable teen movies, Presley showed what he had learned from his painstaking study of both actors.

Hollywood soon proved that you didn't need a Brando, Dean, or Presley to make a teen movie. One of the most successful, Richard Brooks's *Rock Around the Clock* (1955), had caused riots primarily because Bill Haley's music was played over the credits. The basic elements of the genre—teenage nonconformism, rebellion against authority, the clash of generations, handsome young actors teens could identify with or aspire to be, different sexual mores, a hunk of rock music—were clear enough for them to be industrialized.

The genre's flexibility is illustrated by three movies released in the 1950s, the golden age of the teen movie. In the relatively conventional *Rock, Rock, Rock!* (1956), future Presley co-star Tuesday Weld had to raise money to buy a dress for a prom in a story that was essentially an excuse to showcase such acts as Chuck Berry, LaVern Baker (one of Elvis's heroines), and Connie Francis (who dubs Weld's vocals). Jack Arnold's *High School Delinquent* (1958) was much more exotic, with Russ Tamblyn as an undercover cop, a theme song by Jerry Lee Lewis, and enough switchblade fights, drugs, and hep talk to outrage any guardian of morality in the neighborhood. And then came Gene Fowler's *I Was a Teenage Werewolf* (1957), the first feature for Michael Landon (best known as the gorgeous, blubbing patriarch in *Little House on the Prairie*), which proved that fusing the teen movie with horror and sci-fi could be profitable for low-budget studios and directors.

Presley's early films fitted neatly into the mainstream teen genre. *Loving You* certainly rocked, even defending the music—and by implication its star and teenage culture—in a courtroom. *Jailhouse Rock* featured a sneering antihero, whose brushes with authority led him into the slammer—where he was whipped in a thrillingly sadomasochistic scene that symbolized teen torment—and some of the finest rock music Hollywood ever commissioned. *King Creole* fitted even more snugly into the genre. The scene in which Presley confronted his screen father duplicated a similar confrontation in *Rebel Without a Cause*. At the story's heart was a decent but troubled hero most teenagers would have identified with, but the movie also featured more great music and a satisfying knife fight.

Yet none of these films were quite what they seemed. As Alan Fortas astutely observed, all three preached "that the rebel can make it into society but only if he sticks to the status quo." So in *Loving You*, Presley ultimately agreed to be managed by the agent who consistently manipulated him. In *Jailhouse Rock*, he was shocked back to decency by a punch in the throat. And in *King Creole*, the

Dean virtually invented the teen movie—and Elvis wept when his idol died.

death of femme fatale Carolyn Jones mysteriously reconciled the estranged father and son.

This wasn't that unusual—even in *Rebel Without a Cause*, Dean's antihero was reconciled with his parents—but does indicate that Presley's teen movies were softer and more mainstream than such lurid, cultish exercises as Roger Corman's dark satire *Bucket of Blood* (1959), in which a socially awkward busboy became a serial-killing sculptor. American International Pictures, the studio that launched the beach-party flick in the 1960s, released Corman's film.

When Presley returned from the U.S. Army in 1960, rock and roll no longer dominated the charts or the box office. Philip Dunne's *Wild in the Country*, in which he was young, at odds with his father, and on the wrong side of the law, could be described as his last true teen movie.

Some of his subsequent musical comedies resembled beach-party movies, featured plenty of music, and retained a vague air of rebellion (even in *Clambake*, he was on the run from an overbearing father), but he would be eclipsed as a teen idol by the Beatles, when Richard Lester's fresh, spirited, and witty *A Hard Day's Night* was released in 1964. One of many possible inspirations for the Fab Four's name was the Beetles, the biker gang led by Lee Marvin in *The Wild One*.

At first, the British Beat Invasion didn't seem to affect Elvis's box-office fortunes that much. *Viva Las Vegas*, *Roustabout*, and *Kissin' Cousins* (all released the same year as the Beatles' debut feature) were among Presley's top-grossing movies. Yet *Girl Happy*, released in April 1965, was his last big money spinner, although it would make only half as much money at the U.S. box office as the Beatles' movie *Help!*

The studios still made teen movies in the 1960s, though Hollywood's grasp of their young audience's aspirations and desires became progressively hazier as the countercultural revolution spread. "Make love not war" buttons, hippies, LSD, and antiwar protests did not resonate with most Hollywood suits, so they often reverted to the old exploitation formula, pressing the new teen idols into service in movies of varying quality.

Many of these films featured other British acts. Some—like John Boorman's evocative *Catch Us If You Can*, starring the Dave Clark Five—were compelling. Many were even dafter than some of the movies Presley was asked to make. In 1966, Sam Katzman produced *Hold On!*, in which Herman's Hermits belted out seven numbers, NASA decided whether they were worth naming a rocket after, and Fabares, Presley's favorite leading lady, looked on in amusement. The sentimental schooldays epic *To Sir, with Love*, starring Sidney Poitier, was much more successful—it was the eighth-highest-grossing movie of 1967, and the title song, sung by Lulu, topped Billboard's Hot 100.

In the late 1960s, as the old studio system imploded, the teen movie genre mutated into something far more diverse, producing such cultish yet lucrative successes as *Easy Rider*, a biker movie that made *The Wild One* look like "The Mild One," and the schlock melodrama *Beyond the Valley of the Dolls*. Weirdest of all was Bob Rafaelson's messy but underrated *Head* (1969), a Monkees movie that, with the group's gleeful assistance, effectively deconstructs the entire teen movie genre.

As early as 1965, Presley's diminishing box-office prospects had prompted a panicky rethink by his producers. In *Girl Happy*, you can see the first evidence of his producers' ill-advised, cosmetic, and often absurd attempts to make him seem timely and relevant. Rather than try to create something as authentic as *A Hard Day's Night*, the studios tinkered with the formula as if the problem was primarily a matter of presentation.

In Sagal's movie, Presley was cast as the lead singer in a band billed as Rusty Wells & His Combo, and his voice was speeded up on some numbers to make them sound quicker and more contemporary. The precedent set, he was saddled with a band in *Spinout* and *Double Trouble*. Faster numbers—the emphasis here was on quantity, not quality—were ordered from Hill and Range for all three movies.

The strategy of making the King emulate the very acts he had inspired reached a strange, if reasonably entertaining, climax with *Double Trouble*, in which, so the poster proclaimed, he took "mad mod Europe by song." In the movie, the stops on his truncated European tour are London, Bruges, and Antwerp. In reality, Elvis never left MGM's Culver City lot.

The urge to make Presley seem less quintessentially American—and therefore more trendy—presumably explains why three of his leading ladies in the mid-1960s were British: Jocelyn Lane (*Tickle Me*), Suzanna Leigh (*Paradise, Hawaiian Style*), and Annette Day (*Double Trouble*). There could have been more: British pop singer Petula Clark turned down lead roles in *Spinout* and *Speedway*, and immigration difficulties prevented Leigh from returning as the blond villainess in *Easy Come, Easy Go*.

That movie, Wallis's last with Presley, tried to make him seem hipper by casting him as a singing deep-sea diver and surrounding him with a bunch of California hippies so far out, man, that one of them disassembled the hero's car to make an artistic statement. Sadly, this bid for relevance was undermined by lines in which he dismissed this groovy crowd as "kooks."

The only time he seems to share the hippies' values is the final scene. Having spent most of the movie in a hunt for buried treasure, he has a Damascene conversion, singing cheerily that love is more important than money in "I'll Take Love," a song that sounds like a feeble echo of the Fab Four's "Can't Buy Me Love."

The producers didn't try so hard in *Speedway*. The attempt to update the King's image was largely confined to the casting of Nancy Sinatra, who appealed to a hipper, younger crowd, and the creation of the Hangout, a car-themed, Pop Art–style nightclub.

Even a director as dutiful as Taurog knew that such superficial changes would not rectify matters. He had always wanted to direct the King as a cold-blooded killer and suggested to the star that they try a different kind of story—you can see some of that intent in the confused tone of *Double Trouble*—but Presley passed the buck to Parker. Only the comparative commercial failure of such movies as *Clambake*, *Double Trouble*, *Easy Come, Easy Go*, and *Speedway* freed director and star to break out of the old routine, but by then most fans had stopped watching.

In the 1970s, the teen movie foundered as a genre. Such gems as the Martin Davidson/Stephen Verona rambling high school movie *The Lords of Flatbush* (1974), a breakthrough film for Sylvester Stallone, were less interesting to Hollywood because the studios had found new ways to reach the same audience. Gross-out comedies like *Animal House*; summer blockbusters such as *American Graffiti*, *Grease*, and *Jaws*; and the anti-authority violence of Warner Brothers' Billy Jack series, in which Tom Laughlin plays a kind of Navajo, hippie-defending

Dirty Harry were among the decade's biggest earners. One of the most entertaining—and commercially successful—teen flicks of the decade was *The Rocky Horror Picture Show*.

The teen movie enjoyed a renaissance in the 1980s with a series of movies like *Ferris Bueller's Day Off* that took a smart, sympathetic, and humorous look at high school life, but in the ensuing decades, a teen movie came to mean anything from a remake of the dance classic *Footloose* to the fantasy drama *Donnie Darko* or *Spice World (The Movie)*. In the 1950s, the teen movie was a definable, if slightly artificial, genre that made Brando, Dean, and Presley globally famous. By the twenty-first century, the genre had become a demographic.

28

Kissin' Cousins

Elvis Films and the Beach-Party Movie

Who invented the beach-party movie? You could make a case for Elvis. The working title for *Blue Hawaii* (1961) was *Hawaiian Beach Boy*.

You could make an even stronger case for budget director Paul Wendkos, who directed *Gidget* (1959), in which Sandra Dee discovers love and surfing as a teenage girl in search of fun in the sun. Fred Karger, who worked on three Presley movies, wrote the title song. Joe Pasternak, who would produce *Spinout*, had originally wanted to make this picture, with Elvis in the starring role, but Columbia got the rights. The first movie was successful enough to spawn *Gidget Goes Hawaiian* (1961), featuring Deborah Walley (one of Elvis's co-stars in *Spinout*), *Gidget Goes to Rome* (1965), and a TV series.

Yet despite Gidget's success—and even though Elvis had hosted beach parties in *Blue Hawaii* and *Girls! Girls! Girls!* (1962)—most critics say the beach-party movie genre began in 1963 when American International Pictures released the movie *Beach Party*, starring Annette Funicello and Frankie Avalon, one of many pop stars touted as a pretender to the King's throne when Elvis was in the army in the late 1950s.

Estimates of how much *Beach Party* made at the North American box office vary from $2.5 million to $4 million. Either figure represented a substantial profit on a movie that cost AIP less than $400,000 to make.

Movie promoter James H. Nicholson and entertainment lawyer Samuel Z. Arkoff had founded AIP as a budget movie studio in 1954. Galvanized by *Beach Party*'s success, AIP launched six other movies in the same genre: *Muscle Beach Party*, *Bikini Beach*, *Pajama Party*, *Beach Blanket Bingo*, *How to Stuff a Wild Bikini*, and *The Ghost in the Invisible Bikini*. (The fourth and the last films in the series starred Nicholson's wife Susan Hart.)

The plots were even skimpier than in Elvis's movies. Essentially, each film revolved around threats to the romance between Dee Dee/Dolores (Funicello) and Frankie (Avalon) posed by a villain (the most memorable being Harvey Lembeck's Erich von Zipper, a parody of a Marlon Brando *Wild One*–style motorcycling antihero, in *Bikini Beach*), a rival love interest, or both of the above.

The characters idled away their days on the beach and danced through the night, to tunes written or played by such exponents of the surfin' sound as the Beach Boys, Dick Dale and the Deltones, and the Hondells. The soundtrack became more varied as the series progressed: thirteen-year-old Stevie Wonder made his screen debut in *Muscle Beach Party*, and Nancy Sinatra sang in *The Ghost in the Invisible Bikini*.

In *Bikini Beach* (1964), Avalon was given a second role as a British rock star known as Potato Bug (a pun on the Beatles—with beetles being a potato bug), who, despite his glasses, moustache, and British accent, nearly stole Funicello's heart.

Avalon's double act made Elvis's twin roles in *Kissin' Cousins* seem like the work of a singing Stanislavski, but the ploy was recycled in *Pajama Party* (1964). This time, Tommy Kirk took over Avalon's duties as Funicello's partner and played a confused Martian called Go-Go. This movie also featured Elsa Lanchester (the yoga teacher in *Easy Come, Easy Go*) and Teri Garr (who danced in nine Elvis films) and was choreographed by David Winters (*Easy Come, Easy Go*, *Girl Happy*, *Tickle Me*, and *Viva Las Vegas*).

Just when AIP seemed to have lost the plot, *Beach Blanket Bingo* (1965) revived the formula. Avalon sang the classic "These Are the Good Times," a young Linda Evans starred as the Marilyn Monroe–esque singing sensation Sugar Kane (in a part written for Nancy Sinatra), Walley went skydiving, the great Buster Keaton supplied some sublime pratfalls, and director William Asher paid homage to the silent series *The Perils of Pauline* with a scene in which Evans was tied to a buzz saw.

Beach Blanket Bingo marked the apotheosis of the beach party genre. At twenty-six, Avalon was getting a little old to play the eternal teenager and appeared for only a few minutes in *How to Stuff a Wild Bikini* (1965), which was distinguished primarily by Mickey Rooney's scene-stealing turn as an advertising exec. Avalon and Funicello were lucky to escape *The Ghost in the Invisible Bikini* (1966), a shark-jumping exercise in which Basil Rathbone (as a lawyer tastefully named Reginald Ripper) terrorized Walley, rightful heir to the estate left by carnival showman Boris Karloff. Nancy Sinatra did appear in this one but couldn't save the film or the series.

By 1966, when this cycle of AIP pictures came to an end, the movies had sold a lot of surfboards and bikinis. Some say that Funicello's rather ample bikinis introduced America to an item of clothing that had hitherto been regarded as risqué, if not downright sluttish. Millions of teens had been entertained until something better—in this case, the Beatles—came along. AIP's pictures had inspired many imitations, most notably Don Taylor's *Ride the Wild Surf*, featuring past and future Presley co-stars Barbara Eden and Shelley Fabares, a romantic beach-party drama set in Hawaii that has aged rather better than much of the Beach Party series.

When the original formula lost its allure, the studios experimented with the beach-party horror movie (Jon Hall's *The Beach Girls and the Monster*), the dire sci-fi beach-party movie (*The Horror of Party Beach*), and a protofeminist twist on the formula, *It's a Bikini World* (1967), directed by Stephanie Rothman, starring Walley, in her last beach-party movie.

AIP's *Dr. Goldfoot and the Bikini Machine*, starring Frankie Avalon and Vincent Price, is a real curio. Directed by Taurog, this took one of the core elements of the beach party genre—bikini-clad babes—to create a spy spoof that generated few laughs but earned its niche in movie history as one of the sources for Mike Myers's Austin Powers parodies.

AIP wasn't always that inventive, simply moving the beach-party stock company to a ski resort in Alan Rafkin's *Ski Party* (1965) that featured Walley and Yvonne Craig and a talking polar bear. Is this, you can't help wondering, where Parker got the brainwave for a talking camel to save *Harum Scarum*. The timeline works: *Ski Party* came out five months before Presley's mash-up of sword, sandals, and song.

Rafkin's movie must have done reasonably well, because *Clambake* producer Jules Levy says Wallis asked Allan Weiss to write a ski movie for Elvis. That never materialized, possibly because Wallis lost interest in the Memphis Wonder after the indifferent *Easy Come, Easy Go*. Wallis's last Elvis film does feel, at times, like a beach-party movie where the parties have moved indoors.

The philosophy behind the beach-party genre was summed up by Roger Ebert, who said, "The idea of the beach party movies, which had their roots in the Hollywood musicals of the Great Depression, was to sell music, fashions, and sex, seem to be terrifically modern and ignore the problems of the real world." This was, in essence, what most Presley musicals tried to do between 1960 and 1968.

The beach-party movies—like Elvis's formula films—centred on a romantic conflict that had to be happily resolved by the final reel. An attractive young cast, as many musical numbers as the producers could squeeze in, and a generous helping of slapstick humor sweetened the journey to that blissful resolution. The romances were usually pretty chaste. In many films, Hollywood veterans would be cast for novelty value, to raise the overall standard of acting, or provide another viewpoint on the teenagers' antics.

Although Katzman made *Harum Scarum* on a budget so scanty it barely existed, Presley's films usually had more money spent on them than the AIP pictures, and he could usually rely on a more able cast and crew. The one area where the King didn't always compete on equal terms was the music. He relied mainly on Hill and Range's tunesmiths, while AIP and other studios happily featured such acts as the Beach Boys, James Brown, and the Supremes.

The success of beach-party movies exerted a massive influence on the last five years of Presley's film career. Elvis returned to the beach for *Girl Happy*, although there wasn't that much sand in evidence; did the same in *Paradise, Hawaiian Style*; hosted a clambake in *Clambake* and drove a beach buggy; and caught a cold while romancing dotty Michelle Carey on the shore in *Live a Little, Love a Little* (1968).

Elvis was thirty-two when he hosted his last beach party in *Clambake*, six years older than Avalon when he had strolled off Hollywood's beach for the last time. By the end of the 1960s, the sun had all but set on the beach-party genre, although it would enjoy a cultish renaissance with John Milius's underrated surfing movie *Big Wednesday* (1978). Funicello and Avalon reunited for *Back to the Beach* (1987), hailed by some critics as the best beach-party movie of all time. The genre never came back into fashion. Beach-party movies are now fondly regarded as an entertaining, idealized expression of a simpler, happier, more innocent age in the movies and American society, but nobody has yet suggested they are ripe for serious critical reevaluation.

Ebert characterized the beach-party genre as "a tie between harmless and brainless." In that context, the best of Presley's beach-party musicals—especially *Blue Hawaii* and *Girl Happy*—now stand out from many titles in the genre. Elvis may ultimately have been a more successful beach boy than Avalon even if, after *Fun in Acapulco*, he became strangely reluctant to take to the screen in his swimming trunks, was afraid of water and, in his later years, would have to be reminded to sit in the sun by his father.

29

Pieces of My Life

Were the Movies Elvis's Autobiography?

There are three things most of us know about Elvis: he had a manipulative manager, a deeply mourned mother who died when he was young, and he was born a twin.

You will find one or more of these facts reflected in so many of Elvis's thirty-one feature films, it is easy to see why some, notably Douglas Brode in his book *Elvis Cinema and Popular Culture,* have cast him as some kind of auteur and portrayed the movies as an autobiographical statement by their enigmatic star. Before we go any further, it might be useful to remind ourselves how the auteur theory, in general, became so influential.

In the 1950s, the influential French moviemaker François Truffaut suggested that, even though filmmaking was an industrial process, a movie could—and should—reflect a director's personal vision and that directors should therefore be regarded as the auteurs (authors) of a movie in the same way as Herman Melville is the author of *Moby Dick.* Because Truffaut was French, this analysis became known as the *auteur theory,* which does sound significantly more intellectual than its English equivalent, "the author theory."

Expounded at length in the seminal French magazine *Cahiers du Cinéma,* by critics who championed the works of such filmmakers as Howard Hawks, Akira Kurosawa, and Jean Renoir, this theory shaped the writings of American film critic Andrew Sarris in the 1960s and, with the old Hollywood system suffering a crisis of self-confidence, legitimized the challenging work of such directors as Stanley Kubrick, Sam Peckinpah, Francis Ford Coppola, and Martin Scorsese.

Auteurism has had its critics, especially among the screenwriting fraternity, with David Kipen, director of literature at the National Endowment for the Arts, responding with "the Schreiber Theory," insisting that writers get their share of the credit. He later suggested he wasn't aiming to replace one kind of auteur with another but wanted to "overcorrect" the director-centred model of moviemaking.

The great Pauline Kael took issue with Andrew Sarris's suggestion that movies could be judged by the director's technical competence and distinguishable personality. Michelangelo Antonioni didn't have the basic technical skills to direct a film like John Sturges's *Bad Day at Black Rock,* Kael pointed out, yet still made the masterpiece *L'Avventura.* She also argued that the movies that most reflect a director's personality are not intrinsically good because "he falls back on the devices he has already done to death."

As for Sarris's suggestion that movies could be rated according to their interior meaning, produced by the tension between a director and his material, Kael scathingly observed: "These critics try embarrassingly hard trying to give some semblance of intellectual responsibility to a preoccupation with mindless, repetitive commercial products."

The Sarris–Kael standoff has never been resolved although directors still inspire far more reverence, analysis, and criticism than screenwriters. The debate has changed key, with some critics suggesting that most movies are not shaped by any one voice, but are a collaboration of many voices, even if some have more say than others. In 1982, Richard Dyer, professor of film studies at the University of Warwick, argued that some actors were the real auteurs of their films. The examples most often cited are James Cagney and John Wayne. In his biography of Cagney, Patrick McGilligan argues: "An actor may influence a film as much as a writer, director or producer; some actors are more influential than others; and there are certain rare few performers whose acting capabilities and screen personas are so powerful that they embody and define the very essence of their films."

That is certainly true for the Duke. A John Wayne movie became a recognizable commodity whether the star himself, Andrew V. McLaglen, or Henry Hathaway, directed it. As Vincent Canby put it in the *New York Times* in 1971: "In the age of the director, there still are a few actors whose strong personalities can inform the mood, pacing and structure of an entire film. Mr. Wayne's presence, physical as well as emotional, shaped his movies as much as the contributions of the writers, directors, producers, and cameramen."

Can we say the same about Elvis? He doesn't consistently fill the screen like Cagney or Wayne did, but as Cameron Crowe wrote in *Vanity Fair* magazine: "Elvis's catalogue of 31 movies is never less than fascinating, even when he was banging out three a year and barely keeping track of which girl, animal, car, co-star, or guitar he was performing with. Either a performer has built-in screen presence or he doesn't. Most don't. Elvis did, every time he stepped in front of the big glowing camera."

You can see what Crowe means, although Presley's presence is at its most influential, in terms of informing the mood, pacing, and structure of a movie, in the concert documentaries, *That's the Way It Is* and *Elvis on Tour*. From most accounts of Presley's movie years, he had far less overt influence on his roles, scripts, and movies than Cagney or Wayne. Elvis's father told *Good Housekeeping*: "Elvis hardly ever watched the movies he made because he didn't like most of them. He'd been well paid but he had never had script approval or control over the songs in his pictures or over anything else."

This certainly makes it harder to cast Elvis as a classic auteur. There is also, as Kael points out, the issue of quality. TV and music producer Jack Good once summed up the archetypal Elvis musical comedy with unfair but illuminating exaggeration: "Elvis in boat. Elvis waving at girls. Elvis driving up. Elvis driving away. Elvis hitting somebody. Somebody hitting Elvis. And Elvis warbling away in that curious baritone." When you're analyzing movies like *Harum Scarum*, which would, as Parker suggested, have been more entertaining if a talking camel had narrated it, does it make sense to look for hidden meanings?

Yet the movies were, as Wallis has explicitly acknowledged, often built around what the writers, directors, or producers knew about Presley's life and personality. So we are consistently presented with Elvis as a generous, handsome, southern poor boy made good, with a dead mother, an idle father, and a Machiavellian manager. The stereotypical celluloid Elvis has a nomadic spirit, a great rapport with children, and an enduring passion for cars, music, and girls.

Some of the references—such as Elvis's early habit of breaking his guitar strings, highlighted in *Loving You*—are very specific. And others—notably the allusion to his Cherokee ancestors—were known to relatively few people when Presley was alive.

"Why bother to bring the actor to the Method—seems to be the reasoning—when they could just bring the Method to the actor," is how Dundy saw this process. For all the correspondences between the offscreen Elvis and the onscreen star, Presley isn't the instigator of this manufactured Method-ism. Producers, directors, writers, and studio executives tailored many of the movies to suit Elvis, and the pictures were more likely to reflect their view of Presley than his own.

This modus operandi had the advantage of limiting the damage if the star proved to be a bad actor, and made it less likely that the star would be presented with material that was too risky, taxing, or adventurous. The one aspect of Presley's character that everyone who worked with him in Hollywood ought to have been aware of—his burning desire to prove himself a proper actor—was increasingly ignored.

In this context, does it still make sense to cast Elvis as some kind of auteur, or to scrutinize the movies for their hidden autobiographical significance?

It can. Kanter's *Loving You*, for example, introduces many of the familiar motifs—the poor boy made good, the cars, the Svengali figure who asks for 50 percent of his earnings—but casts its central hero in a sympathetic light. Kanter had talked to Presley, watched him on tour, and observed the madness that swirled around him. He distilled his impressions into a sensitive, sympathetic story called "Inside Paradise," published in *Variety*, in which the hero "was enjoying the glamorous, exciting, romantic, soul-stirring [version of] himself that evoked a strange magic on audiences" but, after a year when his future his assured, typically had only one decision left to make on any given day: what to order for dinner. Some of that melancholic tone infused Presley's character in *Loving You*, and it eerily prefigures the singer's last years when he retreated to Graceland.

Brode's quest for deeper meanings does produce some intriguing results. He is surely right to point out that the denouement of *Spinout*, in which Elvis remains a bachelor by wedding his three suitors to other men, is probably a pretty authentic presentation of the star's real attitude to marriage. Asked once, on the set of *Kid Galahad*, why he hadn't married, he replied, "Why should I? I get all I want."

Vernon said once, "I believe that Elvis's marriage failed simply because he realized after the wedding that he didn't want to be married." In contrast, the King looks delighted to be marrying Ann-Margret at the end of *Viva Las Vegas*. Although their romance would cool, for much of 1965 and 1966 many members of Elvis's entourage thought he was more likely to wed her than Priscilla.

Brode's take on Kenny Dornford, Bill Bixby's incompetent girl-chasing manager in *Speedway*, does shed new light on the character. "If we accept car racing as a correlative for Presley's stardom, it is clear that Kenny serves as a one-man symbol for the longstanding Memphis Mafia. In simplified fashion, he represents the coterie of old friends, distant relatives, and hangers-on who served in various capacities such as business managers and enjoyed the spoils of stardom—including the countless young women attracted like magnets to Elvis." That is fine as far as it goes, but the manager's secrecy about how he handles his friend's money—and his gambling habit—makes him an even more effective stand-in for Parker.

Yet there are other moments when Brode seems, as Kael might put it, to be trying too hard. In *Love Me Tender*, he draws parallels between the unfulfilling, possibly unconsummated, marriage between Clint (Presley) and Cathy (Debra Paget) and Elvis's romance with Priscilla. "Cathy becomes uncomfortable in her relationship to the boyish, almost saint-like Clint, She longs for a real man who knows how to hold her and, in bed, satisfy her—rather than treat her as a mother-figure, desiring only to be cradled in her arms," Brode writes. He observes that this "predates and parallels the situation that developed a few years later between Elvis and Priscilla when, before their marriage, they cuddled sensuously but did not engage in the sexual act. After the birth of their daughter, Elvis proved himself unable to accept Priscilla as a total woman—lover, friend, mother, wife—and destroyed the relationship."

The difficulty here is that Brode seems to apply different modes of observation to each situation. Onscreen, he's eager to explore every complexity. Offscreen, Brode seeks a simple, single solution that ignores the possibility, raised by Vernon's comments, the observations of many friends, and his own interpretation of *Spinout*, that the marriage actually collapsed because Elvis never really wanted to get married in the first place.

Yet you can have a lot of fun with this kind of analysis. Just as oranges are famously said to be an omen of death in *The Godfather*, you can make a half-serious case that, in Elvis movies, dogs signify disaster or discomfort.

Elvis's most famous encounter with a dog came in *The Steve Allen Show* in 1956 when , in tux and tails, he was obliged to sing "Hound Dog" to a stupefied basset hound. It was one of the most ludicrous performances of his career, and he made his opinion of the whole charade eloquently clear in the way he wiped his hand on his jacket, as if trying to wipe away the shame.

The twin dogs Elvis owned in *Jailhouse Rock* looked much like the hound on *The Steve Allen Show*, and when hanger-on Mickey Shaughnessy walked them so

The Presley's marriage started in in Las Vegas—and ended in the California divorce courts.

hard their paws bled, it was a sign that the worm was turning and would soon endanger the hero's career with a punch to the throat. In *Wild in the Country*, Hope Lange walked in her back garden with her dog before she decided to commit suicide. Arthur O'Connell nearly fell into Howlin' Devil's Gorge in *Kissin' Cousins* after taking the family bloodhound for a stroll. In *Paradise, Hawaiian Style*, Presley was grounded after a jaunt with a helicopter full of hungry canines went badly awry. And finally in *Live a Little, Love a Little*, Presley's photographer character suffered a terrible cold, lost his job, and hallucinated about dancing with a dog after Michelle Carey's snarling Great Dane has forced him to spend the day in the sea. Okay, the Elvis/dogs/disaster motif is not quite up there with the oranges in *The Godfather*, but it does show where this kind of analysis can lead.

Yet Brode's interpretations do indicate, as Doll has argued, that Presley's movies are worth watching again with an open mind. Many of them offer some intriguing parallels to—and distorted reflections of—the star's life, career, and personality. Yet as we analyze some of these themes, we should remember Kael's caution not to wear ourselves out trying to give an intellectual dignity to repetitive, commercial products where none might exist.

30

"It Keeps Right On a-Hurtin'"

The Absence of Elvis's Mother as Reflected in the Movies

The relationship between Elvis and his mother, Gladys, has inspired a lot of psychobabble by writers who ought to know better, some grotesque tabloid distortion (let's be clear, folks, there was one very good reason mother and son shared the same bed for years: the Presleys could afford only one), and one very good, if flawed, book, Elaine Dundy's *Elvis and Gladys*.

As Dundy suggests, once you strip away the mythologizing, misinterpretation, and misinformation, the story of this famous mother and son isn't, at its root, that unusual: a mother with an extraordinary love for her only son, and a son who reciprocated that even if, as Dundy has shown, he tried from a relatively young age—as early as eight—to draw some lines of demarcation and define a space he could be free in.

The intensity of Gladys's love is, Sigmund Freud would have argued, pivotal to Presley's stardom. As the father of psychoanalysis famously observed: "If a man has been his mother's undisputed darling, he retains throughout life the triumphant feeling, the confidence in success, which not seldom brings actual success."

What neither party could foresee is that the fame that rescued them from poverty would be one of the principal causes of her tragically early death. Gladys was forty-six, not forty-two, as the family and the world believed at the time, when she died on March 24, 1958. The diet pills she took to look good in photographs, her anxiety during her long separations from Elvis (especially after he had been drafted), the alcohol she drank to cope, all assisted her decline. Her son was certainly aware of this, and when he cried, "Everything I have is gone," just after her death, he certainly meant it.

The grief gnawed away at him. As his aunt Lillian told Dundy: "After she died, he changed completely. He never seemed like Elvis again." Gladys's tragedy is one of the keys to Elvis's own tragedy. Scenarios of what might have happened had she lived still haunt his friends and relatives. In Bill Bram's *Frame by Frame*, Bob Isenberg, the actor and assistant to Parker, recalls that Elvis told him on the set of *Easy Come, Easy Go*, "My mommy lived to 42 and I know for a fact I am

The final resting place of Gladys Presley at Graceland. Friends and
family say Elvis never recovered from his mother's death.

going to die at the same age." Isenberg replied, "Don't talk yourself into it."
Later, when Presley did die at the age of forty-two, Isenberg felt, "He just willed
himself to die."

His torment couldn't have been eased by the suspicion that, as his aunt
Lillian had suggested, he was responsible for his mother's death. You can hear
the guilt when, as he lowered Gladys into her grave, he protested, "I lived my
whole life just for you."

This event probably helped trigger the symptoms that would haunt Presley:
addictive behavior, wild mood swings, deep resentment, sleep disorders, and
even, in his final years, an aversion to sunlight. Guralnick says: "The downfall of

Elvis was really the depression he felt, and you can see it increasing in the last four or five years. You see a man in the grip of depression."

Many of Presley's relatives in his maternal line suffered psychological problems. Apart from Gladys, his uncle Travis died of cirrhosis of the liver at age fifty-one; two of his Smith cousins—Bobby and Bobbie Jane Wren—committed suicide; and a third, Junior, died of a haemorrhage or alcoholic seizure when he was twenty-six, after suffering a nervous breakdown while fighting in the Korean War.

For Elvis, Gladys's death was a wound that never healed. You can see the evidence in the movies. Two of his most moving scenes, which show him at his most vulnerable, have mothers at their heart.

In *Flaming Star*, as half-breed Pacer, stung by grief after his mother's funeral, he declared his love for Barbara Eden. Siegel recalled in his memoirs: "Elvis felt he couldn't do the scene and begged for more time to prepare. Almost childlike, he offered me the use of his brand new Rolls-Royce until we had to do the scene. To his amazement and mine, he gave one of his finest performances ever." The vulnerability, hurt, and passion Elvis displayed at this crucial juncture still come as something of a revelation. Siegel referred to his star as a Method actor who jumps out of the screen. That might seem overgenerous to those who have seen only the musical comedies, but in this scene, in this film, he is utterly affecting, having the guts to let his grief and guilt infuse his performance.

His acting in *Wild in the Country* was not as consistently impressive as in Siegel's western, but when he reminisced with Hope Lange about his mother ("That lady, and she was a lady, ma'am"), the regret, resentment, and hint of bafflement that this could happen to him—and her—still ring painfully true.

In *The Lost Country*, the J. R. Salamanca novel this movie was adapted from, the hero's mother is still alive. The change of plot allowed Presley to emote, in a way that may have been cathartic, but the missing matriarch came to define the template for many of his subsequent movies. Elvis has a father and no mother in *Clambake* and *Follow That Dream*, a father and stepmother in *Stay Away, Joe*, a dead father and a mother who is never mentioned in *Girls! Girls! Girls!*, and in *Roustabout* he is an orphan.

The idea that he might even have parents is ignored in eighteen of his films. That is understandable—in the kind of musical comedies Elvis churned out in the 1960s, parents would, unless they were there to be rebelled against, be an unnecessary encumbrance. Yet in only two of his movies made after Gladys's death was Elvis's mother still alive in the final reel: *Kissin' Cousins* (Glenda Farrell, as Jodie's mom) and *Blue Hawaii* (Angela Lansbury). The latter's amusing brand of matriarchal control freakery—and the way it provokes her son Chad (Elvis) into his own declaration of independence—could be seen as a commentary on the bond between Presley and his mother, yet others suggest Lansbury's character owes more to Presley's stepmom Dee Dee Stanley .

If you follow Brode's school of microanalysis, Elvis's first screen mom, played by Mildred Dunnock in *Love Me Tender*, is one of the most notable. Identified in the credits only as The Mother—which bestows an archetypal status not granted to any other member of the cast and suggests she could represent Gladys—she dominates the Reno brothers. When Elvis is asked to sing "Love Me Tender" at a family gathering, Brode notes, "the words 'for my darling I love you and I always will' are addressed to Dunnock before he turns to Cathy half-heartedly proffering a chorus to her."

Is this, as Brode argues, a sign that Hollywood was already aware of Presley's deep attachment to his mother? Or would Kael chastise us for seeking intellectual depths where there are none? Either way, the moment does convey Elvis's paradoxical personality. As Brode concludes: "He was an odd mixture of a hood—the haircut, the clothes, the sullen, alienated look; and a sweet little boy—curiously gentle and respectful."

31

In My Father's House

Vernon, Feckless Dads, and Why the Movies Featured So Many Jailhouse Shocks

If Vernon Presley ever paid much attention to his son's movies, he must have wondered about the way they collectively portray fathers. Elvis's screen dads range from the well-meaning but ultimately ineffectual (Dean Jagger in *King Creole*, John McIntire in *Flaming Star*, Roland Winters in *Blue Hawaii*, Burgess Meredith in *Stay Away, Joe*) to the downright venal (Harry Shannon in *Wild in the Country*). In between, this gallery of patriarchs includes the ornery yet shiftless Arthur O'Connell (*Follow That Dream* and *Kissin' Cousins*) and the decent, if overbearing, James Gregory (*Clambake*).

Many teen movies pandered to adolescent fantasies of rebellion by presenting the son as the real man of the house. This motif ran through Elvis's movies and was given near definitive treatment in *King Creole*. As troubled teen Danny Fisher, Presley explained that he stopped listening to his father because he "ran out of other cheeks," recalling a trip to the circus when his dad let someone smack him in the mouth for no reason. He rounded off the anecdote with a snarl: "When they swing at you, pop, it's not enough to duck, you gotta swing back."

Roland Winters spent much of *Blue Hawaii* ducking, while his wife's domineering behavior drives son Elvis to head to the beach and go into business on his own. The same laudable desire to stand on his own two feet spurred Elvis to strike out from his millionaire daddy in *Clambake*, although in that instance, the problem was that Gregory's oil baron had too much personality, not too little. The only one of Elvis's dads who could be held up as parental role model is John McIntire in *Flaming Star*. Even his decency and stoic bravery couldn't save him, his wife, or his son Pacer from violent death. But do any of these portrayals have anything to do with Presley's real life and his relationship with his father?

Even Dundy, the most sympathetic of Presley's biographers, doesn't have many kind words for Vernon Presley. Although he built the house on Old Saltillo Road, Tupelo, where Elvis was born, Vernon is presented as handsome, mostly well intentioned, but idle ("vaccinated against work" is how one family friend put it). Orville Bean, a local businessman whom Elvis's father crossed, called Vernon "long hungry," a grievous epithet reserved for those who were so lacking in any kind of moral fiber they'd take food out of their family's mouths to ensure they didn't starve themselves.

After Jesse Garon's stillbirth, the most famous event in Elvis's formative years is Vernon's conviction for forgery on May 25, 1938. Having made less money than he hoped by selling a hog to Bean, he had conspired to change the amount on the check. This desperate, stupid idea led to Vernon spending months in custody (his father refused to pay bail) and just under nine months in jail. He was released on February 6, 1939, when Elvis was four.

While Vernon was in prison, the young Elvis responded to this crisis by becoming, in his own mind, the man of the house, often patting his mother on the face and saying: "There, there, little baby." He would accompany her on the long day trips back and forth to Parchman Prison, where, because prisoners were given conjugal rights, he would spend some time talking to and hugging his father before he was left to play with the other children while his parents disappeared into another room.

Those memories would haunt any child, but especially one as sensitive and insecure as Elvis. After Vernon's return, as Fortas says in his book, "the son saw his father as someone to cuddle and coddle." At some point in life, many people end up looking after their parents, treating their elders as if they were children. In Elvis's family, this exchange of roles was accelerated by his startling rise to fame. His father effectively retired in the mid-1950s, looking after the family's accounts—hardly a sinecure, given Elvis's lavish spending habits. With both parents dependent on him, Elvis referred to them as his "babies."

Even as one of Elvis's "babies," Gladys remained the dominant force in their small, tight-knit family. Her death completed the role reversal between father and son, a shift mirrored, to great comic effect, in the courtroom scene in *Follow That Dream* when Arthur O'Connell decided the only way to save the family was to allow his son to speak on their behalf.

In 1960, when Vernon was romancing his future wife Dee Dee Stanley, the two Presleys had an almighty row that ended with Elvis shouting at his father: "You're fired! Get your ass out of here." Vernon stormed out to the office behind Graceland to figure out, as he put it, how a son could fire his father.

The rift didn't last, and father and son would bump along until Elvis's death. Gladys had been her son's confidante, but she also knew how to lay down the law. Vernon was never as close to his son—though they talked more often in Elvis's final years—and nor, though he often tried to advise his son, did he exert the same authority as Gladys. One thing Elvis and Vernon did have in common was that they suffered such severe bouts of loneliness they could be all but inconsolable until their mood lifted. In a touching interview with *Good Housekeeping* in 1978, Vernon comes across as a heartbroken bystander trying to put a brave face on a family tragedy. On June 26, 1979, less than two years after his son's death, Vernon died at the age of sixty-three.

Elvis as Vince Everett in *Jailhouse Rock* (1957). Did the courtroom/jailhouse scenes in Presley's films allude to a family secret?   *MGM/Photofest*

Managing Elvis's finances may have been the only job Vernon ever kept for any length of time. Elvis had no illusions about his father's attitude to work, joking once: "Daddy's had a backache for thirty years. He wouldn't work if you held a gun to his head." In fairness to Vernon, he may not have been the most industrious member of the family (his wife and son both consistently worked to—and beyond—the limits of their endurance), but his idleness, certainly as a young man, was partly dictated by economic circumstance in the Great Depression.

The scene in *King Creole*, in which Jagger, as Elvis's father, was humiliated by an arrogant boss, may well have evoked memories of Vernon's struggles in the workplace. The dynamic between Jagger's weak yet kindly patriarch and Presley's moody son in Curtiz's movie feels more realistic than any other father–son relationship in Presley's movies. There's plenty of love in this clash of generations, but there is also a lot of contempt and incomprehension. Jagger and Presley spark off each other brilliantly, acting out the generation gap the singer's music had helped to create so convincingly that their struggle becomes almost archetypal, saying as much about the conflicts between millions of fathers and sons as about the relationship between Vernon and Elvis.

As Sam Tyler in *Wild in the Country*, Shannon is less interesting onscreen—the principal purpose of his cameo is to exhibit his contempt for Glenn (Elvis)—than in his son's florid description of his feckless behavior. The unequal division of labor in the Tyler family—with the father sitting, drinking, and fishing while the mother toils in the unforgiving sun—is a funhouse-mirror reflection of the Presleys' lives. The script gave Elvis license to explore resentments against his father, who had already met his second wife when this was filmed, that he may have been reluctant to acknowledge.

In *Follow That Dream*, the Kwimpers subsist on relief, much as the Presleys lived on commodities (government handouts of staple goods like beans, cheese, and sugar) in the 1930s. O'Connell's homespun patriarch is much more averse to paid work than Vernon and, judging from his travails with the exploding toilet, isn't as good a housebuilder as Elvis's father. O'Connell's performance was so effective that he recycled it for *Kissin' Cousins*, albeit in in a role too stereotypically one-dimensional to relate to anyone, let alone Vernon.

The other most intriguing fathers in the post-army movies are Winters (*Blue Hawaii*) and Meredith (*Stay Away, Joe*). Winters extracted a lot of comedy from his role as an implausibly meek pineapple tycoon and proved the perfect, quietly exasperated foil for Lansbury, whose blond good looks and southern belle personality owe something to Dee Dee Stanley.

In *Stay Away, Joe*, Meredith's Charlie Lightcloud stood by with quiet good humor as his son turned the family home into a perennial party venue, much as Elvis did with Graceland in the early 1960s. The film's elaborate fights resemble the violent exuberance of the games Presley and his friends played outside Graceland, one of which was known simply as "War." Meredith was equally quiescent as wife Katy Jurado (Elvis's stepmother in the film) redecorated the family home, much as Stanley tried to do at Graceland before the King put his foot down. In the movie, a fight destroyed the Lightcloud house—and Jurado's schemes. Real life wasn't as hilariously melodramatic: father and stepmother moved to a house near Graceland that Elvis bought for them.

As a character, Vernon exerts significantly less influence on his son's movies than Gladys, yet the misjudgement that led to his incarceration at Parchman prison is, Dundy has suggested, at the root of all the courtroom and jailhouse scenes in the Elvis movie canon. This view doesn't have many supporters. Even Greil Marcus, who admired Dundy's writing on Elvis, said, "Her suggestion that Parker contrived the 1957 film *Jailhouse Rock* as a sadistic practical joke, in which the son is forced to walk in his father's shackled footsteps, is worthy of the most inventive students of the assassination of John F. Kennedy."

Here is the story as Dundy presented it. Somehow, Parker discovered the family secret and used it to manipulate or blackmail the Presleys. As minor as the offence might seem now, Vernon was so ashamed he never even told his second wife about it. When discussing the incident in the 1970s with Dr. Nick, Elvis loyally glossed over the crime—saying his father had stolen some groceries after the family went days without food—and made his doctor promise not to tell a soul. Indeed, when the news broke after Elvis's death, it was greeted with such headlines as "The Darkest Secret in the Presley Closet."

In this context, Dundy suggested, is it not odd that, for his third movie, Elvis should be forced to play a pop star who becomes famous after being released from jail and actually uses his disgrace to sell records? Odder still, as she points out, Elvis was twenty-two when he was sent to his celluloid prison—the same age as his father when he was imprisoned.

Although it is widely regarded as one of Presley's best movies, it is unclear whether he enjoyed making this noir-ish musical drama. After shooting, he often visited Shelley Winters and rang home to speak to his mother: "I don't like what I'm doing, I don't like Hollywood, I don't like the film, what should I do?" The answer was always the same: do what the Colonel says.

You can see why he didn't like it. Mickey Shaughnessy, his buddy, cellmate, and first manager in the movie, had made headlines with a nightclub act that included, as *Variety* put it, "forty-five minutes of taking Elvis over the hurdles." The script stuck close enough to Presley's own meteoric rise—and his known personality traits, such as his love for cars, girls, and hamburgers—for many viewers to assume that the callous antihero he plays for most of the movie was the real Elvis. In one scene as Vince Everett, he is gratuitously rude to a motherly maid who has, Dundy suggests, such a strong Tupelo accent she must have sounded like his mother.

Dundy went on to point out how many other Elvis movies feature show trials and jailhouse shocks. In *Loving You*, Lizabeth Scott leads the defence of Presley and his music in a courtroom. In *Wild in the Country*, Elvis starts the movie at a juvenile court and ends it at an inquest (presided over, funnily enough, by a character called Judge Parker), where he is all but accused of manslaughter. (The Salamanca novel that inspired the film features no trial scenes.) In *Follow That Dream*, Presley acts as defense attorney as the state tries to break up the Kwimper family. In *Speedway*, the star has to strike a deal with the IRS to avoid trial after sweating it out in an office that resembles a courtroom. He is sent to the "big house" in *Blue Hawaii* (after a free-for-all in a nightclub), *Roustabout* (after a fight outside a nightclub), and *Harum Scarum* (for plotting to assassinate the king), he breaks into jail in *Girl Happy* (after a free-for-all inside a nightclub), he takes temporary charge of the jail in *Charro!* (for once, no nightclubs were implicated), and he visits jail to reassure an employee suspected of murder in *The Trouble with Girls*.

You can chalk up some of this repetition to the kind of industrialized plagiarism that often typifies Hollywood—especially when producers, directors, and writers are going through the motions. Some of these spells in jail seem perfectly justified by the plot (*The Trouble with Girls*), by the desire to cast Elvis as a rebel (*Jailhouse Rock, Roustabout*), or by the intent to give an impression of conflict were none really exists (*Blue Hawaii*). Even so, for an actor who primarily made musical comedies, that is a lot of time in a cell or in the dock.

If you accept that all these scenes are designed, in a way that only the terrified Presleys and the malignant Parker would recognize, to allude to Vernon's secret crime, you also have to explain how all these references were shoehorned into so many scripts. For that, Dundy has no real answer. And nor do we. Many Elvis fans—Marcus among them—are intrigued by the suggestion that Parker used this knowledge to blackmail the family. Yet the accounts of how Presley's scripts were written are so varied and incomplete that it is impossible to establish a credible conspiracy.

Dundy may not be able to reveal how the conspiracy worked—beyond some dark thoughts about Hollywood's manipulative practices—but she does leave us with one suggestive detail.

In his memoirs, the country musician Gabe Tucker, one of the Colonel's long-standing associates, notes rather randomly that the paper jailhouse used in *Jailhouse Rock* "had been moved squarely into the reception room where Elvis was making *Tickle Me*."

There is no jail scene in *Tickle Me*, filmed in 1965 at Allied Artists, eight years after *Jailhouse Rock*, which had been made at MGM. The Colonel was renowned for his practical jokes, usually staged at someone else's expense, but even by his standards he had gone to some lengths to ensure that Elvis saw the paper jailhouse.

32

Double Trouble

Twins in Elvis Movies

You don't have to look for twins in Presley's movies; you stumble over them. The dual Elvis in *Kissin' Cousins* is only the most extreme manifestation of the theme.

Controversy still rages over how deeply Presley mourned the loss of his twin. Jesse Garon emerged stillborn from Gladys's womb hours after she had given birth to Elvis on January 8, 1935.

Clinical psychologist Peter O. Whitmer has suggested, in his psychological biography *The Inner Elvis*, that the torment defined the singer's identity. A twinless twin wants, Whitmer argued, "to prove his uniqueness, to stand as an individual," but grief is revealed in the dualities. Presley's synthesis of black and white music could, Whitmer proposes, have been achieved only by a twinless twin. Even Presley's famous preference for pink and black as a young man could, he argues, honor the dead brother: "The color pink, soft as an infant, and black, harsh as death."

There is a certain degree of "seek and ye shall find" about such analysis. The combo of pink and black is certainly psychologically suggestive (although another author, Elaine Doss, has suggested the lighter color reflects the King's latent homosexuality!), but the suggestion that Elvis could do what he did musically only because he was a twinless twin seems simplistic, if not reductive. To cite just one example, Bob Wills fused country and jazz to create western swing in the 1930s despite suffering from the disadvantage of having several healthy, musically gifted siblings.

Even among Presley's closest circle of friends and relatives there is little agreement over his attitude to Jesse Garon. The family did visit Jesse Garon's unmarked grave, and, for years, Gladys would set an extra place at the family table in his memory. Yet many of Elvis's friends say he barely mentioned his twin and, if he did, it was often to suggest that his own survival was proof of his destiny.

One of the difficulties is that Elvis, adopting the French writer André Gide's maxim "Please don't understand me too quickly," deliberately shrouded his life in rumor, romance, and mystery. He once assured Lamar Fike that he had had twin toes—a web of extra skin between the second and third toe on his right foot—which was a sign that he had been an identical twin. It's a lovely story, but nobody who ever saw Elvis's feet remembers him having webbed toes.

Anthony Lawrence, who wrote three of his movies and the John Carpenter biopic *Elvis*, told Bram: "He told me about his twin that he had often talked to in the form of his shadow on the wall." Larry Geller, Elvis's hairdresser and confidant, echoes Lawrence's view, saying: "The life and death of Jesse Garon was a precious mystery to Elvis . . . At night, in the dark and silence of his room, he would have conversations with Jesse and later tell people what his brother had said to him."

Yet Priscilla doesn't recall Elvis ever mentioning his brother, and Presley's cousin Billy Smith recalled: "When people read that Elvis had a twin, they'd come up and ask about him and he'd say: "He was born dead, I never knew him." Somewhere in the middle of all those radically different accounts lies the truth about how Elvis really felt about Jesse Garon. The only people who can really solve this particular mystery—Elvis, his mother, and his father—are all dead.

Whitmer is not alone in seeing the stillborn twin as the key to Elvis's story. In the musical drama *Are You Lonesome Tonight?*, British dramatist Alan Bleasdale suggested the death left the surviving twin tragically meek offstage. Bleasdale's play echoes a dream Presley had a few months before his death. In the dream, he and his brother were both performing live in concert and, as Elvis told Geller: "Jesse Garon had a better voice than me."

Presley's story is too complex for any single key to explain it all, but the loss probably marked him in ways he was unaware of. At Sun, Phillips had been struck by Elvis's isolation, saying: "He was a total loner. He felt locked out." The director Sidney Lumet, who once watched the star on set, was reminded of the mythical bird that must hover in the sky until it dies in Tennessee Williams's play *Orpheus Descending*: "It evoked such a memory of what I felt of Presley: something other worldly, unhuman (not inhuman), a kind of restless spirit that could never rest anywhere . . . yet unaware of his separation from the rest of us."

Whatever Elvis felt about his twin, he must have been disconcerted by how often his movies alluded to this tragic fact of his life. The tone is set as early as his second movie, *Loving You*, in which Wendell Corey had the throwaway line "I wish I were twins. I'd have someone to blame for this." When Elvis sang "Mean Woman Blues," a spectator with a similar hairstyle watched him and aped his hand gestures. About two minutes and ten seconds into the song, the doppelganger virtually shared the screen with Elvis and, as if to underline the resemblance, started flicking his head and shaking his shoulders in the same manner as the star.

Some minutes later, the camera panned to show identical twin girls clapping to the music, one twin clapping her right hand into his sister's left. The film's director/writer Kanter had spotted two twins doing this at an Elvis concert in Louisiana and decided to incorporate it into the movie. A similar sighting could have inspired the Elvis lookalike in "Mean Woman Blues." Even so, Kanter had set a precedent that would inspire many other directors.

In *Jailhouse Rock*, the only doppelgangers on display were the twin basset hounds that Elvis's antihero acquires when he becomes rich and famous. The theme recurred in *G.I. Blues* when, at one point, he was surrounded by twin babies. This apparently innocuous musical also featured of the most enigmatic scenes in Presley's film canon, in which he was effectively asked to compete with himself.

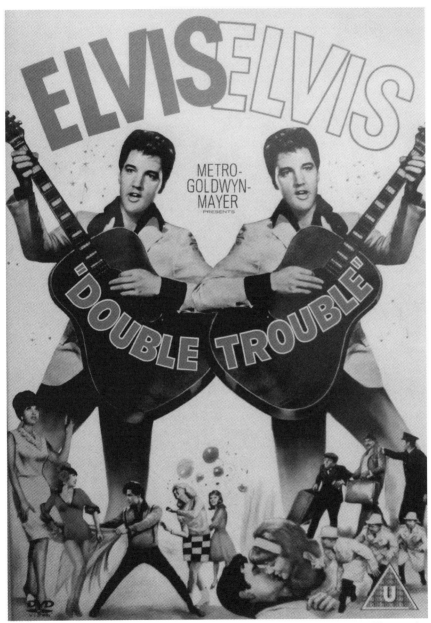

Most of the double trouble in Elvis's movies involved lots of allusions to his stillborn twin.

The new smooth Elvis, crooning "Doin' the Best I Can," found little favor with one soldier who strolled over to the jukebox and selected Presley's "Blue Suede Shoes," provoking the inevitable fight, saying pointedly: "I want to hear an original."

It's difficult to decide whether this scene was meant merely an in-joke, a labored attempt to prove the film's makers have a sense of humor, or a sly dig at the way Hollywood has tamed the star, but such moments do make you wonder exactly what Elvis meant when he famously said: "There were some funny things in that script—I'll have to read it someday." This particular scene may be intended to be funny-ha-ha but comes across as funny-peculiar.

Even when the twinning theme wasn't center-stage, it was often acknowledged in passing. In *Follow That Dream*, Elvis's family adopt twins with rhyming names, Eddy and Teddy, echoing Elvis Aaron and Jesse Garon. In *Girls! Girls! Girls!*, Presley's surrogate father Papa Stavros is a proud patriarch with beautiful twin girls. In *Double Trouble*—an intriguing title, given that Elvis's movies are so full of twinnings—he talks to twin girls in a nightclub. In *Change of Habit*, in which he plays a doctor, a pregnant woman asks him if she's going to have twins.

And then there's *Kissin' Cousins*, in which Presley is blond country bumpkin Jodie and black-haired slick Air Force officer Josh. For whatever reason—and it may just be plain embarrassment at having to utter such lines as "Ah loves you somethin' powerful, lil' old speckled pup"—Elvis doesn't invest Jodie with any personality.

Elsewhere in his movies, you find minor variations on the theme. In *Love Me Tender*, he married his older brother's sweetheart and resolved any potential awkwardness by conveniently dying. In *Flaming Star*, he was separated from his half brother by war and, ultimately, death. In *Fun in Acapulco*, he played a trapeze artist racked by guilt because he accidentally killed his brother. In *Wild in the Country*, he almost killed his brother in the opening scene and later told social worker Lange, "I've got the mark of Cain on me, ma'am."

Given the crime that made Cain notorious, and the fact that Presley often wondered if he had done something in the womb to ensure he survived at his twin's expense, this line could have had a strange emotional resonance for the star that writer Clifford Odets probably never intended.

Hollywood's need to present Elvis as *sui generis* may explain why, so often, his characters have no discernible family. Yet in none of the thirty-one feature films does he have an uncomplicated, fulfilling relationship with a brother. Only twice does Elvis have an enduring happy relationship with a sibling—*King Creole* and *Stay Away, Joe*—and on both occasions that relationship is with a sister.

33

"Elvis Cannot Be Fat or Pudgy Looking"

The Continuing Struggle over the King's Weight

Wallis had a private screening of *Viva Las Vegas* in December 1963 and, although this movie would become one of the King's biggest hits, he was appalled by what he saw. In a letter he quickly fired off to Parker, the producer complained that Elvis didn't look "lean, handsome and rugged" but had become soft, fat, and jowly. The self-proclaimed starmaker added: "In this picture, he plays a lean, tough, hard-hitting guy who rides a motorcycle, works as a roustabout in a carnival show and he cannot be fat or pudgy looking. He must train down to get the look the character requires or the character will not be believable."

The reaction to *Viva Las Vegas* sounds extreme. Presley did not look especially fat in any scene, appearing especially lean when he performed "C'mon Everybody" and "I Need Somebody to Lean On." He had looked beefier before—especially in *Follow That Dream* and *Kid Galahad*—and would look heavier again—when he sang "What Every Woman Lives For" in *Frankie and Johnny* and at certain moments in *Clambake*.

Wallis's tirade was probably inspired, in part, by competitive envy. He was astute enough to sense that *Viva Las Vegas* would be a bigger hit than his recent movies with Elvis. Yet the letter also reflects a continuing battle over Presley's weight that raged for much of his movie career. Parker certainly didn't argue, writing back within hours: "Regarding hair cutting, weight, barber, etc, for Mr Presley, your letter is well taken and I will get the message across to Mr Presley just like you gave it to me." He was good as his word—if not better—interrogating Elvis's friend Marty Lacker and when told that Elvis just ate what he always ate, raised his cane and shouted: "Don't lie to me! Tell me!"

By the time he was forty, Presley's weight problems had become a tabloid joke. After his death, as reports of his typical diet were revealed—and hyped up—he was dubbed "the burger King." His legendary penchant for fried peanut butter and banana sandwiches was, his major domo Joe Esposito said, much exaggerated: "They make it sound like that was all he ever ate. That was a treat once in a while. He didn't eat five or six of them, he ate one." Esposito even got Elvis to eat "pasta with vegetables—broccoli with garlic and stuff," but those meals, because they don't fit the stereotype of Presley as a gargantuan glutton, are largely ignored by the media. There was a certain amount of cultural snobbery behind the ridicule: what else, ran the underlying assumption, could you expect from a southern redneck who became too famous for his own good?

Most of the stories ignored the fact that Presley did have medical problems—notably an enlarged colon—that made him look bloated. (Not all of these ailments were attributable either to his diet or his pills, though many were.) They also overlooked the significance of food in Elvis's life.

Jane Elliot, who had a fling with him during the filming of *Change of Habit*, told Bill Bram: "His eating habits were so bad. He ate no green vegetables, he ate no salads, he ate steak, bacon and eggs, peanut butter. His food obsession was so profound, you just knew this guy was going to run his body into the ground." This certainly wasn't the kind of diet to help a man who suffered from hypertension and a weak heart, but it did reflect an obsession with food that had its roots in Presley's childhood.

Elvis always maintained that, though his family were poor, they never went hungry. Yet he gained twenty pounds in his first year as a performer—which does suggest that he had never been able to eat properly before. Although he was a white millionaire when he recorded "In the Ghetto," he could sing so movingly of the hunger that burned in the song's angry young man because it had burned in him too. The scent of fish always reminded Elvis of his poor childhood, and he wouldn't have it cooked at Graceland. His uncle Vester once joked about taking Elvis's peanut butter and crackers, and whenever he visited the family home, the boy would yell: "Hide them!"

So when Elvis became famous, and could afford to eat, he did just that. His diet became an issue as early as 1957 when Michael Curtiz, the director of *King Creole*, told him he had to lose fifteen pounds to play Danny Fisher. Presley was taken aback, but he did what Curtiz ordered.

The issue of the star's weight was not raised again until Wallis viewed *Viva Las Vegas*. In the United Artist picture *Follow That Dream* and *Kid Galahad*, Presley looked heftier, but the extra weight—and his more natural haircolor—suited his roles, as an innocent abroad and a boxer. In *Roustabout*, he doesn't look as tough as Wallis probably hoped, but he looks sharp enough, though oddly pale in some scenes. He looked trim in *Girl Happy* and *Tickle Me*, but by 1966, when *Paradise, Hawaiian Style* and *Spinout* were released, the extra pounds were starting to show.

In September 1966, Wallis wrote to Parker again, saying that some exhibitors and fans were worried there was something "radically wrong" with the star. John Rich, who was to direct *Easy Come, Easy Go*, said he "couldn't believe the amount of weight he has put on since *Roustabout*." Wallis asked the Colonel to try and get him thinner because, as one memo put it, "Navy men aren't supposed to be fat." Presley must have paid heed, because he looked trimmer as a singing sailor in *Easy Come, Easy Go* than as a singing racing driver in *Spinout*. Rich also took the sensible precaution of dressing his star in black civvies.

Wallis would never make another Elvis movie, but other producers and directors had similar concerns. As Michael A. Hoey, who worked on *Double Trouble*, said in his memoirs: "Elvis looked a lot heavier to me and I learned from Norman [Taurog] that he had a bad habit of pigging out on junk food when he wasn't working and put on lots of weight." One of the star's favorite treats, Hoey wrote, was a dozen assorted donuts from Winchell's Donut shop. Such indulgences could be masked only by diet pills, appetite suppressants (Ionamin was a perennial favorite), and a severe dietary regime.

As Fortas noted: "Usually before a film, Elvis would diet by eating only one meal a day and he could lose fifteen to twenty pounds in two weeks. He had fantastic willpower. He wouldn't eat any sweets or breads and he'd drink plenty of water to flush the fat out of his system." Usually this worked, but when he turned up for *Clambake*, he was thirty pounds overweight. New jackets were ordered, Presley took some more diet pills, and shooting got under way. In the final movie, though Parker reportedly had people report back on the star's weight, Presley didn't look significantly heavier than in *Spinout* or *Paradise, Hawaiian Style*.

Sometimes, you can see Elvis's weight fluctuate between scenes in the same movie, presumably because the longer he was on set, the more weight he lost. In *Frankie and Johnny*, he looks reasonably slender leading the marching band in a rousing chorus of "Down by the Riverside" but looks decidedly plump when he's crooning "What Every Woman Lives For."

It can surely be no coincidence that the King's weight problem abated when he was given a creative challenge. The NBC TV special and the Memphis sessions in 1969 reinvigorated Elvis, and in his last six feature films—*Stay Away, Joe*; *Speedway*; *Live a Little, Love a Little*; *Charro!*; *The Trouble with Girls*; and *Change of Habit*—he was in superb shape. On *Live a Little, Love a Little*, actress Suzanne Covington said: "Elvis always looked perfect. He knew everybody was looking at him when he was on set."

Perfection was hard to maintain. Mesmeric in *That's the Way It Is* (1970), Presley still looked good in *Elvis on Tour* (1972), but the weight was piling back on as the physical and emotional pressure on the star mounted. As a concert schedule that had once been a challenge became a chore, food provided some solace. And the ritual of bingeing and purging that preceded so many movies would be repeated before each major concert tour. His last fast started on August 14, 1977, two days before his death.

34

My Grandmother's a Full Cherokee

Elvis's Native American Ancestry in the Movies

While surrounded by his buddies on the Frankfurt special in *G.I. Blues*, Elvis's hero suddenly announced, apropos of nothing in particular: "My grandmother's a full Cherokee. They don't all sit around smoking corncob pipes, you know!" Emboldened by this revelation, he also revealed that his uncle Charlie—whose real name was Leaping Bear—played a "hot clarinet."

The interjection seems odd because Presley's character does nothing in the movie to make his ancestry even vaguely relevant. Yet Elvis's maternal great-great-great grandmother was a Cherokee named Morning White Dove. The Native American strain in the Presley genes was reinforced in 1903 when Doll Mansell and Bob Smith, first cousins and grandchildren of Morning White Dove, got married. They were Elvis's maternal grandparents, although he would never have remembered them: Bob died in 1931 and Doll in 1935, the year Elvis was born. In photographs of the couple, Bob's Native American roots are particularly evident in his brow, jet-black hair, and dark, deep-set eyes.

Presley was proud of that ancestry. His cousin Billy Smith said: "Elvis knew he had Indian blood in him. He liked that. He said that's where he got his high cheekbones." As Smith noted, many of Presley's maternal relatives, including his mother, "had that Cherokee look . . . Dark skin, dark eyes and high cheeks." Even in the 1930s, the Smith family were still swapping stories about Morning White Dove and her beauty. There was also some speculation in the Presley side of the family that one of the unnamed fathers of the nine illegitimate children born to Rosella, Elvis's paternal great-grandmother, was part Cherokee.

The rest of the world would not discover Elvis's Native American genes until 1981 when Mississippi genealogical expert Roy Walker, helping Dundy research *Elvis and Gladys*, traced the Presley and Smith family trees back to Morning Dove White. Yet the ancestry was known among those close to Elvis and may have been discovered by Parker and some of the star's confidants in Hollywood.

There is a famous story, recalled in Joe Starita's study *The Dull Knifes of Pine Ridge: A Lakota Odyssey*, about Elvis inviting some Lakota actors to Graceland one summer. After some traditional Lakota singing and dancing, Presley asked if he could sing "Jailhouse Rock" for his visitors. The Lakotas then tried to teach him one of their songs and part of their traditional Rabbit dance. This enchanting story is, unfortunately, not corroborated by any other source and is said to have happened in the summer of 1959 when Elvis was serving in Germany. It seems an elaborate tale to invent, so it is conceivable that the year has been misremembered.

His pride in his Native American roots may account for the mysterious outburst in *G.I. Blues* and the initial seriousness with which he took his roles as Kiowa half-breed Pacer Burton in *Flaming Star* and Navajo wheeler-dealer Joe Lightcloud in *Stay Away, Joe*.

On the set of *Flaming Star*, he relished the way the makeup darkened his skin, making him look more like his maternal grandfather Bob Smith. Challenged by Siegel, he threw himself into the role, believing it could signal his final acceptance as a dramatic actor. Though his "torn between two worlds" character was slightly clichéd, playing someone who seemed to fit in but actually didn't, an apparent insider who was really an outsider, had deep psychological resonance for Presley. As Gene Smith, another bodyguard and cousin, wrote in his memoir *Elvis's Man Friday*: "Elvis really got into the role not only because he had some Cherokee blood . . . [but also] because he no doubt remembered the way he was treated in grade school."

In such a downbeat western, which explicitly criticized the expropriation of Native American land, Pacer's death was inevitable. In one of the saddest scenes, his white father (John McIntire) tells him: "I guess folks ain't never been fair to you, Pacer. They take a man for what they think he ought to be, not for what he is." In retrospect, given the prejudices Presley had already overcome and the expectations that would eventually crush him, these words seem particularly poignant.

Though the movie—and Elvis—won many plaudits, it was relatively unsuccessful at the box office. The accolade that probably meant the most to Presley was the decision by Oklahoma Creek entertainer Chief Wah-Nee-Ota to induct him into the Los Angeles Indian Tribal Council in recognition of his "constructive portrayal of a man of Indian blood." Presley was rather impressed with the ceremonial headdress, taking it back to Graceland.

His return to his Native American roots in *Stay Away, Joe*, a film of the bestselling Dan Cushman novel, was much less successful. Cushman's novel was inspired by the author's experiences growing up near the Rocky Boy Reservation in Montana. A book-of-the-month selection in 1953, *Stay Away, Joe* was praised by *Kirkus Reviews* for its "native vitality," yet others—notably the Native American novelist James Welch—were deeply offended by its cast of feckless, irresponsible yet rambunctious Native Americans. Rather than addressing these concerns, Presley's movie tried to sidestep them by playing for laughs.

Elvis described Joe Lightcloud as "part Alfie and part Hud, a wheeler dealer who's always promoting something," but this slapstick comedy, with its flagrantly racist stereotyping of the Navajo characters as drunken, loafing liars, seemed hopelessly dated, reinforcing many of the stereotypes that Presley had challenged in *Flaming Star*. The movie does challenge the liberal, politically correct stereotyping of Native Americans as people whose primary purpose in movies is to suffer, but it doesn't offer any credible alternative.

In many westerns of the era, Native Americans served the plot by suffering. The macho bonhomie of *Stay Away, Joe* at least departed from that stifling norm but unfortunately replaced it with a flagrantly racist stereotyping of Navajos as drunken, loafing liars. This is surely the kind of film that Brando had in mind when, in his refusal to accept the 1972 Best Actor Oscar, he accused the movie-making community of "degrading the Indian and making a mockery of his character."

With all the fights and broad comedy, it is easy to overlook the fact that each Lightcloud personifies, albeit in a clichéd way, a different Navajo response to contemporary American society. At the opposite ends of the spectrum are the grandfather (who flatly rejects assimilation) and Joe's sister who works in a bank and wants to marry a rich young newspaper publisher. Somewhere in the middle are Joe (who flits between both worlds with ease but doesn't quite belong to either), Charlie (who is stranded between his father's traditions and his wife's aspirations) and Annie who longs to be accepted by the modern, "civilized" society symbolized by her potential in-laws.

Nazareth has suggested that Elvis plays his character as a classic Trickster figure. There are some similarities between Joe and the Trickster, the roguish, shape-changing, hero of many Native American myths. Yet surely Nazareth's contention that "the movie is about neo-colonialism and the bourgeois dreams of Third World People, dreams that turn out to be risky fantasies" is giving the writers too much credit, even if the movie does underline, in its ham-fisted way, the perils of Annie's hunger for assimilation.

Stay Away, Joe was still one of Elvis's more enjoyable shoots, but he must have suspected the worst when he was asked to deliver such lines as "She can chew on my moccasins anytime she wants to!" His last appearance as a Native American earned him a different kind of recognition: he was nominated for a Golden Turkey Award for Most Ludicrous Racial Impersonation in Hollywood History. He lost to his idol Marlon Brando, who had played an Okinawan in *The Teahouse of the August Moon*.

Presley would never play another Native American onscreen. Nor, as he became more reclusive, would he show much interest in the Cherokee culture of his ancestors. Onstage, though, his jumpsuits would acquire the flamboyant extravagance of a Native American costume. Indeed, one, which became known as the Indian Feather jumpsuit and can be seen on the cover of *From Elvis Presley Boulevard Memphis Tennessee*, pays a dazzling, intricate homage to his Native American roots.

The movies—and the jumpsuits—have earned Presley a surprising degree of acceptance in Native American culture with novelist Sherman Alexi, Sioux poet

John Trudell, and Kiowa author Thomas M. Yeahpau all acknowledging his influence. As Michael Snyder says, in an essay in *American Indians and Popular Culture*, "one of the biggest reasons Indians might embrace Elvis Presley as Indian is the way he points to the hidden history of American Indians in American popular culture."

The 50 Percent Men

I n *King Creole*, showbiz Svengali Maxie Fields (Walter Matthau) forces promising young singer Danny Fisher (Elvis Presley) to sign his name, as indicated, on a contract that is otherwise completely blank. The contract, to be filled in by the manager later, is supposed to be a sinister symbol of the boss's tyrannical chicanery and the slavery to which the despairing singer has just consigned himself.

This is a compelling image, made all the more resonant by our sense that Elvis often signed real-life contracts as if they were blank sheets of paper, without really knowing what was in them.

According to Jerry Leiber, when it comes to blank contracts, art was merely imitating life in this instance. As he recalled, in an interview with Ken Sharp, author of *Writing for the King*, he was sent a contract for a movie and soundtrack by Colonel Parker: "I took the contract out of one of the manila envelopes and saw nothing but a blank page. Nothing was written on it, except two lines at the bottom where Mike and I were supposed to sign." When he queried this with the Colonel, he was told, "There's no mistake. Just sign it. Don't worry, we'll fill it in later." Leiber's refusal to sign—accompanied by a suggestion that Parker "go fuck himself"—was one of many factors that ensured the songwriters would never do much work for Elvis again.

The story about Parker sending out blank contracts comes as a minor addition to the manager's rap sheet. While many still admire the genius with which the Colonel led Elvis so swiftly to the top, the most high-profile manager in the history of rock and roll has been exposed as a man who conspired with RCA against Presley for financial gain, constructed deals where he made as much money as—or more than—Elvis, gambled up to $30 million away in Las Vegas casinos, and effectively worked the singer to death. When Presley died, his friend Fike said to Parker: "Well, it took you a while but you finally ran him into the ground."

Parker's mysterious hold over Presley has been ascribed—among other things—to the singer's pathological fear of poverty, blackmail over Vernon's "secret" prison sentence, and to a mutual interdependence that meant neither client nor manager had the strength to walk away when the relationship was no longer working—as it so clearly wasn't in the last years of Presley's life.

Parker's flamboyance was eye-catching, a useful sleight of hand to obscure the fact that some of his more ruthless practices weren't that dissimilar from the mob's. From this chilling account by Presley's friend Arlene Cogan of Parker's visits to Graceland, it is easy to see why the singer feared his manager: "The Colonel would just take over the house. He would bring in some of his men and they would screen the telephone calls. Vernon told us that when Parker came to the house and got Elvis locked up for a meeting, he couldn't even talk to his own son till Parker left." Memories like that make Maxie Fields, the Svengali of Bourbon Street, look significantly less outlandish.

Parker had a shrewd habit of renegotiating with Elvis when his client was at his most vulnerable: in 1967, when Presley's movies and record sales were at an all-time low; in 1973, after the divorce from Priscilla; and in 1976, when the singer was emotionally and artistically in the doldrums.

In 1974, Parker set up a company called Boxcar Enterprises to merchandise the King. He owned 56 percent of the shares, his associate Tom Diskin owned 22 percent, and Elvis took the other 22 percent. Two days after Presley's death, the Colonel used Boxcar to sell the rights to market the singer to Factor. The deal was structured in such a way that Boxcar immediately took half the proceeds and the remainder was split three ways: 20 percent to Parker, 20 percent to Elvis, and 10 percent to Diskin. This meant that Parker reaped nearly half the income from this arrangement, while Presley's estate got less than a third. Was this what the manager meant when he said of Elvis's death: "Nothing has changed. Believe me, the show is going to go on"?

Although these arrangements were all written down in contracts, morally there seems little difference between this kind of deal and the old mob practice of skimming. By lying about the take at Howard Hughes's Vegas hotels, the mafia managed to con millions out of the reclusive, deluded billionaire.

Even Parker's legendary business acumen has been called into question since the revelation that Elvis was earning smaller royalties in the 1970s than most artists generating his volume of sales and that the Colonel was so negligent he didn't even include a clause in the contract forcing RCA to audit Elvis's sales. Perhaps he meant to write that in later and forgot.

His persistent objection to Elvis embarking on a lucrative world tour seemed less puzzling when this honorary southern colonel turned out to be Andreas Cornelius van Kuijk, a Dutchman who had immigrated to America illegally in the 1920s (and been discharged for psychological reasons from the U.S. Army). Without a valid passport, it would be hard for Parker to control—and, let's give him the benefit of the doubt, protect—his client.

These revelations, some of which followed Parker's death in 1997, came as a shock to most fans. Even those like Dave Marsh who regarded Parker as "the most overrated person in the history of show business" had generally regarded him as merely mulish, misguided, or mediocre. Yet even when the Colonel was at his peak, in the 1950s and 1960s, his own client's movies were shedding a less flattering light on the questionable tactics employed by Parker and his kind.

In *Loving You*, manipulative agent Glenda Markle (Lizabeth Scott) persuaded naive young genius Deke (Presley) to give her 50 percent of his income. As hefty as this share seemed, it set the benchmark for Elvis's fictional managers. In *Jailhouse Rock*, his cynical cellmate Hunk Houghton demanded the same cut, although when Vince (Elvis) reached the top, he had the sense to ask a lawyer for a second opinion and ended up paying just 10 percent. It's a pity Presley didn't heed the lesson, as he seldom paid Parker less than 25 percent. In *King Creole*, Fields's commission would have been anything he wanted it to be. By the time Elvis made his thirteenth movie, *Fun in Acapulco*, even his twelve-year-old manager Raoul was wise to the deal, demanding—and getting—his half share.

Just for the record, Parker was significantly behind the curve on this issue. He didn't manage to get 50 percent of any part of Presley's earnings until January 2, 1967, when a new deal gave him half of any profits or royalties beyond basic payments from movie and record contracts and half of all special or "side" deals. In March 1973, a new deal between Parker and Elvis split the income from recording 50/50. In a complex new deal, which included the sale of Elvis's back catalog, among RCA, artist, and manager, Parker pocketed $6 million from the label, while Elvis was paid $4 million. In January 1976, the 50/50 split was also applied to revenue from live performances, although Parker waived implementing this until the singer's finances were in order.

The collective impact of these deals was such that, when Presley died, Parker could have been making more money out of the singer than his family. That's one reason the estate felt constrained to sue him.

Even when they weren't demanding half of his earnings, the Parker figures in Elvis's movies were often up to no good. Kanter had spent some time with Parker, but in *Loving You* his exposé of some of the PR ploys used to promote Deke—manufacturing fights, exploiting a dressing room kiss, inventing a widow who wants to give him a car—is done with cynical affection. The tricks don't detract from Deke's—and by extension Elvis's—talent. Kanter was pretty explicit about the model for Scott's agent: "We took the manipulative manager and turned him into a woman."

The switch proved to be inspired, as the rapport between Presley and Scott is central to the movie's enduring appeal. But when Kanter has Deke tell his agent, "That's how you're selling me, isn't it? Like a monkey in a zoo," it's as if the writer is warning Presley about the perils ahead.

In *King Creole*, Matthau's impresario was a sleazy, sinister gangster with a talent for blackmail and a readiness to commit murder. As rival club owner Charlie LeGrand, the only honest man on Bourbon Street, put it: "Maxie Fields, that's a name for you—everything he touches turns to drink."

Although the initial conflict was between Danny (Elvis) and his father, the singer's confrontation with Fields was the movie's climactic showdown. The fact that the manager dies so the singer can live—and redeem himself—seems, given the ultimate fates of Parker and Presley, symbolic and ironic.

In the 1960s, Elvis encountered a few more Svengalis, but these incarnations were more comedic than criminal. In *Kid Galahad*, fight promoter Willie Grogan (Gig Young) exploited Elvis's young boxer with "an ax in his right hand and a bowling ball for a head" but was ultimately redeemed by his love for a good woman and his friendship with his trainer. Though Raoul (Larry Domasin) took a hefty cut of Presley's earnings in *Fun in Acapulco*, he did his entertaining best for his client, virtually staging an auction to get the highest price for his boy and trying to untangle the star's love life.

At first glance, Bixby's incompetent manager in *Clambake* seemed as innocuous as Raoul. He was so comically unsuited to his duties that one incredulous girl asked Steve Grayson (Elvis), "You let him handle all your money?" To which the hero replied, "Why not? I like to live dangerously." He certainly gets his wish, with Bixby losing all of Elvis's winnings at the bookies. That would have been serious enough, but Grayson, like Elvis in real life, was so impulsively generous that a couple of newlyweds and a poor family were dependent on his largesse. Luckily, matters were resolved, kind of, when Grayson was allowed to retain enough of his winnings to keep everyone happy.

Parker had originally been opposed to gambling, telling one associate, "Don't you know how stupid gamblers are? They're all nebos!"—carnival slang for an easy mark. Yet at some point in the 1950s, he became addicted to the dollar slot machines in Vegas, acquiring the habit of staring at a machine as if he could hypnotize them into paying out. By the early 1970s, his addiction was so bad he was losing $1 million a year just at the Las Vegas Hilton (where Elvis spent so much of the decade performing). These losses enraged Elvis, who fumed, after Parker had blown $1.4 million on a Wheel of Fortune in December 1976: "A lot of people don't make that much money in their lives. And how's he going to pay it? I'm his ransom."

It is just possible that Parker saw everyone he did business with—including Elvis—as a potential nebo. During his research for *Roustabout*, writer Allan Weiss recalled, "I spent the weekend with him, to get a bit of circus background. And I got back and Wallis says to me, 'You had an expensive weekend.' It turned out that he'd received a bill from Parker, charging for the time the Colonel spent talking to me." The $25,000 bill was not insubstantial, but the script is so full of carny jargon you could argue it was money well spent.

As good as Elvis was in *Roustabout*, there is a sense in which it was Parker's movie, not his. Apart from Weiss's expensive weekend, the manager wrote to Wallis with other suggestions for the script and some thoughts on casting, and he requested that the film should not denigrate the carnival way of life, a suggestion Wallis certainly adhered to.

In the 1930s, Parker had made his home in Tampa, Florida, where many of America's carnivals spent the off season. His first job as a carny was selling candy apples and popcorn, but he soon did all kinds of chores and worked all manner of attractions. For an illegal immigrant like Parker, the carnival was a perfect place to hide. By tradition, carnies didn't pry into colleagues' previous lives.

Carnivals may have started out as a job for Parker, but they became a lifelong passion. He was, according to his associate Byron Raphael, especially fascinated by midgets, freaks, and bearded ladies and superstitiously respectful of the Tarot readers.

The ensemble in *Roustabout* includes a midget (Billy Barty), a bearded lady, a fortune teller (Sue Anne Langdon), a sword swallower (Lester Miller, auditioned personally by Parker), and, in Harry Carver (Pat Buttram), a carnival owner whose maxims sound suspiciously like the Colonel's views. His relentless focus on the bottom line—exemplified by his insistence that the rival carnival is giving customers too much butter in their popcorn—is worthy of the Colonel. And, oh, novelty of novelties, Carver actually offers his new signing a contract that has some clauses in it.

The one unrealistic touch is the owner's resigned acceptance of his lovestruck star's contract-breaking departure. When Elvis tried to break from Parker in 1974, the Colonel sent the singer a $2 million bill for services allegedly rendered but not yet paid for.

As a carny, the Colonel was famous for painting blackbirds yellow and selling them as canaries, for making chickens dance on a hot plate, and for selling hot dogs with hardly any meat in them. He sold buns that were a foot long but had only a little bit of wiener sticking out at each end. If a customer complained, Parker would point to a piece of hot dog he had dropped in the sawdust that morning and say: "You dropped your meat, boy." Such chicanery is celebrated in *Roustabout* when a boy complains, after discovering that his candy apple—the very product Parker started out selling—has a worm in it. The seller shoots back: "There's no extra charge for the meat—beat it!"

Despite all these correspondences between life and art, writer Anthony Lawrence has vehemently denied that Parker inspired him or his partner Weiss, saying: "I don't think either of us was as fond of the Colonel as to want to do that." This doesn't quite square with the production notes that include a three-page memo from a meeting with Parker in which his feedback included, among a host of suggestions, the worm-in-the-apple story, a midget, and fans to blow the odor of onions and hamburgers down the midway—all of which were incorporated into the movie.

For fans, the most appealing Parker figure in the movies is Walter Hale, the manager of the chautauqua in *The Trouble with Girls*. The novelty being that Hale was played by Elvis. Relatively inexperienced, Hale relied on the counsel of veteran Johnny (Edward Andrews), who bore some physical resemblance to Parker and is cast as slightly more cynical than his boss, more determined not to stand for any "appus crappus." Though Hale shows a kind of Machiavellian genius when he turns a murder to the traveling fair's advantage, the script emphasizes that Elvis's manager has some ethics. When Johnny recruits a stand-in piano player for "the munificent salary of nothing," Hale denies responsibility, assuring shop steward Marlyn Mason in a hurt tone: "I wouldn't hire somebody and not pay 'em."

It feels ironically appropriate that the last in a long line of manipulative Parker figures was played by the star himself, who gives this archetypal character its most sympathetic depiction since Tomasin's boy wonder in *Fun in Acapulco*.

36

Inherit the Wind

Elvis's Secret Wanderlust

There was certain inevitability about the frequency with which cars featured in Presley's movies. As Brode suggests, "Elvis and American car culture are, as signifiers of energy and movement, inseparable—he identified with a means of transportation at the start of each film: horses in the Old West, planes, boats when near a beach, and, in all other cases, a car." Or indeed, in a Greyhound-style bus (*Tickle Me*) and a Japanese motorcycle (*Roustabout*).

Cars were a potent symbol of freedom in the emerging mythology of rock and roll. Presley loved buying them, driving them, and giving them away (he bought around 150 of them as gifts for friends, relatives, and acquaintances). Edward Anhalt, who co-wrote *Girls! Girls! Girls!*, said, "Presley liked cars so a lot of the pictures had to do with cars." He loved motorbikes too, snubbing Paramount's request that he should stop riding them. The American historian William Wright, who spent some time with Elvis in Vicksburg in 1955, told Dundy: "He knew a lot about motorcycles. I think he knew a lot more about motorcycles than he knew about people."

As soon as Elvis became famous, he became synonymous with cars, especially Cadillacs. When he and other artists made their names at Sun Studio, the building was known as "the chicken shack with Cadillacs out back." For Elvis and the other Sun artists, their Cadillacs were tangible, delightful proof that they had made it, and his simple delight in these vehicles may explain why he is so often found driving them (*Viva Las Vegas, Spinout,* and *Speedway*), fixing them (*Kid Galahad, Viva Las Vegas, Spinout,* and *Speedway*), or being given them (the convertible in *Loving You*). As symbols, cars are important for what they say about your status but also, as Brode suggests, because of the freedom they give you.

The clichéd pop-culture image of Elvis casts the star as an obese, lonely recluse, hiding out in Graceland. That may ultimately have been true—the *Memphis Press Scimitar* greeted his death with the headline "A Lonely Life Ends on Elvis Presley Boulevard"—but that was hardly the whole story. He was, Priscilla said once, "a truly free spirit." Bob Dylan, who saw Elvis perform in Vegas, caught this aspect of Presley's character in his song "Went to See a Gypsy" when he said: "Went to see the gypsy staying in a big hotel / He smiled when he saw me coming and said 'Well, well, well.'"

The legend of Elvis's smothering mother has obscured the fact that he started roaming across Tupelo when he was eight; was a pesky boyish presence at WELO radio station, where he idolized country singer Mississippi Slim; hitchhiked 240 miles from Memphis to Meridian to a Jimmie Rodgers festival in May 1953 when he was just eighteen; visited Paris as a G.I., was desperately disappointed not to visit Mexico for *Fun in Acapulco*; was prevented from going on holiday in Europe in 1969 only by the Colonel's paranoia; and, until the concert schedules became physically, artistically, and emotionally punitive in the 1970s, usually reveled in life on the road.

Who knows where else he might have traveled if he had been encouraged, not thwarted, and if he had not become the King with all the trappings—and traps—that entailed. Becoming a professional musician is not just an expression of a gift, it is a statement of ambition, a bid for freedom from ordinary life and the "Earth people," as the carnies call civilians who "aren't with it" in *Roustabout*.

Presley's wanderlust is expressed in many of the songs he sang—from "Long Lonely Highway" (the title song in *Tickle Me*) to "Guitar Man," "Promised Land," and "There's So Much World to See" (from *Double Trouble*)—and in the essentially rootless heroes he plays in movies like *Charro!*; *Double Trouble*; *Girl Happy*; *Live a Little, Love a Little*; *Speedway*; *Spinout*; *Stay Away, Joe*; and *The Trouble with Girls*.

The purest expression of Presley as the frustrated nomad can be found in *Roustabout*, where he plays professional loner Charlie Rogers, who sings a little, chases women, and rides his motorbike from gig to gig or to anywhere there is an off chance of a gig. This freedom is so important him that he rides off from a pretty waitress who has bailed him out of jail and, initially, lingers at the carnival only under protest while his motorbike is fixed. His attempts to seduce Joan Freeman hit the rocks when she tells him, "I like you too, but you're just passing through." The formula dictates that Elvis will redeem himself, save the carnival, and envisage a brand-new day on the horizon. Yet the denouement isn't entirely convincing. You wouldn't be surprised if, in a few weeks' time, Elvis's antihero argues with grumpy putative father-in-law Leif Erickson, mounts his bike, and rides out onto the long, lonely highway.

37

Girls! Girls! Girls!

Elvis as a Very Chaste Kind of Super Stud

E lvis had a libido that would make Jerry Lee Lewis look like a monk,"
said Barbara Pittman, one of the few women to record on the Sun label,
who knew Elvis from childhood. Pittman may be overstating for effect,
but her point is still valid—and makes his record as a screen lover seem even
more curious.

Yet maybe the films just reflect the dichotomy that ran through Elvis's romantic life and his musical career. The King's sexual mores have been dissected by
such biographers as Albert Goldman and Alanna Nash, who wrote *Baby, Let's
Play House*, an epic, voyeuristic, pseudo-psychological account of the King and
the women at his court.

Elvis often found romance on set, certainly with Pamela Austin, Jane Elliott,
Anne Helm, Jennifer Holden, Ann-Margret, Joanna Moore, Joan O'Brien, Juliet
Prowse, and Tuesday Weld. He wooed—but never bedded—Shelley Fabares, who
was married to mogul Lou Adler. Nor was he averse to exploiting his fame in
order to bed fans. As Michael Curtiz told a crew member on *King Creole*: "That
boy he fucks all night long, the girls they line up outside the hotel and he goes
out on the balcony with his friend, he points and tells his buddy, he'll say 'her
and her.' They go down and bring them back and then he goes again, he goes
all night long." Curtiz was notoriously indiscreet when conducting his own affairs
and was amused by such behavior, not appalled.

Yet interviews with many other actresses—most notably Donna Douglas,
Gail Gilmore, Laurel Goodwin, and Deborah Walley—suggest they regarded
Elvis like, as Goodwin put it, "an older brother," albeit one who might expect
them to listen for hours to his views on spirituality and religion or, as Goodwin
remembers, counsel him on his personal problems. And most of his female
co-stars recall him as kind, sweet, and shy if rather isolated.

Mary Ann Mobley, who starred with him in *Girl Happy* and *Harum Scarum*,
said of Elvis: "He put women into two categories. You were either one of the
girls or you were a lady. In Mississippi, he was taught to be kind and take care of
ladies, and then he had the other constantly thrown at him."

Presley's Hollywood career has often been interpreted as a gradual, but
irrevocable, emasculation of the raw sexuality that had thrilled and appalled

America in 1956. Raquel Welch expressed this view most succinctly when she said: "Hollywood took the sex out of Elvis." The truth isn't quite that simple.

Though hugely influenced by such Method masters as Marlon Brando, Presley would never be as brutal to his women onscreen as his idol. As he became less rebellious in the movies, he was more likely to romance as if he were a singing Cary Grant. In some films, notably *Speedway*, he was downright chivalrous.

Yet the Memphis Flash could not be completely sanitized and still raised the temperature with a sexy smooch with Ann-Margret in *Viva Las Vegas*, with a furtive fumble with Hope Lange in *Wild in the Country*, and by encouraging, tongue firmly in his cheek, every woman in the Hangout to let herself go in *Speedway*.

A magnetic performer who looked in his prime like, as one female fan put it, "like a great big hunk of forbidden fruit," Presley liberated millions of women to express their sexual desires and fantasies. As another female fan said, "Kinsey [author of the legendary report on America's sexual habits] told women it was unusual for them to be rapidly or easily sexually aroused. Presley showed us it wasn't. Presley and the Pill brought about women's liberation."

Elvis is at his most uninhibited in *Jailhouse Rock*, where, after one passionate embrace, he is reprimanded by Judy Tyler: "How dare you think such cheap tactics will work with me!" to which he replies, his lip curling beautifully: "That ain't tactics, honey, that's just the beast in me." Later, in a movie within the movie, he can't stop kissing Jennifer Holden even after the director has shouted, "Cut!" The beast reappeared in *King Creole*, where he very nearly lured virginal Dolores Hart into a hotel room and told sexy temptress Carolyn Jones: "That's a pretty piece of material—you ought to have a dress made out of it someday."

G.I. Blues provided the default setting for Elvis's romances in the 1960s musical comedies. His pursuit of Juliet Prowse was impeccably mannered yet strangely passionless. He wooed with more fervor in *Wild in the Country*, where his love scenes with Lange, one rainy night in a cheap motel, had a tender, erotic power. His new chivalrous image was touchingly confirmed in *Kid Galahad* when the star kissed Joan Blackman and immediately proposed to her. Wedding bells also chime in *Blue Hawaii*, *Clambake*, *Double Trouble*, *Tickle Me*, and *Viva Las Vegas*. A nuptial gig is threatened at gunpoint in *Stay Away, Joe* and only averted in *Spinout* when he weds his three suitors to other men.

The predatory pelvis makes a memorable return in *It Happened at the World's Fair*, where he almost encourages Yvonne Craig to relax before her father reaches for his shotgun. This kind of coitus interruptus is a recurring motif in Elvis's films. It's astonishing how many obstacles the King has to overcome as a screen lover. Sometimes his ambitions—to buy a boat in *Girls! Girls! Girls!* and win a race in *Viva Las Vegas*—get in the way. At other times, the plot suffices: in *Harum Scarum*, his true love, a princess in disguise, was understandably put off by the fact that he was hired to kill her father. These complications reach a kind of comic apotheosis in *Girl Happy*, where chaperoning duties, ringing telephones, and masculine guilt conspire to prevent Elvis and his buddies from making the most of their days and nights in Fort Lauderdale.

In *Viva Las Vegas*, the sexual chemistry is obvious when he's dancing with Ann-Margret—performing "C'mon Everybody" and in the nightclub—and in *Roustabout*, he is back to his old lady-killing ways—until he falls for Joan Freeman. She even chastises him in the same style as Tyler in *Jailhouse Rock*: "You kiss every girl you talk to? You kiss the ones you do kiss this soon?" This time his comeback is a tepid: "Why should I explain?"

Yet in many movies of this era, the romantic aspirations of our "sagebrush Lothario" (as he is dubbed in *Tickle Me*) seem to be limited to a quick kiss. In this strange, quasi-celibate state, he is obliged, in movie after movie, to ignore or overlook the allure of such femmes fatales as Joanna Moore (*Follow That Dream*), Stella Stevens (*Girls! Girls! Girls!*), Elsa Cárdenas (*Fun in Acapulco*), Sue Anne Langdon (*Roustabout*), Mary Ann Mobley (*Girl Happy*), Julie Adams (in whose arms he looks hilariously uncomfortable in *Tickle Me*), Fran Jeffries (*Harum Scarum*), Nancy Kovack (*Frankie and Johnny*), Diane McBain (*Spinout*), and Yvonne Romain (*Double Trouble*).

Even when he romances Ursula Andress in *Fun in Acapulco*, the producers' Puritan morality prevented her from wearing a bikini that showed her navel. Oddly, such censoriousness didn't always apply to the scripts. As Dundy has pointed out, the screenplay for *Girls! Girls! Girls!* is sprinkled with jokes about sex ("All men remember small things very big" is one of two Chinese proverbs that poke fun at masculine sexuality), abortions, and Elvis's fly buttons.

Commercially, it made more sense for Presley to woo younger girls who resemble the target audience for these musical comedies. This may explain the casting of unknown British actress Annette Day in *Double Trouble*. A startling scene in which Elvis meets this mystery girl in her school uniform emphasizes the heroine's youth.

One of the bizarre aspects of this confrontation is that Priscilla was a fourteen-year-old schoolgirl when Elvis met her. In the film, he resists Day's advances until she is eighteen and they get married. Such casting—and the romantic choices made by his characters—do oddly echo real life. In the 1960s, Presley was, Fike said once, "fascinated by young teenage girls . . . it scared the hell out of all of us."

Onscreen, Elvis the lover was often marginalized by the producers' curious insistence that he share so much screen time with Hollywood's endless supply of professionally cute children. *Fun in Acapulco*, *Girls! Girls! Girls!*, and *It Happened at the World's Fair* are among the most egregious examples of this device.

Sometimes, as when Elvis sang to the baby in *G.I. Blues*, serenaded a girl with "Your Time Hasn't Come Yet, Baby" in *Speedway*, and cured the autistic girl in *Change of Habit*, these scenes showed Elvis at his most delightful. Such sequences were so frequent you wonder if the producers wanted to sell tickets to the under-tens or were just trying to entertain younger siblings. Whatever the motivation, they often intruded on the romance: in *Paradise, Hawaiian Style*, Elvis couldn't share Moonlight Beach with sultry Marianna Hill without nine-year-old Donna Butterworth proving that three is a crowd.

As the family-entertainment formula broke down, Elvis's romances became more adventurous. He sneaked away from a party with someone else's girlfriend in *Stay Away, Joe*, suggested he and Mason go to bed in *The Trouble with Girls*, and enjoyed some passionate, if fleeting, clinches with Ina Balin in *Charro!* Although we didn't see much of the action, he actually had sex with Michelle Carey in the screwball sex comedy *Live a Little, Love a Little*, the only time this happens in a Presley movie. In his last feature film, *Change of Habit*, as handsome as Elvis looks, he doesn't even get to kiss Mary Tyler Moore.

Yet even in an entertainment as slight as *Tickle Me*, Presley can, as Sheila O'Malley suggests on her website The Sheila Variations, transcend—and subvert—the blandness, performing "It Feels So Right" in the manner of someone who "understands that he is pleasing to look at, who doesn't revel in it a way that is off-putting or vain but who definitely revels in it in a way that seems generous." Although the women's reactions in this scene are so exaggerated they go beyond parody, Presley's performance essentially reminds the audience that sex is fun and it's fun to explore that. The fact that Elvis seems to be in on—and enjoying—the joke only adds to the appeal.

His warmth and wit worked similar miracles with "Let Yourself Go" in *Speedway*, yet even he couldn't salvage "Smorgasbord" in *Spinout*. This throwaway number portrays girls as buffet items to savor, almost as if writers Tepper and Bennett (who never met Elvis) were already privy, in 1966, to the kind of salacious revelations in Nash's *Baby, Let's Play House*.

Nash's explanation for the King's womanizing, drawing on Whitmer's diagnosis, is that Elvis's extreme closeness to his mother left no room for other women—not even his wife, Priscilla—and led him to pursue a long line of women who resembled Gladys with predictably disastrous results. Nash suggests that Presley had the emotional maturity of a fourteen-year-old—Priscilla's age when he met her. This is why, she suggests, he remained so fascinated by teenage girls, who were much easier to mold.

There are certain obvious problems with this hypothesis. While it certainly applies to Priscilla, neither Ann-Margret nor his long-term lover Linda Thompson, two of the women he loved most, resembled his mother, and they weren't teenagers when Elvis met them. The age at which Presley stopped maturing emotionally in Nash's account seems too pat, conveniently mirroring his wife's age when he met her.

The lives of other famous womanizers suggest that it is too simple to blame Gladys. To take two contrasting examples, JFK's attitude to women has often been blamed on his distant relationship with his mother, while Jack Nicholson, one of the last great playboys of the western world, only discovered that the woman he thought was his sister was actually his mother when he was thirty-seven.

Even if you subscribe to Sigmund Freud's Oedipus-complex theory, it seems simplistic to identify mother-and-son relationships as the source of all promiscuity. Many analysts say one of the contributory factors is insecurity, and this, despite his fame, is something Elvis certainly suffered from. Elvis's friend George Klein, the Memphis DJ, has a simpler explanation as to why the star slept with so many women: because he could. Certainly, despite Pitman's remark, Presley's womanizing does not seem so outlandish when you consider the private lives of other famous musicians and actors.

For whatever reason, Elvis invariably ended up with younger women in his movies. One pleasing exception was *Wild in the Country*, where, despite being pursued by Millie Perkins and Tuesday Weld, he fell for Lange and went to college to become a writer.

Although Presley's rapport with Ann-Margret resonated through every scene they share in *Viva Las Vegas*, Elvis was less smooth and more vulnerable in the considerably less glamorous *Wild in the Country*. That very vulnerability makes his love scene with Lange so memorable. Some find their embraces, when they are stranded in a backroads motel on a rainy evening, awkward and stilted, but that, surely, is exactly how their characters would behave in such a situation. Unlike the facile kisses satirized in the famous montage in *Elvis on Tour*, their kiss in the motel meant something, giving us Presley's most compelling love scene.

38

In the Land of Cotton

Elvis the Celluloid Southerner

W ho is that fast-talking hillbilly son of a bitch no one can understand? One day he's singing to a dog, then to a car, then to a cow. They are all the same movie with that southerner just singing to something different."

That was Presley's vitriolic verdict on his movie career. The remark is a reminder of how badly his failure to prove himself as an actor hurt him, but also a pointer to one of the underexplored aspects of his movies, just how thoroughly southern they were.

In W. J. Cash's classic socio-psychological tome *The Mind of the South*, he describes the romantic, hedonistic poor southern white thus: "To stand on his head in a bar, to toss down a pint of raw whisky at a gulp, to fiddle and dance all night, to bite off the nose or gouge out the eye of a favorite enemy, to fight harder and love harder than the next man, to be known eventually far and wide as a hell of a fellow—such would be his focus." And such, once Hollywood had toned it down a bit for the masses and the family audience, was how Presley was presented in many movies.

Presley was born in Tupelo, Mississippi, on January 8, 1935, and grew up in Memphis, Tennessee. The code of conduct he tried to live by—even if he often fell short of the ideal—reflected his vision of how a considerate southern gentleman would behave. He came to embody many of the characteristics that have come to define that elastic concept known as southern charm. Engaging, generous, humble, passionate, polite, spiritual, he virtually became, by the end of his career, the South's ambassador to the rest of America—and the world. This wasn't all show either. Arthur Nadel, who directed him in *Clambake*, said: "He remained a kind of old-fashioned, somewhat courtly person . . . even calling the grips and hairdressers 'sir' and 'ma'am.'"

Although sometimes (notably in *Jailhouse Rock* and *Roustabout*) he acted out the role of the hood who won the fight and the girl, he was more often a prototype Duke of Hazzard, a good old boy who never means any harm. (Indeed, Pam Freeman, a dancer on *Clambake*, reminiscing about Elvis, called him: "Just a good ole boy. A very sweet man.") This persona struck Roger Ebert, who found *Speedway* an intriguing "catalog of the recreations and material possessions prized in 1968, especially by Southerners" and noted what a thoroughly southern icon the star had become: "Elvis races a Barracuda around the Charlotte *Speedway*, lives in an expensive mobile home, drinks pop and keeps his hair combed."

When Presley had jobs other than singing, they often emphasized his southern roots. He was a rodeo rider (*Tickle Me*; *Stay Away, Joe*), stock car driver (*Speedway*), showboat singer (*Frankie and Johnny*); and heir to an oil baron (*Clambake*). In a reminder of the disproportionate number of southerners who have served in the American military over the years, Elvis was a soldier in *G.I. Blues*, just out of the army in *Kid Galahad*, discharged from the army with a back injury in *Follow That Dream*, a U.S. Air Force officer in *Kissin' Cousins*, had just left the U.S. Navy in *Easy Come, Easy Go*, and nearly died in the army (presumably in the Vietnam War) in *Change of Habit*. In *Paradise, Hawaiian Style*, his character had no military connections but, as if to compensate, started the movie in the pseudo-military uniform of a civilian pilot. This recurring theme rebranded Elvis the rebel—none too subtly—as a true patriot (which, to be fair, he was in real life).

Elvis's southern identity is reinforced by the settings for each movie. The eleven Confederate states that seceded from the union in 1860–61 provided the backdrop for ten of his feature films: *Love Me Tender* and *Flaming Star* (Texas); *Clambake, Follow That Dream*, and *Girl Happy* (Florida); *Speedway* (North Carolina); *Kissin' Cousins* (Tennessee); *Frankie and Johnny* and *King Creole* (Louisiana); and *Wild in the Country* (set in the Shenandoah Valley, which spans Virginia and West Virginia).

In *Roustabout*, where Elvis works at a carnival based in some American backwater, he hailed from a "little swamp just outside Shreveport, Louisiana," while in *Blue Hawaii*, the point is made that fun-loving Chad Gates was born in Atlanta, Georgia. The writers take similar precautions in his only two movies set in New York. In *Kid Galahad*, though Elvis's character, Walter Gulick, has dreamed of coming to Cream Valley, he grew up in Kentucky. In *Change of Habit*, Elvis, as Dr. John Carpenter, wears a University of Tennessee sweatshirt and explains that he came north because he owed a debt to a New York sergeant who saved his life.

The presentation of Elvis's southern identity is based on an understanding of the region that rarely delves deeper than a few clichés or tourist images. As Linda Ray Pratt has pointed out in her 1982 essay "Elvis, or the Ironies of a Southern Identity": "Elvis's South was the one that most Southerners really experience: the South where not even the interstate can conceal the poverty, where industrial affluence threatens the land and air which have been so much a part of our lives, where racial violence touches deep within the home, here even our successes cannot overcome the long reputation of our failures."

This is not the South you see reflected in many Elvis movies, although some of this characterization is reflected in *Wild in the Country*. Regional reality might have had a better chance of reaching the screen if Parker hadn't demanded so much money for Elvis to star in Robert Mitchum's *Thunder Road* (1958), his impressive drama about a family of Tennessee moonshiners.

The disconnect between Hollywood's South and the region that Elvis called home becomes hilariously obvious in *Kissin' Cousins*, a movie promoted with playbills that proclaimed: "See The Kittyhawks, The Most Beautiful Collection Of Mountain Cuties Ever."

Producer Katzman decided that, with Elvis "being a country boy at heart," it was time to take him back to the woods or, as things turned out, the hillbilly backwoods. In the movie, Elvis plays two kinds of southern hero. He is infinitely more appealing as Josh Morgan, who escaped the region to make good in the Air Force, than as Jodie Tatum, whose drinking, wrestling, womanizing lifestyle positions him as white trash. Given such lines as "What are you doing wid my face?," Jodie is so oafish you suspect Elvis has decided to descend into country bumpkin cliché by playing, in this instance, a slow-talking hillbilly son of a bitch.

Kissin' Cousins is the kind of movie that reinforces all those prejudices against poor white southerners that disfigured Goldman's biography of Elvis. Maybe that is part of what Elvis meant when he referred to his screen persona as "that southerner." As he observed in a famously candid interview with Pierre Adige and Robert Adel for *Elvis on Tour*, "Hollywood's image of me was wrong and I knew it." So, despite the superficial resemblances between "that southerner" and Presley, the star felt that the stereotype and the man had little in common. As a proud southerner, who (according to his pianist David Briggs) could recite the name of every Confederate general, he probably felt the same about the way his movies depicted the region he was proud to call home.

When he returned to live performance, he would offer his own interpretation of the South by adopting Mickey Newbury's "An American Trilogy" as a personal anthem. As Pratt notes, "Even Elvis could not have sung this at Madison Square Garden before there was some reason for hope and pride in the south." There is precious little hope—or pride—in the hillbillies with which Katzman and his scriptwriters have populated Big Smokey Mountain.

39

There's So Much World to See

The Elvis Travelogues

S ame story, different location." That was Presley's pithy, painfully accurate summary of *Easy Come, Easy Go*, his last picture for Wallis.

At some point in the 1960s, his movies became, as the star put it, travelogues. In a decade when foreign travel was still largely the preserve of an elite known as the jet set, Presley's movies would take his fans to Acapulco, Fort Lauderdale, Hawaii (three times), Las Vegas, New Orleans (twice), a fake Middle Eastern kingdom (*Harum Scarum*), and swinging London (*Double Trouble*, in which the producers threw in a bit of Antwerp for good measure).

Even if the scenery wasn't always picture-postcard perfect, Elvis could still do his bit for the tourist industry, by spending most of a movie at the Seattle World's Fair, singing on a Mississippi steamboat, wooing his beloved in a cable car over a backdrop of the beautiful Rhine, inviting all and sundry to a clambake, helping out at a western dude ranch, working as a roustabout, racing in the Charlotte 500, and winning the Orange Bowl Regatta.

Blue Hawaii was so dedicated to promoting the fiftieth state that Elvis became a tourist guide. His unique approach to customer service involved spanking a troublesome tourist so hard she had to sit on a cushion at breakfast the following morning. In this movie, so many of Hawaii's most famous locales were showcased—including Anahola, Ala Moana Park, the Ala Wai Yacht Harbor, Hanauma Bay, Lydgate Park, Punchbowl, Tantalus, Waikiki Beach, Wailua River, and the Waioili Tea Room—it is as if, as Jerry Hopkins said in his book *Elvis in Hawaii*, "someone had been told to bring Hawaii's best postcards to life."

In *Paradise, Hawaiian Style*, where he played a helicopter pilot flying tourists across the islands, the story—and romance with Suzanna Leigh—were secondary to the landscape. Even when Elvis made an emergency flight to rescue his stranded buddy, the camera was more interested in the landscape than in building any dramatic tension. The triumph of tourism—and travelogue—was symbolized in the finale, when Presley leaned over to kiss Leigh but, even before their lips could meet, was whisked away to perform "Drums of the Island" with an epic cast of natives at the Polynesian Cultural Center.

In four movies—*Blue Hawaii*; *Fun in Acapulco*; *Paradise, Hawaiian Style*; and *Viva Las Vegas*—the destination was deemed so important it was mentioned in the title. It seems no coincidence that, when UK distributors decided British audiences would be confused by the titles *Harum Scarum* and *Spinout*, the movies were renamed *Harem Holiday* and *California Holiday*, respectively.

The celluloid boosterism of *Blue Hawaii, Girls! Girls! Girls!* and *Paradise, Hawaiian Style* helped transform Hawaii's economy. In 1959, the islands welcomed 175,000 visitors. By 1968, that number had soared to 1.2 million. Ironically, the career choice of Elvis's hero in *Blue Hawaii*—ditching dad's pineapple business to become a tourist guide—would be replicated offscreen as the state's economy developed in the 1960s. Sugar and pineapples began to decline, and by 1970, tourism generated around $1 billion for the Hawaiian economy, four times as much as agriculture.

No other locale benefitted as much from the Presley travelogues, although tourists still flock to La Perla, the picturesque cliff that looms so large in *Fun in Acapulco.*

In many parts of the world, fans expected Elvis's movies to have beautiful backdrops. Nitaya Kanchanawan, the Thai academic who is head of the Elvis Presley Fan Club in Thailand, noted: "The 1960s were the best time for Elvis in Thailand. His kind of movies fit the idea of Thai entertainment . . . People were happy when they left the theater. The Thais love to see 'beautiful things' and listen to 'beautiful sounds.'" Emphasizing that "most of his international admirers have never fully understood what he sang or said," she added, "The sound and sight of him made fans happy."

Perhaps Elvis's travelogues—including those fake visits to Acapulco, London, and the Middle East—made him seem less like a purely American icon and more like someone who, as Kanchanawan put it, "spiritually belongs to the world." This kind of thinking inspired many of RCA's subsidiaries and licensees to give him a makeover to suit their markets. The Mexican cover for *King Creole*, for example, shows a very Latino Elvis, with slicker hair, darkened eyebrows, and redder lips.

Setting Elvis in an exotic locale usually paid off at the box office. Of his ten top-grossing movies, four were set in tourist hotspots—*Viva Las Vegas* (No. 1), *Blue Hawaii* (No. 3), *Girls! Girls! Girls!* (No. 6), and *Girl Happy* (No. 8)—while *G.I. Blues* (No. 4) made the most of its German backdrop with cable cars, puppet shows, and exotic nightclubs.

Having promoted major tourist attractions as an actor, Elvis became a global tourist attraction in his own right after his death—not just at Graceland (which has now welcomed almost 20 million visitors), but in Hawaii (the Polynesian Cultural Center is talking about founding an Elvis museum) and at La Perla, the cliff in *Fun in Acapulco* that Elvis's stunt double dived from to impress Ursula Andress.

40

Aloha, El

The Hawaiian Presley

In 1956, Elvis received 400,000 Christmas cards from fans. As a manager who liked to keep track of such things, Parker noticed that 21,000 of them had been sent from Hawaii, which had a population of just 600,000. Having done the math, the Colonel decided that Elvis's next tour should end in Honolulu. Presley played his first gig in front of 14,963 fans in the Hawaiian capital in November 1957 on a trip that ignited his lifelong love of the islands that became America's fiftieth state in 1959.

Presley returned in 1961 to perform for charity and make *Blue Hawaii*. His concert raised $62,000 for a memorial to the USS *Arizona*, a battleship destroyed in the attack on Pearl Harbor with the loss of 1,117 crew. The next day he began filming. *Blue Hawaii* was such a hit that Wallis made two more Presley musicals in this tropical paradise: *Girls! Girls! Girls!* and *Paradise, Hawaiian Style*. In this Hawaiian trilogy, Presley invited us to enjoy the land (*Blue Hawaii*), the sea (*Girls! Girls! Girls!*), and the islands from the air (*Paradise, Hawaiian Style*).

Even after he stopped making movies, Elvis was drawn back to the islands. His favorite karate instructor, Ed Parker, was born in Honolulu. He was a great admirer of actor Jack Lord, the incorruptible cop Steve McGarrett in *Hawaii Five-0*. Elvis's concert at the Honolulu International Convention Center on January 14, 1973, is reputed to have attracted more viewers than the moon landing. The shot of a jumpsuited Elvis singing, with a lei around his neck, became one of the most iconic images of the star's final years.

Presley spent his last holiday in Hawaii, in March 1977, with fiancée Ginger Alden. The vacation (which cost him $100,000) was cut short after fears he had scratched his cornea. Graceland's famous Jungle Room was full of Hawaiian furniture, which Presley bought in about thirty minutes from Donalds store in Memphis. Though Elvis loathed looking for furniture, often buying the first thing he or his current partner liked, the selection does suggest a love for Polynesian culture.

Why did Elvis like Hawaii so much? Esposito says in his book *Good Rockin' Tonight*: "Elvis loved Hawaii. The weather was fabulous and the people treated him with respect. Unlike mainland fans, who hounded him where he went, the Hawaiians left Elvis alone." As Tom Moffatt, a local DJ who interviewed Presley many times in Hawaii, put it: "For someone who was known worldwide, this was

Did Elvis's love of Hawaiian culture inspire the most famous furnishings at Graceland?

a great—and appreciated—change." For once in Elvis's world, the truth may be that simple.

Presley felt at home with Hawaiian music, delivering two of the islands' most famous songs—"Aloha Oe" and "Hawaiian Wedding Song"—with beautiful reverence. Most of his Hawaiian numbers belonged to a genre known as *hapa haole* (half Hawaiian), in which the songs sound western even though they feature Hawaiian words and instruments.

His Hawaiian fans appreciated the way, in *Blue Hawaii*, his character Chad Gates was more intrigued by the islands' culture, rituals, and people than by white American ways. At times, the movie felt as if Elvis was our personal guide, encouraging us to discover the gorgeous landscape, the Hawaiian culture, and the locals, who—judging by the fun-loving local boys in his backing band and the beautiful half-breed princess Miley (Joan Blackman)—were an attractive, unspoiled lot.

This portrayal has its absurd, patronizing, and misleading moments. Ito Eat is an ill-advised comic homage to a tubby local, and the hula Presley performs in the film has no relation to the hula as practiced in Hawaii. Whereas pelvic disruption is central to "Rock-a-hula Baby," the real hula is a system of poetry, movement, and rhythm in which the chants are more important than the dance. In fairness to Elvis, the cliché of Hawaiian hula-dancing beauties who really move that grass around had been established as early as 1927 when Clara Bow played a native wild child in the silent movie smash *Hula*.

Yet when Presley sings "Hawaiian Wedding Song" at the end of *Blue Hawaii*, he starts in English; switches to Hawaiian, as if acknowledging the song's origins; and returns to English for the climax. This lyrical synthesis reflects the reconciliation of whites and islanders, symbolized by the union of Chad and Miley in a lavishly choreographed, yet reasonably authentic, traditional Hawaiian wedding ceremony.

Lansbury provided most of the movie's comic moments for many cinemagoers. Yet Hawaiians, as Hopkins notes, found one beach scene unintentionally hilarious. When Elvis came onto the beach with bongo drums and tambourine and pronounced Kaua'i as if it was spelt "cow eye," many locals couldn't help but laugh.

It May Be Paradise, But It's Not Hawaiian Style

For Hawaiians, *Girls! Girls! Girls!* was a definite step back. There is almost no direct engagement with Hawaiian culture and, as beautiful as the backdrop is, the story of Elvis's quest to buy his father's old boat could have taken place almost anywhere on the American coast.

One of the redeeming features of *Paradise, Hawaiian Style* is that Hawaii does make its presence felt, with song and dance pageants providing some of the film's most stirring moments. Even the infuriatingly catchy "Queenie Wahine's Papaya" can trace its roots back to such traditional Hawaiian songs as "Princess Poo-poo-ly Has Plenty Papaya."

The plot is daffier than ever, and Elvis tries to smile his way through the film, springing into life when he is given the chance to show that the "Drums of the Islands" (a catchy number based on the old Tongan chant "Bula Lai") are still beating in his heart.

Yet as Houston Wood, professor of English at Hawaii Pacific University, has pointed out in the book *Displacing Natives: The Rhetorical Production of Hawaii*, in Elvis's third Hawaiian movie, the islanders are barely individualized. The conspicuous exception is James Shigeta, Elvis's business partner, who is depicted as more adult, responsible, and professional than the hedonistic Presley. The other Hawaiians are presented, Wood writes, as needing "to be safely administered, rather like once-wild animals in a zoo." The focus on a "Euroamerican star acting against a backdrop of local people, who are represented as less intelligent, powerful and charismatic," would recur in *Hawaii Five-O* with Lord in the Elvis role.

Wood doesn't blame Elvis for this, but he argues that since 1966, when *Paradise, Hawaiian Style* was released, not one major movie or TV production has reversed this trope and portrayed the locals as superior to non-Natives. In other words, this movie may offer a vision of paradise, but it isn't really in Hawaiian style.

41

The Shoeshine Boy

Elvis's Duet with a Black Shoeshine Kid and the Racial Politics of His Movies

I n 1957, Louie Robinson, a reporter for the black magazine *Jet*, asked Elvis about a story that, at either a personal appearance in Boston or on Ed Murrow's *Person to Person* TV show, he had once said: "The only thing negroes can do for me is to buy my records and shine my shoes."

Elvis flatly denied the claim: "I never said anything like that and people who know me know that I wouldn't have said it." Other black musicians who had worked with Elvis—notably songwriter Ivory Joe Hunter and pianist Dudley Brooks—told Robinson they were surprised by the story. The fact that Presley had never played Boston or even appeared on Murrow's show made the rumor even more mysterious.

Writing in *Race, Rock and Elvis*, Michael J. Bertrand tracked the quotation down to an article in a Texan magazine called *Sepia*, published in April 1957, which explored how black Americans felt about Elvis. The quotation was not credited to Presley but was one of several remarks in the article by unnamed people in the street and showbiz stars.

As dubious as the story is, the mud stuck. Elvis is quoted by a black cab driver as making this exact remark in V. S. Naipaul's *A Turn in the South* (1989), and the author accepts this apocrypha as a fact. The remark helped reinforce the charge that Elvis deliberately stole black music (he certainly made a lot more money out of it than black rivals such as Little Richard) and made it easier for Goldman to smear Presley as "an unregenerate southern redneck who stopped just short of the Klan." This was some statement for an author who, elsewhere in the biography, dismisses Elvis's friend, the soul singer James Brown, as an "African witch doctor." Goldman's characterization was echoed in 1989 by Public Enemy's Chuck D, who blasted Presley: "straight up racist that sucker was" (though he later retracted this view). All this may explain why, years later, Mary J. Blige would reveal that she had prayed before singing a Presley song because "I know Elvis was a racist."

Although Blige used the word "know," as if she had definitive proof of Elvis's racism, the case that he was is not especially persuasive. Guralnick defended the star, saying: "Like many of our great musicians, Elvis saw no distinction between class and race. He saw people as people. Within the world of entrenched racism, it's unusual to find someone so altogether open."

In the 1950s, when segregation was still dominated life in the American South, Presley dressed like the blacks he saw on Beale Street, hung around black neighborhoods, attended a fund-raiser for needy children at black radio station WDIA, performed on the same bill as Rufus Thomas and B. B. King (whom he told, "Thanks, man, for all the early lessons you gave me"), and had his photograph taken with Bobby Bland and Little Junior Parker. He also publicly acknowledged the black singers who had inspired him—King, Arthur Crudup, Fats Domino, and Roy Hamilton. In 1956, he told the *Charlotte Observer*: "Crudup used to bang his box the way I do now and I said if I ever got to the place where I could feel all old Arthur felt, I'd be a music man like nobody ever saw."

When he became globally famous, he would become friends with Muhammad Ali, James Brown, Sammy Davis Jr., and Jackie Wilson. As Presley's first mentor Phillips pointed out once, if it hadn't been for the singer's lack of prejudice, the revolution in popular culture initiated by rock and roll would never have happened. Elvis's father, Vernon, was stung enough by the suggestion of racism to insist: "We weren't trash, we weren't prejudiced."

Given the enduring appeal of an anecdote that had been rejected as implausible as long ago as 1957, the scene in *Frankie and Johnny* in which Elvis sings "Hard Luck" on a New Orleans street while accompanied by a harmonica-playing shoeshine boy seems more than coincidental.

Shoeshine boys were a popular motif in Hollywood, and it is interesting to compare this scene to the MGM featurette *Shoe Shine Boy* (1943), in which the titular hero (played by little-known jazz musician Mel Bryant) proves he can do more than polish shoes by blowing everyone away with his trumpet playing. Though disfigured by the kind of racism that was all but inescapable in Hollywood movies of the era, the movie is worth watching to see Bryant blow the horn and to appreciate just how old some of the motifs in movies about show business really are.

Bryant is an unassuming genius who, the titles tell us, has a million dollars' worth of talent—the same value Parker famously ascribed to Presley's gifts. Like Elvis in *Loving You*, the poor young trumpeter comes out of the audience to prove his prowess and, as in many Presley movies, soon has agents fighting to exploit him.

Shoe Shine Boy opens with the boy on his knees, frenetically polishing a customer's shoes. In *Frankie and Johnny*, we never see the boy polish shoes, but his occupation is made explicit because the word "SHINE" is chalked in large capital letters on his case. Standing on a street corner, the boy (who, sadly, has not been unidentified) starts playing the harmonica, prompting Presley to lament a life so afflicted by misfortune that his lucky number is thirteen.

Elvis sings the song with—and to—the boy. In this fictionalized nineteenth-century New Orleans, no social barriers separate them. Nor are any implied in the way the scene is shot. As the boy starts playing, Elvis walks over and sits down

In *The Trouble With Girls*, a black boy—and mention of the Ku Klux Klan—gives this Presley movie a distinctive tone.   *MGM/Photofest*

alongside him. Presley all but sings the first verse to the boy, and the two spar off each other for the rest of the song, with Presley more passionate than at any other time in the movie. When the singer strolls off into the night, the boy's bluesy harmonica has the final say.

If Tarantino had directed this movie in the 1990s, this scene would be read as a deliberate riposte to the shoeshine story. Yet it was made in 1965 with Frederick de Cordova, who is still best known as the producer of Johnny Carson's *Tonight Show*, in the director's chair for his last movie. He, writers (Alex Gottlieb and Nat Perrin), conductor Fred Karger, and choreographer Earl Barton hardly seem the type to smuggle subliminal messages into a musical comedy. And yet, given that the scripts allude to so many other aspects of Presley's life, the possibility cannot be ruled out. There seems no other particular point—besides Hollywood's love for this particular cliché—to having Elvis sit on a street corner singing a blues number with a black shoeshine boy who happens to be a virtuoso on the harmonica.

That puzzling scene serves as a suitable introduction to the racial complexities of Presley's movies. The singer seems doomed to be surrounded by inaccuracies on racial issues, and it is often said that Barbara McNair (Sister Irene in *Change of Habit*) is the first black actor to speak in an Elvis film. If this were true—this being his last feature film—it would imply that his movies were, even by the standards of Hollywood in the 1950s and 1960s, unusually racially segregated. McNair was a pioneer in many ways—in 1969, she became the one of the first black performers to host her own musical variety show on U.S. TV—but she was far from the first black actor to speak in an Elvis film.

For a start, it depends on what you mean by talk. Black jazz singer Kitty White cries out "Crawfish!" as a street vendor at the start of *King Creole*, enticing Elvis to duet with her from his balcony. Ruby Goodwin (as Hope Lange's maid Sarah) and Rafer Johnson (as John Ireland's capable assistant) both had speaking parts in *Wild in the Country* (1961). Respected stage actor Joel Fluellen lets Elvis and Joan Freeman have a free ride on the fairground wheel in *Roustabout* (1964) and tells Presley it's a shame he can't keep his mouth shut.

In *The Trouble with Girls* (1969), Pepe Brown plays Willy, a black boy who often greets Elvis's chautauqua manager with the cry, "White folks still ahead," which, in the American Midwest in the 1920s, was probably pretty accurate. Willy has a song-and-dance act with a white girl called Carol. When she is cast in a pageant ahead of the mayor's daughter, the mayor protests, yet adds: "This isn't about the boy. There's no Klan feeling here." For an Elvis movie to even acknowledge such issues is unusual.

In his next movie, *Change of Habit*, McNair does become the first black actor to have such a major part in an Elvis film that she influences the plot. Her defiance of a local mobster earns her a punch in the face and the grudging respect of two local Black Panther figures, who previously advised her: "You're either part of the problem or you're part of the solution." McNair also leads Mary Tyler Moore back to the church so she can choose between Jesus and Elvis.

It is true that Elvis doesn't romance a black actress in any of his movies—although he is chased by Chinese American beauty Irene Tsu in *Paradise, Hawaiian Style*—but, in the context of Hollywood in the 1960s, this was hardly unusual. In 1957, Robert Rossen's *Islands in the Sun* dwelled on interracial romance in the West Indies, but cashier Dorothy Dandridge was allowed only to embrace writer John Justin. As late as November 1968, there was some controversy when William Shatner and Nichelle Nichols enjoyed the first interracial kiss on American TV.

Did Elvis Want to Be a King Creole?

The world of Presley's movies is racially more diverse than it might seem at first glance. He is cast as a Native American in *Stay Away, Joe* and a half-breed in *Flaming Star*, while in *G.I. Blues* he acknowledges his Cherokee ancestry. In *Blue Hawaii*, his bride has Hawaiian and French blood. In *Fun in Acapulco*, his manager is a streetwise Mexican kid and he is wooed by Latin temptress Elsa Cardenas. In *Girls! Girls! Girls!* he is mysteriously at ease with a surrogate Chinese family, and he becomes a chaperone for a young Chinese girl when her uncle disappears in *It Happened at the World's Fair*. In *Paradise, Hawaiian Style*, he partners with Hawaiian pilot Shigeta.

The rationale for these encounters varies enormously. Often they are dictated by locale. Sometimes, as with the Chinese characters, they seem primarily chosen to add novelty value. They are often presented stereotypically. In *Blue Hawaii*, the locals in his band are archetypal happy-go-lucky Hawaiians who count out their lives in beach parties. As patronizing as many of the stereotypes now seem, they are no more demeaning than the portrayal of southern hillbillies in *Kissin' Cousins*. The very title seems designed to allude to the enduring prejudice that the South regards incest as a legitimate indoor sport.

Peter Nazareth, the American academic who has long pondered these complexities, has suggested that, whatever the people who wrote and made Presley's movies intended, the star himself wanted the world to see him as a *King Creole*—a man with a mixed racial heritage who wanted his appeal to transcend such differences.

On record, he could signify this by his exceptional range of styles and voices—one of the aspects of his music that fascinated the young David Bowie. Onscreen, this message was harder to convey. Given the opportunity—as in *Flaming Star*—he could do it through his acting. Yet he didn't get that opportunity all that often, especially in the mid-1960s when he was making three musical comedies a year. Faced with such a treadmill, and that kind of material, it is possible Presley tried to send out his own signals. We know his gestures in the filming of "Return to Sender" were his homage to his close friend Jackie Wilson, the singer reductively labeled "the black Elvis." What we don't know now is what other messages he sent out.

42

"If You're Going to Start a Rumble"

The Importance of the Fight in an Elvis Movie, and a Celebration of the Five Best and Worst

When *Cosmopolitan* interviewer Joseph Lewis visited Elvis on the set of *Stay Away, Joe*, he found the star "bored and bemused," hiding behind a "plastic grin." Presley snapped out of his purposeless splendor whenever there was a fight scene, becoming, Lewis noted, "all sinew and cartilage exploding with kinetic energy . . . At the end of the day, he nurses a bruised cheek and a sore shoulder but he is happy."

Elvis had always nursed a tough-guy complex. This could have been inspired by the bullying he suffered at school or originated as a defensive response to the burden of his extraordinary physical beauty. As a young rock star, whose concerts enthralled women and enraged their boyfriends, he looked like a hood and learned to defend himself—and hire others to defend him. He never stopped trying to be a tough guy, persuading President Nixon to give him a real Drug Enforcement Agency badge, enjoying the company of cops (he half jokingly told Herman's Hermits singer Peter Noone that his favorite group were the Los Angeles Police Department), practicing karate years before Bruce Lee's movies made this martial art fashionable in the West, and collecting guns and riding motorcycles. Even the sideburns reflected this quest, grown to make him look like a truck driver. Nobody ever doubted truck drivers' masculinity, and that was how Presley earned a living until fame changed everything.

In the movies, fights were always useful for raising Presley's morale—he often choreographed them himself with the Memphis Mafia—and as a means of reassuring those fans (especially the men) who had preferred the hard, rocking Elvis that he had not, as one friend of writer Greil Marcus put it, "sold out to the girls." So it came to pass that in twenty-nine of his thirty-one feature films, he threw at least one punch. (The exceptions were *Spinout* and *The Trouble with Girls*—although in the latter he brutally slapped drunken Sheree North.)

The character of the fights varied. They could be slapstick. In *Speedway*, just one punch from the King was enough to send a rival speeding like a bullet across the hotel foyer and into the elevator. Or they could be brutal. In *Jailhouse Rock*, his antihero defended a lady's honor with such vigor that he killed a man with his bare hands. In *Easy Come, Easy Go*, he broke the mold by getting embroiled in an unusual, but dull, underwater fight.

In only one movie, *Kid Galahad*, were the fight scenes essential to the plot, although in *Stay Away, Joe*, the fight scenes nearly replace the plot, with a few moments of comedy, drama, and music thrown in now and then to change the pace.

Part of the fun was guessing where exactly Elvis's buddy Red West, who threw a punch in so many Elvis movies, was going to slug him. It could be anywhere: a restaurant (*Paradise, Hawaiian Style*), a club (*Tickle Me*), a newspaper plant (*Live a Little, Love a Little*), or the family barn (*Wild in the Country*). The formula for these confrontations varied little—Red usually threw the first punch and always lost the fight.

King Creole

"Good boy, fights real dirty." So says gang leader Vic Morrow after his first confrontation with Presley in Curtiz's noir-ish movie. The knife fight between Morrow and Presley was shot and reshot because Curtiz wanted it to look convincing. Filming was briefly interrupted when Morrow accidentally stabbed Presley in the left arm. The wound was superficial, but Elvis needed treatment, joking with the nurse: "He must be a Pat Boone fan." Matthau could have done even more damage, getting so carried away in the scene where he had to break a chair over Presley's head that he picked up a broken chair leg and hit the singer in the mouth.

Flaming Star

In *The Wild Bunch*, one of the movies Elvis loved most, Sam Peckinpah's slow-mo scenes of destruction established him as a poet of screen violence. Eight years earlier, Siegel took a rather more prosaic approach to conflict in *Flaming Star*. Though much of the carnage was traditional horse-opera fare, the manner in which Presley defends his screen mother's honor, by beating up two itinerants, nods toward Peckinpah's 'If they move, kill 'em" mode. As Presley repeatedly slams his opponent face-first into a log, it's hard not to wince. The awkward grace with which Presley leaves the field victorious is superb.

Live a Little, Love a Little

This laudable attempt to revive the screwball comedy genre features one of the longest, most ambitious fight scenes in the Presley canon. Returning to work after four days in a drugged stupor (don't ask), photographer Elvis is so outraged to be fired from the newspaper that six heavies are ordered to escort him from the premises. Inevitably, he has to make a point by taking all six of them on in the press room—and taking all six of them out—before agreeing to leave the premises on his terms. Presley seems much more at home trading punches in the now defunct *Hollywood Citizen News* plant than he does sharing the screen with kooky love interest Michelle Carey.

Roustabout

In one of the most iconic Elvis fights, the star karate chops three uppity college kids into submission. After persuading director Rich to let him do the fight, Presley was determined the scene would go well—which it did until he fell over and stuntman Glenn R. Wilder's heel caught the corner of his eye. Just as things threatened to turn ugly, with West keen to exact vengeance, Presley drove past and urged his friends: "Leave the wild man alone, it was my fault." The star had plastic surgery, and Rich placated the irate Wallis by suggesting they put a plaster over Presley's eye—as if he had been cut in a motorbike accident they had shot—so filming could resume. This fight scene is talked through in the bar in Peter Ormrod's offbeat Irish comedy *Eat the Peach*.

It Happened at the World's Fair

As pilot Mike Edwards, Presley dresses like an aspiring Young Businessman of the Year, but he fights with such speed, panache, and venom that the Swedish censors felt obliged to trim the action. The fights work so well because they seem to happen at least 25 percent faster than in most Elvis films, and the kicks and punches—especially when Elvis takes on the poker players who have taken his buddy to the cleaners—don't seem so telegraphed in advance.

Follow That Dream

The comic ease with which Elvis, as innocent abroad Toby Kwimper, frees himself from the goons ordered to rough him up, is one of many genuinely funny moments in this witty comedy. Elvis adroitly knocks them both out in seconds while never stepping out of character.

Kid Galahad

Despite the best efforts of Mushy Callahan, a former junior world welterweight champion, Presley stands like a karate expert, not a boxer, in most of the fight scenes. Whereas boxers stand so they can always open up an angle on their opponent, Presley's stance was too wide. He did learn to throw a punch like a boxer, and in the finale, he and pro boxer Raymond De La Fuente actually started fighting for real. The big fight is thrilling yet unconvincing and, forgive the pun, packs less punch than the first training session, where Elvis, after taking a battering, lands one knockout blow and, as his big-name opponent lies sprawled on the canvas, asks the trainer: "Hey, mister, do I still get my five dollars?"

And one fight most Elvis fans would rather forget . . .

Harum Scarum

The moment in the film-within-a-film sequence when Elvis kills a leopard with his bare hands is bad enough but is surpassed by the closing confrontation between King Toranshah (Phillip Reed) and his brother Dragma (Michael Ansara), which starts as a fight to the death with swords and peters out with them sitting around a chess table.

43

Even Concrete Cracks

How Actresses Rose to the Ultimate Challenge—Being Sung to By Elvis

W here do you look? How long can you gaze adoringly? At what point should you burst into a smile? These are the conundrums that faced many of Elvis's leading ladies. Obviously if the man himself is belting out a number onstage, you don't have a problem, but what do you do when he's singing to you in a car (*Blue Hawaii, Fun in Acapulco, Wild in the Country*), in a hotel restaurant where it's just you and the janitor (*Speedway*), or in a canoe (*Paradise, Hawaiian Style*)?

The King was embarrassed by his characters' habit of bursting into song, but these scenes were even more problematic for the actresses he was singing to. He did his best to ease the tension. Yvonne Romain recalled that, in *Double Trouble*, he would joke around before they filmed a song to relax himself and his co-star. Some actresses relished the ritual. Diane McBain, to whom Elvis sang "All That I Am" in *Spinout*, told Tom Lisanti, author of *Fantasy Femmes of Sixties Cinema*: "Can you think of anything nicer than be serenaded by Elvis?"

Joan O'Brien certainly could. As Nurse Diane Warren in *It Happened at the World's Fair*, she had Elvis croon "I'm Falling in Love Tonight" to her in the restaurant at the top of the Space Needle. She told Lisanti these scenes were "tedious and hard because he had all the action and I felt awkward. It was very difficult for me—I don't know about other actresses—to be aware of the camera, pay attention to him, and try to look dreamy-eyed and in love. I felt like I had egg on my face most of the time."

Shelley Fabares gave a master class in the difficult art of being sung at by Elvis in *Spinout*. Sitting on a chair, as Elvis and his band performed "Am I Ready" as her birthday treat, Fabares's expression initially suggested her heart was skipping a beat before she settled for an appealing, convincing, blend of adoration and disbelief. Taurog helped her by interspersing the close-ups with shots from the side or behind so she didn't have to hold these expressions for too long, but she made the moment work.

Nancy Sinatra proved just as accomplished in *Speedway*, falling for Elvis when he sang "Who Are You?" As the song started, she looked suitably perplexed by the fact that she was smitten by such an unsuitable suitor—she was working for the IRS and he did owe them thousands of dollars—but she melted slowly, almost hesitantly, before throwing her arms around him.

Sinatra had one advantage: because the song followed an argument, she has licence to emote while Presley is crooning. Mary Ann Mobley made the same emotional journey during "Cross My Heart and Hope to Die" in *Girl Happy*. Livid after being stood up, Mobley tried to keep the Pelvis at bay by playing with a palm frond, slipping away as he closed in for a kiss, and projecting a beguiling combination of anger and hurt with her eyes. She relinquished the frond halfway through the song, a gesture that presaged her surrender.

In *It Happened at the World's Fair*, none of these factors worked in O'Brien's favor. She was sitting next to Elvis at a restaurant table and had to look dewy-eyed for one minute and forty seconds as Presley sang Don Robertson's romantic ballad. At first, she cleverly looked away from Presley, but she soon had to turn around and, apart from stroking his hand occasionally, there wasn't much else for her to do. She did nothing pretty classily, but the camera focused on her face for so long, it's hard not to lose interest. Even so, a dewy-eyed O'Brien was still significantly more watchable than dewy-eyed Annette Day, who fell asleep on Elvis's shoulder as he sang "Could I Fall in Love" in *Double Trouble*. As Day wore the same rictus grin of adoration for most of the song, it came as a relief when she dozed off.

Even Day looks more comfortable being sung at than poor Irene Tsu, who shared a canoe with Presley during the first performance of "Drums of the Island" in *Paradise, Hawaiian Style*. If the Chinese American actress looks bothered and bewildered during the song, that's probably because she is. As she complained to Lisandi, Michael Moore (who was directing his first Presley movie) gave neither her nor Presley any direction for this scene. It showed. Though the scene—like Tsu—is gorgeous, it is painfully obvious that she had no idea where to look.

Sometimes, Elvis's directors tweaked the formula. In *World's Fair*, Yvonne Craig evaded and welcomed Elvis's attentions as he tried to persuade her to "Relax." In *Tickle Me*, Jocelyn Lane shut the window and closed the curtains as Elvis wooed her with "I Feel That I've Known You Forever," a routine rehashed in the "Please Don't Stop Loving Me" scene in *Frankie and Johnny*.

Those actresses fortunate enough to duet with Elvis faced a much less daunting challenge. In *Viva Las Vegas*, Ann-Margret sparred with Elvis during "The Lady Loves Me" and had the final word, pushing him into the swimming pool. In *G.I. Blues*, Juliet Prowse and Elvis turned the ballad "Pocketful of Rainbows" into one of the warmest, most romantic scenes in his films. The song, the setting, Presley's sweet vocal and Prowse's soaring cries of "Rainbow" made this genuinely magical.

Prowse and Elvis, who were having an affair offscreen, had chemistry on it. In *Wild in the Country*, Presley's rapport with Lange (whom he didn't have an affair with) infused their brief duet on "Husky Dusky Day." Lange burst into

O'Brien said she felt like she had egg on her face when being sung to by Elvis in *It Happened at the World's Fair.*   *Photofest*

laughter after losing track of the song, making this sing-along seem natural and spontaneous.

If you can't sing, why not dance? This ploy worked spectacularly for Ann-Margret in *Viva Las Vegas,* Marianna Hill during the "Scratch My Back" routine in *Paradise, Hawaiian Style* (although the way she strutted her legs made Elvis look lackluster), and certainly helped Laurel Goodwin when she joined in with Elvis (and briefly, when the star became visibly erect onscreen, Little Elvis, as the star called his penis) on the endearing, slightly absurd "The Walls Have Ears."

For an Elvis movie to succeed even on its own terms, these songs and scenes had to be right. When they don't work—like "Kismet" in *Harum Scarum,* where even Elvis can hardly keep a straight face—or are skipped completely (as in *Easy Come, Easy Go*), the movies are that much duller. As clichéd as some of the falling-in-love ballads were, they usually provoked a committed performance from Presley, transcending much of the mediocrity that surrounds them.

"Home Is Where the Heart Is" worked beautifully in *Kid Galahad,* partly because Presley wasn't singing the whole song to Joan Blackman. He fiddled with a book and the car, and even when he turned to Blackman, Karlson had the wit to cut to Lola Albright, whose smiling approval helped set the mood. The slightly awkward sincerity with which the King sings this number rings true, and Blackman deserves some kind of acting award for the never taking her eyes off Elvis and never looking forced or false. When the camera zooms in for the killer close-ups, she looks lovely, lovable, and in love. Whatever the critics said, these were the moments that, for millions of fans, defined the pleasure they got from a Presley movie.

44

A New Breed of All-Action Hero

Elvis the Boxer, Race-Car Driver, Speedboat Racer, Stock-Car Ace, and Rodeo Legend

One thing Elvis rarely did in his movies was sit behind a desk. He boxed (*Kid Galahad*), raced cars (*Speedway, Spinout, Viva Las Vegas*) or speedboats (*Clambake*), rode the rodeo (*Tickle Me, Stay Away, Joe*), sailed a boat (*Girls! Girls! Girls!*), flew a plane (*It Happened at the World's Fair*) or a helicopter (*Paradise, Hawaiian Style*), dived off a cliff (*Fun in Acapulco*) or into the deep sea (*Easy Come, Easy Go*), wrestled strangers (*Kissin' Cousins*), and occasionally found time to play American football (*The Trouble with Girls, Change of Habit*), the sport closest to his heart. Elvis rarely contemplated a more cerebral career. He aspired to be a writer (*Wild in the Country*), was a groovy doctor (*Change of Habit*), and, slightly unconvincingly, applied to join NASA in *World's Fair*. As Alf, the cuddly sitcom alien, put it once: "Elvis was a brilliant actor. He could play anything from a singing racing-car driver to a singing deep-sea diver."

No matter how many starlets Presley simpered after or soppy songs he sang, there was usually some kind of all-action sequence for the guys. This could be a race that had to be won against all the odds or a fight in which, like a precursor of Steven Seagal, he confounded his opponents with his martial-arts expertise.

Unfortunately, technology and special effects have improved so drastically since the 1960s that it is all but impossible to understand, today, how thrilling these action-packed scenes were when the movies were first released. The extensive use of back projection, often handled extremely amateurishly, makes these scenes even harder to judge in their historic context.

For all that, the race scenes in *Viva Las Vegas* still work, partly because some really nice cars get wrecked. In *Spinout*, Taurog didn't seem to know whether to play the race for laughs or drama, but for some fans the best thing about the movie was the cars, especially the Fox Five (which was actually a McLaren-Elva racing car from the 1960s).

In *Speedway*, a movie that prefigured the remarkable rise of NASCAR, the racing sequences were enlivened by footage from the 1967 Charlotte 600 and the presence of real-life stock-car legends Richard Petty, Cale Yarborough, Tiny Lund, and Buddy Baker. Despite some spectacular crashes, the scenes were visually not that interesting. Taurog couldn't quite maintain the tension, probably because, as dialogue coach Hoey has since revealed, the director's sight was so bad "he could barely look at the flickering screen where the racing track footage was being projected behind the actors. I would give him a sign at the end of a take if everything went well or if we needed to go again."

In most of his movies, there were too many songs to sing, women to woo, and kids to charm for Elvis to become a true all-action hero. In the 1960s, James Bond's one-man army, summarily dispatching all and sundry, was as tough as mainstream action movies got until spaghetti westerns reached American audiences. Presley ventured into 007 territory with *Double Trouble*, his macho credentials slightly undermined by his need to sing seven songs. *Charro!* was his only stab at a spaghetti western. Neither really worked.

It's a pity Elvis never got to make a proper sports movie. Read Morgan, who starred in *Easy Come, Easy Go*, said: "He always wanted to play in the NFL. He loved football, he wanted to be a wide receiver. He would've been a good one. He was quick and had great hands." He could even have played alongside his friend, the actor and gridiron hero Jim Brown. The football games in *The Trouble with Girls* and *Change of Habit* show Elvis in an entertaining, relaxed mood. Still, this being Elvis, he would probably have ended up starring in a musical comedy about a quarterback who sings in his spare time.

By the 1970s, when Bruce Lee and Chuck Norris were redefining the action movie and paving the way for the likes of Arnold Schwarzenegger, Steven Seagal, and Sylvester Stallone, Presley had retired from the silver screen.

Elvis loved *Enter the Dragon*. Lee's movie inspired him to try to make a karate movie in 1974. Even Wallis was intrigued, paying Anthony Lawrence to develop a storyline, but the studios weren't interested. There was talk of a karate variation on the theme of a gunfighter coming out of retirement and a documentary called *The New Gladiators*, narrated by Elvis, that would become the definitive film about the sport. Usually regarded as the passing whim of an-out of-touch superstar, the project was dear to Elvis. Schilling says, "This was just the kind of challenge he needed and it could have been good too—but he never got the support he needed on it and his health problems got in the way." As the movie was never completed (though a lot of documentary footage has since been released on DVD), we will never know if Presley could have carried it off.

45

Ramblers, G-Men, and 1 Plus 2 + ½

The Role of Elvis's Bands in the Movies

On the set of *Roustabout*, Elvis and his director John Rich had their famous argument over the star's preference for having backing singers on "Wheels on My Heels," an infectious, slightly clichéd ode to life on the open road. When Rich complained that backing singers were unrealistic, Presley suggested that they were no less implausible than the band.

In the musical comedies that dominated Elvis's movie career, realism was a relative concept, but it was often convenient to have him playing with a band. That way, audiences didn't have to wonder where the music was coming from. The group could provide characters to influence the plot—as in *Loving You* and *Spinout*—and, once the Beatles arrived, Hollywood's executives did what their kind have always done, managed creativity by analogy. If the Beatles' movie was a runaway success and they were in a band, then Elvis had darn well better be in a band too.

Not all of Elvis's movie bands had names. In *Girl Happy*, Elvis and his musicians were billed simply as Rusty Wells and his combo. In *Double Trouble*, Guy Lambert (Elvis) was backed by the G-Men—presumably because they were the men behind Guy with a G. In *G.I. Blues*, Presley and his pals formed a trio called the Three Blazes. In *Loving You*, the band with which Elvis becomes famous revels in the name Tex Warner and his Rough Ridin' Ramblers. This outfit made its mark on pop-cultural history. At one point, bandleader Wendell Corey yells to the band: "Okay, ramblers, let's get to ramblin'." This must surely be the inspiration for the cry of "Okay, ramblers, let's get ramblin'" that appears twice in Tarantino's *Reservoir Dogs*.

The name of the band supporting Mike McCoy (Elvis) in *Spinout* is even odder: 1 Plus 2 + ½. As the lead singer, Elvis is presumably the one, and the two guitar players are Larry and Curly, which means that Walley, on drums, is the ½. Is this a sexist dig? (This is the movie in which Elvis sings "Smorgasbord.") Or does it reflect the jokes musicians tell at the drumming profession's expense (e,g., What do you call a guy who hangs around with musicians? A drummer).

The stagey antics of Rusty Wells's combo and 1 Plus 2 + ½ offer a stark, almost embarrassing contrast to the behavior of the Rough Ridin' Ramblers in *Loving You*. In Elvis's second film, the combo backing Deke includes many of the musicians with whom Elvis became famous: guitarist Scotty Moore, bass player Bill Black, drummer D. J. Fontana, and backing group the Jordanaires. Despite the incongruity of Corey's saxophone solos in a fading country-and-western outfit, the presentation of the band is, for Hollywood, reasonably naturalistic, as it was in *Jailhouse Rock*, where two numbers are performed in a recording studio. In *King Creole*, where Danny Fisher (Elvis) is backed by a house band—and, less suitably, the Jordanaires, pretending they know how to play horns after some quick instruction by Charles O'Curran—on the big numbers.

Moore, Black, and Fontana left the screen after *G.I. Blues*, although they played on many soundtracks. The Jordanaires—and the Mello Men, who often accompanied or replaced them—lasted much longer, carving out a profitable niche as the random strangers who left their homes, gardens, or street corners to accompany Elvis, a mise en scène ruthlessly parodied in Woody Allen's *Radio Days*, when all the family joined in as cousin Ruthie sang Carmen Miranda's "South American Way." In *Blue Hawaii*, Chad (Elvis) was backed by carefree Hawaiians friends who knew how to knock out a rock-a-hula.

Before *Roustabout* started production on February 28, 1964, Wallis's associate Paul Nathan asked Brian Summerville, the Beatles road manager, if the group would appear in the film with Elvis. On Nathan's memo, Wallis had written: "1 or 2 numbers—possibly 1 alone and 1 with Elvis." Summerville sounded keen, saying, "the guys are crazy about Elvis," but they were under exclusive contract, in America, to United Artists and couldn't appear in a Paramount picture.

With the Beatles arriving in the United States only on February 7, 1964, Nathan had acted with unusual alacrity, suggesting that someone in the organization had either been entranced by visions of a box-office bonanza or was already fretting about the threat they might pose to the King's reign.

In *Girl Happy*, released three months before the Beatles' second movie, *Help!*, Elvis acquired a combo: two guitarists and a drummer, just like John, Paul, George, and Ringo. Or, as it turned out, not at all like John, Paul, George, and Ringo, because the other members of Presley's combo were about as distinguishable as paper cups. This might explain why music director George Stoll plays a few notes of "Three Blind Mice" whenever the trio appear. Guitarist Jimmy Hawkins does his best to disturb the monotony by hamming it up on a saxophone solo so outrageously he makes Wendell Corley look like Charlie Parker.

MGM refined the *Girl Happy* template in *Spinout* (1966). In this movie, his band 1 Plus 2 + ½ were so clearly delineated that even viewers who weren't paying attention could tell them apart. Guitarist Jack Mullaney spent most of the movie refining his Jerry Lewis impersonation (his casting was obviously designed to aid audience recognition, as he had already done the same shtick in *Tickle Me*). The drummer (Walley) was a girl—and a Cordon Bleu chef. And the other guitarist was saxophone-blowing guitar hero Hawkins from *Girl Happy*, who underlined his versatility by strumming away on a 1965 Gibson double-bass guitar and playing a flute.

The aim was to re-create the kind of goofy bonhomie that MGM executives had perversely concluded was the real secret to the success of such acts as the Beatles and the Beach Boys. It worked up to a point. None of the banter matched the sardonic wit of John Lennon—and Taurog seemed more intrigued by the hordes of dancing beauties in *Spinout*—but the musical did feel faster-paced than many Presley movies of this era.

By 1967, Paramount—and Wallis—had given up. With hopes of a Beatles cameo dashed, they gave Elvis some mediocre numbers and a perky house band in *Easy Come, Easy Go*. Yet MGM persevered, saddling the King with the G-Men in *Double Trouble*, although it is not clear whether the producers wanted to ape the Beatles or their manufactured rivals, the Monkees.

The G-Men sported mop-top haircuts, which the Fab Four had already abandoned but resemble the styles sported by the Monkees' Davy Jones and Peter Tork. They were led by flamboyant Monty Landis, a regular guest on the Monkees, who signified his adherence to Swinging London with a Cockney accent only marginally less ludicrous than Dick Van Dyke's in *Mary Poppins*.

As if that wasn't enough, the final plot owes something to *Help!* (the jewels smuggled in the heroine's luggage are an obvious homage to the ring on Ringo's finger). For all that, *Double Trouble*'s unusual blend of intrigue, comedy, and music makes the film resemble an extended Monkees episode.

MGM would never try as hard again. By 1969, when Presley filmed *The Trouble with Girls*, the studio was content to let him sing in a gospel quartet and play in front of a folk trio. On "Clean Up Your Own Backyard," cleverly shot from a variety of angles that emphasized the ambience and the instruments as much as the singer, Presley was at his most inventive vocally, looking as comfortable in performance as in the NBC TV special. The music, the much more authentic band, and his image (the sideburns had returned in full, anachronistic glory in this film and he looked resplendent in a white suit) hinted at the magnetic performer revealed in *Elvis: That's the Way It Is*.

Here, finally, was proof that the powers that be would surely have done better to ignore the fatal distraction of the Beatles' success and let the King stage his own music, liaising with some of the half-decent choreographers recruited for his films. Too often in his movies, bands like 1 Plus 2 + ½ equaled less than the sum of their parts.

46

The King's Domain

The Movie Music

O n September 4, 1956, the twenty-one-year-old Elvis Presley was standing on a soundstage at 20th Century Fox, singing an ersatz hillbilly number called "Let Me" over a prerecorded background track. That wasn't quite how he had hoped his movie career would start, but symbolically, it prefigured countless indignities as movie producers tried to turn him into all-round family entertainer.

The quality of the song also indicated a change in priorities for the industrial complex behind Presley. The disastrous consequences of that shift would become apparent only in the mid-1960s. Looking back, the tipping point would occur on what seemed, at the time, a moment full of promise: Elvis signing, on April 25, 1956, a contract with producer Hal Wallis for one movie with an option for another six. As Anne Fulchino, RCA's publicity officer, said later, that deal was the moment "when we really lost control." By the mid-1960s, Steve Sholes, who had signed Presley for RCA, felt, as his colleague Joan Deary put it, "the songs Elvis was recording for those movies were not at all strong or commercial." Yet Colonel Parker had organized the singer's career in such a way that the label had little influence, having effectively conceded creative rights to Parker, the people he asked to run the King's music publishing empire, the film studios, and producers like Wallis. Between 1960 and 1970, sixteen of Presley's twenty-eight albums were movie soundtracks. RCA had little control over quality. The label's view was put succinctly once by Deary: "Those soundtrack albums drove me up the wall."

Most directors who have made a rock movie have adopted one of two strategies: create a movie whose primary goal is to showcase the music and the artist—as Sam Katzman did with such cash-in movies as *Don't Knock the Rock* (1957) and *Twist Around the Clock* (1961)—and forget about the plot, or focus on the story and use, as many Hollywood musicals did, the songs to tell that story. Sometimes, if a star has enough talent and all parties are in accord, a director has chosen to ignore the music and make a conventional movie that just happens to have a rock star in it, hoping the performer the talent to cross over and appeal as a genuine actor as Bing Crosby, Dean Martin, and Frank Sinatra did. This option is the most perilous, with Presley (in the fake spaghetti western *Charro!*), Mick Jagger (an entertainingly unconvincing Australian outlaw in *Ned Kelly*), and Madonna (who emotes painfully in the trashy melodrama *Body of Evidence*) all exposing themselves to ridicule. Only Oscar-winning Cher has profitably pursued this strategy in recent times.

Presley's film career veered uneasily between all three approaches. At times he would sing little (*Flaming Star*; *Live a Little, Love a Little*; *Wild in the Country*) or nothing (*Charro!*). In a handful of movies, he would sing a handful of songs (*Change of Habit*; *Follow That Dream*; *Kid Galahad*; *Love Me Tender*; *Stay Away, Joe*; and *The Trouble with Girls*). In most of the rest, he would aspire to sing—and often deliver—a full soundtrack album. As great as some of the songs were—and "Jailhouse Rock," "King Creole," "Love Me Tender," and "Return to Sender" were among his finest recordings—most of the numbers were written to order, to respond to a specific situation.

This was especially true after Elvis returned from the army. In *Loving You*, *Jailhouse Rock*, and *King Creole*, he was cast as a singer, so he could perform any number that his character could plausibly sing in a nightclub or on a TV show. Yet when he returned to Hollywood in the 1960s, he was usually, at best, a part-time singer, using music to kill screen time when the script so required and his job as air force officer, boxer, diver, fisherman, pilot, race-car driver, ranch hand, rodeo rider, soldier, speedboat driver, or trapeze artist allowed. Only in *Girl Happy*, *Harum Scarum*, *Roustabout*, and *Double Trouble* is he cast as a full-time singer. In *Harum Scarum*, his freedom to perform is limited by the need to forestall a plot to kill a king, and in *Double Trouble* he has to sing while dodging metaphorical bullets as he investigates the plot to kill his leading lady. Even in *Roustabout*, he is a part-time carny.

Such casting restricted the scope of the music, forcing songwriters to develop numbers for plots that were often skimpy or absurd, rather than creating tunes with mass appeal. Some writers rose—or sank—to the challenge. Joy Byers, who wrote "Hey, Hey, Hey" for *Clambake*, a number that had to celebrate a mysterious glycol-oxy tonic-phosphate substance nicknamed Gloop, recalled "I remember the script came in and I said, 'You've got to be kidding, there is nothing that rhymes with gloop.' That song got in because it was beneath all the other writers to write. We said, 'We'll write anything, just give us a title.'" In the process, Presley would become—in the eyes of his famous fans the Beatles—a poor man's Dean Martin. And the star himself would finally protest, asking various confidants, "What can you do with a piece of shit like this?"

As an artist in an increasingly competitive marketplace in the 1960s, Elvis's decline was driven by the dross he did record—and the good songs he didn't. In 1962 and 1963, he averaged one nonmovie studio session a year. In 1964, he cut just three songs that weren't for his films. In 1965, every song he recorded was destined for a soundtrack. Only in May 1966, when he returned to Nashville to record "How Great Thou Art," did he and RCA start taking care of business, making his most creative music (though it wasn't especially commercial) since the advent of the Beatles.

When Presley recorded those four songs for *Love Me Tender* in the autumn of 1956, no one would have predicted such indignities. Apart from the title track, the songs were throwaways, but they weren't embarrassing. For *Loving You*, he had better songs—courtesy of Jerry Leiber and Mike Stoller, as well as Karl Mann and Bernie Lowe and Claude Demetrius—and he was actually allowed to record them with musicians he trusted: guitarist Scotty Moore, bass player Bill Black, and drummer D. J. Fontana.

In movies like *King Creole*, Presley was inspired by most of the music he had to record.

Paramount Pictures/Photofest

The *Loving You* sessions set the modus operandi for so many soundtracks to come. Freddie Bienstock and the brothers Jean and Julian Aberbach, the trio who looked after the King's music publishing, would circulate a script to writers with suggestions for songs. Demos would be made—occasionally with a vocal from one of the writers, but more often with a decent professional singer like Jimmy Breedlove, Glen Campbell, or P. J. Proby belting out the tune in a style Elvis could imitate. Sometimes, he would copy these demos almost note for note (as he did with Don Robertson's "No More"); at other times he would revamp or reinterpret them ("Don't Ask Me Why," "Trouble"). For one movie, more than three hundred demos were submitted to Bienstock for consideration. In the long run, the disadvantages of this system would become apparent. If Elvis followed the demo too closely, he would effectively be imitating someone who was imitating him! Yet in 1957, the material was usually so good that such risks seemed remote.

The songs were chosen by an informal committee that could consist of some, most, or all of the following: Elvis, the Colonel, a director (or someone they nominated), Bienstock, Jean Aberbach, a representative from the studio (probably Wallis on a Paramount picture), and someone from RCA. Directors were often disappointed by the choices made—for *Double Trouble*, assistant director Michael A. Hoey detested "I Love Only One Girl" and "Old MacDonald"—but on *Loving You*, the system worked brilliantly.

The vast Paramount soundstage in Hollywood—and the formality of the sessions—didn't really suit Presley, but he still produced such classics as "Got a Lot of Livin' to Do," "Mean Woman Blues," and "Teddy Bear." If anything, the songs for *Jailhouse Rock* and *King Creole* were even better, but the sessions for his third movie also revealed that Hollywood didn't quite know how to handle him.

On May 1, 1957, at the Radio Recorders studio in Hollywood, Presley did something unprecedented: he stormed out of a recording session. In the morning, he had warmed up in his customary fashion, singing gospel songs with the Jordanaires. Returning after lunch, he tried to take up where he had left off, but his backing vocalists were reluctant to join in. MGM representative Jeff Alexander had warned them not to get sidetracked and to focus on the film songs. When he was told this, Presley walked out, staying away the next day and returning only on Friday.

The Jordanaires lead singer Gordon Stoker was baffled by the furor, telling Jerry Hopkins: "What the studio didn't realize was that Elvis hadn't sung in a studio for some while and this was his way of getting in the mood . . . that he might have done all seven songs that afternoon or by the end of the following day. Most singers [would] have taken at least two weeks."

Alexander might not have realized how Elvis worked, but surely the Colonel, who was in the studio that day, could have stepped in to protect "his boy"? This is the same manager who was prepared to wreck a take on location in *Blue Hawaii* by striding across the beach and demanding an extra $25,000 because Elvis was wearing his own watch in the scene. Yet in this instance, when the studios were interfering with the way Elvis did the very thing that made him great and Parker rich, the manager was strangely silent.

Elvis returned two days later for one of the most inspiring record sessions of his life. With Leiber effectively acting as producer on the studio floor, Elvis devoted nine hours to "Treat Me Nice," "I Want to Be Free," "Baby I Don't Care," and "Don't Leave Me Now." Leiber recalled later: "Elvis was deep into our producing style. Our style wasn't anything more than being loose and having fun. Elvis' initial shyness had totally melted away and he was completely in the spirit of the music." Presley was so in the spirit that when Black walked out, frustrated because he couldn't play the bass line, he picked the instrument off the floor and played it himself.

This was the first creative input he had really had since he left Sun and his mentor Sam Phillips, and he would not enjoy counsel of such caliber until he walked into American Studios in Memphis in 1969 to work with Chips Moman.

The Music Goes Flat

Sholes had his own frustrations with the movie sessions, believing Black, Moore, and Fontana weren't versatile enough to play the songs for Elvis's fourth film, *King Creole*. He drafted in extra drummer Bernie Mattinson and asked versatile session musician Ray Siegel and Jordanaire Neal Matthews to help out on bass. The best of the songs—"Hard Headed Woman," "Trouble," "King Creole," and "New Orleans"—were once heard, never forgotten. That wouldn't be the case when Presley returned from the army to record the *G.I. Blues* soundtrack in April 1960.

The songs for this musical comedy were decent but not spectacular. Apart from "Wooden Heart" (which wasn't released in the United States as a single), there was no obvious chart hit. RCA's Hollywood studio didn't really suit Elvis's style or sound. As Ernst Jorgensen notes in his *A Life in Music*: "'Shoppin' Around' came out disturbingly flat. The problem . . . would dog Elvis's soundtrack recordings for the rest of his movie career." The flaws in material and sound quality are partially obscured by Elvis's vocals. His joy at being back in the studio can be heard in his heroic campaign to make the title track sound like the pop classic, it most certainly isn't.

From 1961 to 1963, Elvis showed that he could turn the likes of "Can't Help Falling in Love," "Return to Sender," "Bossa Nova Baby," "*Viva Las Vegas*," and "I Need Somebody to Lean On" into pure gold. When inspired by a challenge—a decent ballad, the Mexican numbers on *Fun in Acapulco*—his voice caught fire. He even did his best to make the fake hillbilly numbers in *Kissin' Cousins* sound as polished as the country-pop crossover Nashville sound that was proving so popular for Jim Reeves in the 1960s.

Yet by 1964, Elvis's enthusiasm had waned. In June, singing an innocuous little ditty called "Spring Fever," he was interrupted by the session's musical director George Stoll, who told him, "It should be a little happier—you're

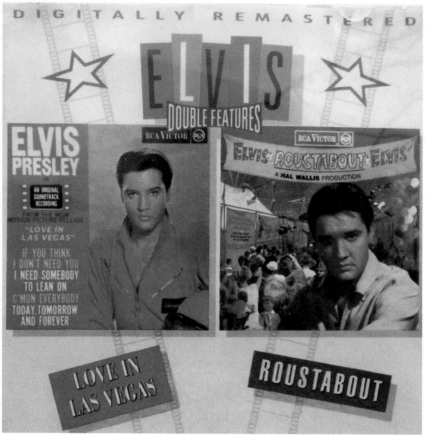

Presley's soundtracks sold well—although oddly *Viva Las Vegas* wasn't released as an album until after his death.

thinking of other things." Presley took this in his stride but complained later about "Do Not Disturb": "That is undoubtedly the weirdest goddam chord change I think I've ever tangled with in my life." After thirty-four takes, assured it was "okay," he replied, "I don't like okay." He had a point: the guitars are still out of key on the master.

In 1965, Elvis recorded thirty-three movie songs. Those tracks had to cover everything from faux Middle Eastern pop (*Harum Scarum*), to Mississippi steamboats in the nineteenth century (*Frankie and Johnny*), to Hawaiian beach party (*Paradise, Hawaiian Style*). The only way you could record such songs in such quantities was to think about something else. That's pretty much what Elvis was doing, talking to his hairdresser Larry Geller about the meaning of life and reading books like *The Impersonal Life* by western mystic Joseph Benner.

Harum Scarum was the first Elvis soundtrack session that musician Charlie McCoy and drummer Kenneth Buttrey had played on. As they had both just finished working on Bob Dylan's seminal album *Blonde on Blonde*, the contrast

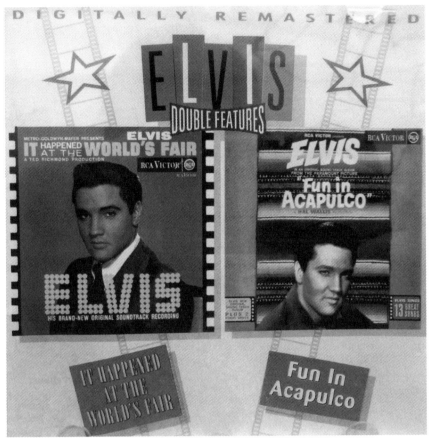

By 1963, the release schedule for Presley's soundtracks had become remorseless.

must have struck them as absurd, if not slightly sinister. When I asked McCoy how he would sum up the atmosphere in the studio for this—and the other soundtrack sessions—he said simply: "Quiet." This wasn't making music, as Elvis understood it, this was a contractual obligation. McCoy and Buttrey were just two of the talented musicians to feature in these sessions. Glen Campbell played guitar on the *Viva Las Vegas* sessions, the great Floyd Cramer was usually on piano—and if he wasn't, the versatile Dudley Brooks often was—and the legendary saxophonist Boots Randolph was a frequent contributor, but the presence of such talent only highlighted how dire many of the songs were.

Scotty Moore played guitar on six Elvis soundtracks. Keith Richards had famously said he'd have died and gone to heaven to play like Moore during the Sun sessions. The Rolling Stone would probably have volunteered to die and go to hell to avoid playing, as Moore did, the *Clambake* sessions.

In the very early days of Tin Pan Alley, some of the songs became so formulaic that songwriters even referred to the most frequently used chord sequences as "Montgomery Ward," "Sears Roebuck," and "Woolworth's." With Hollywood doing its best to ensure that each movie contained, to quote one of the singer's album titles, something for everybody, Elvis's songs were becoming almost as predictable as those Tin Pan Alley chords.

Leiber had seen the writing on the wall long ago, once summing up the musical formula Wallis had established: "You had three ballads, one medium tempo, one up-tempo, and one break blues boogie, usually for a production number. It was too fucking boring. Those assholes only wanted to make another nickel the same way."

The wonder is that Elvis didn't completely give up. Sometimes he consoled himself by behaving like a medieval potentate with his entourage. Bill Cole, a singer on *The Trouble with Girls*, marveled at the manner of the King's entrance when he talked to Bill Bram for *Frame by Frame*: "He was a little late and he came in with an entourage, five or six guys, and we had never seen them before, so we just watched how they did their job. One was carrying the guitar, one set up the area around the microphone Elvis used, one guy hunted for a stool." Presley then picked up a cheroot and teased the flunky holding the cigarette lighter by feigning when he did and didn't want it relit.

More constructively, he maintained his morale by putting his heart into the best ballads—"Am I Ready?," "This Is My Heaven," "Sand Castles"—using them to hone his technique and express his emotions, coming alive in a way he seldom did on the ersatz uptempo numbers. In May 1966, in his first proper nonmovie session in years, he recorded the *How Great Thou Art* album and two beautiful ballads that would be utterly incongruous as bonus tracks on the *Spinout* album: Dylan's reflective "Tomorrow Is a Long Time" and Kui Lee's poignant "I'll Remember You."

Things looked set to improve, but weeks later it was business as usual, with Elvis recording the *Double Trouble* soundtrack on an MGM soundstage that, as Jorgensen put it, "had all the presence of a giant tin can." At one point Elvis cried out: "Lawd have mercy, help!" Even so, he sounded energetic on "Long Legged Girl (With the Short Dress On)" and cool on "City by Night." The *Easy Come, Easy Go* session in September 1966 was much worse; only "You Gotta Stop" seemed to rouse him. This was probably the worst single recording session of his entire career, but his only protest was to turn up late for both days at the Paramount soundstage.

Elvis's faltering return to form in the studio continued in February 1967 when he persevered through twenty takes of the country standard "You Don't Know Me" (but still wasn't satisfied) and breezed through the gutsy "How Can You Lose What You Never Had." The slight improvement was maintained in June 1967 when he recorded the heartfelt "Suppose" and the ballsy "Let Yourself Go" for *Speedway*. The only consolation for Presley at this point was that the studios were so eager to save money they refused to buy songs in the same industrial quantities.

After that movie, his twenty-seventh, the worst was over. For *Live a Little, Love a Little*; *Charro!*; *The Trouble with Girls*; and *Change of Habit* he had fewer, better songs. The material was less formulaic and more contemporary: "A Little Less Conversation," "Almost," "Clean Up Your Own Backyard," and "Edge of Reality" all stand out in different ways. By the time Presley walked out of the studio on March 6, 1969, after cutting four songs for *Change of Habit*, his final feature film, he had resurrected his career with the TV special. For a while, at least, it seemed as if he would live up to the promise he made Steve Binder, the producer of that revelatory show, to never record another song he didn't believe in.

What Do You Do When You're Asked to Write a Song Called "A Dog's Life"?

The Inner Workings of the Presley Music Factory

T his chapter's title asks the rhetorical question that Ben Weisman, who wrote more songs for Elvis's movies than anyone else, once posed to Ernst Jorgensen. The songwriter answered his own question: "Write it," he said. "Because if you don't, someone else will."

That was the modus operandi with which Freddy Bienstock (1923–2009) ensured that Elvis was supplied with the 237 songs he sang onscreen in his thirty-one feature films. The music publisher once proudly boasted, "For the first 12 years of Elvis's career he wouldn't look at a song unless I'd looked at it first."

Bienstock had an office in the legendary Brill Building, a virtual songwriting factory in the late 1950s and early 1960s whose alumni included such writers as Neil Diamond, Neil Sedaka, Gerry Goffin and Carole King, Paul Simon, and Phil Spector. A Swiss Jew, Bienstock had grown up in Vienna but fled Austria after the Anschluss in 1938 to come to America with his brother Johnny (who would later run Big Top Records). In the 1950s, he was hired by his cousins Jean (1910–1992) and Julian Aberbach (1909–2004), two expat Austrian Jews who had founded Hill and Range, a music publishing business that had prospered, in large part, because it dominated the country-and-western market.

It was Bienstock's job to ensure there were enough new songs to meet Hollywood's insatiable demands. In an interview with *Elvis Australia*, he admitted his assignment wasn't always easy: "To be honest, there was never enough time to do them properly. I was given the script and we always managed to find a title song. The scripts never indicated where a song should be and I had to mark up where songs were possible. I would then distribute 12 scripts to 12 teams and tell them to work on certain songs for certain situations. I would get four or five songs for each situation and I would take them to Elvis."

Roy Bennett, who would write around forty songs for Elvis with his partner Sid Tepper, said, "After the movie was in the can, Freddy Bienstock would call in the writers and tell them how they made out. Having the title song was the supreme achievement." He and his partner achieved this twice: for *G.I. Blues* and *Stay Away, Joe*.

As Elvis's movies became more frequent—three a year was pretty typical for the mid-1960s—this operation took on an industrial scale with around seventy writers, teams, or permutations of writers having their numbers sung onscreen. Despite drawing on so many writers, the King's songwriting factory could barely keep up. In 1965, when Elvis recorded nine numbers for *Paradise, Hawaiian Style*, six of them came from the prolific Bill Giant, Bernie Baum, and Florence Kaye. Not entirely uncoincidentally, that album was the first soundtrack to sell fewer than 250,000 copies.

Bienstock's task was complicated by the publishing arrangements he, the Aberbach brothers, and Colonel Parker put in place. They organized two companies, Elvis Presley Music and Gladys Music, which were 50/50 owned by Elvis and the Aberbachs. Whenever possible, these companies would publish Elvis's songs and sometimes, as with the four numbers in his first movie, *Love Me Tender*, demand the singer be given a songwriting credit. Typically, Bienstock suggested, writers were guaranteed that they would get the royalties for a million record sales—if they would give a third of their royalties to Elvis. In the early days of Tin Pan Alley, such a system had been known as a "cut-in." In the 1930s, Jean Aberbach had given himself songwriting credit when selling songs in Europe, so he could earn royalties in Italy. In the 1940s, the same system was used in America as a kind of "payola" to reward bandleaders who agreed to record particular tunes. Most songwriters did agree to an arrangement that became known in the trade as the "Elvis tax," although some, notably Leiber and Stoller and Pomus and Shuman, would eventually write little or nothing for Elvis.

As Dave Marsh points out in his Presley biography, this system proved problematic even when Elvis was at his commercial zenith: "Anyone with an exclusive arrangement with another publisher was automatically barred from having an original number recorded by Elvis Presley. Under these circumstances, it's little wonder that no established songwriter provided Elvis with material—although well-known R&B writers often would, since Presley was an open door to the otherwise restricted pop charts."

Bennett says most writers took the pragmatic view: "We all thought ⅔ of something was better than 1000% of nothing but we didn't like it. I always felt it was the Colonel's idea rather than Elvis's." When Presley was at his commercial peak—with *Blue Hawaii* selling two million in a year—that could be two-thirds of a lot of money, but the deal became even less attractive as songwriters became more commercially astute and Elvis's record sales plummeted. Don Robertson, who wrote "No More," said: "I thought 'God he could have great songs by Johnny Mercer and all kinds of tremendous writers'—except they were too established and too successful to give up a share of their royalties to get Elvis to record one of their songs."

Hill and Range's deal with Elvis was pretty lucrative: in 1965, the company generated $400,000 in profit from Elvis alone ($2.0 million in today's money). Yet by 1966, the conveyor belt of songs was creaking, and by 1970, the Aberbachs and Bienstock would actually be competing for the King's custom when Bienstock launched his own publishing business. The British Beat invasion had transformed music publishing. Jean Aberbach had seen the changes coming, but Hill and Range didn't seem to know how to react. Many of the best new contract writers—like Goffin and King, Barry Mann, and Cynthia Weil—worked with trendier rival publishers like Don Kirshner. With so many successful acts recording their own songs, Hill and Range's business model seemed in peril. At the very point that the Elvis movie machine's demand for new music cranked up, Aberbach and Bienstock were finding good songs harder to come by.

Elvis advertised his disgust, nicknaming Bienstock "Freddy the freeloader." On January 15, 1968, in Studio B Nashville, after cutting "Stay Away," the Tepper/Bennett reworking of "Greensleeves" for *Stay Away, Joe*, Elvis finally rebelled. As Jerry Schilling recalls in *Me and a Guy Named Elvis*, Presley shouted: "Doesn't anyone have some goddam material worth recording?" Jerry Reed, who was playing guitar on that session, jumped in with "U.S. Male." After the recording, Bienstock and Elvis's friend Lamar Fike, who was working for Hill and Range by then, pinned Reed to the wall. The singer/songwriter refused to give up any of his rights and was saved when Elvis strolled past, saying pointedly: "Great tune, man. We need more of that around here."

The system had started well enough, producing songs of the caliber of "Love Me Tender," "Got a Lot of Livin' to Do," "Jailhouse Rock," "Trouble," "King Creole," "New Orleans," "Can't Help Falling in Love," and "Return to Sender." Even in the 1960s, the soundtracks would contain the odd gem—from the desolate late-night ballad "I Need Somebody to Lean On" to the delicious, if ridiculously titled, "Long Legged Girl (with the Short Dress On)" and the rootsy country-blues classic "Clean Up Your Own Backyard." Yet there were too many nondescript tracks where you can almost hear the King longing for the song to end.

The experience of four of the most influential songwriting teams/songwriters sheds some insight into the inner dynamics of the Bienstock/Aberbach songmaking machine and how it shaped Elvis's music.

Leiber and Stoller, the Hipsters Who Spelled Trouble

Jerry Leiber (1933–2011) and Mike Stoller (1933–) are Elvis's most famous songwriters—and probably the hippest. They wrote some of his most famous movie songs: "Jailhouse Rock," "King Creole," "Trouble," "Bossa Nova Baby," "Little Egypt."

The *That's The Way It Is* album featured one song by "Mad Professor" Weisman. *Photofest*

They started out writing for blues stars like Charles Brown (Elvis memorably covered his most famous record, "Merry Christmas Baby") but are probably still best known for writing "Hound Dog," a song inspired by Big Mama Thornton that Elvis turned into a multimillion seller. They were unlikely collaborators for Elvis, and when Jean Aberbach first approached them they insisted they weren't interested. Then they met Presley and realized that he could, as Jorgensen put it in his *A Life in Music*, "discuss, in minute detail, the kinds of obscure R&B records Jerry and Mike thought only they'd ever heard." Impressed by the star's knowledge, passion, and work ethic, they agreed to help.

Even then, they had to be cajoled into action. Aberbach was so desperate for them to write songs for "Jailhouse Rock" that he turned up at their hotel room, pushed a couch in front of the door, laid down on it, and, just before he went so sleep, announced that no one was leaving until he had his songs.

Under such duress, the duo wrote "Baby I Don't Care," "Jailhouse Rock," and "Treat Me Nice."

Leiber and Stoller created some of the best songs for the movie *King Creole*, most notably "Trouble," an almost ridiculously macho Muddy Waters–style blues number they were staggered to see Elvis pull off. Yet they quickly concluded that writing for Elvis's movies wasn't the kind of artistic challenge they wanted and were perceptive enough to see the trap they—and their protégé, whom they described later as a "kind of idiot savant"—might soon fall into.

There was always a tension between their shtick and Elvis's. They loved ironic playlets like "Love Potion No. 9," the Clovers' most famous number. Their "Jailhouse Rock" lyrics were full of irony, but most listeners didn't notice the risqué references or the humor because they were distracted by the visceral thrills of Elvis's howling vocal and D. J. Fontana's relentless drumming. Presley had done something very similar with "Love Me," using his heart and craft to turn their parody of a lovestruck country song into a genuinely moving ballad. They also didn't understand their role at the King's court, and that meant, as far as Parker was concerned, they were looking for trouble.

Although Bienstock insisted that Leiber and Stoller stopped writing for the movies because they didn't want to leave New York for California, the duo actually quit out of frustration and boredom, and the famous incident with Aberbach that had underlined the limits of their influence with Elvis.

The growing friendship between Leiber and Elvis alarmed Parker. His fear that the duo might fill in his boy's head with inappropriate ideas was realized when they suggested to Jean Aberbach that Elvis star in a movie of Nelson Algren's cult novel *Walk on the Wild Side*, which their friend Elia Kazan would be happy to direct. Aberbach consulted Parker and, ten minutes later, as Stoller recalled, "Jean summoned us in. 'Boys, the Colonel sez if you ever dare try to interfere with ze career of Elvis Presley, you vil never work again in Caleefornia, New York, London, or anywhere.' After that we completely lost interest."

Their songs "Dogface" and "Tulsa's Blues," which may not have fitted the new clean-cut Elvis, didn't make it into *G.I. Blues*. Their numbers would still feature occasionally—Presley sang "Bossa Nova Baby" in *Fun in Acapulco* and "Little Egypt" in *Roustabout*—but after *King Creole* they never wrote another new song for an Elvis movie.

There would be good movie songs after they left—many of them ballads—but without their wit, edge, and energy, Elvis's movie music would seldom have as much bite. Presley rarely rocked as hard after their departure, and the rock-and-roll numbers that Bienstock found for his later movies often had a synthetic feel.

Elvis was doubly unlucky because Doc Pomus (1925–1991) and Mort Shuman (1936–1991), who could have filled the void left by Leiber and Stoller, were distracted by their own troubles. Bienstock said, "We expected them to bring us songs every week," and the duo did write such Elvis classics as "Surrender," "His Latest Flame," "Little Sister," and "Viva Las Vegas." But after Leiber's attempted interference, Parker helped make sure that Pomus never met the man he wrote many of his greatest songs for. The songwriting partnership broke up in 1965 when Mort quit to write for Johnny Hallyday, aka the French Elvis, and Pomus fell so badly he spent the rest of his life in a wheelchair. Their last Elvis movie song, the title track for *Double Trouble*, was a nondescript effort.

The withdrawal of such heavy hitters meant there was much more scope for the likes of Giant, Baum, and Kaye; Sid Tepper and Roy Bennett; Joy Byers; Dolores Fuller; Don Robertson, Sid Wayne; and Ben Weisman and Fred Wise. Sometimes the likes of Otis Blackwell; Peretti, Creatore, and Weiss; Batchelor and Roberts; or Aaron Schroeder would supply a song. Yet by 1965, the King's songwriting factory became increasingly reliant on a core group: Byers; Fuller; Giant, Baum and Kaye; Starr; Tepper and Bennett; Wayne and Weisman. Only for his last few movies did new writers like Mac Davis and Billy Strange, and Guy Fletcher and Doug Flett, widen the talent pool.

Giant, Baum, and Kaye: A Brill Trio

Florence Kaye (1919–2006) got a taste for showbiz when she entertained the troops with the United Service Organization and had her own radio show in the 1940s. Returning to her native New York, she met Bernie Baum (1929–1993) outside the Brill Building and agreed to collaborate. Kaye must have impressed Baum, who had already had a U.S. number 1 in 1949 as the co-author of Teresa Brewer's "Music, Music, Music" and was known as "the Golden Boy of the Brill Building."

They wrote some good songs (notably the doo-wop ballad "Heaven Knows Why" for the Four Sensations) but didn't enjoy great commercial success. In 1956 they teamed up with Bill Giant (1930–1987), who is still probably best known for co-writing the delightful Pat Boone novelty "Speedy Gonzalez." (One of Giant's collaborators on that smash was David Hess, who wrote "Come Along," "I Got Stung," and "Sand Castles" for Elvis.)

Working in the Brill Building, Giant, Baum, and Kaye wrote their first song for Elvis in 1961 but must have been disappointed when Elvis decided that "Sound Advice" was so poor it shouldn't feature on the *Follow That Dream* EP. (RCA sneaked it out on the 1965 compilation *Elvis for Everyone*.) But they persevered and ended up writing over thirty songs for the movies with Giant, a frustrated pop star, singing on the demos. Their greatest Elvis movie song was probably "Night Life." Their most painful contribution to the Elvis canon? A tossup between the Hawaiian novelty number "Queenie Wahine's Papaya" and "Beach Shack," in which Elvis invites girls to see his etchings with no irony intended.

Elvis was one of the trio's biggest customers, but he wasn't necessarily getting their best material. In 1965, as Presley recorded six of their tracks for *Paradise, Hawaiian Style*, Giant, Baum, and Kaye were writing songs like "Don't Wait Up for Me, Mother" for Joanne Engel, "Unsatisfied" for Lou Johnson (Edwin Starr's favorite northern soul record), and "A Time to Love, a Time to Cry" (recorded by Marilyn Maye, but better known in Johnson's cover). All of these records had the kind of soul, energy, and charisma that Elvis brought to his best records. But they were hard to fit into a movie plot, especially if your cue you were provided was to write something inspired by Queenie Wahine's papaya.

So Giant, Baum, and Kaye did their best for Elvis—while saving their best songs for other artists and getting involved with production on Johnny Bienstock's Big Top label. From their point of view, it made perfect business sense. Yet if you're an Elvis fan, it's hard not to listen to Johnson's "Unsatisfied," envisage the King on that Radio Recorders stage in Hollywood trying to work miracles with "House of Sand," and weep for what might have been. To get a glimpse of this alternate universe, just play "The Power of Love" from Elvis's Memphis sessions, a saucy number delivered with passion and wit. That was written by Giant, Baum, and Kaye and fortunately never made it into a movie. As performed by Elvis at his most committed, it has the same kind of power and soul as Johnson's "Unsatisfied."

Their last Elvis movie song was a strange gem: the quirky "Edge of Reality," which almost captures the essence of *Live a Little, Love a Little* better than the script does. Giant, Baum, and Kaye would bow out from the King's world with the impassioned, slightly overdone ballad "The Sound of Your Cry."

Tepper and Bennett: The Good, the Bad, and the Lovely

In 1957, Tepper (1918–) and Bennett (1918–) wrote "Lonesome Cowboy," their first Elvis movie song, for *Loving You*. Ten years later, Elvis recorded his last Tepper/Bennett track, the children's lullaby "Five Sleepy Heads," for *Speedway* (although it was cut from the film). To understand how varied—and variable—the duo's material for Elvis was, just watch him singing "New Orleans" and "Confidence." It's difficult enough to believe the same man is performing both songs. It's even more astonishing to think that the duo who encouraged Elvis to howl and stutter his way through that masterpiece in *King Creole* also asked him to sing, "With a C, and an O, and an N, and an F and an I and an D and an –ence," for *Clambake*.

Raised in Brooklyn, where they met, Tepper and Bennett were yet another Brill Building team. They wrote over three hundred songs between 1945 and 1970. Their first big hit was Vaughn Monroe's "Red Roses for a Blue Lady," which reached number 4 on the Billboard charts in 1948, and they wrote "Naughty Lady in Shady Lane" for Elvis's idol Dean Martin. In 1961, they penned "The Young Ones," the biggest hit for Cliff Richard, a singer who had originally been billed as the "British Elvis" and would, like the King, make a string of movies that left critics distinctly underwhelmed.

Tepper would have preferred to write for Sinatra, but Ol' Blue Eyes was, the songwriter observed, "a professional stickler," and Elvis could sing a much greater range of material. A frustrated vocalist, Tepper sang on the demos. He made a point not to sound like he was imitating Elvis. He was impressed by

Presley's ability: "He'd listen to the demos once or twice and sing it like he'd sung it his whole life." Like Pomus, neither Tepper nor Bennett ever met Elvis or visited his sets.

Tepper and Bennett wrote five songs for Elvis's biggest-selling album, *Blue Hawaii*—the most entertaining being "Beach Boy Blues"—but none were released as singles. As prolific as the duo were, they never wrote a massive hit for Elvis, though "Puppet on a String," the best ballad from *Girl Happy*, peaked at number 14 on Billboard's Hot 100. Their charming fairground number "It's a Wonderful World" (from *Roustabout*) was considered for an Oscar nomination.

With the exception of "New Orleans," their strongest numbers were ballads, with "Angel," "All That I Am" (covered by Tony Bennett), "Stay Away," and "A House That Has Everything" among the best. They brought rare humor to "The Lady Loves Me," the Elvis duet with Ann-Margret, although their lyrics aren't as sophisticated as the performances. Yet many of their songs sound like album fillers. Bennett has admitted that he and his partner once wrote five Elvis songs in one afternoon. Mind you, if you have to set your minds to creating music that honored Western Union, gardeners' daughters, and shrimp, you probably need to work at that kind of speed. And sometimes—notably on the entertaining "Fort Lauderdale Chamber of Commerce"—they surpassed their brief.

Yet when you hear "Confidence," a pale imitation of "High Hopes" that featured in *Clambake*, it's hard not to wish that Elvis, like Sinatra, had been more of a stickler. Bennett has defended the songs, saying: "Of course there were songs of varying quality but it should be recognized that these songs were written for specific spots in the movies and the topics therefore were limited to particular situations and locales." That is all true but still doesn't quite excuse some of their bottom-of-the-barrel material.

In 1970, the year Elvis's last feature film was released, Tepper had a heart attack and gave up songwriting, disillusioned with the music industry, feeling that the new songs weren't as meaningful as they had been. Coming from the man who was half responsible for "Song of the Shrimp," this may sound perverse, but that was how he saw it. With his partner out of action, Bennett effectively left the music business too.

Ben Weisman: The Mad Professor

Ben Weisman (1921–2007) wrote more songs for Elvis—fifty-seven, count 'em!—than anyone else, yet only hardcore fans have heard of him or his songs. The irony is that Weisman is more famous today for "The Night Has a Thousand Eyes," a hit he wrote for Bobby Vee, than for any number the King sang.

Raised in Brooklyn, Weisman was a musical prodigy who studied under the classical pianist Grace Castagnetta and spent World War II as a music director for the U.S. Army Air Force. After the war, he headed to New York, where he played the piano, teamed up with various songwriters in Tin Pan Alley, and was spotted by Jean Aberbach. In 1955, Weisman's first big hit, "Let Me Go Lover,"

The songwriting team of Leiber & Stoller. From left; Mike Stoller, Elvis, and Jerry Leiber at MGM Studios during the recording of "Jailhouse Rock" in the Spring of 1957. Leiber and Stoller's rapport with Elvis was so good Parker felt obliged to end it.

made the Top 100 for four different artists, including Patti Page, Gladys Presley's favorite singer. By then, Aberbach was already schooling his protégé to broaden his repertoire. During one famous argument, when Weisman had insisted he couldn't write country songs, the publisher waved a check in the air and said: "Go out and buy the top ten country albums now!" The songwriter got the point.

Weisman's plaintive ballad "First in Line" featured on Presley's second album. For *Loving You* and *Jailhouse Rock*, he successfully pitched "Got a Lot of Livin' to Do" and "Don't Leave Me Now." He flew to Hollywood in 1957 to see Elvis record the *Loving You* soundtrack. As Weisman recalled later, Presley got so carried away singing "Got a Lot of Livin' to Do," he forgot to sing into the mic. Though overwhelmed by the experience, the writer admitted, "In my wildest dreams I never imagined the impact he would make on the world." Nor did he imagine that he would write more songs for this phenomenon than anyone else.

Weisman took a different approach to writing for Elvis: "It was like I was walking in his musical shoes." Knowing that Presley's talent spanned genres, he strove to infuse the songs with country, pop, rock, and blues. He tailored his demos to the singer, using a soundalike, similar vocal backing, and the same kind of rhythm section. So many of his songs were chosen that Elvis grew accustomed to Weisman's presence in the studio and, amused by the writer's studious demeanour, nicknamed him "the mad professor." In the early 1960s, Weisman took Aberbach's advice and moved to California to get closer to the action. His proximity came in handy during the filming of *It Happened at the World's Fair*, when he was assigned to write the finale, "Happy Ending," primarily because he was the only writer in the vicinity. Weisman was so dedicated he didn't even object when the singer could barely stop laughing long enough to record "A Dog's Life."

Weisman had quite a few collaborators, most notably Dolores Fuller ("Rock-a-hula Baby"), Buddy Kaye ("Change of Habit"), Schroeder ("Got a Lot of Livin' to Do"), Sid Wayne ("Happy Ending"), and Fred Wise ("Pocketful of Rainbows"). Calling on such a variety of partners, he was a versatile songwriter who refused to be daunted by the subject matter. He had worked wonders with the unusual opener "Crawfish" for *King Creole*, but his transformational touch deserted him with "A Dog's Life" in *Paradise, Hawaiian Style* and "Dominic," the notorious song about a bull, chosen for *Stay Away, Joe* without Elvis even being consulted.

While some songwriters expressed frustration with their lot, or became defensive about the quality of their work, Weisman's enthusiasm never dimmed. He was rewarded with seven title songs for the movies (the most notable being "Follow That Dream" and "Fun in Acapulco"). His strike rate was remarkable: twenty-four of the King's movies featured a Weisman number. He even had a hand in the ballad "Twenty Days and Twenty Nights" that appears on the *That's the Way It Is* album (though it isn't used in the movie). His biggest seller for Elvis was "Wooden Heart," although the cast of songwriters on that number included Fred Wise, Kay Twomey, and Bert Kaempfert. Yet for many fans the best song Weisman ever wrote for Elvis is the quiet gospel number "We Call on Him."

Why Was Elvis Caught in a Trap?

Like Giant, Baum, and Kaye; Pomus and Shuman; and even Weisman, some of the King's other songwriters made the most of their freedom when they weren't restricted to stock situations or locales. Sid Wayne, who had collaborated with Weisman on twenty movie songs, returned to New York as Elvis's film career tapered off and won a Grammy for "It's Impossible" (which Elvis later sang in concert). Buddy Kaye, who co-wrote three of the songs for *Change of Habit* with Weisman, penned "Little by Little" for Dusty Springfield. Brill Building stalwart Sherman Edwards, who wrote "Home Is Where the Heart Is" with Hal David, was so disgusted by the "Elvis tax" that he gave up rock and pop to write the classic musical *1776*.

As the movies came and went, the only person who remained locked into this system was Elvis. The filming of movies—and recording of movie songs—dominated his schedule. Though the musical comedies spawned fewer bigger hits—"Puppet on a String," released in October 1965, was the last movie single to grace the Billboard Top 20—the soundtrack albums outsold studio albums until 1968, when *Speedway*'s shocking sales made everyone realize things had to change.

Yet what few can understand—and many can't forgive—is why Elvis didn't rebel over the songs. Feeling obligated because you had signed a contract was one thing, but nowhere in those contracts did it say he would be forced to sing about rhumbas in sports cars. Marsh suggests: "If he was bold enough to imagine that he could convert any trashy song into something palatable, he was also humble enough to suspect he might deserve nothing better."

There are times when you can hear him trying to transcend the material. His perfect, teasing vocal on "One Boy, Two Little Girls" gives the ballad a resonance that neither the lyric nor the situation merit. Yet on many of the later movie songs, he would sound disenchanted ("The Love Machine"), embarrassed ("Dominic"), or like a man impersonating himself ("I'll Be Back").

It is possible, as Marsh hints, that his fear of poverty persuaded him to toe the line. Certainly the fear that his success could crumble overnight came to haunt him as early as 1958. Elvis's friend Marty Lacker says Parker explicitly warned the singer that if he didn't do what the studios want, "you'll ruin your career and go back to being a poor kid." He must also, as Harbinson suggested in his illustrated biography, have experienced a colossal loss of confidence by the mid-1960s. While the acts he inspired were dominating the charts and setting trends, he was appearing in a succession of musical comedies that constituted, in Harbinson's words, an oblique form of retirement.

The cruel paradox here is that a man who had come to symbolize freedom—Bob Dylan famously remarked "The first time I heard Elvis, it was like busting out of jail"—had been subjugated to such an extent that he was working for the man as surely as any shop-floor worker. The big difference being that he was much better paid. His predicament may ultimately be put down to his personality. Director Gene Nelson said he always felt Elvis had more confidence as musician than as a human being.

Yet in retrospect, it is clear that some kind of rebellion had been brewing in Elvis since May 1966, when he had rediscovered his joy for music in recording "How Great Thou Art." In September 1967, he returned to the studio to record some pertinent music: "Guitar Man," "Big Boss Man," "Hi-Heel Sneakers," and "You Don't Know Me." He followed that, in January 1968, with the session where, in desperation, he cried out for new material and cut "U.S. Male."

Nobody will ever know how far Presley would have pushed things, because he didn't have to. With sales falling and no studios interested in new movie contracts with Elvis, Parker was forced to act. The return to live performance—and the artistic renewal represented by the TV special and the 1969 Memphis sessions—freed him to be himself again. Disputes over publishing rights would still bedevil him, but he would never have to sing another song about papayas, shrimps, and racing cars.

48

Fifty Million Reasons Why the King Can't Stop Singing

Who Needs Money? Presley and Parker Do

In 1971, music and TV producer Jack Good called the King's movies a "criminal waste of talent." Yet even he had to admit that, commercially, the run had been phenomenally successful. Certainly until 1965 the movies lived up to Colonel Parker's dictum that, as Harbinson put in his biography, "If Elvis stops singing, the cash tills stop ringing and there ain't another thing to discuss."

For Parker and Presley, the commercial arguments for making movies were overwhelming. They could earn up to a million dollars from each film—and half of the profits. The income from one movie was much greater than their annual royalties from RCA. By recording the soundtracks, they generated recording royalties and publishing revenues because they owned the songs and fulfilled their contractual obligations to RCA. There was a catch here, which Elvis finally cottoned to: this model was most effective when he recorded ten or twelve songs for a movie. In other words, if he tried to fulfill his ambition to be the next James Dean, everyone—himself included—stood to lose money. There was always the chance that a breakthrough performance in a dramatic picture could generate more box-office revenue, but that would have seemed, to Parker, an unacceptable risk when you were guaranteed a million bucks, 50 percent of the profits, and all the other fringe benefits.

The sad truth is that, as bad as some of the movie soundtracks were, the promotional push they generated meant that, for most of his career, they outsold Elvis's studio albums. Either deliberately or through sheer stubbornness, Parker made it even harder for the studio albums to compete by insisting that these releases omit such multimillion sellers as "It's Now or Never" or "Are You Lonesome Tonight?" What other major recording artist would have squandered such massive promotional opportunities? (Later, Parker would give the same trick a different spin when he put "Burning Love," Elvis's last U.S. chart topper, on a budget compilation with songs from his movies, a bizarre decision that seemed to belittle the star, the song, and the fans.) So *Elvis Is Back!* sold just over

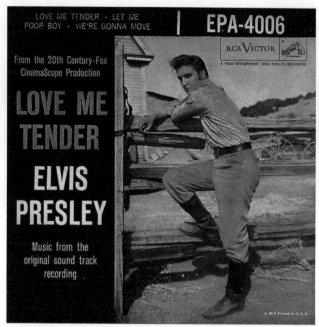

Elvis's movie debut spawned a multi-million selling single, "Love Me Tender."

200,000 copies, less than the *Paradise, Hawaiian Style* soundtrack, and *From Elvis in Memphis*, the most creatively satisfying album of his career, sold 100,000 copies less than the *Girls! Girls! Girls!* soundtrack.

The movies spawned eight singles that sold a million or more ("Love Me Tender," "Teddy Bear," "Jailhouse Rock," "Hard Headed Woman," "Wooden Heart," "Can't Help Falling in Love," "Return to Sender," and, counting the Junkie XL remix, "A Little Less Conversation") and two million-selling Extended Play records (*King Creole, Jailhouse Rock*). Two of the singles—"Love Me Tender" and "Jailhouse Rock"—sold over two million copies and were among his biggest sellers of all time.

The films also gave Elvis the most commercially successful album of his lifetime, *Blue Hawaii*, which sold two million in its first year and was listed by *Billboard* as the second-biggest-selling album of the 1960s behind *West Side Story*. No movie soundtrack quite matched that success, but *G.I. Blues* (700,000), *Girls! Girls! Girls!* (600,000), *That's the Way It Is* (500,000), *Roustabout* (450,000), and *Girl Happy* (400,000) were strong sellers. A slew of soundtracks—*Fun in Acapulco, Harum Scarum, It Happened at the World's Fair, Kissin' Cousins*, and *Spinout*—all sold around 300,000. *Frankie and Johnny* sold 250,000, 25,000 more than *Paradise, Hawaiian Style*, and 50,000 more than either *Double Trouble* or *Clambake*. Rock bottom was reached when *Speedway*, the last soundtrack album, sold 100,000 copies or less. If RCA had released a soundtrack album for his biggest box-office smash, *Viva Las Vegas*—instead of an EP that sold 150,000 copies—they might have had a bigger hit than *G.I. Blues*. The failure to do so seems a colossal misjudgment by the label and Elvis's manager. By 1964, Parker's Midas touch was not quite as sure as it had been, but he had hitherto always been able to spot when his golden goose (Elvis) had laid a golden egg.

Sales figures for Elvis's records are largely driven by the U.S. market. Yet as separate research by Alan Hanson and Nick Keene has suggested, Elvis's movies sold records in significant, but hard to quantify, numbers across the world. "Bossa Nova Baby," for example, went to number 1 in Belgium, while "No More" was a number 1 hit in Italy. Hardly the kind of chart-topping action the Colonel or RCA had in mind, but it does suggest that the King's global sales success may have been underestimated. To take a nonmovie example, Keene's research suggests that Presley's 1970 single "The Wonder of You" sold 995,000 copies in the United States and 2,200,000 in the rest of the world. Analyzing the performance of several singles, Keene concluded that up to 70 percent of their sales derived from outside the United States. Hanson's research also suggests that fans in other countries were slower to reject Elvis as the quality of product began to drop. For example, between 1963 and 1965 in Australia, Elvis's soundtrack singles "Bossa Nova Baby," "Viva Las Vegas," and "Do the Clam" all reached number 4, while "Kissin' Cousins," "(Such an) Easy Question," and "I'm Yours" made the top 10. In other words, the movies were probably significantly more lucrative for Elvis and his manager than anybody probably realized. That may partly explain why Parker, especially, was so keen to stick to this strategy even when, by 1966, it was proving increasingly ineffectual.

49

That Curious Baritone

And Why Did They Speed His Voice Up in *Girl Happy?*

I f you spend much time on an Elvis fan forum, you will inevitably stumble across a heated debate about the sound of Elvis's voice in *Girl Happy*. There is no doubt that Elvis's voice was speeded up on the title track, but the argument still rages about whether the same treatment was applied to any other tracks on the album and indeed why anybody would want to do such a thing. The most common explanation is that Elvis's voice was speeded up to make him sound higher, younger, and hipper, able to slug it out in the pop charts with the Beatles. The only flaw in this theory is, as a fan called Kiwi Alan asked on the For Elvis CD Collectors Forum, how would making Elvis sound like Mickey Mouse beat the Fab Four?

Such fiddling was far from unusual. In his book, Schilling recalls a drive down to the Mississippi in the mid-1960s when Presley, hearing his new single come on the radio, suddenly turned around and drove back to Graceland at a hundred miles per hour, disappearing for two days. When he resurfaced, he asked Schilling to buy the new single. The two of them sat in Graceland's famous TV room and compared the commercial release to Elvis's acetate. As Schilling tells it: "Even a non-musician like me could tell the difference—there was a marked drop in punch and volume. His voice was forward in the mix and the band and the background vocals had just about disappeared. To put it bluntly, the song had lost its balls."

Elvis historians would love to know exactly which single had been so emasculated, but Schilling can't remember, concluding, "Sadly, the reason my memory's foggy about this single, is that the scene happened more than once." Presley is known to have complained to RCA about the sound on "Are You Lonesome Tonight?" and "Guitar Man," but he may well have been dissatisfied with the mix on many other records.

The rationale, expressed by Parker, was that fans were more likely to buy an Elvis single if they could hear Elvis on it. This was a gross oversimplification, but there was some crude commercial logic to it. And sometimes, he had a point. As good as it is, Elvis's cover of *Hawaiian Wedding Song* would be far more effective if the Jordanaires had been politely shown the studio door.

When Elvis turned up at MGM's Radio Recorders studio in Hollywood in June 1964, he had had only had one million-selling single, "Return to Sender," in the last two and a half years. His soundtrack albums were selling less than 500,000 copies each, and it was already clear that the Beatles, who had had a dozen singles on the Hot 100 in April 1964, were the biggest threat to his crown since 1956. In this context, the King's instincts no longer seemed infallible to RCA or Parker. The label didn't have the clout to demand Hill and Range find better material—although the Colonel did so belatedly before *Spinout* started shooting in 1966—so it was easier to tinker with the sound of the King's music.

Elvis may inadvertently have instigated the tinkering on *Girl Happy*. He was embarrassed enough by the title track to beg the movie's producer Joe Pasternak not to bring his vocals up in the mix. It was a curious request, because when the backing vocalists shut up, there's only Elvis and a pretty thin instrumental backdrop. Instead, somebody—and we'll probably never know who—decided to speed up the master tape by 8 percent. Elvis's vocal isn't quite Mickey Mouse— though it is heading that way—but it does sound very soggy. The title track is not the best of an underwhelming set of songs, but it did sound better when released at its natural speed on the *Follow That Dream* label. What makes all this jiggery pokery seem really pointless is that "Girl Happy" wasn't even released as a single.

After recording the *Girl Happy* album, Elvis would not return to the recording studio for eight months. RCA would never again speed up an Elvis song by 8 percent, but the quality of production on the soundtrack albums didn't necessarily improve. McCoy has a simple explanation for the *Harum Scarum* soundtrack's peculiar sound: "They were supposed to add the echo track later. They forgot." Quite a few movie soundtracks sound like that. And on some later tracks—notably "City by Night" in *Double Trouble*—you can hear evidence of a ham-fisted attempt to bring Presley's vocal to the fore. Luckily, by 1968 Elvis was back in the studio to record some proper songs. Onscreen, Elvis would sometimes still sing in what Jack Good called "that curious baritone," but at least he would never again sound like Mickey Mouse on record.

50

Nice Strategy

Shame about the Songs

E ight months after Elvis's death, the soundtrack album to the 1950s musical *Grease* was released. After selling 18 million copies very quickly, it would eventually become the sixth-best-selling movie soundtrack album of all time, shifting around 28 million units. The movie didn't do too bad either, becoming the most successful movie musical of all time with a worldwide gross of $394 million.

Grease was cleverly constructed to appeal both to those who could remember the 1950s and to those who couldn't. Presley's ghost hung over the story—at one point, during "Look at Me, I'm Sandra Dee," Elvis is warned to keep his pelvis at a safe distance—and it is intriguing to wonder what Colonel Parker made of its success. Gross receipts, millions of units shifted—these were the kind of metrics that Elvis's Svengali intuitively understood.

This was exactly the kind of cross-promotional pay dirt he had envisaged when he first took his client to Hollywood. They'd never achieved success of that magnitude. *Blue Hawaii* had come close—spawning an album that topped the U.S. charts for twenty weeks, producing a million-selling single, and raking in $38 million at the box office (at today's prices). You couldn't really compare *Grease* to *Blue Hawaii*, but you could see the Warren Casey/Jim Jacob musical's blockbuster success as a vindication of Parker's hard-nosed commercial strategy.

The system Parker created to market Elvis in Hollywood harked back to the 1930s—and forward to the 1970s and the emergence of a strategy some industry analysts call the "total entertainment complex."

In the 1930s, the incredible promotional power of the movies—and the popularity of morale-boosting musicals during the Great Depression—had all but turned Tin Pan Alley into a subcontractor that spent most of its time churning out songs for its musicals. Hollywood didn't just influence American popular music—it defined it. That cozy arrangement collapsed in the 1940s and 1950s when radio surpassed the movies as a medium for selling songs.

Presley's music was revolutionary, yet the tactics Parker used to sell it to the masses were anything but. Taking a leaf out of Hollywood's old playbook, he turned that part of Tin Pan Alley owned by the Aberbachs into his own production house (while keeping a share of the royalties), used the movies to showcase the songs, and persuaded RCA to release them as albums and singles. There was nothing wrong with the strategy—indeed, if you were Parker or Presley it worked beautifully, guaranteeing income from the publishers, studios, and RCA—but after 1961 the execution began to go awry. There was little point in Hill and Range publishing songs that nobody but Elvis wanted to sing, showcased in movies that a rapidly diminishing audience wanted to see, and released on records that only completists and diehards wanted to buy.

Robert Stigwood, who produced *Grease*, would learn the same painful lesson. In 1978, the same year John Travolta and Olivia

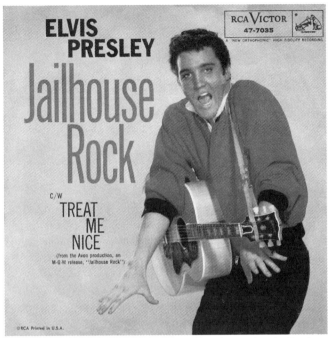

Parker's strategy to sell Elvis's movies and music was ahead of its time.

Newton were selling millions of records, Stigwood presided over the $18 million extravaganza that was *Sgt. Pepper's Lonely Hearts Club Band*. Hailed by one critic as having "a dangerous resemblance to wallpaper," this Beatles musical with no Beatles in it took just $11.4 million at the U.S. box office. If *Grease* had been Stigwood's *Blue Hawaii* (only far, far bigger), *Sgt. Pepper* was his *Easy Come, Easy Go* (only far more expensive).

Yet Parker and Stigwood had proved a point. Today, the commercial synergy between movies and music is exploited ruthlessly. The soundtrack to Whitney Houston's movie *The Bodyguard* sold 42 million copies, an all-time record. The success of the *Titanic* soundtrack is even more remarkable. It does feature Celine Dion's "My Heart Will Go On," but this album of mainly orchestral music has shifted 30 million copies.

In his way, Parker was behind the times—and ahead of them. The entertainment industry would learn from his successes and mistakes. Today, entertainment empires like Sony own their own music publishers, movie studios, and record labels. Parker wouldn't have liked that. You can't play off one against the other if the other doesn't exist.

51

"Could I Fall in Love?"

The Best of the Movie Ballads

C ontractually obliged to get the girl so the movies could fade out with the expected embrace, Elvis ended up singing more than his fair share of ballads in his thirty-one feature films. Once Leiber and Stoller had left the scene after *King Creole*, songsmiths like Tepper and Bennett; Giant, Baum, and Kaye; Don Robertson; and Wise and Weisman were instinctively more at ease with love songs than hard rock. So no matter how dire things got onscreen, most Elvis movies—*Easy Come, Easy Go* being the dismal exception—featured at least one listenable ballad. The aching "So Close Yet So Far" briefly redeems even the outlandish *Harum Scarum*. As the soundtracks came thick and fast, these were the songs that intrigued him. They did at least allow him to give the music the emotional resonance that he couldn't invest in many of the uptempo songs or the novelty numbers.

"Can't Help Falling in Love," *Blue Hawaii*

Astonishingly, this haunting variation on the eighteenth-century French melody "Plaisir d'Amour" almost did not make it into *Blue Hawaii*. Luckily, Hugo Peretti, Luigi Creatore, and George Weiss's intimate ballad, one of the best numbers to come out of Hill and Range, was spotted by Elvis, who suggested it might be good for the movie. He was so smitten with the song he completed twenty-nine takes at Radio Recorders Hollywood studio until he was satisfied. Take 13, where you can hear how hard Elvis is trying to do justice to the lyric, is a beauty.

In the movie, he sings the first lines accompanied only by Dudley Brooks's celeste, giving the song a genuinely Polynesian feel. In the studio, the celeste was used for accenting, with Alvino Rey's steel guitar weighing in and the piano arpeggios coming to the fore. Colonel Parker's continual complaints about the mix on Elvis records are pertinent here as, at times, the Jordanaires sound like they're vying with Elvis rather than backing him. Yet this can't detract from Presley's subtle, beautiful phrasing. This may be light-years away from the kind of music Elvis made at Sun, but the mysterious yearning that intrigued Sam Phillips is still evident in his voice.

The beauty of the original is often overshadowed by the speeded-up, tongue-in-cheek renditions with which he closed his concerts. The line "Some things are meant to be" often seemed to particularly amuse him, but he usually refocused on the song and came back for a barnstorming finale. In concert on March 30, 1977, less than five months before his death, he forgot the words and quipped: "Wise men know, when it's time to go . . . "

"I Need Somebody to Lean On," *Viva Las Vegas*

Elvis never sounded as sophisticated on record as on this wistful Doc Pomus/ Mort Shuman ballad. There are no mannerisms or melodramatics on this gentle slice of Sinatra-style late-night melancholy, just Elvis at his most authentic, singing with what Guralnick called "a quiet, earnest sincerity that belies the stagy showiness of the rest of the film."

In the movie, the song starts as an interior monologue, as he drifts through a casino that is about to close up for the night. The mood and the milieu are reminiscent of the "Is That All There Is?" scene in Martin Scorsese's *After Hours*. When the King does start singing onscreen, you get a glimpse, as Guralnick said, of the "things he felt and the movies he could have made."

"I Just Can't Help Believin'," *Elvis: That's The Way It Is*

The artistic perfection of Presley's definitive Vegas ballad is still a joy to listen to. The interaction with his backing singers is worth the price of admission.

"In My Way," *Wild in the Country*

One of the most beautiful ballads Elvis ever recorded. It's just the King himself and a guitar, singing with a simplicity that recalls "My Happiness," the recording he made at Sun in the summer of 1953 to impress his mother. Short yet magnificent, this tender yet cynical number is sung so effectively by Elvis—after he had heeded a producer's advice not to project too much—that when he sings, "Smile when you kiss me, for tomorrow you will cry," he sounds as if he's saying something profound about the human condition.

"Love Me Tender," *Love Me Tender*

Elvis was the most famous singer on the planet when he recorded this iconic ballad based on the folk air "Aura Lee," which had been sung brilliantly by the troubled actress Frances Farmer in the drama *Come and Get It* (1936). Yet at twenty-one, and already on his way to being a multimillionaire, Presley sings it with the naive, romantic manner of a lovestruck boy. Even the fact that you could hear him breathing somehow only added to the power of the performance.

This wasn't smooth balladry, but it was authentic and sweet, almost as if he had deliberately set out to disarm those self-appointed panjandrums who regarded him as a threat to the very fabric of society.

He returned to the song twelve years later in the NBC studio in Burbank for his TV special. That performance starts off with a gag, "You have made my life a wreck—complete," but the parody soon gives way to something much more powerful. Elvis's richer, deeper voice gives the number such emotional depth that the performance transcends the plain but slightly trite lyrics to create something compelling, mysterious, and moving.

"Almost," *The Trouble with Girls*

Elvis looks more at ease tootling on the piano in this number at the end of *The Trouble with Girls* than he did in many other movies where he was forced, for reasons no one has been able to fathom, to strum miniature toy guitars. This delightfully low-key Buddy Kaye/Ben Weisman ballad has a gentle swing to it, and Elvis sounds at his most nostalgic as he bemoans what could have been. Performance and song would be far better known if it had appeared in a more commercially successful movie and if it hadn't been overshadowed, musically, by Elvis's return to his roots in Memphis in 1969. The undubbed version—released on the *Live Little* double soundtrack CD—is even better because Presley's effortless, elegant regret is even clearer.

"Young and Beautiful," *Jailhouse Rock*

Although the title song is the standout number in Elvis's third movie, the track that touched millions of his female fans was "Young and Beautiful," a fine Abner Silver/Aaron Schroeder ballad made memorable by the swinging arrangement (especially Dudley Brooks's fine piano work) and Elvis's touching vocal. When he asks the girl to fill his lonely arms, he sounds genuinely bereft. His plea for her to take his heart is passionate, desperate, and sincere. He rehearsed it for *Elvis on Tour*, performing it with enough affection you almost wish he had performed it onstage, yet he probably felt, rightly, that this is a young man's ballad.

"Wild in the Country," *Wild in the Country*

The Peretti/Creatore/Weiss team, which created "Can't Help Falling in Love," also penned this heartfelt title track for Elvis's seventh movie. After various arrangements and experiments—some of his notes recalled the falsetto used in his cover of "Blue Moon at Sun"—Elvis opts for a simple, understated vocal that makes this genuinely haunting. In the UK, the song was preferred to the bluesy "I Feel So Bad" as the A side of the single and reached number 4 in the charts. So delicately arranged and sung, this ballad is almost too efficient for its own good.

"As Long as I Have You," *King Creole*

A timeless ballad, artfully contrived by Wise and Weisman to sound as if Carolyn Jones's sluttish nightclub singer could have performed it and still provide a suitable finale for *King Creole*. Elvis took to the song instantly, and the lyrics, especially the plea to focus on the future and forget the past, fit his near recon-ciliation with the virginal Dolores Hart. The King's drawl makes lines like "Let the stars fade and fall" sound like the poetry of the street. In his appreciation of *King Creole*, critic Gerald Peary says the song and performance have the potent irony of Marlene Dietrich singing "Falling in Love Again."

"Doin' the Best I Can," *G.I. Blues*

The classiest song in *G.I. Blues*, Pomus and Shuman's delicate doo-wop is often overlooked—even in the movie, a fight abruptly curtails the song. This is a shame because, as Jorgensen notes, it is the only song on the soundtrack that would have made the cut at a regular RCA session. Elvis is at his sweet, silky best on this idiosyncratic ballad, trying so hard to please, much like the lover in the song. You can hear the influence of Dean Martin and the Ink Spots, but it's hard to imagine anyone doing this better than Elvis.

"They Remind Me Too Much of You," *It Happened at the World's Fair*

The best song in Elvis's twelfth movie almost didn't make it because the melody was deemed too close to "Chapel in the Moonlight." Luckily, the songwriter Don Robertson was playing piano on the session and fiddled around with the open-ing notes, singing a phrase to Elvis, and the song stayed in. One of the classiest Elvis movie ballads, "They Remind Me Too Much of You" almost prefigures "I Need Somebody to Lean On" in *Viva Las Vegas*, with the number presented as an interior monologue. Robertson's ballads suited Elvis, who sounds vulnerable and lovelorn, bringing his most delicate phrasing to such lines as "If these lovely things don't hurt you . . . " The accent on the word "lovely" is sublime.

"Loving You," *Loving You*

Leiber and Stoller's title track for Elvis's second movie is brilliantly crafted, right from the dark piano arpeggio with which Dudley Brooks gets things under way. With Scotty Moore and Bill Black at the peak of their game, and Elvis in rich, resonant voice, this ballad exerts a hypnotic spell but mysteriously never quite catches fire in the way that the same duo's "Love Me" did. A clip of Elvis singing this in the farmyard in the film was broadcast on *Top of the Pops*, to mark his death, the only obituary in the British TV show's forty-two-year run.

"This Is My Heaven," *Paradise, Hawaiian Style*

The best song to make it into *Paradise, Hawaiian Style*, this mellow Giant, Baum, and Kaye ballad isn't brilliantly used in the movie, but on record it stands out from an admittedly mediocre soundtrack. The harmonies are lovely, Elvis's delicate vocal is beautifully judged, and the Hawaiian flavor—the gentle percussion, the deliberate pacing, and Bernal Lewis's steel guitar—feels more authentic than in most of his other numbers in this vein.

"Marguerita," *Fun in Acapulco*

Physically unable to go to Mexico for *Fun in Acapulco*, Elvis did travel across the border musically, smoldering his way beautifully through Don Robertson's finger-snapping ballad. Sweetened by Herbert Alpert–style Tijuana horns, and driven on by the castanets, this urgent ballad is the perfect expression of Elvis as a sinuous Latin lover, drawn like a moth to the flame that is Ursula Andress (who, in reality, wasn't his type). A delightful concoction.

"Am I Ready," *Spinout*

On many of the songs in *Spinout*, Elvis sounded like one of his own demo singers. Yet on "Am I Ready," a Tepper/Bennett ballad that draws on American composer Edward MacDowell's classical piano piece "To a Wild Rose," Elvis is at his intimate best, sounding almost as if he is having a conversation with the listener. Aided by some of Floyd Cramer's smoothest piano playing, the King has seldom sounded more charismatically indecisive.

"Angel," *Follow That Dream*

There ought to be nothing extraordinary about this modest Tepper/Bennett ballad sung at the finale of *Follow That Dream*, but Elvis transforms what could have been a harmless piece of fluff into a teen ballad that sounds like it belongs to a David Lynch soundtrack. It's partly the way he adds an extra syllable into "Angel"—"Ay-ayn-gel"—but it's also the way he plays with the inflections in his voice to create a sound that transcends the cheesy arrangement and the half-decent lyrics. Millie Kirkham's angelic soprano helps too, making this sound more distinctive than it really is.

"Could I Fall in Love," *Double Trouble*

The King duets with himself on Randy Starr's pretty variation on the "I'm Falling in Love Tonight" formula as he wonders whether he really could be smitten by Annette Day. Perhaps relieved to be singing something half decent, Presley is smooth and sincere.

52

Hard Rock

The Most Intriguing Rock Songs in His Movies, from "Party" to "Long Legged Girl"

In April 1956, the *Waco News Tribune* referred to Presley as "the new 21-year-old King of Rock and Roll." As Presley's record sales grew exponentially, the title stuck, to the envy of rivals such as Jerry Lee Lewis and even his future 'son-in-law' Michael Jackson, who frequently asked: "They called Elvis the King, why not me?" When the reigning monarch of rock went to Hollywood, the fans expected him to cut loose onscreen. And so he did, in three out of his four pre-army movies. In the 1960s, as his image and the roster of songwriters changed, he didn't rock the joint as often—or to such devastating effect.

His second movie, *Loving You*, is probably the closest we can now get to the experience of watching him in concert in his 1950s heyday. Rock songs like "Got a Lot of Livin' to Do" and "Let's Have a Party" feel less dated than many of his movie songs from the 1960s. Yet even in 1957, there were signs of the quality-control issues to come: "Hot Dog" has all the lasting impact of the snack it's named after.

In *Jailhouse Rock*, Elvis is at his most regal, inspired by the breathtaking title song, "Baby I Don't Care," and "Treat Me Nice" (all from the pen of Leiber and Stoller). There are a few purists who still insist that Elvis was at his greatest before they put drums on his records, but for almost everyone else, the sheer power, attack, and audacity of "Jailhouse Rock" is impossible to resist. You can hear the sneer in "Baby I Don't Care" and "Treat Me Nice." Commercially, this hard-rock approach paid off, with *Jailhouse Rock* eventually selling over two million copies, topping the charts in the UK and United States, and the EP selling over a million copies.

King Creole didn't rock quite as hard, but the title track, "Hard Headed Woman," and "Trouble" were all gems. The first verse of "King Creole" is probably one of the most iconic passages in the entire Elvis canon. The last two numbers in the film—"Young Dreams" and "As Long as I Have You"—are both ballads, a nod to a smoother future. Was Parker—who Schilling said was uncomfortable with the raw, rebellious Presley—already looking ahead to Elvis the all-round entertainer, who would be so wholesome critic Bosley Crowther would marvel that he must have "honey in his veins instead of blood"?

There was rock in *G.I. Blues*, but of the sweeter, softer variety exemplified by "Shoppin' Around" and "Tonight Is so Right for Love." In the same perfectly acceptable vein were "I Slipped, I Stumbled, I Fell" and "King of the Whole Wide World" (though the latter hardly repays the 31 takes devoted to it). "Rock-a-hula Baby" and "Bossa Nova Baby" were inserted at the last minute to exploit current teen crazes. Yet in many army movies, Elvis barely broke sweat. In the early 1960s, the decision to disconnect Elvis from his pelvis reflected a pop market dominated by ballads. That changed in 1964 with the Beatles. His *Kissin' Cousins* album was released in April 1964, the same week that the Fab Four had monopolized the top five on Billboard's Hot 100. Rock was back in fashion, albeit with a British accent. Millions of record buyers saw Elvis as a king of the past, and *Viva Las Vegas*, his best, rockiest single since "Return to Sender," peaked at number 29 on the charts.

The obvious response to the threat of the Beatles would have been to give the King better material. Yet the music-publishing machine was either unable or unwilling to deliver. From *Roustabout*, released in November 1964, until *Easy Come, Easy Go*, which opened for (not very much) business in March 1967, the best rock song Elvis performed onscreen was "Put the Blame on Me," a funky uptempo number originally recorded in March 1961 and recycled for *Tickle Me* in 1965.

The plots didn't help. Elvis could hardly be expected to rock his way through the kingdom of Lunarkand (*Harum Scarum*), a nineteenth-century Mississippi riverboat (*Frankie and Johnny*), or exotic Hawaii (*Paradise, Hawaiian Style*). *Spinout* was full of faster numbers, but not even "Adam and Evil," the best of the bunch, rocked as credibly as "Put the Blame on Me."

After the nadir of *Easy Come, Easy Go, Double Trouble* provided a thrilling surprise: the short, punchy "Long Legged Girl (with the Short Dress On)." From here on in, when Elvis did rock, he did so with conviction. "Let Yourself Go," "A Little Less Conversation," and "Clean Up Your Own Backyard" all pointed the way to a more contemporary rock sound. In *Change of Habit*, he gave soulful distinction to the joyous, infectious nonsense of "Rubberneckin'."

His demonic "Polk Salad Annie" in *Elvis: That's the Way It Is* gave us a mesmerizing glimpse of what might have been. Although fitting that kind of energetic swamp rock into an adventure set in Lunarkand would have troubled even the King's most slapdash scriptwriters.

"Jailhouse Rock," *Jailhouse Rock*

This really shouldn't have worked. Leiber and Stoller's ironic playlets, this one even hinting at a homosexual affair between two jailbirds, were perfectly suited to the Coasters. Scotty Moore and D. J. Fontana wanted to create an intro inspired by Verdi's famous Anvil Chorus and the sound of men smashing rocks on a chain gang. Bill Black had a new electric Fender with which to try out his walking bass figures. And Elvis? He was in such impassioned form that from the moment he declares that the warden has thrown a party, all the contradictions were rendered utterly, magnificently irrelevant. In the movie, Hollywood tried to enhance the song with such sophisticated interjections as "Lay it on me, daddy-o!" from Elvis's faux cellmates. Whitesnake singer David Coverdale, who heard "Jailhouse Rock" when he was about eight, captured its effect on kids rather well when he said: "You don't know what it is but it gets you fluffed up."

"King Creole," *King Creole*

With such lines as "When the king starts movin' it's as good as done," this could be as much about Elvis as Danny Fisher or any other monarch of Bourbon Street. Certainly, he is a "hip-shaking King Creole," if you take Creole as a metaphor either for his own American Indian roots or for the way his music has helped dismantle racial boundaries. For whatever reason, the song resonates with Elvis, whose electric vocal—supported by one of Scotty Moore's finest guitar solos—all but ensured this would replace "Danny" as the title song for his third movie. On film, Elvis's performance is so compelling it's even possible not to be distracted by the Jordanaires, looking hilariously out of their comfort zone as fake house musicians in a New Orleans nightclub.

"Polk Salad Annie," *Elvis: That's the Way It Is*

Making Elvis rock on celluloid wasn't that complicated. Just put him onstage, give him a classic swamp rock number by Tony Joe White, a body where he seems to be able to rearrange every molecule at a nanosecond's notice, and a drawling southern Dean Martin accent and you're most of the way there. Crazed, soulful, exhilarating, and exhausting, this is was Elvis's wildest moment onscreen since he rocked that jailhouse.

"Viva Las Vegas," *Viva Las Vegas*

Arguably the most challenging vocal Pomus and Shuman ever gave Elvis. With the complicated lyrics and rollicking rhythm, the King barely has anything to hang a note on, but he soars above the dense, pounding backing, giving such an exhilarating portrayal of the thrills to be had in Las Vegas that the city's tourist board must have been ecstatic. So iconic that it has been covered by Springsteen, the Dead Kennedys, ZZ Top, and, of all people, Engelbert Humperdinck, this has become a modern standard.

"Hard Headed Woman," *King Creole*

Claude Demetrius's best lyrics have the fun and fizz of Leiber and Stoller's. The rhythm in this smash hit is so relentless it's a miracle Elvis has time to tell us about a king who was doing swell until he messed around with "that evil Jezebel." Driven on by a brilliant horn section, Elvis gives one of his fastest, most iconic performances.

"Got a Lot of Livin' to Do," *Loving You*

Weisman's rocker, one of the signature songs in Elvis's second movie, made it into the film after Wallis heard it. You can understand the producer's enthusiasm. The number allows Presley to play with his own image, inviting his baby to "pitch a little woo" with him. Though the King took a while to get this right in the studio, the master version has a freedom and energy that many of his movie rock songs would later lack.

"Let's Have a Party," *Loving You*

With its mysterious boast that the narrator knows how to shake a chicken in the middle of the room, this distinctive rocker, written by Jessie Mae Robinson, is at the musical core of *Loving You*. The first version—where he tells his other half to paint her lips and regulate her wig—sounds like an invitation to a much wilder party than later iterations where the meat is on the stove. The song's only serious flaw is that it's a bit too short.

"Treat Me Nice," *Jailhouse Rock*

Would Elvis ever sound this arrogant on record again? (Possibly—in some ways, his 1973 cover of Rosco Gordon's "Just a Little Bit" feels like a companion piece to this Leiber and Stoller number.) Here he spells out, in no uncertain terms, the behavior he expects from his girl. A compelling slice of chauvinism made enjoyable by the panache with which it is performed and the sense that Elvis isn't taking this too seriously.

"Put the Blame on Me," *Tickle Me*

Co-authored by TV comedy writer Norman Blagman, "Put the Blame" is a blues-tinged number that sounds a bit like "A Mess of Blues" but has enough quirky charm to catch the ear. Recorded in March 1961—and conscripted into *Tickle Me* to save money—it's a pleasure to hear the new smooth Elvis volunteering to take the blame for something, let alone being enough of a threat to upset his girl's parents. The electric keyboard gives the song an unusual flavor. In the early takes, Elvis is much wilder and bluesier, almost in the fashion of Little Willie John.

"Long Legged Girl (with the Short Dress On)," *Double Trouble*

The title may be long, but for one minute and twenty-six seconds this stomping rocker never lets up. Opening with Elvis's impatient shout of "All right," "Long Legged Girl" has a harder edge than any movie song he had cut since *Viva Las Vegas*. Though the production lacks finesse, you can hear why Billboard thought this might be a winner (it wasn't peaking at number 63). J. Leslie McFarland (co-author of "Stuck on You") and Winfield Scott (Otis Blackwell's co-writer on "Return to Sender") should have collaborated for Elvis more often.

53

So Close, Yet So Far

The Songs That Never Made It—One of Which May Have Inspired "Imagine"

The selection of songs for Elvis's movies could be a chaotic process. So many parties had a vested interest, and so many demos were submitted, that a committee effectively created the soundtracks, with inevitable mixed results. Often songs would be cut from the films incorporate feedback from audience previews. "Summer Kisses, Winter Tears" was edited out of *Flaming Star* because audiences laughed when Elvis sang it around the campfire. As good as the song is, that was probably just as well. Often, the process was so haphazard that the best songs ended on the cutting-room floor.

"Suppose," *Speedway*

This quiet, chilling ballad offers a rare insight into Elvis's musical soul—which is probably why it wasn't recorded for *Easy Come, Easy Go* and was then cut from *Speedway*. He sang it, in a slightly overwrought fashion, around the piano at Graceland (this version is available on *The Home Recordings*) and recorded it in RCA's Studio B on March 20, 1967.

With some subtle piano work from David Briggs, and Millie Kirkham's ethereal soaring soprano, the King gives a measured yet committed performance, sounding more engaged that at any time since the "How Great Thou Art" sessions in 1966. The pause after "Suppose I have no wish . . . " is just beautiful. Jorgensen suggests the sound was too similar to "Indescribably Blue," which had just been released as a single, to generate any enthusiasm at RCA. Whatever the reason, "Suppose" was eventually released as a bonus song on *Speedway*, Elvis's last soundtrack album.

"Suppose" was an unusual song for Elvis to discover. Co-writer Sylvia Dee had worked with Ben Weisman on "Moonlight Swim" but was best known for "Chickery Chick," a novelty number about a chicken who brightens up his day by repeating the same idiotic catchphrase. She wrote "Suppose" with George Goehring, who is most famous for "Little Donkey." Luckily, the only animals mentioned in "Suppose" are the birds that may not cross the sky.

The story of "Suppose" doesn't end there. Some fans have suggested it inspired John Lennon's utopian anthem "Imagine." The timings certainly work—Lennon's classic was written in 1971, three years after "Suppose" was released. But how would Lennon have heard it? Would he really have bought the soundtrack album for *Speedway*? He might have, if only out of ironic curiosity to see what indignities his hero had been forced to suffer. Fellow Beatle George Harrison was still listening to Elvis in the late 1960s, going so far as to quote the lyrics of "Clean Up Your Own Backyard" in an interview.

The similarities between the songs are striking. In both songs, the singer runs through a list of things that might not exist. In both songs, the singer is alone at the piano, contemplating the world. Both lyrics have lines that start with the same repeated word. And at one point, Elvis even sings that it's impossible to imagine a world without a star or a world without his love.

The official inspiration for "Imagine" was Karl Marx's *The Communist Manifesto*, but if you play "Suppose" and "Imagine" in succession, it's hard not to be struck by the resemblance.

"Sand Castles," *Paradise, Hawaiian Style*

By 1965, the quality control on Elvis's movies was so haphazard that the better a song was, the greater chance it had of being cut. This beguiling lullaby, written by David Hess and Herb Goldberg, was one of the victims. If commercial necessity dictated that the King sing children's songs in his movies, why couldn't they have been as good as this? Beautifully arranged, with the King at his most laid-back, this song has a haunting fairy-tale quality and is easier to listen to now than such contemporary children's fluff as "Puff the Magic Dragon."

"Summer Kisses, Winter Tears," *Flaming Star*

"Summer Kisses, Winter Tears" is an unforgettable, regretful ballad sung with great tenderness and delicacy. Ben Weisman's unusual lyrics—and Presley's pure tones—give this a poetic, quasi-philosophical, air. Cut from *Flaming Star*, where its impact was lessened by a strange use of Native American drums, the song was deservingly rescued from obscurity by members of Elvis's UK fan club, who voted for it to be reissued on the 1977 compilation *Elvis in Demand*.

"Let's Be Friends," *Change of Habit*

This quiet Chris Arnold, Geoff Morrow, and David Martin ballad deserved better than to be the title track on a Camden budget album. Cut for *Change of Habit*—the lyrics obviously allude to the autistic girl who is cured by Presley—this flows so naturally, resistance is futile. The gorgeous melody and the tender lyrics obviously appeal to Elvis, who is smoky, sincere, and soulful, indulging in a little unstrained vibrato.

"I Don't Want To," *Girls! Girls! Girls!*

Janice Tarre and Fred Spielman's ballad is a slight variation on the formula—for once, Elvis isn't trying to seduce but is being drawn into love against his will—and it was certainly one of the stronger tracks filmed for *Girls! Girls! Girls!* Unfortunately, it was cut due to a late panic about the movie's pacing. The finished film was criticized for containing too many songs, but Elvis is in such good voice it's a pity this didn't make it at the expense of such fluff as "Dainty Little Moonbeams."

"You're the Boss," *Viva Las Vegas*

This could have been the King's sexiest duet, but with Parker fretting that director George Sidney was turning an Elvis film into an Ann-Margret movie, it got the chop. Originally recorded by Jimmy Ricks and LaVern Baker (whom the King idolized), this number sizzles, with Elvis and his co-star in fine voice. The exchange of compliments is steamy enough—especially when Ann-Margret compares him to a horse—but at the very end, when she laughs and says: "Ah, tell me about it," it's as if we're eavesdropping on their affair.

"Forget Me Never," *Wild in the Country*

Sacrificed to let the story flow, this stripped-down Fred Wise/Ben Weisman ballad is short, sweet, and memorable. Many fans prefer "Lonely Man," but that feels slightly stilted and self-conscious in comparison to this gentle lament.

"How Can You Lose What You Never Had?," *Clambake*

As touching as "The Girl I Never Loved" is, that ballad is essentially a reprise of "You Don't Know Me." *Clambake* might have benefited from the inclusion of this gutsy, pertinent, if slightly predictable blues-tinged pop number on the same theme by Ben Weisman and Sid Wayne.

"Where Do You Come From?," *Girls! Girls! Girls!*

A slow, aching ballad that starts a bit like "As Long as I Have You," this Ruth Batchelor/Bob Roberts number intrigued the King. He swoons his way through this, almost hypnotizing himself. Dudley Brooks's sublime piano adds to the song's mystical air. Rejected from *Girls! Girls! Girls!*, this featured on the B side of "Return to Sender."

"Wisdom of the Ages," *Harum Scarum*

Despite the obligatory references to sages, sands of time, and the hand of fate, this Giant, Baum, and Kaye number is one of the few songs in *Harum Scarum* that couldn't have been performed as ably by a talking camel. The Middle Eastern flavor sounds more convincing than on most tracks, and Presley's voice is so charismatic than when he beckons us to listen to the wisdom of the ages, we feel obliged to do so. The number didn't make it to the U.S. or UK release, but fans in Brazil mysteriously got to see this—and "Animal Instinct"—in their version.

"Night Life," *Viva Las Vegas*

This fast-moving number is rightly celebrated for a line about long-legged women out to give you all a trimming. Giant, Baum, and Kaye's catchy number would have enriched any of the soundtracks that followed.

54

The Songs They Should Have Cut

In Other Words, How Did "Old MacDonald" Stay In?

Watching Elvis record some of the movie songs in the 1960s, the Jordanaires' Gordon Stoker was struck by the change in the King's style. As he told Jorgensen: "How many times have I seen him sit as far from the microphone as possible? The material was so bad he felt like he couldn't sing it." Given some of the dreck he was asked to sing, it's a wonder he didn't walk out more often. Some of these songs have been compiled on a bootleg CD called *Elvis' Greatest Sh*t*, a kitsch selection that reveal the compiler's lack of taste by putting the exquisite "Can't Help Falling in Love" in the same bracket as "Old MacDonald."

Every fan has a playlist of movie songs they wish Elvis had never recorded. Here are ten that are at the very bottom of the barrel.

"Old MacDonald," *Double Trouble*

With a moo-moo here and an oink-oink there, this farmyard frolic prompted one diehard Elvis fan to say it made him want to kick the stereo around the room. Songwriter Randy Starr should have been fricasseed—as should the bright spark who decided this was worthy of releasing on the misleadingly titled budget release *Elvis Sings Hits from the Movies* (which featured some songs that were hits but weren't in the movies, and other numbers that were in the movies but weren't hits).

"Yoga Is as Yoga Does," *Easy Come, Easy Go*

How can we take this song serious, when all it does—for Elvis and us—is give us a pain in our posterior? Gerald Nelson, who wrote this and "The Love Machine" (with Fred Burch), thought the instruction to write a song about yoga was joke and admitted later: "It turned out to be the absolute worst song I ever heard."

"Dominic," *Stay Away, Joe*

The oddest song Weisman wrote for Elvis, this ditty about a bull had Presley begging RCA's Harry Jenkins to skip this one. The star recorded it with great reluctance after producer Felton Jarvis promised it would never be released—in which case, why bother to record it? When that promise was finally broken in 1994 both Presley and Jarvis were dead.

"A Dog's Life," *Paradise, Hawaiian Style*

Julie Parrish, the actress Elvis sings this to in *Paradise, Hawaiian Style*, recalled: "Elvis hated the song. He couldn't stop laughing while he was recording it." The King flatly rejected the idea that the song would be improved if he added a "bow-wow." The pity is that he agreed to record it at all.

"Queenie Wahine's Papaya," *Paradise, Hawaiian Style*

RCA executive director Joan Deary's first thought when she heard this song was: "How did Elvis sing this without laughing?" Somehow, he did, making this monstrosity vaguely charming until the tempo mysteriously speeds up—possibly because the King was anxious to get this one over as soon as possible.

"Clambake," *Clambake*

"Claaaaa-mmbake, got have Clambake!" Easily the King's worst title song, this did provoke one of the seminal Elvis studio moments. After recording an energetic, but turgid, master take of this, Elvis broke off to strum a few chords of it on his guitar. In a scarily plausible, bluesy, twenty-second acoustic version, he sings the couplet about hanging around the brightest lights in town and bursts into laughter at the absurdity of it all. What makes this even dafter is that Winfield Scott wrote an alternate theme, which, even though it runs through his girl's vital statistics, sounds so much better than the Weisman/Wayne number.

"The Love Machine," *Easy Come, Easy Go*

The single from Hal Wallis's last Elvis film isn't outrageous or absurd, it's just dull. The boredom in his voice is so obvious it's almost a coded appeal to the faithful not to buy this song. Luckily for Elvis, most of them didn't.

"Barefoot Ballad," *Kissin' Cousins*

Dolores Fuller, who co-wrote this hoedown with Lee Morris, was the muse and girlfriend of Ed Wood, who is semi-officially known as the worst director of all time. A puzzling meditation on toes accounts for one verse and is then repeated just to make it even more excruciating. Semi-officially, the worst hoedown in Hollywood history.

"Petunia the Gardener's Daughter," *Frankie and Johnny*

This fake oldtime vaudeville Tepper/Bennett song works well enough in the film but should never have been recorded. The lyrics in which he dances when she plants her two lips (geddit!) on him are bad enough, but Eileen Wilson's overdubbed vocal is about as subtle as a punch in the nose.

"Hey Little Girl," *Harum Scarum*

Byers's worst Elvis song? Quite probably. In the movie, the fact that he Presley is singing this to a girl young enough to be his daughter is troubling enough. On record, it's just painful to hear him trying to force some life into such an artificial rocker.

55

"I Sing All Kinds"

Jazz, Country, Blues, and Gospel in Elvis's Movie Music

W hat kind of singer are you?" Marion Keisker, Phillips's secretary at Sun Records, had famously asked the eighteen-year-old Elvis. To which he even more famously replied: "I sing all kinds."

Although Presley had far more say in his own destiny than the Goldmans of this world give him credit for, even he could not have foreseen how many genres, in twenty-one years as the most famous man in the world, his peerless pipes would be asked to span. As the legendary record producer Jerry Wexler put it, "Presley's registration, the breadth of his tone, listening to some of his records, you'd think you were listening to an opera singer. But it's an opera singer with a deep connection to the blues." And a deep connection to country, pop, and gospel. That breadth would prove extremely useful onscreen as Hollywood tried to broaden his appeal, presenting him with a variety of songs that touched on blues, calypso, country, gospel, Hawaiian music, jazz, pop, and rock. Yet on the best of these numbers you can hear that unique combination that singer Patti Page identified recently: "He performed like a rock star. He was loud, he was boisterous, yet he had that down-home country quality that came from some of his gospel music. He wasn't afraid of anything; that was him singing and that was what he wanted people to hear." Sensing this, the King's tunesmiths encouraged him to experiment in almost every major musical genre—with varying results.

Jazz

In the 1920s, jazz was demonized as a subversive threat to society as we know it, being greeted with the same opprobrium as rock and roll in the 1950s. The *Ladies Home Journal* had dismissed jazz as "originally the accompaniment of the voodoo dancer, stimulating the half-crazed barbarian to the vilest deeds . . . That it has a demoralizing effect on the human brain has been demonstrated by many scientists." Yet in the 1950s, modern jazz had become a critically acclaimed art form that was no longer resonating with teenagers like Elvis, who once confessed, "I don't understand jazz." Jazz didn't dig him either, with critic Alan Kurtz once flatly declaring that the King didn't have a sophisticated bone in his body—he had obviously never heard Elvis sing "I Need Somebody to Lean On" or "Fever."

The changes Presley wrought in popular culture meant that jazz would never hold center stage again. The shift wasn't entirely his fault—modern jazz, like progressive rock, was never likely to prosper in the commercial mainstream—but he got much of the blame for it. The competition between jazz and rock was satirized in *Jailhouse Rock*, where Vince Everett (Elvis) is invited to a party where his girlfriend's parents are playing a record by the latest hepcats. Asked whether atonality really is a passing phase, Elvis's antihero snarls, "Lady, I don't know what the hell you're talking about," before storming out.

Though Elvis never swung too often on record, he was attracted to the nightclub jazz perfected by performers like Peggy Lee, loved Billy Eckstine, and idolized Dean Martin. In the studio, he covered "Fever" with style and wit. In the movies, even though he spent an entire film in New Orleans, he rarely sang jazz. Even a song like "New Orleans," decked out with jazz's instrumental trappings, is really a big hunk of bluesy Dixieland rock. The opportunity for some true, if anachronistic, Dixieland jazz is largely squandered in *Frankie and Johnny*. The closest he comes to real jazz onscreen is the surprisingly accomplished "City by Night" in *Double Trouble*.

"City by Night," *Double Trouble*

Characterizing Bruges as a city that never sleeps—take that, New York!—"City by Night" is the kind of smoky nightclub number you might expect Bobby Darin to sing, Driven by Richard Noel's muted trombone and Floyd Cramer's tinkling piano, with some intriguing tempo changes, this is a hidden gem. The production is patchy—at times, the band sound like they're in another studio—but Elvis interprets this beautifully.

Country Music

Although Elvis always insisted that rock and roll had its roots in blues and gospel, when he was starting out he cited Ernest Tubb, Hank Snow, and Roy Acuff as influences, and even before he left Sun he had recorded the country standard "I Love You Because." He never lost his love for country and western—the genre dominated his private record collection—and he once told the singer Wanda Jackson that he sang country music with a beat but it wasn't a music that Hollywood instinctively understood. Hill and Range had made its name in the genre, but Tinseltown's imperfect grasp of country becomes hilariously clear in *Loving You*, where Tex Warner (Wendell Corey), the leader of the Rough Ridin' Ramblers, plays the saxophone, hardly a typical hillbilly instrument.

"Teddy Bear" and "Jailhouse Rock" were country number 1s, but the genre would become so neglected in the movies that, from 1958 to 1969, not one Elvis single featured on Billboard's country charts. Even when the King went back to the country for *Kissin' Cousins* and recorded the album in Nashville, only Pomus and Shuman's bonus track "Long Lonely Highway" (which later featured in *Tickle Me*) had an authentic country feel. It's a shame, in retrospect, that he didn't get the part of doomed country great Hank Williams in *Your Cheatin' Heart* (1964). Hank's widow Audrey vetoed his casting, fearing that Elvis would become the focus of the picture. George Hamilton stepped in and did a decent job, but it would have been fascinating to hear the twenty-nine-year-old Presley sing such Williams classics as "Long Gone Lonesome Blues."

Elvis's passion for country—especially Jerry Reed's feisty take on the genre—inspired his artistic renaissance in the late 1960s. His interpretation of "You Don't Know Me" is one of the highlights of *Clambake*, while "Stay Away," sung over the credits of *Stay Away, Joe*, has a nice country vibe. One of the many paradoxes of Elvis's movie career is that a music that had inspired him since he was a teenager—and would inspire one of his greatest albums, *Elvis Country*—became so marginalized onscreen that millions of moviegoers could easily have assumed Hawaiian songs were closer to his musical soul.

"You Don't Know Me," *Clambake*

A hit for Eddy Arnold (who wrote it with Cindy Walker) in 1956, and Ray Charles in 1962, this plaintive ballad roused Elvis. He struggled through twenty takes without really nailing it in February 1967 but after returning to RCA's Studio B in Nashville that September, inspired by recording more gutsy material such as "Guitar Man," he rose to the challenge, conveying, as Harbinson put it, "a very real sense of nobility and loss." Arnold had once been managed by Parker, and his material always seemed to inspire Elvis's competitive spirit. The King covered several of the singer's hits—most impressively, "I Really Don't Want to Know"—and never did a bad job on any of them.

"You Gave Me a Mountain," *Elvis on Tour*

Elvis had shared the bill with Marty Robbins on his ascent to stardom and, after the breakup of his marriage, used one of the country singer/songwriter's trademark songs, a Top 30 hit for Frankie Laine in 1969, to express his anger, bafflement, and grief. His powerful rendition in *Elvis on Tour* is free of the histrionics he later brought to the song and all the better for it.

Blues

In the mid-1960s, probably roughly about the time Elvis was contemplating his next musical comedy set in Fort Lauderdale, on a dude ranch, or in a fictional Middle Eastern kingdom, the great Muddy Waters said of him: "That boy made his pull from the blues, if he's stopped, he's stopped, but he made his pull from there."

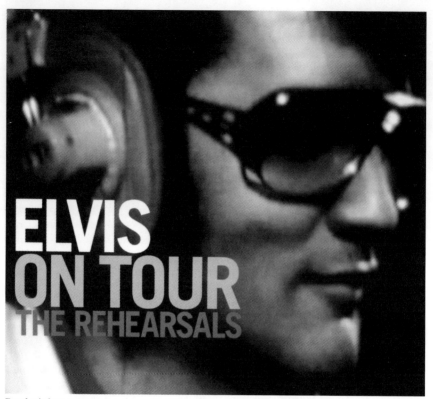

Presley's last concert movie majored on country music and ballads.

Waters was absolutely right. Presley owned records by LaVern Baker, Ruth Brown, the Clovers, Arthur Gunter, Lowell Fulson, and Lightnin' Hopkins. He also publicly acknowledged his debt to Arthur Crudup (who wrote "That's Alright Mama"), Bobby Bland, Sonny Boy Williamson, and Howlin' Wolf. His instinctive grasp of the blues had made his first rock records sound much more authentic than either Bill Haley's or Pat Boone's.

When Elvis came to Hollywood, the blues was one aspect of his music his filmmakers could not ignore. There was no way to squeeze the genre into the Civil War melodrama *Love Me Tender*, but *Loving You* was a different matter, and although Claude Demetrius's "Mean Woman Blues" wasn't classic R&B, it certainly, as Waters might say, made its pull from there. In *King Creole*, Presley attacked "Trouble" and "New Orleans" with gusto.

R&B was too raw for the post-army, sanitized Presley but his songwriters did their best to indulge him, creating such lighter blues numbers as "All I Needed Was the Rain," "Beach Boy Blues," and "Hard Luck." He rehashed "It Feels So Right" for *Tickle Me*, sounding significantly less bluesy than he did on *Elvis Is Back*. Though "Beach Boy Blues" is Hollywood's commercial take on the blues,

Elvis obviously enjoys singing it, especially the line "Only 30 days and 90 years to go." He almost tries too hard on "Hard Luck," but the Weisman/Wayne number is easily the best thing in *Frankie and Johnny*. The gentle country blues "All I Needed Was the Rain" works better on record than onscreen, where the scene is played for broad comedy.

Though a vastly inferior song, "All I Needed Was the Rain" has aged better than Elvis's frenetic cover of the Ray Charles classic "What'd I Say," where he is competing with Randolph's sax, Calvin Jackson on the organ, and two sets of backing singers on a version that, for all its incidental pleasures, ends up feeling like watered-down R&B.

The best blues song Elvis sang in his 1960s movies is probably "Clean Up Your Own Backyard." The highlight of *The Trouble with Girls*, this song straddles almost as many genres as Elvis. As the Teardrop Explodes' founder Julian Cope put it in his enthusiastic review: "'Clean Up Your Own Backyard' rides along on a bluegrass-flavored soul groove, the gospelly 'Amen' and 'Hallelujah' backing vocals providing an ironic counterpoint to the lyrics which preach against hypocritical preachers. If only all Elvis's soundtrack material had been this good." If all his celluloid blues had felt as authentic as this Mac Davis/Billy Strange number, Presley's prowess as a blues singer might be more widely recognized.

"Trouble," *King Creole*

Leiber and Stoller's macho classic has probably had greater cultural impact than any other Elvis song. It became a kind of anthem for the man himself, when he resurrected his career in 1968, and it has been covered or referenced by everyone from Robbie Williams to Britney Spears and the model Amanda Lear, one of Salvador Dali's muses, who featured on the cover of Roxy Music's glam-rock album *For Your Pleasure*. Leiber and Stoller had thought it would suit Muddy Waters better than Elvis, but he attacked the song with such ferocity they changed their minds. The way he lets rip on "green-eyed mountain jack" is still spine-tingling. When Waters heard the performance, he was reminded of his own "Hootchie Cootchie Man" and said: "I better watch out. I believe whitey's picking up on things I'm doin'."

"New Orleans," *King Creole*

Tepper/Bennett's finest Elvis song encourages the King to stretch out the word "Loo-oosy-oosy-anna" for so long you worry his vocal cords might snap. Although the Jordanaires have no right to feature on this kind of song, their interaction with Presley encourages him to try all kinds of vocal pyrotechnics, shouting, stuttering, almost rapping, and, to cap it all off, sounding delightfully sinful when he says the Cupid doll queens will make you awful glad you were born a man. A bit gross, but still good to listen to.

"Mean Woman Blues," *Loving You*

Demetrius was an incredibly versatile songwriter who had already penned songs for Louis Jordan, B. B. King, and Elvis ("I Was the One") when he wrote this stirring twelve-bar blues for *Loving You*. Onscreen and in the studio, Presley makes the most of the playful lyrics, a tribute to a woman who is so tough she scares black cats. An inspirational performance, this ought to have been a hit for Elvis and not for Roy Orbison, who reached number 5 with it in 1964.

Gospel

Elvis was born and raised on gospel music. Throughout his life, sacred music was balm for his troubled soul, its healing power providing one of the most moving moments in *Elvis on Tour* as he watches J. D. Sumner and the Stamps sing "The Light House" before joining in to sing "Lead Me, Guide Me." Yet in the 1950s, gospel was regarded as a poor man's music. The genre seemed so separate from the rest of the music business that when Weisman wrote "The Robe of Cavalry," he had to use a pseudonym because Hill and Range thought a gospel song written by someone with a Jewish name wouldn't sell.

Elvis publicly declared his love of gospel by singing "Peace in the Valley" on Ed Sullivan's show in 1956, but he would wait a long time before he sang a spiritual number in his movies. God wasn't the kind of character to pep up the plot of the average musical comedy, so Elvis didn't sing his favorite music until *Easy Come, Easy Go* (1967). Looking for a number to get him out of a party, he shakes a tambourine and sings "Sing You Children." The LaVern Baker classic "Saved" was considered for this spot, but luckily it was saved for the TV special. Though no classic, "Sing You Children" is the second-best song in the movie.

In *The Trouble with Girls*, Elvis performed "Swing Home Sweet Chariot," which he had recorded on the 1960 album *His Hand in Mine*. In the movie, as the stand-in for a gospel quartet singer struck down by laryngitis, he looks resplendent in his white suit, clapping his hands and snapping his fingers, as he drives the song on. He looks glad to be up there, and the scene must have brought back memories of his own frustrated ambition to join a gospel quartet.

Elvis returned to the church for his last feature film, *Change of Habit*. It seemed oddly fitting that he should bow out, as an actor, in fine voice, leading a congregation in the upbeat, inclusive religious number "Let Us Pray," co-written by Weisman, who, on this occasion, didn't have to use a pseudonym.

"Swing Down Sweet Chariot," *The Trouble with Girls*

If Elvis had been accepted into the Songfellows Quartet in 1954, the history of popular culture might have been very different. After his audition, they decided he was fine as the lead singer but struggled to harmonize when asked to sing baritone or tenor. He worked on the harmonies, but he had already signed for

Sun when he got his second chance to join. When he leads the Jordanaires in this rousing feel-good version of "Swing Down Sweet Chariot," he sounds utterly at ease, engaged, and in control, almost as if he's relishing making up for a missed opportunity.

King of the Whole Wide World

Elvis's World Musical Tour—From Hawaii to Germany and Back Again

W hen Elvis Presley called his movies travelogues, he could have been referring to the music as much as the scenery. He may never have performed live outside North America, but his movies drew on musical influences from all corners of the globe, from Giovanni Martini's "Plaisir d'Amour" to Hawaiian Queen Lili'uokalani's "Aloha Oe," to Mexican composer Pepe Guízar's "Guadalajara."

This could have been a cunning marketing strategy—fans of the King in Brazil, France, Germany, Hawaii, Italy, and Mexico could hear echoes of their country's music in his movies. More likely, it reflected the volume of songs his publishers had to find to service the movies and the fact that they could save money by repackaging material in the public domain. Yet this multiplicity of influences also reflected the singer's interests. The singers he admired varied from Crudup to Johnny Ray and Charlie Rich to Mario Lanza. He became fascinated by Charles Boyer's *Where Does Love Go* (1966), in which the actor sang—all right, talked—through famous love songs in a French accent. Presley was inspired by the Mexican-flavored soundtrack for *Fun in Acapulco*, and his interest in Polynesian music went above and beyond the movies, as he showed by recording Lee's romantic ballad "I'll Remember You" and incorporating it into his *Aloha from Hawaii* concert.

Here are eight movie songs that draw on the rest of the world's music in inspirational, magical, and sometimes downright puzzling fashion.

"Aloha Oe," *Blue Hawaii*

In a movie in which his character marries a Hawaiian princess, it seems only appropriate that the King should cover a classic written by a real Hawaiian princess, Lydia Kamekeha Lili'uokalani, who wrote this in 1878, thirteen years before she became the first and last queen of Hawaii. The song is about two parting lovers—the title means "Farewell to thee" or "Until we meet again"—and reached number 10 in the U.S. charts in 1924 when it was covered by Hawaiian guitarist Frank Ferera. Elvis sings this beautifully, almost reverently. This kind of music won't change the world, but it is incredibly evocative. You can almost feel the sea breeze when you play this.

"Drums of the Island," *Paradise, Hawaiian Style*

Elvis's third celluloid sojourn in Hawaii wasn't especially significant, but this Tepper/Bennett number, based on the old Tongan chant "Bula Lai," is at least driven by the native rhythms of the Pacific. Elvis and the Jordanaires breeze through this and sound so engaged, you wouldn't be surprised if the island's drums were really beating in their heart. In the film's finale, the number inspires a perfect pop-video moment, in which Elvis seems to transcend the mediocrity of much that has gone before and unite cultures with his sheer presence. Offscreen, the Samoans and Tongans were arguing over what kind of canoe should have been used and who had the right to paddle in it.

"Guadalajara," *Fun in Acapulco*

In a soundtrack full of *amigos, dineros,* and *muchachos,* Guízar's popular mariachi song provided Presley with his greatest technical and linguistic challenge. He rises to it, enunciating almost every Spanish word perfectly (although the words "como las tardes" do sound more like "como les tatter"), and channeling Lanza to soar above a clamorous backing, the Amigos and the barflies of Acapulco. Known as the musical painter of Mexico, Guízar (1912–1980) was determined to make the world listen to Mexican music. Although Presley's version takes its arrangement from Nat King Cole's cover, this magnificent curio from *Fun in Acapulco* proves Guízar had succeeded.

"Hawaiian Wedding Song," *Blue Hawaii*

Elvis sings this seductive ballad in the spectacular finale to *Blue Hawaii.* Originally written by Charles E. King for his operetta *Prince of Hawaii* in 1926, the song was called "Ke Kali Neau Au" (which means "Waiting Here for Thee") and was a Hawaiian standard long before Elvis sang it.

Recorded in 1928 by the great Hawaiian soprano Helen Desha Beamer, the song was covered, in English, by Bing Crosby in 1951. Seven years later, Al Hoffman and Dick Manning wrote some new English lyrics to give Andy Williams a hit. Elvis sang these words in *Blue Hawaii,* although he acknowledges the song's antecedents by singing in the Hawaiian language (and you can hear how seriously he is taking the pronunciation) before returning to English for the climax.

The song is at the heart of one of the most compelling spectacles in Presley's movies, selling Hawaii to the world as the quintessential, romantic tropical paradise. As he marries Joan Blackman's Hawaiian princess, the King looks so Hawaiian it's as if he's gone native. Musically, he hasn't had a complete

Polynesian makeover, though. Elvis's version of "Hawaiian Wedding Song" is a perfect, hugely enjoyable *hapa haole* ("half Hawaiian") song.

"I Love Only One Girl," *Double Trouble*

Tepper and Bennett's catchy crowd-pleaser for *Double Trouble* has its roots in a much raunchier number called "Auprès de ma Blonde" ("Next to My Girlfriend"), a drinking song popular with French soldiers during the reign of Louis XIV (1643–1715). While we cannot entirely rule out the possibility that Tepper or Bennett were experts on the Franco-Dutch War (1672–78), which inspired this song, it seems more likely they remembered it from Doris Day and Claude Dauphin's song and dance in the 1952 musical comedy *April in Paris*. Like the French soldiers, the King loves one girl in every town, although he seems as intrigued by Maria's lasagna as by her *amore* for dessert.

"No More," *Blue Hawaii*

This Don Robertson/Hal Blair ballad from *Blue Hawaii* was originally recorded by the great Italian tenor Ferruccio Giannini (1868–1948). "No More" is based on "La Paloma," written by Basque composer Sebastián Yradier while he was traveling in Cuba in the 1850s. Giannini recorded his version in 1896, but by then "La Paloma" had almost become a folk song, its popularity spreading across the world.

The song gave its name to a 1936 musical movie romance in which it is sung by the tenor Charles Kullmann. The *New York Times* reviewer noted: "The famous La Paloma sounds just about as well in a German picture as when sung in its original Spanish." Repurposed by Robertson for *Blue Hawaii*, "No More" sounds even better with Elvis—who did thirteen takes and still didn't sound satisfied—in tender, powerful voice.

"Please Don't Stop Loving Me," *Frankie and Johnny*

One of the best songs from Elvis's riverboat romance, this Byers ballad is probably the only Presley soundtrack number to be influenced by a Eurovision Song Contest winner. In 1964, the lovely Gigliola Cinquetti won the competition with her song "Non Ho L'eta" ("Per Amarti"), which can be roughly translated as "Too Young to Love." The song launched Cinquetti's career and, although the chorus is completely different in "Please Don't Stop Loving Me," the similarity between the melody and the verses is striking. Given Hill and Range's habit of scouring Europe for songs they could transmogrify for Elvis, the resemblance probably shouldn't surprise us.

"Wooden Heart," *G.I. Blues*

Commercially, the most successful product of Hill and Range's global quest for material was this catchy crowd-pleaser inspired by an old German folk song. Based on Friedrich Silcher's "Muss I Denn Zum Städtele Hinaus," which he wrote in 1827, "Wooden Heart" was created by German bandleader Kaempfert, one of the pioneers of easy-listening music, and three American songwriters: Wise, Weisman, and Twomey.

Elvis sings the song in *G.I. Blues*, in a scene showing a disarming, if not slightly disturbing, facility for interacting with Punch and Judy puppets. Indeed, the more you watch the clip, the harder it is to shake off the impression that he shows more rapport with the female puppet than with some of his subsequent leading ladies. Oddly, the song was not released as a single in the United States, allowing Joe Dowell to top the Hot 100 with his kitsch cover in August 1961. In Europe, RCA were quicker off the mark: the single sold well over a million copies

Wooden Heart single cover in German. This should have been a Presley chart topper in the US—but Joe Dowell beat him to it.

with German fans unable to resist the King singing in their language. Although he cracked up in the studio at some of his mispronunciations, Elvis's German in the master version is delicately sung.

"Wooden Heart" polarized opinion. Many were appalled by the idea of Elvis singing to puppets, but others are won over by its innocent charm. One young fan, Tom Petty, loved it so much he covered it at Sun Studios in 1993. "That was the first album I ever owned," Petty said. "The music meant so much to me."

57

Shake That Tambourine

Dance Crazes in Elvis Movies

The 1960s were a decade when dance crazes came and went faster than headlines about Liz Taylor's love life. Elvis's natural moves didn't suit any craze or style—they were just his. Outraged guardians of morality regarded him as little better than a burlesque act. Yet in the 1960s, in their desperation to present Presley as in touch, up-to-date, and thoroughly groovy, his film producers often obliged him to temper his rhythms to fit in with a new fad. Mercifully, he was never asked to do the Pony (popularized by Chubby Checker), the Mashed Potato (referred to by Connie Francis in her 1962 hit "V-A-C-A-T-I-O-N"), or the Chicken (in which dancers flap their arms and kick their legs like Colonel Sanders's favorite bird).

That said, if you watch many of the songs in Elvis's movies—especially those performed at a party or in a nightclub—you can't help but marvel at some of the shapes the dancers are cutting. This is especially true in *Spinout* when Elvis is performing the title track, "Beach Shack," and "Smorgasbord." In the latter number, Dodie Marshall steals the scene with some frenetic dancing that does look as if it belongs in a burlesque show.

The dance craze Elvis looks most at home with in the films is the Climb, the Forte Four's nightclub number in *Viva Las Vegas*. The King is obviously relishing a dance that enables him to get nose to nose and knee to knee with the curvaceous Ann-Margret.

The Twist

"You move as if you're putting out a cigarette with both feet. Then you move your arms as if you just stepped out of the shower, stretching a towel behind you, drying off your butt to the music." That is the Twist, according to Chubby Checker, and even though some of us may not recognize the dance from his description, who are we to argue? Checker introduced the craze to the public on Dick Clark's *American Bandstand* in 1960, and his single "The Twist" sold three million copies between 1960 and 1962.

Three million sales made it all but inevitable that the Pelvis would be required to Twist. Weisman, Wise, and Fuller rose to the challenge, deciding

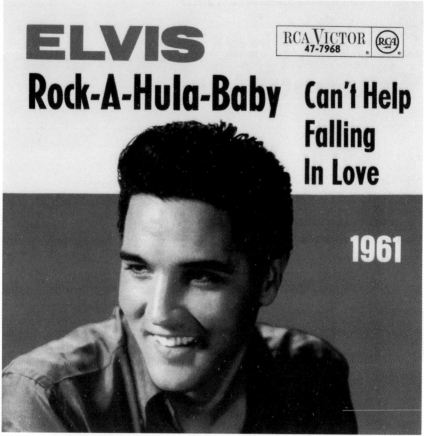

ELVIS

RCA VICTOR
47-7968

Rock-A-Hula-Baby **Can't Help Falling In Love**

1961

This is what happens if you encourage Weisman to blend the twist and the hula.

that, as Weisman put it, "the twist and the hula were perfect together. Out of that combination. "Rock-a-hula Baby was born." With its story of a girl who would rather dance than romance, it is a Hawaiian counterpoint to "Dixieland Rock" in *King Creole*.

There isn't a lot of twisting onscreen, although if you accept that the spirit of the craze is to dance with freedom, express yourself, and react to the music in a visceral, creative fashion, you could say Elvis is inspired by it. Though no classic, the song is likable and energetic enough for Presley to relish the rare opportunity to cut loose. He really lets rip in the slowed-down finale—a trick known in the trade as the Elvis Ending and celebrated in the "Poor Poor Pharaoh/Song of the King" number in the musical *Joseph and His Amazing Technicolor Dreamcoat*. At one point, Elvis starts to spasm as if he's been knifed in the back by a maniac—a trick he used to circumvent the censors when they filmed him from the waist up singing "Don't Be Cruel" on *The Ed Sullivan Show* in 1956.

The Bossa Nova

The fusion of samba and jazz that became known as *bossa nova* (literally, "new trend") had been created in Rio, not Acapulco, but with characteristic disregard for the subtleties of Latin American popular culture, Hollywood decided that Presley's Mexican adventure would be enhanced by this kind of rhythm. They were right. Kind of. The Leiber and Stoller classic gives the King the chance to click his fingers, shake his hips, and tap his feet, but none of his moves have much to do with the bossa nova as it has been practiced at dance schools across the world. In other words, a stupid idea that inspired a great performance.

The Clam

David Winter choreographed *Viva Las Vegas* brilliantly, so it seems only fair to regard "Do the Clam" as the inevitable bad day in the office. The attempt to launch a dance craze didn't work, as, despite the combined efforts of Wayne, Weisman, and Fuller and Randolph's sax solo, millions proved strangely reluctant to gather round to the bongo sound. Elvis does his best, especially when he urges listeners to "Grab your barefoot baby by the hand," powering the record to number 21 in the Hot 100.

The resistance may partly reflect the fact that, in the movie, apart from the signature moves—which involve some fake digging and making some clam shapes with your hands—the clam seems to involve all kinds of acrobatics with skilled exponents tumbling backward over a mound of sand. The other odd thing about this craze is that the mollusk it is named after is hardly famed for being poetry in motion.

The Jerk

Ever wondered why the dancers surrounding Elvis in *Spinout* are making those bizarre arm-chopping motions? Probably not—after all, these are hardly the most outlandish dance moves to be performed by the thousands of extras who gyrated across the screen in an Elvis film. But in *Spinout* these dancers were doing the Jerk, a dance craze inspired by the Larks' single of the same. The band even released an album dedicated to the craze in 1965. Representative titles include: "Jerkin' USA," "Keep Jerkin," and "Mickey's East Coast Jerk." One of the prime promoters of this craze—he has even been described as creating the Jerk—was David Winter, the choreographer of *Viva Las Vegas*, *Tickle Me*, and *Girl Happy*. He didn't work on *Spinout*, though; Jack Baker did.

58

Who Are You?

Exploring the Theory That Elvis Used His Movie Songs to Pay Homage to Such Heroes as Harry Belafonte and Jackie Wilson

E lvis greatest ambition, Marsh wrote, "was to unify all of the popular music he heard around him." That didn't interest his first mentor, Phillips, and for a while that lofty aspiration was all but invisible as Elvis rocked the world. His post-army conversion, though dismissed as a sellout by such disappointed fans as John Lennon, was initially driven by that ambition. With its beguiling blend of rock, gospel, blues, country, and pop, *Elvis Is Back*, his first album of the 1960s, was a purer expression of his musical personality than anything he cut at Sun—albeit much less revolutionary.

Presley had never made any secret of his regard for certain singers, often insisting that Fats Domino was the real king of rock and roll, and putting his admiration for Jackie Wilson on the record—and on record, at the million-dollar quartet sessions in Sun Studios in 1956 and when he cut "Return to Sender."

In his essay *Elvis as Anthology*, Peter Nazareth has suggested that Presley used his movie songs to honor his heroes, most especially Harry Belafonte, Nat King Cole, Sam Cooke, and Wilson. The idea is worth exploring, although, given the limits of Elvis's influence on his own movies, it would seem difficult to position him as some kind of musical auteur.

Jackie Wilson

There is no doubt that "Return to Sender" was Elvis's tribute to Wilson. As Guralnick wrote in his sleevenotes to *Elvis: The Great Performances, Volume 2: The Man and His Music*: "Elvis gives back a witty, almost flawless interpretation of Wilson's act with this rich r&b flavored Otis Blackwell song. The hand gestures, the boxer's shuffle that stands in for the Twist, the self-amused little shoulder shrugs, even the facial expressions, all suggest Wilson."

Presley had first seen Wilson perform in Las Vegas in 1956, with Billy Ward and his Dominoes. Wilson's cover of "Don't Be Cruel" so impressed Presley, he recounted the story for Jerry Lee Lewis and Carl Perkins when he dropped into Sun Studios in September, even imitating Wilson's distinctive vocal theatrics.

The King even had the generosity to admit that Wilson's version was "much better than that record of mine." Ten years later, he dropped in to see Wilson at the Trip on Sunset Boulevard, and the two met again on the *Double Trouble* set when Wilson watched Presley at work. Schilling says that some of Elvis's moves when he is singing in the film echo Wilson's trademark gestures, and there are certainly some uncharacteristic moves during the King's performance of "Long Legged Girl."

Harry Belafonte

Nazareth has suggested that Presley pays homage to another favorite singer later in *Girls! Girls! Girls!* Even for an Elvis movie, "Song of the Shrimp" is an odd number, a pretty little calypso about a crustacean sung with astonishing sincerity by a star who, Nazareth suggests, is acknowledging the influence of the calypso king Harry Belafonte. Tepper and Bennett's song is certainly crafted and arranged in such a way it's hard not to think of Belafonte, and it is sung with great delicacy by Elvis. The two legends never met, but Elvis did sing a snippet of Belafonte's hit "Banana Boat Song" (number 5 on the Billboard charts) in the studio in May 1957.

Nat King Cole

Cole and Elvis both broke down racial boundaries in America in the 1950s. Cole was a black artist who broke into a pop chart dominated by white singers. Elvis was the white artist who paved the way for black musicians like Little Richard to make their own commercial impact. You can hear Presley's reverence for Cole in his version of "Mona Lisa," sung as a slow ballad at home in the 1950s, while Cole performed a swing version of "Jailhouse Rock" on his TV show. Both artists covered "Guadalajara," and, although the arrangements are very similar, Presley's Latin-influenced vocal is completely different. The King's real homage to the crooner came when he recorded "Love Letters" in May 1966, a year after Cole had died. The song had been covered by Cole in 1957, and you can hear his influence in Presley's impeccable vocal.

Sam Cooke

In 1963, the great soul singer swaggered his way through "Frankie and Johnny." The sublime, jazzy version is held by Nazareth to have influenced Elvis's rendition. It's hard to directly compare the two versions, because Cooke's is beautifully arranged and Elvis's is hardly arranged at all. (Apparently Weisman had to fill in as the conductor when it was recorded.) The other difficulty is that Cooke's version is modernized with references to Ivy League and Jaguar sports cars, so it sounds much less dated than Elvis's Mississippi steamboat shtick.

But can you hear Cooke's influence in Elvis's vocal? And is the part where Presley sings "Frankie, I beg please don't shoot me" an allusion to Cooke's untimely demise? (He had been shot in suspicious circumstances on December 11, 1964.) Although the official, and not entirely convincing, version was that the singer had been shot by a woman defending herself from a sexual assault, Parker told Elvis that Cooke had been killed by mob hit men and disgruntled RCA image makers, an explanation Presley often referred to. If you follow this reading, Elvis was more likely to be singing for his own life, begging not to be shot by whoever had killed Cooke. All that said, you can hear echoes of Cooke in Presley's vocal. Unfortunately, as this isn't one of the King's finest performances, you can also hear him sound lost, as if he doesn't really know where the song is taking him.

59

Operettas, Elvis, and Al Jolson

The Rules of Singing in the Movies

They should call them operettas. The philosophy seemed to be, don't say if you can sing it." That was how Yvonne Craig, who starred in *Kissin' Cousins* and *It Happened at the World's Fair*, saw Elvis's movies. Presley may have influenced her verdict. He had become increasingly embarrassed by scripts that insisted he burst into song whenever a child needed cheering up (*World's Fair*), when he inadvertently landed in jail (*Blue Hawaii*), or after he caught a load of fish (*Girls! Girls! Girls!*). Now that we are accustomed to the pop video—and characters in *Glee* who rarely walk down a corridor at McKinley High without belting out a tune—the songs in Elvis's movies, rather than the way he is forced to sing them, are more likely to strike us as absurd.

The rules that define how an actor sings in a movie date back to the first sound picture, *The Jazz Singer* (1927). In that groundbreaking musical, Al Jolson follows a convention known as "song as performance," which means he starts warbling a tune only when he performs, rehearses, or sings to his family. Although he sings six songs in eighty-nine minutes, this was essentially a Jolson's-greatest-hits-show. His numbers didn't relate to the plot or express his characters' emotions. That convention was challenged in the early 1930s when Warner Brothers persevered with the musical genre even though rival studios had lost interest. In 1932, in Busby Berkeley's backstage musical *42nd Street*, Bebe Daniels sings "You're Getting to Be a Habit with Me" as she tries to decide which partner she would most like to dance and smooch with. (For the record, Wallis was one of the uncredited associate producers on that musical, and Una Merkel, who plays a streetwise showgirl in this trailblazing picture, made her last movie appearance in *Spinout*.)

Ever since then, producers and directors have felt free to select songs that advance the plot and/or illuminate character (in Elvis's movies these are usually variations on "I'm Falling in Love Tonight," although "Clean Up Your Own Backyard" does shed light on the murder mystery in *The Trouble with Girls*) or feature those—like "Jailhouse Rock"—that exist for no other purpose than to thrill the audience.

The simple fact that characters sing, rather than speak, has consistently troubled a minority of the cinemagoing audience who balk at this lack of realism. Elvis was one of those cynics, troubled by "playing the guy who gets into a fight, then starts singing to the guy he beat up." That same concern had inspired Rodgers and Hammerstein to devise a naturalistic opening, worthy of August Strindberg, for the stage production of *Oklahoma!* (1943), in which the first thing the audience saw was an old woman churning butter. And when Curley sings to Aunt Eller, he does so realistically because he actually says: "I've come a singing to ya" and bursts into "Oh, What a Beautiful Mornin'," which sounds like something he has known for ages or just invented. Hammerstein was convinced that if the audience found these characters—and this scene—realistic, they were more likely to accept what followed.

None of Elvis's directors went quite so far in their quest for realism as Hammerstein. The songs in *Jailhouse Rock, King Creole,* and *The Trouble with Girls* all have reasonably believable cues. At the other extreme, in *Stay Away, Joe,* Elvis's roguish hero Joe Lightcloud mysteriously decides that the best way to encourage a recalcitrant bull to fulfill his mating duties is to sing to it, a choice that says nothing about character—apart, perhaps, from to suggest how dumb Lightcloud is—and everything about the need to squeeze another song in. To be fair, even in mainstream musicals, the rationale for characters bursting into song could be something of a moveable feast.

No matter how realistic the rationale, Elvis wouldn't have been entirely happy. He hadn't come to Hollywood to star in a slew of interchangeable musical comedies. He aspired to be the next James Dean, who was one of Hollywood's most influential role models in the 1950s. Elvis was just one of many actors who aspired to be him. Dean's most iconic role was as troubled adolescent Jim Stark in *Rebel Without a Cause* (1955), but that same year, he could so easily have won a completely different part—as Curley in *Oklahoma!* Luckily for Dean's reputation as the coolest actor in movie history, Gordon MacRae beat him to it.

60

Shrimps, Income Tax, and Chambers of Commerce

The Most Unusual Songs in Elvis Movies

lthough the plots of so many Presley's films were all but interchangeable, they presented his songwriters with all kinds of challenges, as this selection clearly proves.

"Song of the Shrimp," *Girls! Girl! Girls!*

Impeccably sung ditty about a tragically naive, newspaper-reading shrimp, which, onscreen, is actually 17 percent less excruciating than watching Elvis sing "Dainty Little Moonbeams" with the Chinese moppets. Tepper and Bennett strike again.

"Fort Lauderdale Chamber of Commerce," *Girl Happy*

To some, this Tepper/Bennett number is a tragic waste of talent. Yet a minority reluctantly admires the way the tunesmiths have contrived to create a song where the name of a chamber of commerce forms such a catchy hook. Even in the carefree 1960s, the idea that young men in Fort Lauderdale are automatically arrested if they're not stalking a "cute female" was not part of the city's penal policy.

"Yoga Is as Yoga Does," *Easy Come, Easy Go*

"Well, I can see that you and yoga will never do." That's the opening line—and it gets weirder from there. If only Elvis had blown this particular scene a lot sooner.

"He's Your Uncle, Not Your Dad," *Speedway*

Consider this a kind of comic kissin' cousin of George Harrison's irate "Taxman." This production number is endearingly odd, a lament about the IRS's tyranny that still periodically celebrates Uncle Sam.

"Queenie Wahine's Papaya," *Paradise, Hawaiian Style*

This novelty number starts rather conventionally with a couplet about selling seashells on the shore, but then before you know it, Elvis is singing about pineapples, pumpkin, and pickle salads.

"There's No Room to Rhumba in a Sports Car," *Fun in Acapulco*

This lovers' lament significantly reduced the amount of fun to be had in Acapulco. Sadly, the song gives us no guidance on the kind of vehicles it is safe to rhumba in.

"Ito Eats," *Blue Hawaii*

A Tepper/Bennett novelty number that doesn't do anything for *Blue Hawaii* except add some goodnatured broad comedy about fat boy Ito O'Hara. This soundtrack sold two million copies in Presley's lifetime. How many copies could it have sold without this song about a man who eats all night and day?

"Edge of Reality," *Live a Little, Love a Little*

Unforgettable, incomprehensible, a song by Giant, Baum, and Kaye that lives in a parallel universe—and is all the better for it.

"Smorgasbord," *Spinout*

Even for Elvis, this Tepper/Bennett number is a bit much. The good news—for girls watching—is that the King loves all kinds of women. The bad news is that he likens sex to a Swedish open sandwich.

61

They Also Sang

The Other Singers Who Shared the King's Limelight

Elvis did most of the singing in his thirty-one feature films, but every now and then someone else, usually his leading lady, would get a turn. Sometimes it worked—as when the lovely Liliane Montevecchi took to the stage in *King Creole*—and sometimes, such as when Glenda Farrell croaked her way through "Pappy, Won't You Please Come Home?" accompanied by a dog, it really didn't.

Dolores Hart: *Loving You*

As the innocent Susan Jessup, Hart wraps her tonsils around "The Yellow Rose" and "Detour," an old Patti Page hit. She does well enough with "Detour" to make you want to hear more.

Wendell Corey: *Loving You*

The leader of Tex Warner's Rough Ridin' Ramblers, Corey and his band get to perform a forty-second instrumental version of "Candy Kisses."

Mickey Shaughnessy: *Jailhouse Rock*

Shaughnessy's slow country ballad "One More Day" is the first song in *Jailhouse Rock*. Not quite as soulful as it would like to be, the number's weary tone lingers in the memory.

Liliane Montevecchi: *King Creole*

The French ballerina brings some exotic allure to Bourbon Street's nightspots as she coos her way through "Banana," a novelty number laden with enough innuendo to make Carmen Miranda blush. Fruit have seldom been sexier.

Stella Stevens: *Girls! Girls! Girls!*

After reluctantly agreeing to play chanteuse Robin, Stevens does at least get to sing some quality songs: "Never Let Me Go," "The Nearness of You," and "Baby Baby Baby." *Sing* is overstating it: she does perform them on set, but the vocals you hear in the film are by the ubiquitous Marni Nixon, dubbed "the ghostest with the mostest" because she also replaced the voices of Natalie Wood (*West Side Story*) and Audrey Hepburn (*My Fair Lady*).

Glenda Farrell: *Kissin' Cousins*

Although Farrell's lament for Pa Tatum is far from the worst musical moment in this hillbilly romp, it certainly slows proceedings down.

Ann-Margret: *Viva Las Vegas*

When you watch the bombshell flounce through "My Rival" and "Appreciation," you can see why Parker was so enraged. Co-written by Bernie Wayne, whose biggest hit was "Blue Velvet," the songs allow her to show off her vivacity while poor old Elvis has to stomp his way through "Yellow Rose of Texas."

The Forte Four: *Viva Las Vegas*

Groovier than most real dance crazes, "The Climb" is a bluesy, soulful nightclub number that, incredibly, wasn't available anywhere until the Follow That Dream release of the movie soundtrack in 2003. The Forte Four's complete lineup is Dan Anthony (vocal/guitar), Jack Shaeffer (sax and vocals), Ernie Earnshaw (drums), and Guy Watson (on bass). They recorded with one of Elvis's session guitarists, Glen Campbell. Sadly, they were so nervous on set, their vocals were dubbed by the Jordanaires.

Nita Talbot/Shelley Fabares: *Girl Happy*

Although Margret had threatened to steal the limelight in *Viva Las Vegas*, the film's commercial success convinced producers that it might help if Elvis's leading ladies stepped up to the mic occasionally. Fabares had already had a number 1 hit in the United States with Johnny Angel and, after being shown the ropes by Nina Talbot's nightclub act, performs the striptease number "Read All About It" with sexy aplomb.

Donna Butterworth: *Paradise, Hawaiian Style*

Child actress Butterworth murders the classic "Bill Bailey, Won't You Please Come Home?" and then declines an encore on the grounds that you always leave the audience wanting more. In this case, movie audiences wanted a lot less.

Nancy Sinatra: *Speedway*

Sinatra's enigmatic producer/songwriter partner Lee Hazlewood wrote "Your Groovy Self" for her to sing in the Hangout. Cool, quirky, and fun, this number suits Sinatra just fine, even if it's not equal to the same duo's "Did You Ever?" This is the only song by another singer to feature on the first release of a Presley soundtrack album.

The Elvis Soundtrack That Was Ahead of Its Time

How *The Trouble with Girls* Broke the Mold

A merica the Beautiful," "Camptown Races," "The Darktown Strutter's Ball," "Susan Brown" . . . These are not the kind of songs you expect to hear on an Elvis soundtrack, but they all add to the charming ambience of *The Trouble with Girls* even if none of them are sung by Elvis. (For the record, these four songs were played by: kids on a kazoo, a precocious one-man band, two child stars, and a local folk trio.)

Somebody—presumably Billy Strange, who was in charge of the music, with the backing of director Peter Tewksbury—had decided to break with Presley travelogue tradition. This being an Elvis movie, the King has to sing a few numbers—and, for once, the story actually makes their presence vaguely credible—but the period setting is enhanced by the sight of college boys trying to divert an impatient rural audience with a chorus of "On, Wisconsin!," Elvis crooning gently about "Gentleman songsters on a spree," and a folk trio, credited on the cast list as the Farmhands, singing the square-dance number "Hello, Susan Brown" and the beautiful "Fourth Day of July," which starts, "So the cuckoo is a pretty bird," but is obscured in the movie by a firework explosion. Strange took these numbers very seriously. One song required forty takes, and by the time he was satisfied, Kathy Rainey, who sang and played tambourine in the group, had a sore arm.

This is hardly *O Brother Where Art Thou?* territory—although "Hello, Susan Brown" and "Fourth Day of July," selected from Alan Lomax's book of folk songs, would have not sounded out of place on that multimillion-selling album—but, given the time, the place, and the context in which the movie was made, this soundtrack was a refreshing change. Conventional wisdom had hitherto dictated that the music in an Elvis film should emanate almost entirely from the man himself or a few privileged guest stars (Stella Stevens, Ann-Margret, and Nancy Sinatra). This philosophy had even been applied when, as in *Frankie and Johnny*, the milieu and period meant that the king of rock couldn't rock at all. By using songs and snatches of songs from an ensemble cast to convey a genuine feel for time and place, *The Trouble with Girls* quietly departed from the norm—and is the only Elvis film to have something resembling a modern movie soundtrack.

Sing It, Fella

The Best Use of Elvis's Music in Other Movies

he King's songs have been a regal presence on the soundtrack of a surprising array of movies—from *Big Fish* to *Forrest Gump*. Here are six of the best examples.

"Mystery Train," *Mystery Train* (1989)

Jim Jarmusch's anthology of drifters and outsiders bursts into life with one of Presley's most inspiring numbers, "Mystery Train," and ends with Junior Parker's version of the same song. Elvis is, as one Memphian gripes, "fucking everywhere" in this movie, haunting the troubled lives of a Japanese couple, an Italian woman, and an unemployed Englishman. Jarmusch depicts the King's hometown as a place where lost souls live in limbo. The fact that he closes with Parker's "Mystery Train" has been read as evidence of the director's purism. It could equally signify his pessimism. Elvis's reiteration is driven by rebellious exhilaration, whereas the weary resignation in Parker's original is a suitably somber signoff.

"Blue Moon," *Desert Hearts* (1985)

Donna Deitsch's thoughtful lesbian romance between a buttoned-up English professor and a ranch owner's daughter in 1950s Arizona showcases some sumptuous desert scenery and haunting period music, including Elvis's eerie falsetto cover of the standard "Blue Moon," recorded at Sun in August 1954. Phillips hadn't been in the studio that day and was so nonplussed by the performance he never released it. RCA did, and Elvis's evocative rendition accentuates the yearning at the heart of this underrated movie.

"Jailhouse Rock," *Rio das Mortes* (1971)

Rainer Werner Fassbinder's enjoyable exploration of German youth's discontents, in which two best friends—played by Michael König and Gunter Kauffman—spend most of the time trying to raise the money to fund their dream of visiting Rio das Mortes in Peru and discovering a hidden Mayan treasure, features the director, as a bar fly, dancing with König's girl Hanna Schygulla to "Jailhouse Rock." Pop-cultural references abound, with Schygulla reading a chunk of Lana Turner's biography.

"Don't Be Cruel," *Diner* (1982)

"Sinatra or Mathis?" asks Steve Guttenberg over the table in Barry Levinson's *Diner*. Mickey Rourke replies: "Presley." "Elvis Presley," Guttenberg hits back. "You're sick . . . " The first installment in Levin's celluloid biography of Baltimore, essentially one long male bull session, baffled the studio, which released it with little fanfare, but has become a critics' favorite. A stellar cast— Guttenberg, Rourke, Paul Reiser, Ellen Barkin, Kevin Bacon, and Kevin Spacey— was matched by a sparkling soundtrack that featured "Don't Be Cruel." This is the moment Hollywood reconnected with Elvis's music, and his songs would recur in Levinson's Baltimore cycle, with "His Latest Flame" featuring in *Tin Men* and "Blue Moon" gracing *Liberty Heights*.

"Summer Kisses, Winter Tears," *Until the End of the World* (1991)

The bittersweet ballad from *Flaming Star* was a natural for the David Lynch/ Angelo Badalamenti *Twin Peaks* treatment. Sung in Julee Cruise's distinctive airy style, it is one of the more memorable moments in Wim Wenders's intriguing, if inexplicable, road movie.

"Promised Land," *Men in Black* (1997)

It's always a pleasure to hear Elvis's turbocharged interpretation of the Chuck Berry classic, and it prompts one of the funniest exchanges in this blockbuster sci-fi comedy. K (Tommy Lee Jones) plays the song as the agents are driving through a tunnel. J (Will Smith) says, "You know Elvis is dead, right?" only to be told, flatly, "Elvis is not dead, he just went home."

"Santa Claus Is Back in Town," *The Long Kiss Goodnight* (1996)

Renny Harlin's action thriller, in which housewife Geena Davis hires Samuel L. Jackson to investigate a past she can't remember, is a pretty decent movie, but Elvis fans will always remember it fondly for the inspiring blast of "Santa Claus Is Back in Town," his naughtiest Christmas song, that kicks off proceedings.

64

A Dozen Seriously Underrated Movie Songs

From "Return to Sender" to "Beginners Luck"

Yes, Elvis did record some awful movie songs. But they weren't all bad, and, once you've discovered the obvious greats ("Jailhouse Rock," "King Creole," etc.), there are some seriously underrated gems worth listening to.

"Return to Sender," *Girls! Girls! Girls!*

Can a million-selling global chart topper ever be said to be truly underrated? Certainly if that song is "Return to Sender," the catchy Otis Blackwell classic that was the highlight of *Girls! Girls! Girls!* A great rock single from a King who was about to abdicate, "Return to Sender" is often overlooked because it lies betwixt and between the two most influential phases of Elvis's career: the trailblazing 1950s and the live-in-concert 1970s. This perfect slice of pop-rock bursts into life with Boots Randolph's baritone sax before Elvis takes charge with an effervescent, tightrope-walking vocal and a memorably idiosyncratic pronunciation of the word "sender." Even Parker recognized the quality when he heard it, promising Blackwell it would make it into the movie "because it's a great song." Elvis was just as enthused, taking the recording back home to Bel Air and telling a friend, "You've got to hear this. I love this song." A work of genius that deserves much more airplay.

"Clean Up Your Own Backyard," *The Trouble with Girls*

The normally reliable Jorgensen says that Billy Strange's association with Elvis produced "nothing successful or artistically significant." Yet many would beg to differ, citing this nugget of country soul penned by Strange and Mac Davis. Half singing, half talking, Elvis breezes through the complicated lyrics, his voice

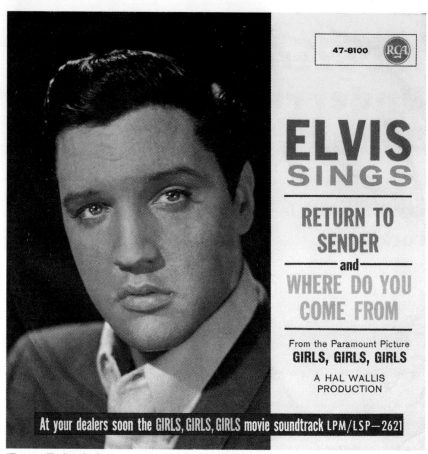

"Return To Sender" was arguably Presley's greatest movie single of the 1960s.

soaring superbly when he warns, "Ah, don't you hand me none of your lines." The Dobro guitar that gives this song such an authentic flavor was played by Gerry McGee, one of the prime movers in the instrumental rock band the Ventures.

"A Little Less Conversation," *Live a Little, Love a Little*

The Junkie XL remix of this funky number topped the charts in nine countries in 2002, giving him his eighteenth number 1 in the UK (putting him one ahead of the Beatles). Yet the original version, though a tad brief, packs more punch, with Elvis back to his macho, swaggering best as he dares his girl to satisfy him, baby. The song was recorded for the 1968 TV special but never used. Played back today, the 1968 version (available on the *Memories* CD) sounds like a harbinger of the remix to come, with a much harder, heavier sound than the original.

"Crawfish," *King Creole*

Even on the first listen, it's hard to resist the urge to gatecrash Elvis and Kitty White's lovely duet by crying out, "Crawfish!" The best opening number to any Elvis movie—and easily the best of the King's songs about fish. Delightfully quirky, driven by an unusual drumbeat, this demands a lot of Elvis vocally, and he shows off his range, soul, and control. Clash frontman Joe Strummer described this as one of his favorite Elvis songs.

"Baby I Don't Care," *Jailhouse Rock*

Often neglected because of the sheer magnificence of the movie's title track, "Baby I Don't Care" is a hard, driven, cynical rock song about love. When Elvis breaks into his mumble, it feels as if he's pointing us back to "Baby Let's Play House," his last Sun single. In "Let's Play House," he berates his love's worldly ambition—in "I Don't Care," he bemoans her square ways—but in neither song are such flaws considered fatal.

"Edge of Reality," *Live a Little, Love a Little*

Julian Cope sums up "Edge of Reality" as "a big production that takes itself very seriously indeed, all mystical lyrics, haunted backing vocals and dramatic orchestral riffage. Very easy to mock but taken on its own terms, oddly appealing." This is probably the oddest song Giant, Baum, and Kaye ever wrote for the King, a crypto-psychedelic ballad with staccato strings and a chorus that sticks in your head after one listen—even though you have no idea what it, or the rest of the song, means.

"C'mon Everybody," *Viva Las Vegas*

A happy, feel-good rocker from Elvis's best musical of the 1960s. "C'mon Everybody" has a catchy hook, an infectious beat. and enough half-decent lines (it's fun to hear El singing that there's nothing wrong with the "long haired music" from Beethoven to Bach) to make it stick in the memory even if you haven't seen it thrillingly performed by Elvis and Ann-Margret. Although some have argued the song needs a rougher edge from Elvis, the vocal seems perfectly judged for the sentiment of the song and its place in the movie.

"You Can't Say No in Acapulco," *Fun in Acapulco*

Penned by Sid Fuller (who conducted and arranged many of Ray Charles's hits), Dolores Fuller, and Lee Morris, this is a smoochy gem. In the movie, it is hard not to be distracted by the bathing beauties doing their Esther Williams impersonations in the swimming pool. On record, it is easier to focus on the finer nuances in Elvis's breezy vocal and his delightful repetition of the "don't say no, you can't say no" motif.

"Let Yourself Go," *Speedway*

Joy Byers's fine song is a hedonistic blast in which the King offers to teach any and every beauty in the vicinity how to let themselves go. While Presley gives this performance plenty of power, he has the sense to make it slightly tongue in cheek for the movie, as he dances, sings, and kisses his way around the Hangout. The version he cut for the 1968 TV special is much raunchier, but the sequence in which he sings the number in a bordello was deemed too steamy and was withdrawn from the original broadcast at the request of the show's main sponsor, Singer Corporation.

"I Got Lucky," *Kid Galahad*

In this sweet, uplifting rocker. the King gets to snap his fingers and shake his hips in an affectionate allusion to the Twist. Elvis's songwriters were often criticized for writing songs to a formula, but Dolores Fuller, Wise. and Weisman hit the jackpot here. The song fits Presley like a glove and is catchy enough to have been a hit for many lesser pop stars. In a similar vein to the same team's "Rock-a-hula Baby," but much mellower.

"Puppet on a String,"*Girl Happy*

Bennett says this is his favorite of the songs he and Tepper wrote for Elvis. Elvis certainly looks happy enough singing it to Shelley Fabares as he squires her around Fort Lauderdale. The ballad would probably have made a better lead single than "Do the Clam" for *Girl Happy*. Tepper and Bennett adapted the melody from the song "Hush, Little Baby," and the King's light vocal touch turns it into a charming teen ballad that repays relistening.

"Beginner's Luck," *Frankie and Johnny*

As this lilting ballad starts, Elvis is singing virtually a capella. Luckily, he's in such fine voice that this above-average Tepper/Bennett schmaltz sounds like a classic. The number becomes more predictable as the musicians and the Jordanaires weigh in, and the sound quality isn't exactly top-notch, but the King sounds utterly at home, making each line count. One fan added echo to this track and says it sounds much better. Even without the echo, this works.

The King is Dead, Long Live the King!

Presley's Intriguing Influence on Directors

Elvis was a man of many eras—rock-'n'-roll Elvis, G.I. Elvis, beach-boy Elvis, Vegas Elvis—so celluloid allusions to his cultural impact come in various forms. It seems safe to assume that Elvis's movies were resonating in the mind of short-lived comedy writer-director Andrew Bergman when he penned his 1992 hit comedy *Honeymoon in Vegas*, as the climax hinges on a team of skydiving Elvis impersonators. Luckily, some filmmakers wishing to reflect, honor, or abuse the King's memory have not gone quite as kitsch.

Jim Jarmusch

In the 1989 cult classic *Mystery Train*, Jarmusch certainly can't be accused of taking the King superficially. Named after the Junior Parker classic that Presley covered at Sun, Jarmusch's moody drama is set in a moth-eaten Memphis hotel that doubles as an Elvis shrine. The movie is drenched in Presley references, from lead character Jun's quiff to the hotel rooms adorned with the King's portraits and a gag about his weight—we are reliably informed he would have weighed 649 pounds if he had died on the planet Jupiter. Debate still rages over what it all means and whether the King is a pernicious influence in the lives of the film's characters.

David Lynch

American auteur Lynch once said, "Elvis swims in our minds, and in the emotions all through time." He proved his point in the cult road movie *Wild at Heart* (1990). With his jet-black quiff, southern drawl, and hip-swinging swagger, Nicolas Cage's character Sailor embodies young Elvis. Laura Dern, who played Sailor's girl Lulu, said she and Cage went on a road trip to Vegas to understand their characters. Dern said, "We agreed Sailor and Lulu needed to be one person, and we would share it. I got the sexual, wild Marilyn Monroe, gum-chewing fantasy female side; Nick got the snakeskin, Elvis, raw, combustible, masculine side." Lynch studied Elvis's repertoire of greatest hits before deciding Sailor should serenade Lulu with "Love Me" and "Love Me Tender."

Cameron Crowe

As Crowe began his career writing for *Rolling Stone* magazine, it's no surprise Elvis has pervaded his movies. Soundtracks are always a key feature of Crowe's films, and he enlivened *Jerry Maguire* (1996) with Presley's neglected gem "Pocketful of Rainbows." Presley played a crucial role in the development of *Vanilla Sky* (2001). This film—dismissed as a bombastic mess by some critics—was a reworking of Alejandro Amenabar's *Open Your Eyes* (1997), yet Crowe says the adaptation was inspired by the King, "I once heard a taped radio interview with the young Presley, conducted after one of his first concerts. Presley attempted to tell a probing and skeptical DJ how his explosive new popularity was affecting him. 'I feel lonely,' Presley said, 'even in a crowded room.' It was that idea that began my adaptation." Crowe recently claimed to be working on a script about a fictional lost Elvis Presley movie called *Blue Seattle*. He already has a soundtrack of Presley-like tunes written and recorded with his ex-wife Nancy Wilson of the band Heart.

Robert Zemeckis

Despite making his feature film debut in 1978 with *I Wanna Hold Your Hand*, a movie about a group of Beatles fans on their way to see the Fab Four in New York, Zemeckis says he "converted to Elvis in his teens." In his second feature, *Used Cars* (1980), central character Rudy (Kurt Russell) is an Elvis fan, and a statue of the singer takes pride of place in the character's bedroom. Russell was a smart choice, having enjoyed his cameo in *It Happened at the World's Fair* (1963). Russell couldn't escape Presley's ghost, portraying Elvis in the John Carpenter TV movie about the King and an Elvis impersonator in *3000 Miles to Graceland* (2001).

A special-effects expert, Zemeckis brought Elvis back from the dead in his smash, *Forrest Gump* (1994). As the Gump family's young lodger, Presley is taught to dance by a leg-brace-wearing Forrest and goes on to shock America with that routine while singing "Hound Dog" on TV. Peter Dobson plays Elvis, although, inevitably, Kurt Russell supplies the voice. The scene left Jon Michael Spencer, professor of music and American Studies at Richmond University, wondering if Zemeckis was trying to airbrush history, complaining, "Those syncopated leg and body movements are not attributable to Forrest Gump but to the rhythms that underlie African-American music."

Aki Kaurismaki

One of the trademarks of maverick Finnish filmmaker Kaurismaki is his eclectic use of soundtracks, which typically draw on 1950s rock 'n' roll. His cult favorite *Leningrad Cowboys Go America* (1989) is steeped in Elvis culture. The comic antiheroes of this odyssey are arguably the most ineffectual rock band to tour America. Yet what they lack in talent, they make up for in black pompadours, winklepicker shoes, and passion, especially when they make their homage to Sun Studios, the greatest Presley shrine after Graceland. Like the King in real life, they suffer from their manager's iron whims. The America they discover—a stream of decaying gas works and seedy strip clubs—feels like a dismal parallel to the America that Presley crisscrossed in his endless 1970s tours.

Quentin Tarantino

What's inside the case? That was the question that vexed many cinemagoers after watching Quentin Tarantino's *Pulp Fiction* (1994). The answer for many movie aficionados was Val Kilmer's gold Elvis suit. Having begun his Hollywood career in 1988 as a Presley impersonator in an episode of sitcom *The Golden Girls*, Tarantino genuflected to the King with his script for *True Romance* (1993). Book clerk and film buff Clarence Worley (Christian Slater) is a fervent Elvis fan who is counseled by the King, albeit in the unlikely guise of Kilmer. The film's director, the late Tony Scott, said Kilmer wanted to play Clarence but agreed to spend eight hours in makeup to be transformed into Elvis, or "the Mentor" as Tarantino called him to avoid litigation. Clarence's girlfriend Alabama later bludgeons gangster goon Virgil (James Gandolfini) over the head with a statue of Presley. Like many true fans, Clarence named his and Alabama's son Elvis.

So what was really in the case, and why is it so prized by crime lord Marcellus Wallace? We do know it contained a golden, mysterious something or other, but that doesn't get us very far. It could be gold, Marcellus's soul, an Oscar statuette, or Kilmer's suit—as a tongue-in-cheek reference to the director's earlier work. The suit is certainly possible—Tarantino drops in enough allusions to *Reservoir Dogs*—but the man himself, when asked what was in the briefcase, would say only, "It's whatever the viewer wants it to be."

Elvis does feature in that famous deleted scene from *Pulp Fiction*, with Uma Thurman's Mia Wallace claiming everyone can be classified as an Elvis person or a Beatles person. She thinks Vincent (John Travolta) is an Elvis man—some critics have even suggested he has been cast as the Elvis to Samuel L. Jackson's Chuck Berry. What is not in doubt is that Vincent prefers Presley to the Fab Four. Like Tarantino.

Selected Bibliography

Books

Biskind, Peter. *Easy Riders, Raging Bulls* (Bloomsbury, 1999)

Biszick-Lockwood, Bar. *Restless Giant: The Life and Times of Jean Aberbach and Hill and Range Songs* (University Of Illinois Press, 2010)

Bram, Bill. *Elvis Frame by Frame* (Wingspan Press, 2007)

Braun, Eric. *The Elvis Film Encyclopedia* (B. T. Batsford, 1997)

Bret, David. *Elvis: The Hollywood Years* (Robson Books, 2001)

Brode, Douglas. *Elvis Cinema and Popular Culture* (McFarland, 2006)

Brown, Peter, and Pat Down Broeske. *At the End of Lonely Street: The Life and Death of Elvis Presley* (Arrow Books, 1998)

Carr, Roy, and Mick Farren. *Elvis: The Complete Illustrated Record* (Eel Pie, 1982)

Cash, W. J. *The Mind of the South* (Vintage, 1941)

Chadwick, Vernon. *In Search of Elvis: Music, Art, Race and Religion* (Westview Press, 1995)

Clayton, Rose, and Dick Heard. *Elvis Up Close: In the Words of Those Who Knew Him Best* (Virgin Books, 1994)

Cohn, Nik. *Awopbopaloobopalopbamboom: The Golden Age of Rock* (Grove Press, 1969)

Dick, Bernard F. *Hal Wallis: Producer to the Stars* (University Press of Kentucky, 2004)

Doll, Susan. *The Films of Elvis Presley* (Publications International, 1991)

Doss, Erika. *Elvis Culture: Fans, Faith, and Image* (University Press of Kansas, 1999)

Dundy, Elaine. *Elvis and Gladys* (University Press of Mississippi, 2004)

Dunne, Philip. *Take Two: A Life in Movies and Politics* (Limelight, 1992)

Fortas, Alan. *Elvis: From Memphis to Hollywood* (Popular Culture Ink, 1992)

Geller, Larry. *If I Can Dream* (Simon and Shuster, 1989)

Guralnick, Peter. *Careless Love* (Little, Brown, 1999); *Last Train to Memphis* (Little, Brown, 1994)

Guralnick, Peter, and Ernst Jorgensen. *Elvis Day by Day* (Ballantine Books, 1999)

Guttmacher, Peter. *The King and His Movies* (Metro Books, 1997)

Halberstam, David. *The Fifties* (Fawcett, 1994)

Harbinson, W. A. *Elvis: An Illustrated Biography* (Michael Joseph, 1975)

Hazen, Cindy, and Mike Freeman. *Memphis Elvis-Style* (John F. Blair, 1997)

Hoey, Michael A. *Elvis, Sherlock & Me* (Bear Manor Media, 2007)

Hoffman, Elizbeth Delaney (editor). *American Indians and Popular Culture* (Praeger, 2012)

Hopkins, Jerry. *Elvis* (Abacus, 1974); *Elvis in Hawaii* (Bess Press, 2002)

Jackson, Howard. *Treat Me Nice* (Anchor Print, 2011)

Jorgensen, Ernst. *Elvis Presley: A Life in Music* (St Martin's Press, 1998)

Keogh, Pamela Clarke. *Elvis Presley: The Man, the Life, the Legend* (Atria Books, 2004)

Klein, George. *Elvis: My Best Man* (Virgin Books, 2010)

Lisanti, Tom. *Drive-in Dream Girls: A Galaxy of B-Movie Starlets of the Sixties* (McFarland, 2012); *Fantasy Femmes of Sixties Cinema* (McFarland, 2001)

Marcus, Greil. *Dead Elvis: A Chronicle of a Cultural Obsession* (Viking, 1991)

Marling, Karal Ann. *Graceland: Going Home with Elvis* (Harvard University Press, 1996)

Marsh, Dave. *Elvis* (Times Books, 1982)

Nash, Alanna. *The Colonel: The Extraordinary Story of Colonel Tom Parker and Elvis Presley* (Aurum, 2004); *Elvis Aaron Presley: Revelations from the Memphis Mafia* (Harper Paperbacks, 1995)

Osborne, Jerry. *Elvis Word for Word* (Osborne Enterprises/Word For Word Publishing, 1999)

Plasketes, George. *Images of Elvis Presley in American Culture 1935–1977: The Mystery Terrain* (Harrington Park Press, 1997)

Presley, Donna. *Precious Memories* (Southern Publishers, 1997)

Schilling, Jerry. *Me and a Guy Named Elvis* (Gotham Press, 2006)

Siegel, Don. *A Siegel Film: An Autobiography* (Faber and Faber, 1996)

Simpson, Paul. *Rough Guide to Elvis* (Rough Guide, 2nd edition, 2004)

Slaughter, Todd, with Anne E. Nixon, *The Elvis Archives* (Omnibus, 2004)

Stanley, David E. *The Elvis Encyclopedia* (Quay Wray, 1997)

Stern, Jane, and Michael Stern. *Elvis World* (Bloomsbury, 1987)

Tatham, Dick. *Elvis* (Phoebus, 1977)

Thomson, David. *A Biographical Dictionary of Film* (Knopf, 1994)

Torgoff, Martin. *The Complete Elvis* (Putnam, 1984)

Victor, Adam. *The Elvis Encyclopedia* (Overlook Duckworth, 2008)

Werner, Steve. *Elvis and the Apocalypse* (Xlibris, 2000)

Worth, Fred L., and Steve D. Tamerus. *Elvis: His Life from A to Z* (Corgi, 1989)

Websites

Elvis Australia
www.elvis.com.au

Elvis Presley History Blog
www.elvis-history-blog.com

The Elvis Information Network
www.elvisinfonet.com

ElvisBlog
www.elvisblog.net

Elvis Women
elviswomen.greggers.net

Elvis Presley On-line Fanclub Magazine
www.elvisnews.com

Elvis Presley: Original Versions of Songs He Sang
davidneale.eu/elvis/originals

For Elvis CD Collectors
www.elvis-collectors.com

The Sheila Variations
www.sheilaomalley.com

Flickdom Dictum
Flickcomdictum.blogpsot.co.uk

The Mystery Train Blog
themysterytrainblog.com

Internet Movie Database
www.imdb.com

Turner Classic Movies
www.tcm.com

Magazines

Elvis: The Man and His Music
Elvis Monthly

Index

THE FAQ SERIES

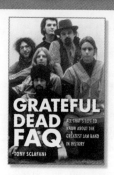
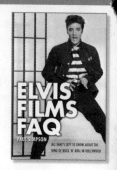

Armageddon Films FAQ
by Dale Sherman
Applause Books
978-1-61713-119-6.........$24.99

Lucille Ball FAQ
*by James Sheridan
and Barry Monush*
Applause Books
978-1-61774-082-4......$19.99

The Beach Boys FAQ
by Jon Stebbins
Backbeat Books
978-0-87930-987-9...$19.99

Black Sabbath FAQ
by Martin Popoff
Backbeat Books
978-0-87930-957-2....$19.99

James Bond FAQ
by Tom DeMichael
Applause Books
978-1-55783-856-8....$22.99

Eric Clapton FAQ
by David Bowling
Backbeat Books
978-1-61713-454-8......$22.99

Doctor Who FAQ
by Dave Thompson
Applause Books
978-1-55783-854-4....$22.99

The Doors FAQ
by Rich Weidman
Backbeat Books
978-1-61713-017-5.........$19.99

Fab Four FAQ
*by Stuart Shea and
Robert Rodriguez*
Hal Leonard Books
978-1-4234-2138-2.......$19.99

Fab Four FAQ 2.0
by Robert Rodriguez
Hal Leonard Books
978-0-87930-968-8.. $19.99

Film Noir FAQ
by David J. Hogan
Applause Books
978-1-55783-855-1......$22.99

Grateful Dead FAQ
by Tony Sclafani
Backbeat Books
978-1-61713-086-1.......$24.99

Jimi Hendrix FAQ
by Gary J. Jucha
Backbeat Books
978-1-61713-095-3......$22.99

Horror Films FAQ
by John Kenneth Muir
Applause Books
978-1-55783-950-3....$22.99

KISS FAQ
by Dale Sherman
Backbeat Books
978-1-61713-091-5.......$22.99

Led Zeppelin FAQ
by George Case
Backbeat Books
978-1-61713-025-0.......$19.99

Pink Floyd FAQ
by Stuart Shea
Backbeat Books
978-0-87930-950-3..$19.99

Elvis Films FAQ
by Paul Simpson
Applause Books
978-1-55783-858-2.....$24.99

Elvis Music FAQ
by Mike Eder
Backbeat Books
978-1-61713-049-6.....$24.99

Bruce Springsteen FAQ
by John D. Luerssen
Backbeat Books
978-1-61713-093-9......$22.99

Star Trek FAQ
(Unofficial and Unauthorized)
by Mark Clark
Applause Books
978-1-55783-792-9......$19.99

Star Trek FAQ 2.0
(Unofficial and Unauthorized)
by Mark Clark
Applause Books
978-1-55783-793-6 $22.99

Three Stooges FAQ
by David J. Hogan
Applause Books
978-1-55783-788-2......$19.99

U2 FAQ
by John D. Luerssen
Backbeat Books
978-0-87930-997-8...$19.99

Neil Young FAQ
by Glen Boyd
Backbeat Books
978-1-61713-037-3.........$19.99

Prices, contents, and availability subject to change without notice.

FAQ.halleonardbooks.com